CULTURES COLLIDING

JOHN R. HADDAD

CULTURES COLLIDING

*American Missionaries, Chinese Resistance,
and the Rise of Modern Institutions in China*

TEMPLE UNIVERSITY PRESS
Philadelphia • Rome • Tokyo

TEMPLE UNIVERSITY PRESS
Philadelphia, Pennsylvania 19122
tupress.temple.edu

Copyright © 2023 by Temple University—Of The Commonwealth System
 of Higher Education
All rights reserved
Published 2023

Library of Congress Cataloging-in-Publication Data

Names: Haddad, John Rogers, author.
Title: Cultures colliding : American missionaries, Chinese resistance, and
 the rise of modern institutions in China / John R. Haddad.
Description: Philadelphia : Temple University Press, 2023. | Includes
 bibliographical references and index. | Summary: "This book tells the
 history of how and why American missionaries started building schools,
 colleges, medical schools, hospitals, and YMCA chapters in China before
 1900"— Provided by publisher.
Identifiers: LCCN 2022029435 (print) | LCCN 2022029436 (ebook) | ISBN
 9781439911600 (cloth) | ISBN 9781439911617 (paperback) | ISBN
 9781439911624 (pdf)
Subjects: LCSH: Missions, American—China—History—19th century. |
 Missions, American—China—History—20th century. |
 Christianity—China—History—19th century. |
 Christianity—China—History—20th century. | Missions—Educational
 work—China—History—19th century. | Missions—Educational
 work—China—History—20th century. | Women in missionary
 work—China—History—19th century. | Women in missionary
 work—China—History—20th century. | China—Intellectual life—Western
 influences.
Classification: LCC BV3415.2 .H34 2023 (print) | LCC BV3415.2 (ebook) |
 DDC 266.00951—dc23/eng/20221013
LC record available at https://lccn.loc.gov/2022029435
LC ebook record available at https://lccn.loc.gov/2022029436

Printed in the United States of America

9 8 7 6 5 4 3 2 1

Contents

Acknowledgments		vii
A Note on the Spelling of Chinese Names		ix
Map of Missionary Activity		xii
	Introduction	1
1	Into the Crucible: Shandong Missionaries Face Resistance	15
2	An Exercise in Futility: The Struggles of Missionaries in the South	39
3	Christ versus the Demons: Encounters with the Chinese Supernatural	60
4	Cutting the Cord: Chinese Ministers Out on Their Own	81
5	Crisis Breeds Invention: The Emergence of New Missionary Models	97
6	The Spirit of Debate: The Missionary Conference of 1877 and Aftermath	121
7	A New Kind of Man: Experiments in Hybrid Identity	137
8	Challenging Convention: Single Women Enter Missions	166
9	Transforming Health: Female Doctors Enter Medical Missions	188

10	Hybrid Healers: American-trained Chinese Women in Medicine	206
11	Extroverted Evangelists: The Student Volunteer Movement and the YMCA	220
12	Ivory Pagodas: The Rise of Christian Colleges	236
	Conclusion: Into the Twentieth Century	263
	Notes	273
	Bibliography	307
	Index	321

Acknowledgments

This book would not have been possible without good people and good institutions. Penn State Harrisburg University, my professional home for nearly two decades, supports me in numerous ways. I wish to express gratitude to the administration, who have always been in my corner—Chancellor John Mason; Omid Ansary, Senior Associate Dean for Academic Affairs; Jeffrey Beck, the Director of the School of Humanities; and the late Mukund Kulkarni, our wonderful former Chancellor. In American Studies, I have benefited greatly from the assistance of my colleagues Charlie Kupfer, Anthony Buccitelli, Anne Verplanck, Mary Zaborskis, Jeffrey Tolbert, and David Witwer. I must not leave out our incredible library, where I have found resources and friendship. Special thanks here go to Glenn McGuigan, Heidi Abbey Moyer, and Bernadette Lear. Finally, I wish to acknowledge Penn State's Institute for the Arts and Humanities and its former director, Michael Bérubé. Thanks to its Resident Scholars Program, I was able to take time away from teaching and advance the project considerably.

Every book needs a great editor. I had one of the best. I want to express maximal gratitude to my editor at Temple University Press, Shaun Vigil, who guided me every step of the way. Shaun was a true joy to work with, as was the whole team at Temple.

Finally, I would like to thank friends and family members. I am fortunate to have great friends—Kim Chasse, Mike Szabo, and Daniel Medwed—who always buck me up with their good cheer. My parents, Richard and Betsey, offer encouragement and support every step of the way. So too do my brother, Rich, his wife, Sandy, and their three boys, Tim, Alex, and Sam. Similarly, I am grateful to my wife's family in China—in particular, my parents-in-law, Wang Qingyi and Yang Xiurong—who epitomize the Chinese tradition of respecting scholarship. As for my wife, Catherine, and my children, William and Elizabeth, I am most appreciative of you. The three of you provided the joy and laughs that proved to be indispensable to this venture. It is no exaggeration to state that I could not have written this book without you.

A Note on the Spelling of Chinese Names

The romanization of the Chinese language poses problems for historians because, for any given word or proper name, several different spellings can exist. In the 1950s the Chinese adopted Pinyin as the state's official system on the grounds that its spellings most closely approximate the true sound of Mandarin Chinese. For this reason, this book uses the Pinyin system as its default system. That said, there are two exceptions to this rule. First, some Chinese personal and place names, when converted into Pinyin, appear unrecognizable to many of today's readers, who are more familiar with an older spelling (for example, most readers recognize Sun Yat-sen but not Sun Yixian). In these cases, I have opted to leave the names in their older form. Second, when certain names repeatedly appear one specific way in primary source materials, I have elected to retain these spellings. For example, since nineteenth-century American sources referred to the city of Dengzhou as Tengchow, the latter spelling is used here. Likewise, Guangzhou appears as Canton, Fuzhou as Foochow, and Shantou as Swatow.

CULTURES COLLIDING

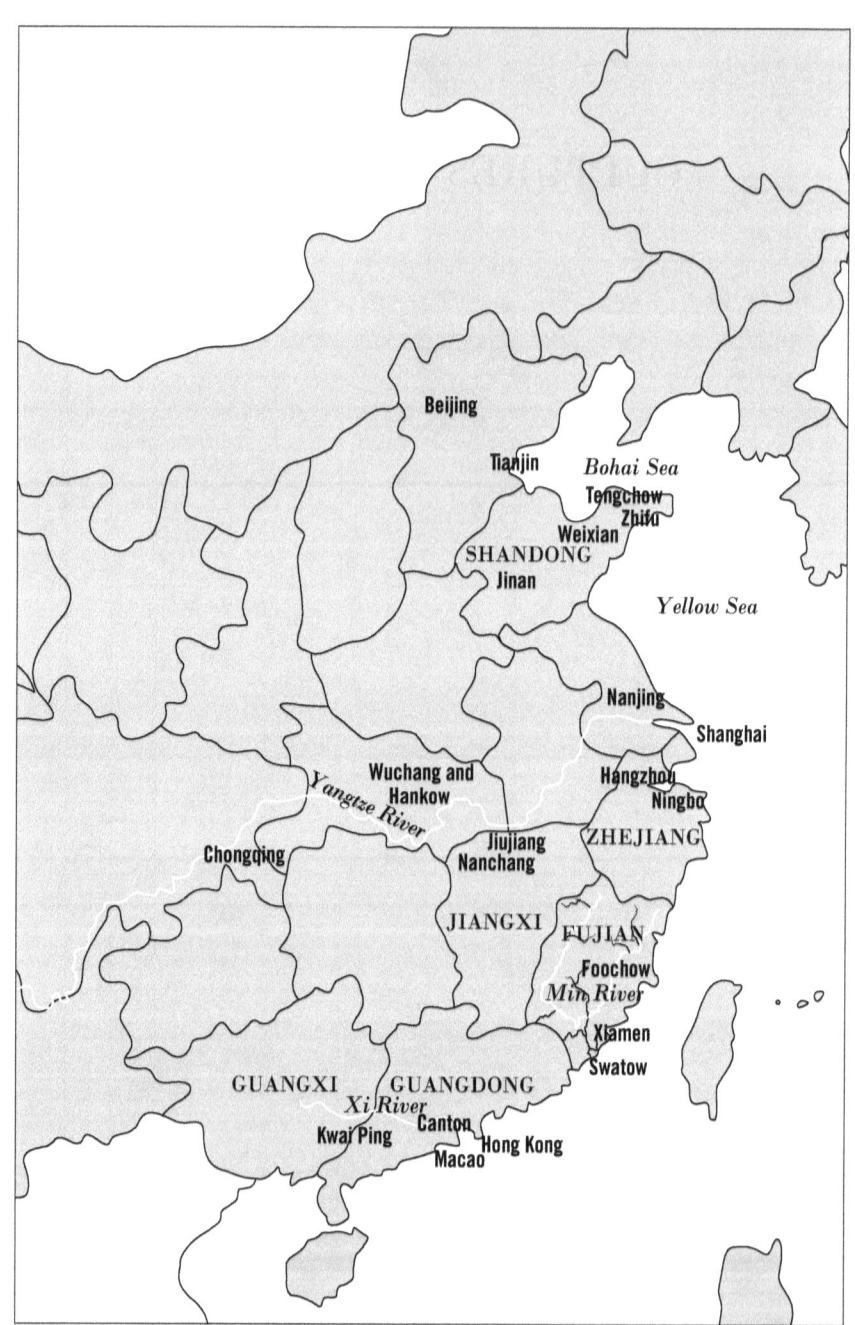

Map Showing Locations of Missionary Activity

Introduction

It is no small matter to try to reproduce one's own institutions in another country. Yet in China in the late 1800s, American missionaries attempted to do exactly that. By 1900, they had committed to an ambitious project to establish schools, colleges, hospitals, medical schools, museums, presses, and chapters of the Young Men's Christian Association (YMCA) in many parts of the country. Some of these institutions have long since vanished. Others have not only survived China's turbulent twentieth century, they have evolved into elite institutions. Beijing University, Qinghua University, and Peking Union Medical College stand out as salient examples, but there are others. Taken collectively, these institutions contributed to China's modernization in the twentieth century. None of this was a part of the missionaries' plan at the start. Back in 1860, when foreigners first gained access to the Chinese interior, the zealous men and women who streamed into the country intended only to spread the Gospel and prospect for souls. Fixated on this holy purpose alone, they established circuits, opened chapels, and delivered sermons. Eschewing other forms of evangelism, they could not imagine a future in which they would oversee large institutions with budgets and bureaucracies. But by 1900, American missionaries—a group not exactly known for its flexibility—had reinvented their entire enterprise in China. How and why did this transformation take place, and what were the consequences of it? This book answers these questions.

We can better understand this transformation by meeting two missionaries who were active in China during this period of change: Absalom Sydenstricker and Henry Winters Luce. Today, both men are best known not for their missionary work but for raising children who achieved global fame. Sydenstricker's daughter, Pearl Buck, wrote *The Good Earth*, a best-selling novel that won Buck the Pulitzer Prize in 1932 and established her as America's foremost literary voice on China. Luce's son, Henry Robinson Luce, created a media empire in the twentieth century that included the magazines *Time*, *Life*, *Fortune*, and *Sports Illustrated*. But we are concerned here not with the celebrity children but with the obscure fathers. Each one of these men, in terms of his traits and method, perfectly captures a certain missionary type. Thus, a snapshot of each helps us to understand the larger transformation within China missions.

Absalom Sydenstricker represents the older missionary model, one that dominated for decades before losing out. In an effort to understand what made her father tick, Pearl Buck devoted an entire book, *Fighting Angel* (1936), to his monomaniacal drive to save the Chinese "heathen." Absalom's missionary operation, which he launched in 1880, worked something like this. On top of his white donkey, he would toss his bedding roll and whatever supplies he needed. He would then don his loose-fitting Chinese gown, which, when combined with his long, braided hair (required of Chinese men in the Qing Dynasty), made him appear somewhat Chinese. But not really. His great height, white skin, protruding nose, and glassy blue eyes gave him away. Bidding his wife and children farewell, Absalom would head out for several days . . . or weeks . . . or months.[1]

Out on the road, he must have presented quite a sight—as giant men on small donkeys always do. Though his feet nearly dragged in the dirt, he remained erect in the saddle, utterly oblivious of or impervious to the smirks and snickers of the Chinese watching him clip-clop by. But most striking would have been the evangelical fervor that glowed in his eyes. "There is fire in him," a Chinese man observed. "The flame in his soul leaned over and caught at the flame in me." Indeed, Absalom entertained not a single doubt as to the cosmic significance of his life's work. He was "a spirit made by that blind certainty," his daughter wrote, "that pure intolerance, that zeal for mission," and "that high confidence in heaven." Frighteningly austere and unyielding as iron, Absalom was exactly how people who dislike missionaries imagine them to be. Yet within his rigid frame radiated a warm heart. He adored the Chinese. And they, for the most part, loved him back.[2]

After reaching the preselected town, Absalom would set up shop and wait. Before long, a crowd of people would materialize, eager to see the strange visitor. Capitalizing on their curiosity, he would try to establish friendly relations by engaging in good-natured banter and handing out his Christian literature. If lucky, he might generate immediate interest in the Gospel. But if not, it was no matter. He would hover in the area, returning to the village again and again to build trust and familiarity in the people. He would also rent a simple structure to serve as a chapel. Here he did not require much—just a spacious room, some wooden benches, and a table to serve as a pulpit. He would then preach in the chapel long enough to secure a handful of converts, at which point it was time to move on. Before departing, he would install as minister of the new chapel a convert from a different village whom he had trained. Twice a year, he would return to each town on his circuit to check on its progress, handle complaints, and conduct baptisms. For fifty years, Absalom conducted missionary work in roughly this fashion. He represents the traditional itinerant minister, and when he began his career in 1880, this model enjoyed the support of nearly all missionaries. But its reign would not last. By the 1890s, when Henry Luce reached China, it was already on the way out.[3]

Henry Luce represents a different model—the model that won out. After he graduated from Yale College and Princeton Seminary, his mission board deployed him to China. Though devout like Sydenstricker, Luce employed a diverse array of strategies in his effort to expand God's kingdom. Instead of traveling along a circuit, Luce remained stationary, working primarily at a college founded by his mission. There he taught Physics and served as department head. He also introduced a new sport called basketball and arranged games between students and faculty. A natural organizer, he oversaw the move of the college to a new city where it joined a consortium of other institutions that included a medical school and a theological college. The mission board, recognizing his people skills and administrative abilities, appointed him vice president of the institution and dispatched him on fundraising tours in the United States. Affable and persuasive, Luce locked up commitments from big donors, many of whom were linked to the industrial fortunes of the Gilded Age. Armed with capital, Luce expanded the infrastructure of the college, creating a campus complex rivaling any in America. He gave his life to this model of missionary work, and in his view it was worth it. The goal of a mission, after all, was not just to save souls but also to improve the physical and intellectual well-being of the people, generate prosperity, and increase China's global standing.[4]

Between 1860 and 1900, China missions underwent a seismic shift. Collectively, missionaries moved away from the itinerant model epitomized by Absalom Sydenstricker and toward the institutional model perfected by Henry Luce. Though Luce focused on college education, other sorts of institutions flourished as well. By century's end, missions had witnessed a Cambrian explosion of evangelical diversification, one that generated a sudden variety of institutions. In addition to colleges, missionaries founded museums, printing offices, hospitals, medical schools, nursing schools, mental asylums, schools for the blind and deaf, famine relief agencies, and YMCA branches. Historian Daniel Bays has called these institutions "the single most impressive visible result of the missionary labors of the late nineteenth century."[5] The transformation was stark.

Why did America's China missions turn away from Sydenstricker's model and embrace the one exemplified by Luce? Why, in other words, did missionaries engage in large-scale institution-building near the century's end? This was the question I set out to answer. Like most historians, I embarked on my research harboring a theory that was really more like a hunch. I expected that the sources, once examined, would support a narrative of *gradual but inevitable evolution along a continuum*. That narrative, I predicted, would follow this general arc. After pioneering missionaries like Sydenstricker succeeded in establishing a beachhead in China, institutional missionaries like Luce would follow in their wake. This latter group would fortify Christianity's expanding presence by erecting schools, colleges, and hospitals. They would pay for all of this building by drawing philanthropic funds from America's growing pool of wealthy donors—families that had struck it rich during the country's industrial expansion. In this narrative, in other words, I saw Sydenstricker and Luce as representing consecutive and complementary phases of a single initiative intended to Christianize China and Americanize its institutions. As I delved into missionary sources, I expected to find a self-confident people, the Americans, with superior resources inexorably imposing their will over the Chinese. I began, in sum, from the assumption that Americans held the advantage.

I was in for a rude awakening. In missionary accounts, I did not find proud declarations of well-laid plans coming to fruition. Rather, from these pages resounded the plaintive howls of men and women collectively agonizing over their emotional and physical pain. Instead of glorious triumph, missionaries wrote mostly about devastating setbacks: violent mob attacks, burned-down churches, desecrated graves, lethal diseases, dying family members, extreme isolation, mental depression, physical exhaustion, stingy mission boards, and their utter inability to win converts. Generally speaking, I was discovering not a record of success but rather the *existential shock of a grand dream going awry*. The evidence compelled me to reassess my preliminary assumption that missionaries wielded superior power and that institution-building had been in the cards all along. It was time to script a new narrative.

This book proposes a radically different storyline. It argues that the wave of institution-building was never inevitable and that missionaries like Luce were not in the original plan. Instead, missionaries lurched abruptly in the new direction in response to a crisis of such mammoth proportions as to threaten the viability of China missions. To understand this new narrative, we must look back to the moment of initial Protestant penetration. To missionaries, all had seemed promising back in 1860 when a treaty ratified during the Second Opium War allowed them, for the first time in history, to leave China's coastal cities and proselytize in the interior. They had no plans, at this time, to build institutions other than churches and the occasional small school to be run by a missionary's wife. Holy crusaders, they marched into rural China predicting rapid success—and why not? They had divine wind at their backs. God Himself had guaranteed victory—or so they thought.

They were not prepared for what happened next. In the interior, they met with what we might call the "real" China—a rural population with entrenched systems of belief. The countryside abounded with vernacular religions featuring a colorful array of gods, ghosts, and demons. In an already crowded supernatural landscape, there was little room for God and Jesus. Missionaries also confronted the governing class, the local scholar-officials whose knowledge and authority flowed out of Confucianism. For centuries, this philosophy had informed Chinese statecraft, dominated the education system, organized society, and molded values. Since Christian missionaries and Confucian scholar-officials both claimed a monopoly over eternal truth, they could not coexist in peace. They became "natural enemies," in John King Fairbank's words, like "cats and dogs."[6] Viewing missionaries as unwanted disruptors in a social order over which they presided, Chinese officials dug in. Conflict ensued. As the collective efforts of missionaries crashed against a wall of Chinese resistance, anti-Christian violence spiked. Most missionaries suffered from low morale, if not outright depression. Some quit. Others died. And many quietly formed an opinion that, years earlier, would have been unthinkable: *that traditional itinerant preaching did not work*. China had become less a land to be conquered and more a crucible to be survived.

It was time to regroup. Though some missionaries refused to modify their method, others responded to crisis with innovation. Starting in the 1870s, they abandoned their circuits and began experimenting with new evangelical models. After making visible gains, these pioneers presented their new models at a major missionary conference held in Shanghai in 1877. Receiving just enough endorsement from colleagues, they returned to their work to continue developing their experimental operations. At this point, they had a stroke of luck. Back in the United States, two grassroots movements triggered a flow of hundreds of new recruits into China. Starting in the 1870s, the Woman's Foreign Missionary Society sent to China a whole new category of missionary—the single woman—which brought a much-needed focus on Chinese women and girls. A decade later, a second movement exploded on college campuses—the Student Volunteer Movement (SVM). Hundreds of young graduates (a group that included Luce) signed up for missions work instead of heading into the usual professions. Casting aside the old-fashioned itinerant model, these young men and women infused the newer experimental models with their vitality and numbers. Some of them delivered very few sermons and undertook no itinerating at all. They were far more likely to teach science or math, head a college, treat patients, or run a YMCA chapter.

Thus far, our narrative appears somewhat one-sided, with Americans acting on China. In fact, the agency of Chinese people played a powerful role in effecting the transformation of missions. Their first major act, of course, was to repulse the initial missionary advance. After that, they continued to exert influence by expressing their preferences to a suddenly receptive missionary body. Indeed, repeated failure had taught missionaries a crucial lesson: one could not simply impose one's religion onto the Chinese and expect them to embrace it. To ensure Chinese "buy in," a missionary needed to cater to the needs of the Chinese, especially those who were not benefiting from the Confucian social order. Though the status quo in China satisfied many people, others derived little advantage from it. Large numbers fell through the cracks. Those left out were open to alternative ways of living, worshipping, learning, and self-actualizing—if only missionaries would listen. In the 1870s and 1880s, some missionaries did exactly that. They built the kinds of schools, churches, hospitals, and organizations many Chinese wanted. As reciprocal needs, Chinese and American, fit snugly together, the two sides tacitly recognized the interlocking nature of their interests.

But the Chinese did more than just avail themselves of institutions—they changed them from within. As more Chinese joined the new institutions, Americans started to see themselves less as permanent fixtures on the Chinese landscape and more as catalysts: they would spark the formation of churches, schools, and hospitals before receding. As the role of foreigners shrank, the Chinese role expanded at a commensurate rate. The Chinese started to preach the sermons, teach the classes, treat the patients, and run the organizations themselves. By century's end, some Chinese were forming American-style institutions on their own. It is hard to imagine this Chinese agency when it remains abstract. A third biographical sketch allows us to attach this concept to a real man.

Meet Yen Yung Kiung.[7] Born in 1838 to a poor family in Shanghai, Yen flashed signs of the kind of intelligence that inspires parents to dream. Might their son one day become a scholar-official? That dream, however, would require expensive schooling in the Confucian classics, something Yen's father could not afford. Fearful that the boy's talent would go to waste, the parents made the fateful decision to enroll him in an Episcopal boarding school run by missionaries. Better to send him to a Christian school, they reasoned, than to no school at all. But it was at this point that the parents lost control of Yen's destiny. For though he would rise, it would be along a non-Confucian track. At school, he impressed his American teachers with his precocity, so much so that the mission decided to invest in his future: it sent him to the United

States in 1854 to continue his education. After high school, Yen matriculated at Kenyon College, where he played sports, joined a secret society, and dominated the curriculum. In 1861, he graduated as class valedictorian. Returning to China, Yen discovered that America had altered him profoundly. He had acquired a hybrid identity, one that fused together Chinese attributes and American ones. He also realized how extraordinarily rare he was—very few people like him walked the earth. Missionaries, of course, welcomed Yen's metamorphosis. Bilingual and bicultural, Yen could work effectively among both Chinese and Americans. They perhaps even imagined him as the prototype for a new kind of missionary. He was God's secret weapon.

Except Yen did not feel like a weapon. What he felt was lonely. He had lived overseas for too long and now was paying the price. He could no longer relate to his fellow Chinese, and the Americans failed to comprehend his inner turmoil. This was the downside of being an prototype: no one could empathize with him because nobody else had shared his experience. He was alone. But instead of quitting, Yen hunkered down. Over time, he found ways to express his formidable talents through the missionary apparatus. He engaged in some conventional preaching and translation work, but his largest contribution lay in education. He loved Kenyon and aspired to give Chinese youths access to a comparable education. In what is now Wuhan, he opened two schools, one of which evolved into a university. In Shanghai, he helped found St. John's, the first college in China started by an American mission. As the college's first dean, he had a hand in constructing its curriculum, building its administrative apparatus, defining its culture, and forming its vision. Yen's many achievements, a missionary observed, showcased the "possibilities of a cultivated, Christianized, Chinese mind."[8]

While Yen clearly embraced many things American, he remained thoroughly Chinese. Nationalism smoldered in his core. When Europeans treated Chinese people as second-class citizens in Shanghai, Yen demanded fair treatment. Before his death in 1898, he bemoaned to his children that he would not live to see a resurgent China. "Well, my sons," he said, "I am sorry that I shall not in my lifetime have the chance of seeing our country become rich and powerful, but you of the younger generation will . . . witness a New China."[9] This, after all, had been his purpose all along: to use American knowledge and systems to build "New China."

Yen's agency did not cease with his death and so neither does our story. Ralph Waldo Emerson defined an *institution* as "the lengthened shadow of one man."[10] These words certainly apply to St. John's, whose graduates carried Yen's vision into their careers. As industrialists, engineers, physicians, statesmen, educators, filmmakers, and intellectuals, they became the builders of modern China. Many of these alumni, born after Yen had died, knew nothing of the man or his role at the genesis of their alma mater. To them, he was only the mysterious name attached to Yen Hall.[11] But another group knew exactly who Yen was. Like Luce and Sydenstricker, Yen had descendants who enjoyed illustrious careers. His son, W. W. Yen, recalled his father leading his children on tours of American and Chinese battleships and factories out of "eagerness" to have them "see all that was possible in the way of modern inventions." W. W. Yen studied at the University of Virginia before teaching at St. John's. He then went on to edit China's Commercial Press, a major conduit for Western knowledge, and serve as president of the Republic of China in the 1920s. Like his father, W. W. Yen helped develop a college, Qinghua, which is today an elite university.[12] Yen Yung Kiung also raised his nephew, F. C. Yen, who graduated from St. John's and Yale Medical School before pioneering in public health. Like his uncle, F. C. Yen spent his life building up institutions. He taught and administrated at Yale's medical school in Hunan Province, helped establish the Central Medical College in Shanghai (now Shanghai Medical College of Fudan University), became the first Chinese vice president of Peking Union Medical College, and served as Minister of Public Health in the 1930s.[13] There were many others who bore the imprint of Yen Yung Kiung's influence. However, if we were to try to identify them all, the endeavor would overwhelm us and consume this entire book. Would it be an exaggeration, therefore, to say that Yen Yung Kiung—the small boy deposited in a mission school by desperate parents—succeeded in grafting his DNA onto modern China?

This book, like Yen's life, is as much about Chinese agency as missionary action. In the pages ahead, we venture inside the lonely chapel of a fearless Chinese minister who is determined to plant Christianity in a hostile village without any help from missionaries. We meet a former pirate who uses the church to cure his opium addiction before launching a ministry centered on sin and redemption. We visit a mission school where the local Chinese pastors oust the American teachers who refuse to tailor the curriculum to their demands. We meet three teenage boys who radically alter their life trajectories by volunteering to accompany their missionary teacher back to America. We encounter equally courageous Chinese girls who request admission to a male-only missionary medical school. We venture inside a major missionary hospital to witness a Chinese doctor performing an operation never before attempted in China. In the countryside, we witness Chinese Christians who, without missionary sanction, perform exorcisms to rid the supposedly possessed of demons. Last, we follow a bold Chinese minister who, in a village suffering from drought, pits God against local deities in a winner-take-all contest to see which supernatural entity can deliver rain.

All of these stories take place after the Opium Wars and before 1900. This was a turbulent period in China, one that saw the Qing government cling to power in the face of intense foreign aggression. What did this aggression look like? Bryna Goodman and David Goodman have described it as a "piecemeal agglomeration" comprising "a diversity of colonial arrangements." There were unequal treaties, won through war, that conferred special rights to the Western powers. One such right, extraterritoriality, allowed foreigners accused of crimes against Chinese civilians to be tried in their own tribunals. Treaties also engendered a system of treaty ports, "forcibly-opened sites for foreign trade" that "dotted China's coastal areas." In addition, the foreign powers seized territories, "coercively leased" properties where "Chinese sovereignty was suspended," and created spheres of influence, special zones where they enjoyed the right to mine for minerals and build railroads.[14] Yet despite this exploitation, China never relinquished sovereignty. "While the chaos and poverty of China as a whole . . . is beyond question," observes Daniel Vukovich, China "retained its political sovereignty at all times aside from various cantonments and concessions."[15]

That China was never formally colonized has presented scholars with a dilemma. What nomenclature should one employ when trying to conceptualize China's predicament? While scholars wisely avoid calling this a "colonial period," the West's metastasizing influence prevents them from classifying China as "independent." China's status lay somewhere in between. Goodman and Goodman note that many scholars have, in "formulaic fashion," settled on *semicolonialism*, a term first used by Vladimir Lenin, as a way to comprehend China's ambiguous status.[16] Marius Meinhof, Junchen Yan, and Lili Zhu observe that other scholars favor *colonial modernity*, a term that "entangles colonial logics" with Chinese "projects of modernization." "Even after the Opium Wars," these authors point out, Chinese officials seeking to modernize "did not simply receive foreign influences." Rather, "they actively traveled abroad, investigating the Western powers" in their search for "strategies to rescue the country."[17] Though these terms differ from one another, they all reflect the fact that China was subjected to extensive foreign aggression but preserved a degree of autonomy at the governmental level.

What about the nongovernmental levels where the missionaries operated? There is no denying that, in a practical or logistic sense, missionaries benefited from Western imperialism. Indeed, they could access China's interior only because of privileges attained through war. Once inside, they availed themselves of their own government's infrastructure, such as consular offices, and invoked treaties when they felt their rights were violated. What is more, the same gunboats that protected foreign residents and assets provided missionaries with security as well. Though clearly the beneficiaries of imperialism, missionaries did not see themselves this way. Most not only decried it, they conceived of their movement as the antidote to it. They saw "Western expansionism," William Hutchison wrote, as an "inexorable force" that must be "tamed" or replaced with "fine spiritual imperialism."[18]

Though missionaries viewed the religion, education, and medicine they brought as unambiguously noble, they were nevertheless imposing their culture, which they deemed superior, on the Chinese. For this reason, past scholars have understood missions as a form of "cultural imperialism." The idea to link missions to nationalism and imperialism, writes Dana Robert, "proved to be an irresistible thesis" starting in the late 1950s.[19] The American attempt to project military power in Indochina in the 1960s convinced more historians to subscribe to this thesis.[20] Robert cites Paul Varg as an example of an historian who produced excellent scholarship within this paradigm. Varg set out to explain why missionaries failed to Christianize China. He argued that their religious and philanthropic project got "caught in the vortex of nationalistic crosscurrents." Believing in the supremacy of their own culture, they brought what they "believed to be [China's] needs" and not "what the Chinese themselves felt to be needs."[21]

Scholars like Varg have a point. Let us imagine that we are somehow able to summon Absalom Sydenstricker from the dead and ask the stalwart evangelist if his purpose in China was to eradicate indigenous belief systems and replace them with Christianity. He would probably scoff with disgust at the obvious nature of our question before responding, "Of course, that is exactly what I meant to do." Pearl Buck agreed that a form of imperialism propelled her father through life. Animated by an "imperialism of the spirit," she wrote, Absalom "set forth into the universe to make men acknowledge his god to be the one true God, before whom all must bow."[22] Furthermore, if we could somehow deploy a satellite, send it back to 1860, and program it to take photographs over China for several decades, the pictures from this eye-in-the-sky would reveal the steady expansion of American institutions. The photographic sequence, in other words, would look a lot like cultural imperialism.

However, there is more to the story. When we zoom in with our hypothetical satellite's camera lens, reaching the level of person-to-person interaction, the cultural imperialism narrative does not fade, but a different story emerges alongside it. We see that the Americans, though initially the aggressors, are repelled by the Chinese. They experience emotional and physical anguish as the people they had come to save reject them. Unable to impose their will, the Americans acquire a much-needed dose of humility. For some, it does wonders. Previously inflexible, they start to bend in response to pressure from the Chinese, who seem much stronger than the victims of cultural imperialism ought to be. After regrouping, some Americans rally and return to the field, ready to build institutions other than churches. Crucially, the institutions they erect end up reflecting an unspoken compromise: while advancing the evangelical objectives of the missionaries, the institutions also serve Chinese needs. They do exactly that, and the Chinese do not hesitate to use these institutions to better their lives. Mothers and fathers lacking educational options (like Yen's parents) send their children to free schools. The sick obtain medical attention at no charge. The inquisitive read about the outside world in missionary magazines. Young men flock to their local YMCA, which channels their energies into community building, social improvement, and sports. Our close-up shot, in short, reveals the presence of new institutions that were less about imperialism and more about mutual benefit. They contributed to what Xu Guoqi has called "a shared history."[23]

Our camera's zoom feature also affords us a closer look at Chinese identity. From out of these missionary institutions, a new kind of human being emerged. No longer shaped exclusively by Chinese influences, these individuals exhibited *hybridity*: their identities fused together Chinese and American knowledge, culture, and values. They were, in every sense of the word, "new" men and women who did not previously inhabit the earth. Since this book is filled with these kinds of people, readers must decide how to conceptualize them. One option is to comprehend them as the unwitting subjects of cultural imperialism and see their hybrid identities as evidence of their colonized minds. This interpretation is valid and applies in certain cases. It does, however, fail to take the agency of Chinese individuals into account. In the pages ahead, readers will meet many Chinese who, instead of submitting passively to a dominant institutional power, actively constructed identities by making deliberate choices. They saw the American presence as an opportunity and seized advantage. For example, many Chinese who attended American schools availed themselves of instruction in math, science, and English but passed on Christianity. They reserved the right to pick and choose and, by doing so, exercised a form of power within their negotiation with Americans.

Those American missionaries were not immune to change themselves. When we train our camera on them, we find that that they too evolved. Even Absalom, when we zoom in, carries much less cultural arrogance than we initially supposed. According to Pearl Buck, he came to be motivated by a fierce "intolerance" for white "race superiority." He acquired respect for the Chinese and despised any foreigner who treated them as lesser. Absalom also argued that "Chinese Christians should have full powers of self-government" in their churches and "should be free of . . . domination from the missionaries." Missionaries needed to back off, in other words, and cede power to their converts. He even believed in giving the Chinese the latitude to modify church creeds to "fit their own souls," on one condition: they must keep the Holy Trinity intact. Even Absalom, it turns out, was not the uncompromising zealot many thought him to be.[24]

This book is certainly not the first to push beyond the cultural imperialism paradigm. Back in 1980, Jonathan Spence eloquently remarked that missionary activity took place in "that indefinable realm where altruism and exploitation meet."²⁵ More recent scholars have tended to view this paradigm as an excessively blunt instrument with which to treat a nuanced topic. Ryan Dunch has observed that cultural imperialism, as a blanket theory explaining missions, "reduces complex interactions to a dichotomy between actor and acted upon, leaving too little place for the agency of the latter."²⁶ Dunch's own research on the Protestant missions of Fujian Province reveals how Chinese converts used the intellectual offerings of missionaries to imagine a modern Chinese state.²⁷ Daniel Bays, in his history of Christianity in China, identifies a progression of increasing Chinese ownership of church governance: "The Chinese Christians were first participants, then subordinate partners of the foreign missionaries, then finally the . . . sole 'owners' of the Christian church."²⁸ With Ellen Widmer, Bays also edited a collection of essays on Christian colleges that emphasizes not these institutions' imperialistic nature but their hybridity; American educators and Chinese students each adopted some of the other's ideas in these "bicultural" settings.²⁹ David Hollinger, in his recent book, sees the "missionary project" as a "dialectical event," one involving exchanges of ideas, through which the "world we call modern was created."³⁰ Going even further, Lian Xi has argued that missionaries exposed to Chinese culture underwent a "transformation of thought and attitudes" that amounted to a "conversion" to "Oriental life."³¹

This book recounts the unexpected origins and rapid rise of American institutions in China. It does so by telling the stories of the Americans who established the institutions and the Chinese who changed them from within. The approach, in sum, is biographical. I make no pretensions toward offering an exhaustive account; indeed, the size and scope of the American project in China precludes a comprehensive treatment. By 1905, China was host to 1,304 American Protestant missionaries who came primarily from the Presbyterian, Methodist, Baptist, and Episcopal denominations. These men and women established 1,888 stations, which were often churches or chapels. In education, they founded 966 primary schools that enrolled 19,884 Chinese children. Their 187 high schools and colleges offered instruction to 9,130 students. In the area of medical services, Americans built 70 hospitals and 67 dispensaries, which combined to treat over 500,000 patients annually.³² Given the sheer number of institutions, I have had to be selective in choosing the cast of characters for this narrative. To this end, I have kept my focus squarely on *innovators*—Americans and Chinese whose experimental ideas gained traction, attracted followers and imitators, and assumed brick-and-mortar form as institutions.

Our story starts in 1860 and proceeds chronologically to its end around 1900. Chapters 1 and 2 depict the missionaries' first foray into the Chinese interior, an advance that meets with stiff resistance and yields frustration, sickness, and death rather than converts. In Chapter 3, missionaries confront something unexpected on the countryside: cases of demon possession. While these encounters baffle missionaries, their converts find ways to exploit the demon phenomenon. In Chapter 4, some missionaries experiment with a new evangelical model that de-emphasizes the missionary's role and devolves responsibility to the Chinese. Chapter 5 focuses on a handful of creative missionaries who respond to their crises with innovation; their new evangelical models spur a missionary recovery in the 1870s. In Chapter 6, we take a front-row seat at a major missionary conference where these innovators present their models to colleagues. Chapter 7 examines three Chinese men who, after receiving educations in America, return to China with hybrid identities and use institutions to pass American-style education to the next generation. Chapters 8 and 9 describe the transformative role that single women play in schools and hospitals after the advent of the Woman's Foreign Missionary Society. Chapter 10, a mirror image to Chapter 7, presents three Chinese women who study medicine in America before running hospitals in China. Chapter 11 describes two organizations, the Student Volunteer Movement and the YMCA, that fill missionary ranks with a new type of recruit. In Chapter 12 we examine perhaps the most influential of all institutions—the college.

By 1900, the transformation was complete. In the space of four decades, the needle on the missionary spectrum had moved dramatically in the direction of Henry Luce and Yen Yung Kiung. Americans like Luce could function effectively in bureaucratic settings that rewarded collegiality, fundraising, and social organization. Chinese in the mold of Yen could filter all of the Western learning streaming into China, identify the knowledge the country needed in order to modernize, and disseminate this through institutions. Absalom Sydenstricker could not flourish in this new environment. Nor did he want to. As institutions rose up around him, Absalom stuck to his circuit. He performed missionary work in the twentieth century much like he had in the nineteenth—with one notable exception.

It turned out that even Absalom could modernize just a little. At some point, he traded his white donkey for a mule and hired a carpenter to build a custom-made wagon, a vehicle unlike any other in the world. The new wagon could transport him, his bedding, his boxes of Christian books, and his ministerial accoutrements from village to village. Wheeling around in his ecclesiastical contraption, Absalom became the envy of the countryside. Peasant farmers would stop their field labor to watch as he "clattered up and down" the dirt roads "in great content." But fame would not be his friend. When word of the God mobile got out, a gang of thieves decided they coveted it. One day, after Absalom set out, robbers ambushed him on the road, seized possession of his vehicle, and hurled his books into a ditch. Not one to back down from a fight, Absalom struck the thieves with his whip. And using his height to great advantage, he "cracked a lot of their heads together." But there were too many assailants to fend off, and eventually they overwhelmed him. Bruised and bloodied, Absalom walked thirty miles home to his wife and children wearing only his underwear (they stole his shoes and clothes too). Was he defeated? Hardly. He could not run a board meeting at a hospital or university. But he could survive—and perhaps somewhat enjoy—a nasty scrape with bandits. Absalom was indomitable.[33]

But he was living in the wrong time. By the twentieth century, he had become a living antique, a crusty holdover from a bygone era. What would have been his optimum time to shine? In 1860, missionaries advanced into the Chinese interior for the first time. Though God no longer took the form of a pillar of fire as in the Old Testament, these men and women sensed His presence at their backs, supporting their holy venture. Victory seemed assured, until . . .

1

Into the Crucible

Shandong Missionaries Face Resistance

In 1857, five missionaries in Shanghai put on their finest clothes for what they thought would be a historic photograph. The five were Charles Mills, Rose Mills (Charles's wife), Lucy Mills (Charles's sister), Samuel Gayley, and Sarah Mills Gayley (Charles's other sister and Gayley's wife). This group would attempt to establish the first Presbyterian mission in Shandong Province. In the photograph, their faces reflect their deep resolve and commitment to the work lying ahead. That is because each one planned to spend an entire career spreading Christianity in the Chinese hinterland. Though the photograph conveys some hopefulness, its optimism is tempered by something vaguely ominous. In selecting a pose, the five decided to seat themselves in a row, with each one clasping the hand of a neighbor. Though trusting in God, their linkage of hands suggests they saw solidarity as key to survival. They were bracing themselves for the unknown.[1]

In May of 1861, Samuel and Sarah Gayley and their young son Charles set out for Tengchow, the site of the mission. They were accompanied by another missionary couple, Joshua Danforth and his wife. It did not take long for tragedy to strike. In September, Mrs. Danforth died after suffering from poor health. Her passing left her husband "shattered in both mind and body" and in no condition to continue. He sailed for America, never to return. The mission was reduced by two. The following year, a deadly invisible foe launched its attack. In July of 1862, Charles and Rose Mills, planning to join the Gayleys in Tengchow, departed Shanghai for the port of Zhifu with their two young sons. They arrived with only one: cholera claimed one boy during the voyage.² Landing in Zhifu with the small corpse, the devastated Mills family learned that the same cholera epidemic was ravaging the entire region. "From morning to night," one missionary recalled, "we could hear ... sounds of weeping and wailing while new-made graves could be seen in every direction." Another missionary called the area the "chamber of death."³ In Zhifu, the Mills family accepted the hospitality of an English doctor while they awaited overland conveyance to Tengchow. Tragically, he contracted cholera himself as he cared for the overwhelming number of Chinese patients. The Mills family watched in horror as cholera claimed the doctor and his daughter on consecutive days.⁴

Samuel Gayley, hearing of the stranded Mills family, left Tengchow for Zhifu to lend assistance. Upon arriving, he arranged for a wagon to convey the Mills family to Tengchow. Gayley warned them not to "spend another night amidst the plague" but to depart immediately. He would stay behind to bury the dead and would rejoin them later. Four miles into their journey, Charles, Rose, and their surviving son stopped in the home of an American missionary who was mourning the recent death of his wife, a victim of the scourge. After catching up with the Mills family, Gayley prepared the wagon to resume the trek to Tengchow. Before the party headed out, the Mills's other son contracted cholera and died the same day. The grieving parents placed him in a small box and resumed their journey to Tengchow. On the road, Samuel Gayley began showing symptoms. With no hospital in the vicinity, Charles and Rose Mills had no choice but to make haste for Tengchow. Shortly after the party arrived, Gayley expired. Days later, the disease attacked Gayley's daughter, not yet two years old, and she died also. Distraught, Sarah Gayley left China with her surviving child, never to return.⁵ After the surviving missionaries buried their dead, vandals broke into the foreign cemetery and desecrated the graves. The message was clear: missionaries were not welcome.⁶ This was how the Shandong Mission got its start.

Chapters 1 and 2 examine the obstacles and hardships that Protestant missionaries faced in the 1860s and 1870s. Along with disease, missionaries contended with low morale or outright depression caused by their extreme isolation and failure to win converts. That said, their poisonous relationship with China's ruling class provided the largest source of strife. Despising the Christian intruders, local officials choreographed mob violence in an effort to repulse them. Given the centrality of this conflict, this chapter begins by describing, in general terms, the treaties that allowed missionaries to penetrate the interior and the ideological underpinnings of the Chinese leadership. The chapter then pivots from the general to the specific, presenting portraits of four missionaries who arrived in the wake of the group that had been waylaid by cholera: Hunter Corbett, John Nevius, and Calvin and Julia

Mateer. Their stories capture the extreme crisis that defined the missionary movement in its early years.

China's Legal and Cultural Topography

The Rights of Missionaries

Before the 1860s, the Qing government's policy toward foreigners effectively bottled up the missionary movement. When the first American missionaries arrived in China in 1830, Qing law forbade foreigners from traveling outside of Canton. Geographically confined, these missionaries chafed at the bit. They yearned for the day when God would blast China open for evangelism. With the First Opium War (1839–1842), they got their wish. Behind powerful British forces, missionaries discerned the hand of God. They thought it strange that God would use the morally foul opium trade to pry open China; however, they did not question the methods of a Lord who moved in mysterious ways. The resulting Treaty of Nanjing opened four additional treaty ports—Xiamen, Foochow, Ningbo, and Shanghai. The missionaries swooped in, establishing bases at these ports. But here their movement stalled. They could preach in the city streets, but the vast Chinese interior remained inaccessible.[7]

The Second Opium War (1857–1860) blew the lid off of China. In 1858, the United States was one of four Western powers to secure treaties with China at the end of this war's first stage. The Treaty of Tianjin opened the Chinese interior to American evangelism. From the five treaty ports, eager missionaries shot out along vectors. After establishing stations in cities, they next sought to string together outposts in the countryside, which they would periodically visit by traveling along ever-expanding circuits. This was called itinerant preaching. Though they knew the work would test them, they proceeded with confidence. After all, God had chosen this moment in cosmic time to convert China to Christianity. As they streamed into the interior, they had faith that He hovered approvingly over their holy enterprise, guaranteeing its ultimate triumph.[8]

While God's role remains murky, missionaries were aided by special legal rights contained in the Treaty of Tianjin that protected missionaries and their converts: "Any persons, whether citizens of the United States or Chinese converts, who . . . peaceably teach and practice the principles of Christianity shall in no case be interfered with or molested." Should molestation occur, the treaty compelled Chinese officials to take prompt action. In the event of a mob attack, a local official must "dispatch a military force to disperse the rioters," arrest "guilty individuals," and "punish them with the utmost rigour of the law." Should an official's failure to protect result in injury or in damage to property, the missionary could alert his consul, who would file a claim with the Chinese government. If the claim were legitimate, the Chinese government would provide monetary compensation for losses. Chinese officials may not have wanted to enforce missionary rights, but the treaty was legally binding. What choice did they have?[9]

The legal gate did not swing both ways. In a case involving an American accused of a crime, a Chinese plaintiff could not easily gain satisfaction, even though the alleged infraction had occurred on Chinese soil. A privilege spelled out in the first Sino-American treaty, the Treaty of Wangxia (1844), exempted an accused American from prosecution under the Chinese justice system. Instead, his own consul would convene a tribunal to try him. "Extraterritoriality," as this article was called, gave the American living in China near immunity to Chinese law.[10] Taken together, these two treaties emboldened the missionary in his dealings with local officials. The latter, even if they questioned—or rejected outright—the legitimacy of treaties linked to unjust wars, were forced to protect the missionary and lacked the legal authority to prosecute him. Given these advantages, the missionary constituted an entirely new entity on a landscape. Along with his white skin, he glowed brightly as an alternative source of power, one that brought to an end the Chinese official's monopoly on the same.[11]

Ordinary Chinese noticed the sudden appearance of this strange new figure. For some, access to the missionary's power rendered conversion more appealing. They believed that, if they embraced the new faith, some of the missionary's legal privileges would rub off on them. In 1875, Ho Ching, the governor of Fujian Province, noted scornfully that Chinese Christians had imbibed the "erroneous idea" that Chinese laws no longer applied to them. "They know . . . that the missionaries give a ready ear to their stories and that the Consul is there to manage matters for them." Emboldened by a false sense of "impunity," they defy "constituted authorities" within the government.[12] In 1878, the Zongli Yamen in Beijing, the office responsible for handling China's relations with foreign nations, produced an official report highlighting this problem. "Among the missionaries are some who . . . arrogate to themselves an official status," the Zongli Yamen observed, and then proceed to "interfere" with "business" that local officials ought to handle. Their converts then follow their lead by seeing their church membership "as protecting them from the consequences of breaking the laws of their own country."[13] The mere presence of missionaries, in short, disrupted society by encouraging Chinese to challenge the status quo.

Backed by treaty privileges, missionaries aggressively advanced into China. Their penetration is reflected in the statistics they kept on their own activities. Before the Treaty of Tianjin (1858), missionaries had established 97 stations in four coastal provinces. Between 1858 and 1890, missionaries added 362 stations spread out over twenty-one provinces, many located in the interior. Only Hunan Province, famous for its hostility to foreigners, succeeded in keeping the Gospel out.[14] At these hundreds of sites, missionaries collided with an existing social order. Though *legally welcome*, they were *culturally despised*. American bulls had entered the China shop.

The Confucian Social Order

In every village, the missionary intruded upon a social and intellectual ecosystem predicated upon the philosophy of Confucius (551–479 B.C.). Without a review of his life in detail, it suffices to say that the tumultuous times in which he was alive shaped his philosophy. He lived near the end of the Spring and Autumn Period, an era devastated by social and political upheaval that left the empire broken into warring states. Current rulers, Confucius believed, had caused the unrest by forsaking the beliefs and rituals that had previously glued society together. A return to tranquility, therefore, would require a rebirth of older ways. Confucius dedicated his career to mastering the wisdom and ways of antiquity, to persuading leaders to adopt such wisdom and old ways in governance, and to teaching disciples who could pass the knowledge down to posterity.[15] After his death, different Confucian sects collected philosophical fragments written not by the sage himself but by his students. They consolidated these shards in a single text—*Analects*.[16] This and other works formed the Confucian canon, which provided the blueprint for an orderly, peaceful, and moral society.

At the level of the individual, Confucianism stressed the cultivation of a moral and ethical life. If one were willing to work hard and receive instruction, such a goal was not only possible but realistic, since Confucians judged humanity to be innately good. This hopeful idea is conveyed by the poem that opens the *Three Character Classic*, a text that parents and teachers used to teach children grammar, memorization skills, and Confucian ethics:

> *Men at their birth, are naturally good.*
> *Their natures are much the same; their habits become widely different.*
> *If foolishly there is no teaching, the nature will deteriorate.*
> *The right way in teaching, is to attach the utmost importance in thoroughness.*[17]

In just these few lines, we can identify a major hurdle that missionaries would have to overcome if they were to convert a population raised on Confucianism. Christians viewed humanity as innately sinful following Adam and

Eve's transgression in the Garden of Eden. This point becomes abundantly clear when we juxtapose the above lines with those that open the *New England Primer,* an early American textbook, which every Puritan child memorized: "In Adam's Fall / We sinned all." Given humanity's fallen nature, Protestants believed that only a radical renovation of the human interior—wrought by an infusion of the Holy Spirit—could save the sinner from damnation. Far less invasive, Confucians required only that dedicated teachers help dutiful students live up to the promise of their inborn good natures.[18]

A crucial part of Confucianism focused on human relationships, especially those within the family. Confucian leaders strove to build an orderly society held in place by a strict hierarchy based on gender and age. Everyone—from the emperor down to the peasant—understood his place and how to behave when interacting with others. Though all social relationships held significance, Confucians viewed the family as the key building block of a healthy society. Within the family, the father occupied the top of the hierarchy. His wife, as a female, owed deference to her husband, but as a parent she enjoyed a privileged position over her children. According to the doctrine of filial piety, children must follow parental instruction with unquestioning obedience and place their parents' needs above their own. A child's deference to a parent extended even beyond the latter's death, as the child was expected to continue the veneration by making sacrifices at a household altar—a practice called ancestor worship. Hierarchy also governed relationships among brothers and sisters. Boys commanded more respect than girls, and younger children owed deference to their older siblings. It was obviously a privilege to be the first-born son. Why did Confucianism place so much emphasis on the family? A son raised to revere his father and mother at home was likely to carry proper behavior into society. He would follow laws, respect his superiors in his work, and never seek to overthrow the government.[19] In this way, every Confucian household, itself a spinning gyroscope of stability, contributed to an orderly Chinese society.

Across the centuries, Chinese governments understood the utility of Confucianism in safeguarding the state against insurrection. The various dynasties found ways to graft Confucianism onto statecraft, rendering the two inseparable. Qing rulers, as earlier dynasties had done, incorporated the Confucian canon into the civil service examinations that aspiring young men were required to pass in order to achieve prestigious careers as scholar-officials. In doing so, the Qing channeled the energies of intellectuals, a potentially subversive group, toward productive state-building.[20] Once in office, officials tried to become the living embodiments of Confucian ideals. Toward this end, they performed numerous social functions resembling the French practice of noblesse oblige: they cared for the poor, organized militias when bandits threatened, paid for the upkeep of Confucian temples, and established schools. Each school adopted a curriculum based on the Confucian canon, since it would inevitably be judged according to how well its graduates performed on the state examinations. In modern parlance, the schools taught to the test.[21] The Qing also established state cults whereby the emperor, scholar-officials, and gentry would worship the great sage twice a year in elaborate ceremonies held in temples located in Beijing, the provincial capitals, and the county seats.[22]

Not just for officials, Confucianism suffused the lives of ordinary Chinese. Qing rulers went to great lengths to inculcate Confucian values widely. The aforementioned schools accomplished some of this objective with their curricula steeped in Confucianism. In addition, at Beijing's request, officials promulgated Confucian values in every town and village through state-sponsored lectures. To ensure that even illiterate farmers understood the basics, officials would speak using the local dialect. They would also boil the complex philosophy down to its bare-bones essence so that audiences could easily grasp it. By taking such deliberate measures, the Qing sought to eliminate almost any distinction in the minds of the people between Chinese values and Confucian values. *Chinese culture was Confucian culture.* As a result, Confucianism came to animate every emperor's edict, official's ruling, textbook recitation, exam question, father's scolding, and child's deferential bow.[23]

Clash of Ideologies

Whenever a missionary trundled into town atop his donkey, no one rued his arrival more than the local official. The official did not view the newcomer as an innocent traveler in need of hospitality. Instead, he saw him at best as a disruptor and at worst as the advance guard of an ideological siege. The official recognized instantly that he had the most to lose if the foreigner were to establish a presence in his jurisdiction and disseminate an alternative ideology that rivaled the Confucianism out of which his power, status, and authority flowed. Nor were his fears misplaced: missionaries did not come in the spirit of friendship. The majority of Protestant missionaries, believing their religion to be exclusive, could not envision Christianity coexisting peacefully with Confucianism. Rather, they saw Christianity's victory as requiring Confucianism's destruction. It was a zero-sum game. "Protestant missionaries and the Chinese local elite were as natural enemies as cats and dogs," wrote John King Fairbank. "Both were privileged" and "teachers of the cosmic doctrine. Rivalry was unavoidable."[24]

Missionaries brought to China something we might call a *delete-and-replace model*. Missionaries fully expected the Chinese to *delete* belief systems like Confucianism and *replace* these with Christianity. They "require the site to be cleared," wrote one Western observer, "the destruction of what already exists."[25] Stephen Johnson, a missionary in Foochow, characterized Christianity as a "blaze of light" over a "benighted" Chinese landscape. "The proud and skeptical disciples of Confucius," he predicted, "will yet humbly learn of Jesus" and become "devoted heralds of the gospel."[26] Some missionaries deployed violent language to describe the ideological clash. In 1864, William Ashmore, a missionary in Swatow, announced that a winner-take-all battle was underway: "The age of collision of the hard death-grapple with Confucianism is beginning."[27] Calvin Mateer, a subject of this chapter, defined missionaries' collective purpose as "to destroy heathenism and to cause Christian faith and morals to interpenetrate the whole structure of society." Mateer likened missionaries to an "army" whose "object is . . . to subdue the nations as a whole to Christ, to pull down the fortifications of heathenism" and to "destroy the faith which supports it."[28] Arthur Smith, Mateer's colleague, understood the massive disruption he and his colleagues were causing. "The many ways in which Christianity cut across Chinese customs," he wrote, "and the social complications thus caused rendered the avoidance of collisions most difficult."[29]

Chinese officials correctly identified the newcomers as threats to their dominance. And they dug in. When missionaries appeared in their districts, they would mobilize the people for some form of defensive action. The "ultimate responsibility for every popular uprising," wrote the missionary Chester Holcombe, "must be laid upon the shoulders of the literati," whom he described as "an intensely hostile and dangerous force."[30] Following the official's lead, villagers would treat the foreigner as a dangerous pathogen invading a healthy host: they would swarm around the unsuspecting outsider and subject him to vitriol and violence. Noting these patterns of behavior, historian Sidney Forsythe aptly called the rural Chinese a "rejective" society.[31] The missionary Hunter Corbett experienced the full ferocity of the rejection—and barely survived.

Hunter Corbett

Hunter Corbett knew hardship before his life in China. Growing up on a Pennsylvania farm, Corbett passed his childhood engaged in strenuous and sometimes dangerous agricultural labor. When just a boy, he fell into a threshing machine where, for several moments of extreme agony, the grinding teeth of the revolving wheel "chewed" off "inch bites of flesh" from his body. He escaped alive but severely scarred. Others around him were not as fortunate. He lost his sister to scarlet fever and his best friend to a freak accident—crushed by a falling tree. Corbett reacted to loss by withdrawing into himself and embracing strong religion. It was a harsh childhood, to be sure, but one that equipped him for the missionary life: he had formed a strong bond with

God, had developed a high threshold for pain, and thrived on being alone. While studying at Princeton Theological Seminary, Corbett received his "call"—the silent voice of God summoning him to Christian service overseas. On July 3, 1863, he boarded a ship bound for Shanghai with his new bride, Lizzie Culbertson, and his future colleagues, Calvin and Julia Mateer. As the vessel drifted out of New York harbor, the Battle of Gettysburg raged in Corbett's home state. It would be 100 days before the group would learn the outcome of the war's bloodiest contest.[32]

The Corbetts and Mateers were in for an ordeal of their own. The six-month ocean voyage included an abusive sea captain, rancid food, stormy seas, and fetid drinking water. After reaching Shanghai in December, they boarded a steamship bound for Zhifu, Shandong's largest port. Unfortunately, darkness and an untimely snowstorm limited the captain's visibility.[33] After he ran the vessel onto the rocks along the coast, the small missionary party commenced a brutal twenty-eight-mile trek across frozen terrain. During the journey, the desperate party sought warm shelter, but Chinese inns refused to offer lodging. Most concerning, Hunter Corbett and Julia Mateer contracted intestinal illnesses that would impair their health for decades. When the Corbetts and Mateers finally reached Tengchow, they needed a stable situation in which to recuperate. They found exactly the opposite.[34] The mission, established in 1861 by Gayley and Danforth, was in shambles. During the cholera outbreak, missionaries and their family members had dropped like flies. Exacerbating the situation, the local population had turned hostile. China, Corbett could plainly see, would severely test his stamina and will.[35]

No stranger to adversity, Corbett resolved to soldier through it. He and Mateer attempted to rent suitable living quarters, a seemingly simple task that proved challenging. To keep foreigners out, Chinese officials instructed local property owners not to lease space to them.[36] Repeatedly turned away, Mateer and Corbett were compelled to accept their only offer: a priest, desperate for money to purchase opium, agreed to rent his temple.[37] It was far from ideal. "The Mission premises here [are] very inconvenient," wrote Mateer, "and we find ourselves very uncomfortably fixed." Adding to the unsettling feeling, the couples learned that vandals had broken into the foreign graveyard and smashed headstones, yet another sign that the local population wanted them out.[38] Displeased with the temple, Mateer started building a house with a makeshift woodburning stove to provide warmth in the winter.[39] The Corbetts left Tengchow altogether, moving to a "hostile village" outside of Zhifu where they rented a house with a dirt floor. They were fortunate to get it: it was only available because villagers suspected it was haunted.[40]

To stave off depression, the Corbetts immersed themselves in language study. By taking a slow approach, they differed from other missionaries in the 1860s who, in their zeal to commence God's work, ventured out knowing only a few "broken phrases." According to another missionary, these over-eager evangelists imagined themselves to be preaching coherently, but were actually only "uttering some sounds wholly unintelligible to the hearers." They brought not the Gospel, but "gibberish."[41] In contrast, the Corbetts hired a language teacher and devoted themselves to a year of intensive study. Though Hunter lacked aptitude, he hunkered down and became good enough. In 1865, the couple left their haunted house and moved to a new residence in Zhifu. From there Corbett launched his traveling ministry into the Shandong countryside.[42]

Corbett epitomized the itinerant missionary. After mapping out a route, he would leave Zhifu on a mule and embark on a long circuit ride that might last as long as two months and cover as many as 1,200 miles. Methodical and organized, Corbett kept statistics of his itinerating. "During the past two months," he once recorded, "I have traveled on mule upwards of 700 English miles."[43] His objective was to visit as many villages as he could to spark interest. Then by making repeated visits to each locale, he hoped to establish a permanent presence, which meant renting a space to serve as a chapel, securing converts, and training them to continue the work in his absence. Thus, his later visit to a given town would involve not drumming up interest but monitoring existing operations and supervising the Chinese Christians. If all went well, the chapels would eventually run themselves, with Corbett providing only modest oversight. This was the plan, anyway, in ideal form. In reality, Corbett met with discouraging apathy and sometimes violent hostility.

One bleak December day in 1873, Corbett and his horse clip-clopped across the countryside on their way to a remote missionary outpost. If ever there was a day in which Corbett needed a favorable site visit, it was this one. His spirits were low since he had recently suffered two devastating losses. His fourth son, Ross, had died in 1871, one year after his birth. His passing had precipitated the next tragedy—the physical and emotional collapse of his wife. Lizzie Corbett had died earlier in 1873 after a decade of poor health and a bout with depression following Ross's death.[44] Her passing left Corbett bereft of companionship and tasked with the care of three young boys. In fact, they accompanied him on this trip because he did not deem it prudent to leave them alone in Zhifu with only their Chinese nanny for protection. To all outward appearances, Hunter Corbett did not pose a threat as he approached his destination. How could he, a sad man with his children in tow, strike fear in the heart of anyone?

And yet, Corbett's arrival provoked a strong reaction. As his bedraggled party approached a village, people started to materialize, with many of them shouting, "Hi-ya! Here come the great devil and the little devils, too." As long as the hostility remained verbal, Corbett had little to worry about. After all, he had been called "devil" countless times. Unfortunately, his antagonists decided to ratchet up the abuse—in response, he believed, to earlier inroads he had made. On previous trips to this district, Corbett had preached effectively, distributed Christian literature, conducted baptisms, and left helpers behind. He had, in sum, established a Christian presence. Uncertain as to his reception, Corbett decided to leave his children and their nanny in a nearby village as a precautionary measure. He then headed out alone to a different village to conduct a service. Along the way, he passed through a market town where the people, alerted to his coming, lined the streets armed with rocks. As he moved through the "volley of stones," a projectile struck his horse, which immediately bolted forward out of his control. Corbett was nearly killed. Though one might expect the authorities to intervene, Corbett was convinced that a local official had deliberately neglected to post a proclamation forbidding the people from antagonizing foreigners. This official's lack of action had almost ensured that Corbett would find trouble.

Bruised but not defeated, Corbett, following the advice of his Chinese helpers, traveled to a village where a local temple was holding a festival. Since a festival would attract people, Corbett would enjoy a substantial audience when he preached—or so the reasoning went. As he began his street sermon, an ominous crowd gathered around him. When the stones started flying, Corbett ducked into the temple seeking refuge. Thinking himself temporarily safe, Corbett discovered, to his horror, that the mob had followed him in. Cornered, Corbett feared for his life. At this moment, a Chinese man saw his dire predicament and elected to intervene. "You must get out of harm's way," the stranger urged Corbett. When the missionary replied that he had "no way to get out," the quick-thinking man seized Corbett's riding whip. Cracking the whip, he plunged into the mob, opening up a temporary passage. "Now rush for your life," he called back, "and I will try to keep the crowd from overtaking you." After reaching his horse, Corbett raced out of the village amid a "shower of stones." Returning to his children, he learned of a plot to attack their temporary residence that very night. Resolving to flee immediately, the party slipped out into the "bitter cold" as soon as darkness fell, with Chinese helpers carrying the children on their backs. Later, Corbett received news that his residence had been ransacked.[45]

Corbett presented the case to his consul, who took up the matter with the Chinese government. In the end, the offenders were punished and Corbett received compensation for his losses.[46] Though he could take solace in the legal victory, success as a missionary continued to elude him. A full decade into his missionary career, the fierce resistance showed no signs of dissipating. Corbett was failing. And he was not alone.

John Nevius

John Nevius believed in order. That someone as self-disciplined as Nevius would stumble through his early years in China shows just how difficult missionary work was. Born in western New York, Nevius received his theological training at Princeton. It was here, in 1853, that a recruiter from the Presbyterian Board of Foreign Missions sparked his interest in foreign missions.[47] It was also at Princeton that Nevius, like Benjamin Franklin a century earlier, endeavored to impose strict order over his life. Nevius believed that human appetites, if left unchecked, could reduce productivity or even engender a life out of control. To combat his own natural tendencies, Nevius developed a philosophy of self-mastery, which he codified in his journal as "Rules or Resolutions for Regulating my Life." His twenty-four rules (outdoing Franklin by eleven) covered religious exercises, human relations, time management, food intake, and sleep (never more than seven hours). The mere act of compiling such a list aligned nicely with rule nineteen—"Do everything systematically."[48] This impulse to systematize would define his missionary career.

John and Helen Nevius embarked for China in 1853. They started their work in Ningbo, a treaty port, but moved to Shandong in 1861 to join the fledgling mission after the Treaty of Tianjin opened China to evangelism. "We missionaries now felt," Helen wrote, "that the time had come for extending our efforts to those regions from which we had until then been excluded."[49] In Shandong, Nevius launched his itinerant ministry. A lover of exercise in the great outdoors, he covered as many as forty miles in a day.[50] In this way, he penetrated hundreds of villages, observing each closely. Helen, who experienced chronic illness, stayed home.[51] After several years, he started to discern the invisible power structures shaping life in the typical Chinese village. This knowledge lent him special insight into the missionary movement—which, a few sporadic successes notwithstanding, was failing to gain traction. Missionaries, after sprinting out of the gate in 1860, had gotten bogged down.[52] What had gone wrong?

Nevius endeavored to diagnose the problem. He did so by thinking of village resistance not as unpredictably chaotic but rather as adhering to a common pattern. He developed what amounted to a flowchart to understand the phenomenon. When the missionary first appears in a village that has never before beheld a white man, schools empty and shops close as "the whole town is thrown into a state of excitement." A "jostling crowd" materializes "to catch a sight of the strange apparition." "Every thing connected with us is an object of curiosity," Nevius wrote, including "the color of our eyes and hair" and "the material of . . . our clothes." After locating a suitable platform upon which to preach, the missionary finds himself "surrounded by an immense crowd." His sermon finished, the tired missionary cannot simply retreat to his inn; the crowd follows him wherever he goes. Were he to try "barring the door against the crowd," his action would "likely result in a mob" and "the breaking down of the doors." However, if he patiently responds to inquiries with "kindness and politeness," he can later retire to his inn with "sanguine hopes of great and perhaps speedy results"—or so he thinks at the time.[53]

But those "speedy results" seldom materialize. As soon as the missionary departs, "darker shades" emerge from the background. A Chinese official intent upon sabotage addresses the villagers with a speech that, according to Nevius, sounds something like this:

> It is a pity that you should have been carried away by excitement, and treated this foreigner with so much respect, and spoken of his new and dangerous doctrines so flatteringly. The religion which he would introduce is exclusive, intolerant, revolutionary. It strikes at the root of all our cherished civil and social institutions. It would destroy every temple in the empire . . . and abolish even the homage paid to the Emperor, to Confucius, and to deceased ancestors.

Though the speech is designed to subvert the missionary's efforts, Nevius did not disagree with its essential facts. "These conclusions are literally true," he admitted, because "Christianity is an exclusive religion, and it must supplant all others." Both sides, in other words, understood what was at stake: the Christian missionary and the Confucian official were competing in a winner-take-all contest.[54]

In the final phase, the missionary returns to the village full of hope, only to confront a disturbing new reality. The "former excitement" has vanished, and he finds only "suspicion, alarm, and . . . studied coldness." "No crowds follow us in the streets," Nevius wrote, and those who are "desirous to learn more" about Christianity cannot inquire openly "for fear of the reproach and opposition of their people."[55] The villagers, in sum, give the missionary the cold shoulder. In some cases, the Chinese official instructs the people to do more than shun the missionary. He may, as Corbett discovered, urge them to subject the outsider to physical assault. Either way, only a missionary with iron resolve can maintain a presence in a village so hostile to his designs. Given the ubiquity of this pattern of resistance, Nevius did not have to wonder why missions reported such slow progress.

Resistance was not limited to the local official. Though that individual played the role of ringleader, Nevius found that Christianity faced a different form of opposition within the homes of potential converts. On several occasions, Nevius invested time in a candidate, only to watch that person's will collapse under intense family pressure. Nevius cited the example of his language teacher, a recovering opium addict named Swun. Swun verged on converting but then suddenly reversed course, renouncing his belief in the Bible and dismissing the resurrection as "foolishness." After Nevius probed with "searching questions," Swun backed off his declarations and shared his real reason for abandoning the faith. On a piece of paper, he jotted down the obstacles blocking his conversion: the vehement opposition of his mother, the loss of friends, and his inability to find work in a society determined to exclude him. Swun, in short, did not wish to be ostracized. After reading the list, Nevius tried to allay some of Swun's concerns. Observing that the Confucian mandate to honor one's mother weighed heaviest on Swun, Nevius shrewdly deployed the doctrine of filial piety to his own advantage. "Your filial duty to your mother," Nevius contended, "requires you . . . to save her soul." Convinced by this logic, Swun reentered the Christian tent—but the victory failed to hold. Swun's sister turned his own son against him. If that were not enough, she also threatened to commit suicide if Swun joined the church; to demonstrate her resolve, she "seized a large knife and cut her finger to the bone." For Swun, it was too much to bear, and his resolve folded. He quit working for Nevius, suffered a relapse with his opium addiction, and faded from view. Helen Nevius believed that the microstory of Swun's aborted conversion shed light on the macrostory of missionary failure in China. "To understand the real trials of a missionary's life," she explained, one must recognize "that cases such as this of Mr. Swun are frequent."[56] Promising candidates faced irresistible familial and societal pressure to renounce their faith; as a result, missionaries were losing the struggle for the Chinese soul.

With his analytical mind, Nevius had discerned the underlying patterns of Chinese resistance. With these patterns, he could explain why an entire town could turn against a missionary and why promising candidates tended to backslide. Identifying problems was one thing; fixing them was another. "I prosecuted the work laboriously, making long tours over the same ground every spring and autumn," he wrote of this period, "but for five years had not a single convert." These early years consisted "chiefly of failures and disappointments," as prospects like Swun, "who seemed almost persuaded to be Christians, went back and were lost."[57] Nevius could identify the problems that plagued missions but the antidote eluded him. His colleague Calvin Mateer was not faring any better.

Calvin Mateer

Calvin Mateer had iron resolve. As a boy growing up in rural Pennsylvania in the 1840s, he was scared of ghosts. For this reason, an abandoned church near his home both fascinated and terrified him. Looking through a window, he could see the Bibles, desks, and chairs left undisturbed since the day the church closed; they remained eerily frozen in time like a museum exhibit. Adjacent to the church was an overgrown cemetery that was said to be haunted. Witnesses claimed to have seen white apparitions hovering over the graves, and legend had it that a headless ghost wandered the surrounding woods at night. The place filled Mateer with dread. If he happened to be passing the church after sunset, his heart would pound and he would quicken his pace. One night, however, Mateer decided to confront his fear. Sneaking out of his home, he walked to the graveyard, perched himself on the fence, and sat alone in the darkness all night while an owl hooted. By the time dawn broke, he had mastered his fear. Throughout his life, Mateer would make a habit of confronting the sorts of things most people swerved to avoid: an area of personal weaknesses, a challenging situation in which he might fail, or anything provoking fear.[58]

He followed this philosophy when choosing both his first job and his life's work. After graduating from Jefferson College, located outside of Pittsburgh, in 1857, Mateer fielded an offer to teach at the highly regarded Lawrenceville School in New Jersey. Staying true to character, Mateer turned down Lawrenceville precisely because it presented the best option. He deliberately chose the worst option—the chance to run a dilapidated school in Beaver, Pennsylvania, that was hemorrhaging students. "I found it run down to almost nothing," Mateer wrote, but "I was . . . determined not to fail." Mateer proceeded to build up the academy by promoting it in the community, teaching the classes himself, and providing sturdy leadership. When he left the school, he had quadrupled the student body and restored the institution to health. At this point, the sequence of events that would send Mateer to China were set in motion. Deciding upon a ministerial career, Mateer matriculated at Western Theological Seminary in Pittsburgh. There he heard a recruiter speak on campus, and he started to think. Missionary work, he informed his mother, would necessitate the forfeiture of all "prospects which I might have had at home" and offer instead a life of "trial and self-denial." What was not to love? Mateer volunteered. While he awaited his deployment, he preached at a church in Delaware, Ohio.[59]

There he met Julia Brown, a young woman who also headed a school. Born on the Ohio frontier, Brown had experienced hardship early in her life. "Pioneer farm life," Calvin Mateer's brother later wrote, prepared her for the "rough and trying" missionary experience by providing "valuable training in service and self-denial."[60] When she was eight, her mother's death signaled the end of her childhood: she would have to assume a larger role in managing the homestead. When her father died seven years later, she was thrown completely onto her own resources.[61] After graduating from seminary, she became the successful principal of a country school. After she married Calvin in 1862, their mission board assigned them to China.[62] "I have given my life to China," Calvin Mateer said in his farewell address to his church. "I expect to live there, to die there, and to be buried there."[63]

As this chapter has already shown, the couple's journey to China and first months there presented only adversity. Calvin Mateer would not have it any other way. For him, the trials afforded by illness, physical deprivation, and angry villagers provided yet another proving ground. And he got to work. After constructing a house in Tengchow with his own hands, he and Julia commenced a rigorous study of the Chinese language. Mateer discovered that the language was extremely hard, and he lacked linguistic aptitude. "I have been studying pretty regularly this week," Mateer wrote in 1864, "yet to look back over it, I cannot see that I have accomplished much. Learning Chinese is slow work." The difficulty of the language, he complained, forced the missionary to devote his "best energies" not to evangelism but to preparation. "It is as if a mechanic should spend half his life . . . getting his tools ready."[64]

Mateer persevered. Two years later, in 1866, he prepared to open his first church in Tengchow. Securing this property had not been easy; obstructionist local officials, Mateer felt certain, had quietly ordered landowners not to rent him space. Given this skulduggery, Mateer felt justified in resorting to deceitful measures himself. He convinced three Chinese men to rent a house from a landlord for the ostensible purpose of opening a grocery. After securing a lease, they sublet the property to Mateer, who converted it into a church.[65] After declaring the venue ready, Mateer thrust the doors open to the public. He was not prepared for what followed. A "crowd of rowdies" waiting outside greeted him with a shower of rocks. Outraged villagers next demonstrated in the streets, and vandals desecrated the nearby missionary cemetery.[66]

In Mateer's view, this was exactly the sort of behavior that the Chinese government was legally required to rein in. Invoking his treaty rights, Mateer contacted E. T. Sandford, the U.S. consul stationed at Zhifu, who referred him to Robert Townsend, commander of the *U.S.S. Wachusett*, an American gunboat anchored in Tengchow. To remind the Tengchow prefect of his obligations to foreigners, Townsend ordered his men to march, fully armed, in front of the official's office. After this display of muscle, Mateer presented a list of demands to what must have been an incensed prefect. He sought the immediate arrest of the troublemakers and money to repair the damaged tombstones. Unfortunately for Mateer, his plan to defeat Chinese officials with a show of legal and military force backfired. Later that day, Townsend's men ran amok in Tengchow, committing crimes and assaulting civilians. In Beijing, the Zongli Yamen learned of the incident and was appalled. It turned the incident into an embarrassment for the United States. It reprimanded Sandford and Townsend for terrifying civilians and accused Mateer of concocting "artful plans." The Americans, the office scolded, ought to be ashamed of themselves. Mateer himself acknowledged the counterproductive nature of the whole affair. "Since the departure of the *Wachusett*," he reflected, "our position has been tenfold more embarrassing than it was before." Mateer had taken a step back, but he had learned a lesson: one could not force the Chinese to accept Christ through legal or military means.[67]

But if consuls, treaties, and gunboats did not work, what would? Mateer decided to hunker down and focus on itinerant preaching. Like Hunter Corbett, Mateer planned to establish a Christian presence by running an ever-expanding circuit through villages and towns; he would visit each site periodically to monitor progress, disburse funds, perform baptisms, and train Chinese clergy. For as long as three months, Mateer traveled across the Shandong countryside, usually in a *shentza*. For *shentza* travel, he strapped two parallel wooden poles across two mules; he then tied roping to the poles, creating a makeshift seat for himself and a compartment for his belongings. Since mules never synchronized their gaits, *shentza* travel entailed constant jostles.[68] If the days were hard, night afforded little rest. Mateer would stop at flea-infested inns where he tried in vain to sleep on mud brick platforms while being kept awake by a "musical concert," "free to all the guests," composed of the "tune" of braying mules and donkeys blended with the "swearing of the muleteers." He had not lost his sense of humor.[69] In this way, Mateer traversed the countryside. And since he quantified his evangelical activity with careful record-keeping, we know that between 1864 and 1873, he logged fifteen thousand miles between 102 different towns and villages. In 1866 alone, he distributed nearly two thousand pounds of Christian literature. He was, if nothing else, indefatigable.[70]

If the travel was not grueling enough, Mateer faced multiple forms of opposition when he preached. "Every village I come to, the term, 'devil!' 'devil!' comes ringing in my ears," he wrote. As for the size of his audience, that varied from place to place. Sometimes, he preached before gatherings of two hundred; other times, he attracted only eight or ten. "In one village I failed entirely to get anyone to listen," Mateer recalled. "One boy ventured to ask where we came from, when instantly a man . . . reproved him for speaking to us." As this anecdote indicates, social pressure often prevented the curious from approaching. When not preaching, Mateer would spread out his Christian books on a cloth and either sell them or give them away. Here again he found that, while many wanted a book, they felt "ashamed to accept it from the hated foreigner" within sight of neighbors. In one village, a local fortune-teller charged at Mateer with a spear, shouting "Ah! I'll kill you!" Though we do not know the motivation behind the attack, the man perhaps saw Mateer as a spiritual rival trespassing on his territory. In handling the attack, Mateer invoked one of his guiding rules: never capitulate to threats, because if you do, you set the precedent that they work. Mateer, who never traveled unarmed, drew his revolver. Yet instead of discharging his weapon, he seized the man's spear and warned him not to take another step. The assailant retreated, unleashing a stream of invective and cautioning others not to accept the foreigner's books. A local official, expressing concern for Mateer's personal safety, urged the missionary to depart. Mateer, though shaken by the incident, returned to his work to prove a point both to himself and the village: he could not be intimidated.[71]

Mateer could pride himself for not backing down. However, the frequent exposure to danger would have been easier to accept were it accompanied by progress. Unfortunately, Mateer's early years were mostly barren.[72] Equally discouraging, the few converts he had frustrated him by smoking opium, worshipping idols, and skipping the Sabbath. One of the "great discouragements," he acknowledged, was that "even those who profess the name of Christ" remain "under the power of sin." Thus far in his life, Mateer had not failed at anything he had set his mind to. But after years of trying, he was unable to gain traction in the countryside. Though stoic in the face of hardship, Mateer possessed a deep reservoir of Christian feeling. When preaching, he was known to choke up with emotion and require a moment's pause before regaining his composure. While he sang hymns, tears would stream down his cheeks.[73] It was this sentimental side that prompted a colleague to describe him as a "block of granite" with the "heart of a woman."[74] His morale plummeting, Mateer longed for uplift. He needed something to make him believe again in that single idea that had impelled him to China: that the Chinese could feel Christ as profoundly as he did. In short, Mateer yearned to give the gift of Christianity to someone who could match his own spiritual depth. In the late 1860s, he got his wish—or so he thought.

During one of his junkets, Mateer introduced the Gospel to a man named Miao Hua-yu. In 1869, Miao invited friends and family to his home to share exciting news. Calvin and Julia Mateer stopped in to hear the bombshell. "I have sent for you," Miao began, because "I had an important matter to tell you. It is this: I have led you in serving the Devil" but have now "left the service of the Devil." Speaking from the heart, Miao pleaded with his loved ones to follow his lead. "I want to show you the way . . . to the true God. Examine for yourselves," he entreated, and "know that I am not deceiving myself nor you. This doctrine of Jesus is absolute and unmistakable truth." Calvin Mateer wept tears of joy. Before his eyes, a promising convert had evolved into a charismatic exhorter of the faith. The effect on the community was electric. The "whole village" and many from "neighboring villages" streamed into Miao's home, where they heard Mateer conduct a service. "We preached to them nearly all day," Mateer recalled, "keeping it up far into the night." One man's embrace of Christian faith had rendered the entire town receptive to missionary influence. The event verged on miraculous.[75]

With the help of Mateer, Miao rented a building to serve as a chapel. By doing so, he tripped an alarm and soon ran afoul of a local official who summoned him to his office. In the ensuing exchange, the official charged Miao with the "crime" of "attempting to propagate false, corrupt and dangerous doctrines." After Miao cited protections afforded by the Treaty of Tianjin, the official moved to challenge his faith: "Then Jesus really suffered in your stead—did he?" After Miao answered in the affirmative, the official punished him with fifty lashes. With "blood flowing freely" from Miao's wounds, the officer mocked his religion: "Can Jesus bear *that* for you?" When Miao refused to denounce Christianity or plead guilty to any crime, the official transferred him to another city, where a magistrate issued fresh charges: Miao, working in league with a "Mr. Mateer," had wrongly taken possession of a house and employed "mysterious arts to deceive the people" with the intent of fomenting "insurrection."[76] Rushing to Miao's aid, Mateer beheld his "Christian brother with a chain around his neck and his body disfigured for the gospel's sake." Miao was a martyr. To end his persecution, Mateer appealed to his consul, even though he had regretted taking such action in the past, and secured Miao's release.[77]

An inspirational story like this had the potential to jump-start Mateer's career. Instead, it only exacerbated his growing crisis. Though Miao excelled at sensational martyrdom, he showed little patience for the more prosaic side of Christianity. "His religion endured persecution much better than quiet study," Julia Mateer observed. "He neglected his books," "ceased coming to church," and "had to be excluded." Miao also, the Mateers later learned, used his lofty standing in the missionary community to achieve leverage over Chinese elites. He was friends with the missionaries, he boasted, and enjoyed access to their power. In sum, Miao was lost and Mateer devastated. He had, as Irwin Hyatt explained, invested all his emotional reserves in Miao, only to see his hopes dashed.[78] This singular disappointment left Mateer grappling with questions. If Christianity had failed to achieve a lasting hold on one as promising as Miao, how could he continue to entertain hope for the general population? And if a decade of exhausting itinerating had yielded so little fruit, should he simply continue with the same method? Was it time for the indomitable Calvin Mateer to contemplate what was once unthinkable—that he should quit?

Julia Mateer

Julia Mateer was not faring any better. Since itinerant preaching called Calvin away for months at a time, she decided to operate a boarding school in his absence. Her decision was consistent with convention; missionary wives often ran small schools as sidebars to their husbands' itinerant preaching.[79]

Julia was especially suited for educational work because she had previously headed a school in Ohio. In Tengchow, Julia's school started small—only six boys when it opened in 1864—and saw only trouble during its first ten years. Most worrisome, the school failed to win over local families, as the following story illustrates. A missionary visiting Tengchow recalled witnessing a strange scene in the school's front yard. "A schoolboy was being pulled towards the gate by his father," he recalled, "while Mrs. Mateer gripped the boy on the other side to retain him in the school." That a boarder wished to run away from school hardly surprises. The unexpected part of this story concerns the father who, after signing a contract committing his son to six years, suddenly wished to remove him. Though Julia prevailed in the tug-of-war, this was no isolated incident. During the school's early years, many boys tried to run away, and some parents broke their contracts by withdrawing their sons.[80]

Why did parents experience a change of heart? Many regretted consenting to the unspoken agreement that defined the school's relationship with area families. That agreement went something like this. *Your son will receive a free education, including room and board, which features training in the Chinese language. In exchange, you must commit to six years, during which time we will expose your son to Christianity.* Though the school seemed like a good idea to parents in theory, many had second thoughts upon realizing that Christianity would hinder their sons' ability to find work, get married, and lead normal lives. Other parents faced pressure from their communities to renege on the six-year commitment. "When my parents first sent me to school," a graduate recalled, "there was a great protest from all the village. They tried to scare my mother by saying that the foreigners were vampires who could extract the blood of children by magic arts." Though this family refused to back down, others wilted under pressure.[81] The opposition was so strong as to compel Julia to abandon her greatest hope: that her students would carry Christianity into their homes and communities during holidays. After ten years, she reported that "We have not known one individual instance of the friends or relatives of the boys being brought under the influence of the gospel by the school." Sadly, home visits often yielded the opposite result. Boys showing interest in Christianity had it "laughed out of them," a humiliating experience that served only "to harden them against Christian influence" and render them discontented when they returned to school. Between 1864 and 1872, attrition rates were disturbingly high and conversions alarmingly low. By all measures, the school was failing.[82]

Who would fix the problems? Since Calvin was seldom at home, Julia ran the school alone. "Just think," she wrote, "of having to watch thirty boys every day, to see if their rooms are swept, their beds made, their heads combed," and their "faces washed."[83] Though the physical labor was demanding, Julia suffered more from the mental stress. There was a "strain put upon her mind," another missionary recalled, "by the constant stream of troubles and worries."[84] Perpetually overworked, Julia could barely manage to keep the school operational. When it came to solving its serious problems, she had no energy in reserve. Like her husband, she found herself in crisis and did not know how to extricate herself.

The Death Blow

Far from being anomalous, the vampire rumors swirling around Julia's school formed part of a larger phenomenon threatening missions. In 1870, Calvin Mateer and John Nevius witnessed a disturbing antimissionary hysteria ripple across not just Shandong, but all of China. They traced the mass xenophobia back to its catalyst—*Death Blow to Corrupt Doctrines*. This incendiary pamphlet, they asserted, "has been secretly used as a powerful engine against us."[85] What was *Death Blow*? For anyone looking for salacious stories of missionary corruption, bloodlust, or sexual deviance, *Death Blow* offered rich source material. The author, likely a member of the literati, had collected fabulous anti-Christian stories, some dating back to the 1600s, and packaged them together.[86] Nevius and Mateer believed that a coordinated effort on the part of officials moved *Death Blow* systematically through the various strata of Chinese society: after magistrates provided copies to local officials, the latter distributed them to schoolteachers and gentry, who disseminated the ideas to students and ordinary people. So that "none should fall into the hands of the Christians," the same system operating in reverse could collect all copies. When one copy slipped out, Nevius and Mateer obtained it.[87]

Death Blow had perhaps contributed to a horrific act of violence committed against Christians earlier that year. The Tianjin Massacre shocked people around the world and pushed missionaries into a state of panic. The event had its origins in the Second Opium War, when French forces occupying imperial grounds in Tianjin began construction of a colossal—and from the Chinese perspective, culturally offensive—cathedral. In this new French zone, an order of nuns operated an orphanage that took in diseased, dying, and unwanted children. As children went in, never to reappear, locals started to fixate on the great mystery: *What were the nuns doing to the orphans? Was something sinister going on behind the walls?* A rumor that the French were harvesting children's eyes and organs to use in magical concoctions won believers and soon provoked mass hysteria. An angry mob gathered around the cathedral and went on a rampage, burning the cathedral to the ground and murdering twenty-one nuns, all the while crying, "Kill the French first, then the other foreigners."[88]

Nevius and Mateer felt certain that the "vile and slanderous stories" of *Death Blow* had fueled the mob action in Tianjin. "We believe," they wrote, that it "sheds important light on the means by which the recent massacre at Tien-tsin was brought about." They may have been right: *Death Blow* explains in graphic detail both how missionary alchemists extract silver from lead by mixing it with Chinese eyeballs and how they "cut out the ovaries of girls, emasculate boys, and use different methods to obtain the brains, hearts, [and] livers . . . of children." Indeed, in the nightmarish Christianity depicted in *Death Blow*, wicked missionaries mutilate children, hold wild orgies in churches, drug and rape Chinese women, and paint their own faces with menstrual blood, all the while professing the sanctity of their religion. On this point, *Death Blow*'s author cautions readers not to be fooled by missionaries' high-minded speech because their ultimate goal is truly evil: to "exterminate" the Chinese and "take possession" of China.[89] Interestingly, *Death Blow* proved effective because it offered not pure lies but an amalgam of truth and fabrication. According to Paul Cohen, the pamphlet's hybrid nature made it difficult for readers to figure out "where fact ends and falsehood begins." To illustrate, Cohen cited the pamphlet's description of the Sabbath. On this day, Christians gather in a church where a preacher "extols the virtues of Jesus" and the congregation "mumbles through the liturgies." Were the account to stop here, readers would have an accurate portrayal of a Sunday service. But the description continues, claiming that, after liturgies, "they copulate together in order to consummate their joy."[90]

Later in 1870, missionaries heard rumors that a coordinated attack—a potential Tengchow Massacre—was in the offing. "Warnings were frequently conveyed to us," Nevius wrote, "that our safety could be secured only by a speedy departure." At any other time, missionaries might have dismissed the rumor and carried on with their labors. However, with *Death Blow* in their possession, the Tianjin Massacre occurring just weeks earlier, and the lives of women and children at risk, the missionaries took the threat seriously. Believing an attack was imminent, they informed consul Samuel Holmes of their decision to evacuate.[91] Mateer, who loathed fleeing confrontation, held out the longest but eventually agreed to depart.[92] With no American warship anywhere in the vicinity, the consul arranged for two British warships to deliver the missionaries to Zhifu. There Nevius and Mateer handed British consul W. F. Mayers their translation of *Death Blow*. Nevius, Mayers wrote, "has placed in my hands a copy of a Chinese publication of most mischievous tendencies, which the missionaries find to have been widely circulated throughout this province." "It is probable," he continued, that the pamphlet "contributed to the popular excitement at Tien-tsin."[93] With all agreeing on *Death Blow*'s malignant influence, missionaries departed for Shanghai to have it published as evidence of the highly organized resistance they faced.[94]

Death Blow was not unique. "From 1860 on," Cohen observes, China "was deluged with a growing torrent of violently anti-Christian pamphlets."[95]

Plenty of evidence suggests that many Chinese believed what they read. In 1871, paranoia struck Fujian Province when villagers suspected missionaries of releasing poison into food and water supplies. When ill Chinese women approached missionaries looking for a cure, the story went, they became sexual partners against their will.[96] That same year, mass hysteria erupted in Guangdong Province—the "Shan Sin Fan" scare. An anti-Christian group distributed what they called "gods and genies" powder throughout cities and villages, telling the people it would ward off "calamity and disease." Once hundreds of thousands had consumed the elixir, the organizers posted placards informing them they had all been duped. The "foreign devils," the placards proclaimed, had concocted the powder, which was actually poison. Chinese who did not obtain the antidote from foreign physicians would "swell" up and die. But there was a catch. To receive the cure, one had to join the church, where missionaries would force female converts to engage in the "vilest deeds." The violence that flared up in Guangdong took its toll on missionary operations. The plot "to drive missionaries and their assistants away from every county station," the missionary-published *Chinese Recorder* reported, has "to a large extent . . . succeeded."[97]

Why did ordinary Chinese, in the words of Nevius and Mateer, "drink in such stories" with "ready credulity"? To answer this question, we must look through Chinese eyes at the two most visible types of foreigner—the merchant and the missionary. The Chinese easily grasped the merchant's motivation for coming to China: he pursued riches through trade. Even opium importation, foul business though it was, seemed consistent with human nature. After all, human beings are known to abandon morality when profits are to be had. In contrast to the merchants, missionaries presented an enigma. When the Chinese asked the missionary why he had come, he responded with a story that, truthful though it may have been, left auditors incredulous. In response to a "call" from God, the missionary had left family and friends, endured hard months at sea, and set up a residence among China's poor, all toward what purpose? *To tell them about a man who was nailed to pieces of wood two thousand years earlier.* From the Chinese perspective, the story defied belief. According to Nevius and Mateer, the Chinese judged the "idea that Christianity is propagated from benevolent motives" to be "inconceivable." Viewing the missionary claim of self-sacrifice without personal gain as misaligned with human nature, the Chinese dismissed it.[98] Its rejection created an intriguing informational void: *if what the missionary claims is false, what then is the hidden agenda lurking behind his enterprise?* In this way, the missionary became a blank white screen upon which any outlandish story could be projected—and believed. It is little wonder then that the fantastical claims of *Death Blow* found a receptive audience.

Conclusion

They were all failing. American missionaries had come to Shandong with grandiose dreams to serve God and save China. Though never expecting the work to be easy, they had carried to China the firm conviction that, at their backs, an almighty God guaranteed His crusaders' ultimate triumph. But now the rout was on. Forces beyond the missionaries' control were undermining—even overwhelming—their efforts. China simply presented too many traps and too much misfortune: deadly diseases, conniving officials, an angry populace, and inflammatory pamphlets. Shandong was not the only locale where missionaries began with evangelical promise only to see their dreams disintegrate. In the southern provinces, missionaries also stormed into China with holy ambition, only to become paralyzed by problems and opposition.

2

An Exercise in Futility

The Struggles of Missionaries in the South

In 1864, William Ashmore made a stunning proclamation. The Baptist missionary from Ohio announced that he had detected "signs" of a "Coming Dawn in China," when conversion to Christianity, previously an "isolated" occurrence, would become "contagious." A single conversion, like a falling domino, would cause other Chinese to topple before the Lord, and before long Christianity would cascade across the land.[1] Ashmore's optimism was surprising for two reasons. First, Christianity had witnessed only glacial progress in China up to this point. Second, Ashmore himself had experienced more hardship than success. Physical and emotional pain—not conversions—had defined his first years in Asia. After the passing of his wife in 1858, he struggled with grief and loneliness. Making matters worse, a prolonged bout with dysentery left him "broken in health." Despite these trials, he somehow summoned the strength to found the first American mission in Swatow, a port city in Guangdong Province, later that year.[2] Ashmore "sniffed the battle from afar," a colleague later wrote, and "plunged into it, reckless of strength or of safety."[3] Having established his mission, Ashmore sounded his bold prediction of a "Coming Dawn." And why not? His faith taught him that God backed the missionary enterprise, and there was no force on Earth that could resist God's will.

One force insisted on trying. "The officials and the gentry," Ashmore recalled of these trying times, "watched us like hawks" and frequently choreographed acts of violence. "We were mobbed . . . in the district cities" and "mobbed in the large towns." "We got so used to being pelted with mud and gravel and bits of broken pottery, that things seemed strange if we escaped the regular dose." Angry mobs also destroyed property. "It went badly with our chapels," he continued, where our "roofs were broken up, doors were battered in and furniture was carried off." In some locales, missionaries were "driven out" entirely. China had become less a land to be conquered and more a crucible to be survived. Though Ashmore was determined to outlast his antagonists "as an anvil sometimes wears out a hammer," this state of perpetual conflict took its toll. "The Swatow people," he summed up, "are good haters."[4]

Hatred was not peculiar to Swatow. Indeed, the most *extraordinary* aspect of Ashmore's story is how *ordinary* it was. We have already explored the resistance to missions up north in Shandong. Missionaries in the south, from Shanghai down to Canton, did not find conditions any easier. Along with malicious officials and raging mobs, they contended with the death of family members, funding problems, isolation, and low morale. This chapter presents the trials and misfortunes of four missionaries: Nathan Sites, John Kerr, Adele Fielde, and Young J. Allen. The chapter closes by examining a contentious debate that took place within missionary circles after a controversial essay asked a question that, just a few years earlier, would have been unimaginable: Was it time to end the Protestant experiment in China?

Nathan Sites

Nathan Sites was a man of sudden action. He moved decisively and with alacrity to execute any task he deemed a moral imperative. While an undergraduate at Ohio Wesleyan in the late 1850s, he stumbled upon a curious scene at a saloon near the campus. Peering inside, he observed a group of women engaged in an act of organized violence. All members of a temperance association, they were smashing liquor bottles and breaking kegs in an effort to save their community from alcohol's destructive power. As Sites looked on, the women methodically converted the proprietor's entire stock into a wet mess of glass shards, splintered wood, and foaming puddles. Eventually, they met with a beer barrel that "defied their best strength." No matter how hard they tried, they could not penetrate the unyielding wood. Inspired by their righteous fervor, Sites could restrain himself no longer. Abandoning his role as spectator, he picked up an axe, drove the blade into the resisting barrel, and watched its contents spill onto the floor.

It was this tendency to react impulsively to someone else's zeal that launched Sites's missionary career. In 1859, Robert Maclay, a missionary on furlough from Foochow, delivered an address that Sites attended. Then a junior preacher for the Methodist Episcopal Church, Sites sat spellbound by Maclay's impassioned rhetoric. Standing nearby, the bishop noted the intensity with which Sites drank in the speech. He knew an opportunity when he saw one. He scribbled a question onto a slip of paper and thrust it into Sites's hand: would Nathan go to China? When Sites read the note, it "thrilled" him "through and through." He viewed the event as divine in origin—as "God's call." Sites's interpretation notwithstanding, it is likely that Maclay, always in need of recruits, had asked the bishop to remain vigilant for promising candidates in the audience. Regardless, Sites took immediate action. He first approached his mother, who approved of his decision but also delivered an ominous prophecy: "We shall never meet again in this world." He next met with his girlfriend, Sarah Moore, who agreed to a hasty wedding. Prior to departure, the couple attempted to study the "mysterious country" where they planned to spend the rest of their lives. "We tried, in public libraries, to find books on China," Sarah wrote, but "there was almost nothing to be found." In 1860, they ventured off, not just to China but also into the thick fog of their own ignorance.[5]

As one of the original treaty ports opened after the First Opium War, Foochow had hosted missionaries since 1847. Astoundingly, it took ten years for the Methodist Episcopal Mission to secure its first convert. The "first breach" in the "stone wall of Chinese conservatism" having been achieved, missionaries set their sights on future harvests. Unfortunately, disease, overwork, and poor living conditions perpetually undermined any hope for progress. During the twelve years preceding the arrival of Sites, twenty-four men, women, and children sailed for China. Out of this group, three missionaries and two children died. Six others left the country as "invalids," with one dying at sea and another upon reaching America.[6] After a dozen years in China, missionaries confronted a disturbing statistic: their own dead outnumbered their converts.

Amazingly, the Methodist Episcopals did not lose heart in the 1860s. On the contrary, they ambitiously plotted their expansion. Feeling boxed in by other denominations' missions, they shifted their gaze beyond Foochow proper, targeting inland populations away from the port city. Robert Maclay, who had returned to China, summed up his group's position and laid out a strategy. "Eastward is the sea, northward we trench on the territory occupied by the Ningpo missions," and "southward we enter the appropriate sphere of the Amoy [Xiamen] missions," he explained, talking like a field general studying a map. If "we grow at all," the "expansion of our work will necessarily be westward." The mission resolved to penetrate the interior by sending itinerant ministers to the countryside.[7] Nathan Sites was perfectly suited for this kind of work. Though not much of a scholar, he possessed the necessary traits for any frontier: he was passionate, fearless, and willing to suffer.[8] "He delighted in pioneer work," his colleague Stephen Baldwin later observed, because he enjoyed venturing "into new places to preach the Gospel where it had never before been preached."[9] In the 1860s and 1870s, the mission sent Nathan and Sarah Sites to remote locations to work by themselves.[10]

Though the Gospel was always a tough sell, opium compounded the difficulty. In the previous decades, Fujian Province had absorbed vast quantities of opium, and addiction was widespread. The opium scourge tore through the fabric of Chinese society, and European and American traders bore the blame. Unfortunately for Sites and other missionaries, the Chinese did not draw a distinction between foreign opium smugglers and missionaries. They did not, in other words, indict the former and exonerate the latter. Instead, they imagined foreigners as a monolithic entity that imported two things: narcotics and religion. "God knows," an exasperated missionary wrote, "how often and often" our Christian message is "contemptuously thrown back in our face" with the following rebuke: "You destroy us with your opium, and now you insult us with your offer of . . . salvation." The Chinese insistence upon linking Christianity with opium, he complained, had "rendered abortive" the missionary enterprise.[11] In some towns, outrage against opium trafficking mixed with the standard xenophobia organized by scholar-officials to yield a roiling witch's brew of anger and resentment. Is it any wonder that Sites nearly lost his life when visiting this sort of town?

The town of Yen-p'ing had already taken a firm stand against missionaries by the time Sites arrived in 1879. In 1875, the American Methodists opened a chapel where a Chinese preacher held services and a bookseller, Chang, sold Christian texts. The gentry, viewing the chapel as the beachhead for a larger Christian invasion, organized opposition. A mob attacked the chapel, razed it to the ground, beat Chang senseless, and dragged him to a local prefect claiming falsely that he had kidnapped women. The prefect, siding with the mob, expelled Chang from the city. Clearly, the anti-Christian denizens of Yen-p'ing had thrown down the gauntlet. Not willing to back down, missionaries contacted their consul, who pressed the case with higher Chinese authorities. The settlement favored the missionaries: the government agreed to rebuild the chapel, pay for damages, lift the scurrilous charges against Chang, remove the prefect from office, and order the townspeople to allow missionaries to work unmolested. Missionaries had won, but Yen-p'ing remained a wasp's nest of anti-Christian sentiment.[12]

Nathan Sites would feel the full force of the town's animosity. When he arrived on a Wednesday in early December, the town's gentry launched, with the prefect's approval, what Sarah Sites called a "preconcerted and carefully organized plan." The plan's first phase manifested itself on Saturday, when inflammatory placards appeared all over town, urging residents "to bind, beat, and toss out the foreigner." At Sites's request, the local magistrate had the placards taken down. He also admonished Sites not to preach the following day. Though Sites prudently canceled his Sunday service, this preemptive action failed to forestall the plan's next phase. On Sunday afternoon, Sites ventured out into the countryside on a long walk that ended in the vicinity of the rebuilt chapel. Ominously, a crowd of men dressed in black surrounded the building. Before Sites could slip away, the assassins entered into pursuit. Recognizing his peril, Sites made a run for the magistrate's office one-half mile away—but it was too far. About to be overtaken, Sites ducked into a building, hoping to find decent people willing to protect him. But the building was abandoned and Sites was trapped. Armed with rocks and clubs, the black-clothed men entered the building, surrounded Sites, and beat him mercilessly. One man, intending to gouge out Sites's eyes, thrust a two-pronged fork into his face, causing blood to stream down. Somehow freeing himself, Sites fled onto the road. In no condition to run, he was easily overtaken, and the assault continued. This time, his attackers tied his feet together, bound his hands behind his back, and threw him headfirst onto the stone road. His face submerged in a pool of his own blood, Sites turned his head slightly to breathe and played dead. He then reminded himself that God had not forsaken him. What else could he do?

Assuming Sites to be dead, his assailants debated their next move. Some wished to pelt the lifeless body with stones while others favored throwing the body into the river. Before they could reach consensus, however, the arrival of an official with armed soldiers forced them to disperse. The official transported Sites to the chapel where the missionary could make out the sobbing voice of his Chinese preacher. The next voice he heard was that of the chapel's "cook-boy," who calmed Sites's frazzled nerves by saying, "Teacher, everything is safe." All night Sites's converts remained at his side, applying cold water to his wounds. The next morning, an official arrived to express regrets and have Sites removed by boat to Foochow where he could receive medical attention. After describing the incident to the American consul, Sites vowed to return. "My Bible teaches me to bless them that curse me," he said. "I want to go back to Yenping as soon as I am well."[13]

Sites would return two years later. However, Yen-p'ing had made its stand. By destroying church property and nearly committing murder, the town had sent missionaries a resounding message of total defiance. Thanks to unequal treaties, foreigners enjoyed the legal right to proselytize. However, Yen-p'ing compelled them to factor into their decision-making the total commitment of the people to resist missions through organized violence. In essence, the town forced missionaries to answer a fundamental question: *you may possess the legal right to preach the Gospel here, but is it worth your trouble?*[14]

As Sites recovered, he was unexpectedly waylaid by tragic news. In the spring of 1880, he received a letter from his daughter Belle, then finishing her first year at Wellesley College. She urged him not to become "discouraged" in his work because she would come to help him. Days later, a "hard, cold" cable arrived that turned Sites ashen gray: "Your daughter is dead." Without warning, typhoid fever had struck her down. Nathan and Sarah tried to find solace in the notion that her soul was now with Jesus, but the anguish overwhelmed them.[15] Stories of personal misfortune like this one provide important context to our larger narrative of missionary failure amid Chinese resistance. Human beings, in order to maintain morale, must find positivity in some part of their lives. Had missionaries won more converts, this progress would have rendered the personal pain easier to bear: they could comprehend personal loss as the sacrifice one made to advance God's larger design. But where could a missionary look for hope and meaning when all aspects of life seemed to fail at once—when family members died but still the converts did not come? Disturbing questions like this one haunted the mind of Adele Fielde when a jarring tragedy derailed her mission before it started.

Adele Fielde

As Adele Fielde's ship approached Hong Kong in 1866, she took comfort in the fact that a harrowing journey had come to an end and a new life was beginning. Somewhere in the Indonesian archipelago, a highly contagious "jungle fever" had infected nearly everyone onboard. Ten sailors had perished, and Fielde too had contracted the fever. "A chill like that of ice in the veins," she recalled, "was followed by scorching fever . . . and wild delirium," which were "succeeded by collapse, utter helplessness and possible coma." While lying motionless, "I was thought to have died." As the death ship drifted into Hong Kong harbor, a fellow passenger lifted Fielde out of bed and helped her put on a white gown. This was to be her wedding day.[16]

Despite feeling wretched, Fielde must have enjoyed a moment of complete satisfaction as she gussied herself up. After all, she was stout, highly intelligent, and free-thinking at a time when these traits were thought to damage a woman's chances for matrimony. She had also become something of a feminist after her abolitionist beliefs led her to the view that women, like slaves, suffered under a form of bondage. Her friends went so far as to predict that she would live out her years as an "old maid."[17] Far from being insulted, Fielde agreed with this forecast. That is because it was consistent with a lucid childhood dream that lingered in her memory. In the dream, she walked through a forest until she reached a lonely log cabin. Peering in the window through a veil of cobwebs, she saw a room that was empty save for an old woman with black eyes "who knew my fortune." The "witch," who communicated telepathically, told her she would live a "long and eventful life" but remain completely alone. Not entirely gloomy, the prophecy also foretold that the solitary life would yield "honors and uncommon happiness."[18]

Defying both the witch's augury and her friends' predictions, Fielde fell madly in love with a man who reciprocated her affection. The devout Cyrus Chilcott, the brother of her college roommate, was preparing for his mission in Bangkok under the auspices of the American Baptist Missionary Union (ABMU). Though located in Thailand, the mission focused on the expatriate Chinese community, not the local Thai. William Dean had founded the mission in 1832, when China was still closed. At that time, the ABMU had viewed Thailand as a learning laboratory for missionaries eventually headed to China, a place where they could preach to Chinese people and study the language.[19] William Ashmore had spent seven years there learning Chinese before eventually founding the Baptist mission in Swatow.[20] After becoming engaged, the young couple made arrangements: Cyrus would head out alone to Thailand to establish himself; after one year, Fielde would sail to Hong Kong where the two would wed before starting their life together in Bangkok. Having reached Hong Kong, Fielde awaited her fiancée in her wedding gown. Unfortunately, the small boat approaching Fielde's ship carried not Cyrus but—ominously—two solemn men.[21]

Cyrus was dead. He had contracted typhoid fever shortly after his arrival in Bangkok. As Fielde stood in a daze, the awful significance of the news sank in. Her entire life's plan—romance, marriage, children—evaporated in an instant. When word of the tragedy spread, she became an object of concern for those around her. The captain proposed that she sail home with him, and the other passengers urged her to accept his offer. Fielde, however, held back her consent. One hour later, she informed everyone of her plans: she would continue to Thailand to see the place where Cyrus had worked and now was buried. This, she hoped, would provide closure. She then collapsed and spent three weeks recovering in a hospital.[22]

In Bangkok, Adele Fielde struggled to put her life back together. When William Dean led her to Chilcott's grave, she fainted. And as she entered the dwelling where he had died, she felt overwhelmed by "inexpressible darkness." After regaining her composure, she informed Dean of her immediate plans: she would move into Cyrus's house and continue his work.[23] Though the decision was made, formidable hurdles remained. Fielde was attempting to become a single female missionary at a time when mission boards strongly favored married couples. Men, the thinking went, could not succeed in a challenging environment without a wife to provide companionship, offer moral support, and handle housekeeping. Boards also frowned upon the sending of unmarried women, out of fear that the latter would become romantically involved with the people they sought to convert.[24] Had word of Chilcott's death reached the ABMU prior to Fielde's departure, it would have assigned someone else to fill the vacancy. That Fielde had already reached Asia presented the ABMU with a conundrum. Could she, a single woman, handle the rigors of missionary work? With some reluctance, the ABMU elected to keep her in Bangkok under the supervision of Dean.[25] However, since hers was an anomalous case, Fielde and Dean would both need to adjust. For Fielde, adjustment meant inventing an entirely new category—the single female missionary. In order to prove that an unmarried woman could shoulder this burden, she would need to show progress, exhibit strength, and avoid controversy. As for Dean, the ABMU expected him to supply mentorship and exercise patience while Fielde figured things out.

Both failed miserably. Dean believed, as a core conviction, that only married people should undertake missions work. He grew leery of an arrangement that asked him to accommodate a single woman. Instead of providing support, he endeavored to uncover evidence of Fielde's inadequacy. As for Fielde, she sensed (correctly) that Dean despised her and so felt isolated as a result. Her typical day, she wrote, was a sad one: "I *sleep*, I *eat*, I *work*, I live *alone*." It did not help that she earned half the salary of the men.[26] As Fielde slid into depression, she started to make questionable decisions that called into doubt her ability to model either proper female behavior or appropriate Christian decorum. After observing local people smoking hashish, she succumbed to the temptation to experiment: "I . . . decided to test upon myself the effect of the narcotic." Obtaining a small quantity of the "herb," she withdrew to a secluded village to smoke without risking detection from a "white person."[27]

She experimented with the drug repeated times, entering into "separate states in consciousness" each time. The hashish transformed her first into a "musical instrument, a complex arrangement of strings and keys, trembling in rapture while sending forth enchanting melody." In another session, Fielde described the narcotic as splitting her consciousness, producing an astral self with limitless ability to assume new forms. "My duplicate became a boundless sea, ravishingly cool, utterly free." Becoming next a "continent," she felt her "vital forces working in every blade of grass and every spreading tree." "The thrill of growth," she said, "was ecstasy." During her final experience, she "lost all power to judge" time. When she attempted to walk across the room to "close a door," it "seemed to have been millions of years in reaching it."[28] Dean never found out about Fielde's experimentation with a hallucinogenic substance. However, the episode pointed to a missionary career rapidly careening off the rails.

The next transgression would bring about her removal. Feeling unwanted among missionaries, Fielde sought friendship in the diplomatic community. She formed a close relationship with the American Consul to Bangkok, visiting him for lengthy stays when his wife was absent. She even filled the role of hostess for his celebration of Washington's Birthday. Though the relationship may have been innocent, it appeared highly inappropriate, if not scandalous, to the ABMU. It was Dean, unsurprisingly, who reported her behavior.²⁹ Fielde passed her time "with unbelievers," he informed the board, referring to the expatriate community, at "dancing parties and card playing" that lasted late into the night.³⁰ Furious, the ABMU recalled Fielde to the United States and ordered that a hearing be held in Boston. She departed Thailand in 1871, passing through the Chinese port of Swatow on her way home.³¹

In Swatow, Fielde's luck improved. For one week, she stayed with William Ashmore, who took an immediate liking to her. Impressed by her intelligence, vitality, and oratorical skills, he urged her to return to Swatow once the storm clouds had dispersed. Feeling like she belonged, Fielde vowed to do exactly that—provided, of course, that she survived her hearing.³² In Boston, Fielde convinced the executive committee to drop its charges. Though she spoke eloquently on her own behalf, she also benefited from a fortuitous development within the Baptist Church. Female Baptists had recently announced plans to form a missionary society of their own that would send single women overseas. Fearing that the new organization would seize a share of the finite funding that supported missions, the ABMU saw the strategic value of keeping Fielde, a single woman, in its ranks.³³ Letters from Ashmore and the consul in Bangkok also buttressed Fielde's case. The consul reassured the committee of the innocent nature of his relationship with Fielde, and Ashmore attributed the fiasco in Thailand more to Dean's controlling personality than to Fielde's indiscretion. Crucially, Ashmore also proposed that Fielde be reassigned to Swatow. In its deliberations, the ABMU recognized that Fielde was too talented to lose. While stateside, she had impressed everyone with her oratorical and fundraising abilities. Audiences listened with rapt attention as she described the plight of the Chinese woman. That being said, the ABMU viewed Fielde with ambivalence. "Her powers are of no common order," the secretary of the ABMU wrote to Ashmore. "And yet I see there is something in her that may thwart all these powers . . . unless a tender and loving human interest shall hold her in a gentle restraint." In the end, the ABMU ordered Ashmore to provide that "gentle restraint." His job would be to mentor Fielde in a way that accentuated her gifts while suppressing her flaws.³⁴

As Fielde embarked for China in 1873, she probably reflected on her missionary career up to this point. If so, she likely arrived at the conclusion that, now thirty-four years of age, she had little to show for her seven years of service, most of which had been consumed by personal crises brought on by awful luck and poor decision-making. Though she might have pioneered a pathway for single women in missions, her impact thus far had been negligible. The male-dominated ABMU, though forgiving, still regarded the single female as a liability, and her example had only reinforced that view. Fielde, in sum, had yet to unleash her potential. But as Swatow drew near, she must have wondered if God were giving her a second chance. With it, she could prove that women could accomplish things in China beyond the capabilities of men. Certainly, male missionaries in Swatow desperately needed help. The "mob-spirit," Ashmore wrote of these dark days, was perpetrating "outrages on person, property, and converts. Houses and chapels were sacked and burned."[35] A new missionary model, one that featured women appealing to women, could conceivably circumnavigate this violent clash of men. But what form would this new model take?

John Kerr

Rash Decisions or God's Call?

In one crucial respect, John Kerr differed from the missionaries discussed in the first two chapters. He was a doctor, not an itinerant preacher. This means that his story does not follow the usual pattern. His experience in China did not involve, for example, meddlesome officials inciting violent attacks. In fact, the opposite was true. Far from wishing to drive John Kerr off, Chinese officials and ordinary people sought him out for his medical skills. That being said, Kerr suffered setbacks during his early years in China, much like the other missionaries. And even though he had a viable model—he was a medical missionary—he struggled to make the modifications to this model that would allow him to both heal bodies and save souls.

John Kerr's career in China was born out of, and later shaped by, a singular character trait. Whenever a new idea illuminated his mind, he would interpret it as a divine sign and then, with little deliberation, fully commit to it. Was God truly calling, or was John Kerr simply prone to rash decision-making? Regardless of the answer, Kerr's tendency yielded a career filled with bold plans and abrupt changes. Indeed, if one were to chart his life on graph paper, one would sketch not a gently curving line but a sequence of zigzagging segments, with each pivot point representing the moment a mere thought had prompted a life-altering course of action.

Born on an Ohio farm in 1824, Kerr experienced his first immaculate idea while studying at the Granville Literary and Theological Institution (later Denison University). One evening in 1840, the students gathered in the chapel for a mandatory prayer session. During these meetings, students would typically read out loud the inspirational stories of missionaries taken from magazines. On this night, one of the youngest students, a sixteen-year-old freshman, abruptly rose to his feet and urged the gathering to pray for him. "We were amazed," recalled one student, who would later write an account of the strange event that followed. The freshman was John Kerr, and he was having the religious experience that would alter his life's course: he must devote his life to God's service.[36]

As the gathering prayed for "little Kerr" something remarkable happened. Kerr's spontaneity triggered a chain reaction. "In a little while," the student continued, "seven or eight" of the young men "broke down, and sobbing, begged" for the group "to pray for them." In the ensuing days, the students held additional prayer meetings that packed the chapel with still more soul-searchers. One by one, the human dominoes began to tumble. "The student to my right fell helpless" during the first verse of a hymn, one student recalled, while "the one on my left hand held on till we were in the second verse when he, too, gave it up and went down." Among those witnessing the spontaneous revival was William Ashmore, then a teenage student.[37] Up to this point in his life, Ashmore had declared his firm intention *not* to preach. "I'll not become a preacher," he had said, "if I can help it." But the awakening sparked by Kerr stirred something deep inside the reluctant Ashmore, and he received his calling too: "Here am I, send me."[38]

Though Kerr had committed his life to God, the details of that commitment remained vague. Kerr knew neither the location of his service nor the form it would take. In 1842, Kerr felt the sudden inclination to become a physician—and his life altered course again. Since Granville did not offer medical training, he abruptly quit without graduating. When God spoke, one could not be bothered by something as trivial as degree completion. He matriculated at Jefferson Medical College in Philadelphia, earning his degree in 1847. Dr. Kerr then practiced medicine in Ohio for six years, before he experienced a third epiphany—the one that would steer him to China.[39]

In the spring of 1853, Kerr stumbled across an intriguing announcement. A Chinese man would be speaking in the town hall on the state of medicine in China. At this time, one rarely saw a Chinese person in Ohio, and so Kerr probably attended partly out of curiosity. As he sat spellbound, the speaker enumerated the many problems of Chinese medicine. Chinese doctors were "ignorant," he claimed. Unfamiliar with surgery, they treated physical ailments easily cured by operations by prescribing ineffective herbal remedies. As a result, the "death rate" in China exceeded that of all European countries combined. The speaker concluded by exhorting Western-trained doctors to come to China, heal the sick, and teach Western medicine. Though the lecture probably intrigued many in the audience, one man decided instantaneously to reconfigure his life around its message. "Why should not I go to China?" Kerr asked himself. "What is there hindering me from doing so?"[40] Of course, he could think of nothing. The next morning, Kerr made arrangements for another doctor to take his practice. Shortly thereafter, he submitted his application to the Presbyterian board and found a wife—Abby Kingsbury.[41] To his delight, he learned of an immediate vacancy. Peter Parker, the celebrated missionary-physician, was heading home after two decades of running the Canton Hospital. The couple arrived in Canton in 1854.[42]

Chinese Medicine

When missionaries arrived in China, they confronted not an empty lot, as far as religion was concerned, but a thick forest of existing belief systems. Similarly, John Kerr met not with the absence of a medical tradition but rather with one that had evolved for centuries on a parallel track. The Chinese based their healing system on the foundational concept that a duality of opposites defined the universe—*yin* and *yang*. Applying the concept to the human body, healers assumed that a disparity of these two forces caused illness and, fittingly, prescribed treatments designed to restore proper balance. In addition, they linked health to the five elements believed to make up the world, associating each one with a specific organ: wood (liver), water (kidneys), metal (lungs), earth (stomach and spleen), and fire (heart). Attributing poor health to the improper proportions of elements (too much of one and not enough of another), practitioners devised remedies aimed at restoring "equilibrium."[43]

Who was this Chinese practitioner and how did his medicine work? When Dr. Kerr regarded a Chinese doctor, he did not see someone who resembled himself. As historian G. H. Choa explains, a Chinese doctor entered the profession after training under a mentor. At no point during this apprenticeship did he sever human skin with a scalpel, peer inside a body, or perform a dissection. After starting his own practice, he saw patients not in a hospital but in an herbalist's shop. When a patient entered, the "scholarly-looking" doctor would seat him at a table, observe his overall appearance, listen closely to his voice, and measure his pulse. Once he formed his diagnosis, he would write out a prescription on paper with brush and ink. The consultation complete, the patient would hand the paper to the "dispenser," who would package the ingredients and explain how they were to be mixed and consumed.[44] Western medicine obviously did not look anything like this. Unable to see merit in the Chinese system, some foreign physicians disparaged their Chinese counterparts. When a patient arrives, a missionary magazine wrote, the doctor "looks at the patient's tongue," "feels his pulse," and then prescribes "cockroaches, rhinoceros skin, silk worms, crude calomel, asbestos, rhubarb, full-grown roses, moths, maggots, centipedes, shell fish, caterpillars, toads, [or] lizards."[45]

This belittling characterization aside, Chinese medicine probably worked at least as well as Western medicine in the 1800s for many ailments. Thus, if medical missionaries were to win converts through healing, they would need to identify specific health areas where Western medicine enjoyed an advantage. Their answer was to venture where Chinese medicine refused to go: *inside the human body.* By the mid-nineteenth century, Iris Borowy writes, Western medicine was "clearly superior in knowledge of anatomy and surgery."[46] Using surgical tools, foreign doctors amputated infected limbs, performed delicate cataract operations on the eyes, removed painful bladder stones, and excised cancerous tumors.[47] Traditional Chinese medicine, though providing a veritable storehouse of herbal knowledge, did not perform invasive operations such as these. "In the domain of Surgery," wrote a medical missionary in Swatow, the Western physician "has the field almost entirely to himself." The "immediate results are so striking to the Chinese," he continued, "that there is no question as to supremacy." The Western doctor's only real challenge lay in managing expectations—to remind patients "there is a limit to our power."[48] The Chinese expected miracles, so overwhelming was the Western advantage in surgery.

The Canton Hospital

John Kerr's first stint in China, though short and sad, was productive. In Canton, he confronted circumstances completely unlike what other missionaries were experiencing. Whereas many of them had to shield themselves from airborne stones, the Chinese threw at Kerr not projectiles but their ailing bodies. In 1856, Kerr handled 377 surgical operations, more than one per day.[49] He was assisted by a Chinese doctor, Kwan Ato, whom Peter Parker had trained.[50] Unfortunately, forces beyond Kerr's control interrupted his practice. First, Kerr's wife Abby died of illness in 1855 and, just days later, he learned of the passing of his mother. For a grieving Kerr, who was predisposed to interpret coincidences as God's will, these losses prompted unpleasant soul-searching. "In the loss of my beloved companion," he wrote, "God has taken away my only earthly source of comfort & support . . . among these heathen people." And when God added to the "burden" by taking away his mother, Kerr "felt that God indeed had a controversy with me." The dual blow compelled Kerr to question his role in a world that suddenly seemed to lack meaning. He called himself "a stranger in the earth" and a "sojourner in a vain and empty world" (underlining in original). Dejected and confused, Kerr returned to America after just two years.[51]

America brought rejuvenation and new prospects. Kerr spent much of 1857 in Philadelphia, updating himself on the latest developments in medicine at Jefferson Medical College. He also found a second wife, Isabella Mosley, who joined him when he sailed for China in 1858.[52] Back in Canton, Kerr met with additional challenges and sorrows. While he was stateside, hostilities had erupted between China and two European powers, England and France (the Second Opium War). One of England's bombardments had caused a conflagration in Canton. Though this fire did not reach the Canton Hospital, a second fire of mysterious origin destroyed most European and American buildings.[53] The Canton Hospital collapsed in the blaze. Quite possibly, the Chinese had set fire to the foreign district as an act of retaliation. Regardless, Kerr faced the daunting prospect of rebuilding the entire facility.[54]

He also confronted personal tragedy and evangelical disappointment. Concerning the former, Isabella gave birth to three children, and all of them died, two succumbing to diphtheria.[55] During this prolonged period of loss, Kerr contended with his utter failure as an evangelist. Between 1861 and 1872, the Canton Hospital treated 409,000 patients but reported only twelve conversions.[56] If he had been so brave (or perhaps masochistic) as to do the math, he would have confronted a devastating ratio: he secured one conversion for every 34,000 patients. Kerr, in short, healed many bodies but saved few souls. He was a devoted missionary who had come to China to use his medical expertise to spread Christianity. However, his early years were defined mostly by disease, death, and destruction.

Young J. Allen

Kerr, Fielde, and Sites were not the only missionaries to struggle. Young J. Allen stormed into China full of Christian passion, only to see circumstances beyond his control douse his evangelical fire. Allen was born in Georgia in 1836 to a slave-owning family. Since his father died before his birth and his mother died twelve days after it, Allen was raised by his aunt, who treated him as her own son. Amazingly, Allen learned he was an orphan only after he turned fifteen. Allen's defining religious experience occurred in 1851. While listening to an especially fiery sermon, he all of a sudden became overwhelmed by a sense of his own sinfulness; he jumped through a church window and sprinted into the nearby woods. He filled out the rest of his Christian identity at Emory College. It was at Emory that he acquired the austere appearance of a missionary—perhaps even of a holy man. According to a fellow student, his "erect" posture, "long flowing beard," and eyes "like an eagle's" made him "the most striking figure" on campus.[57]

Though Allen had become devout, he never allowed his mind to become exclusionary. Indeed, college awakened other academic interests that harmonized with his Christian faith. The inquisitive Allen found himself in an intellectual orchard, and he happily ate the fruit. Emory's emphasis on a classical education ensured that Allen would consume a steady diet of Ancient Greek, Latin, and moral philosophy. He also took courses in the natural sciences and mathematics. Composition, which would become Allen's greatest strength, suffused the entire curriculum.[58] Allen's education also strengthened his conviction regarding women's rights. An avid book collector, he amassed a library of three hundred volumes dominated by biographies, many of which featured the lives of accomplished women.[59] Thanks to this rigorous academic training, Allen could, when presented with a problem, draw solutions from multiple intellectual systems—not just Christianity. His mental agility would serve him well after his missionary career got off to a rocky start.

Interestingly, Allen gave very little thought to the single biggest decision of his life—becoming a missionary. Neither he nor his new wife, Mary Houston, had so much as contemplated China when, in 1858, a missionary recruiter uttered a mere five words: "What think you of China?"[60] Astoundingly, the couple volunteered to join the Southern Methodist Episcopal Mission in Shanghai, and in 1859 they embarked with their infant daughter. As Allen stood on the ship's deck holding her in his arms, he confronted for the first time the disturbing implications of his rash decision. Why had he decided to spend his life in China, given the "vastness" of that country and his own "insignificance"?[61] If Allen entertained doubts during the journey, his early months in China would only magnify them. When he reached Shanghai, the Treaty of Tianjin theoretically allowed him to evangelize in the interior—but circumstances confined him to the treaty port. China was then in the throes of the Taiping Rebellion (1850–1864), a massive civil war pitting Qing forces against a rebel army started by Hong Xiuquan, a religious fanatic who claimed to be the son of God. Since Taiping forces posed a constant threat to Shanghai, Allen could not venture out to rural areas to prospect for souls.[62] Missionaries, Allen wrote, were "hovering on the border" waiting for China to become "quiet and safe in the interior" so that they could "possess the land." Hemmed in, Allen had "to learn to wait." With little else to do, he studied Chinese, following a regimen that included reading the texts that taught Confucian ethics to children. By doing so, he acquired respect for Chinese learning. The *Three Character Classic*, he observed, offered "more learning . . . than I had previously given it credit for." After completing this text, Allen moved to other classics, venturing as deeply into the Chinese canon as his language proficiency would allow. In this way, the ever-curious Allen added Confucianism to the knowledge base he first nurtured in college.[63]

If the Taiping Rebellion were not enough, another civil war plagued Allen's fledgling ministry with financial trouble. On April 12, 1861, the Confederate Army's attack on Fort Sumter signaled the start of the American Civil War. When Lincoln ordered the blockade of southern ports, Allen's mission board cut off his funding. Though commanded by God to proselytize, Allen faced a more immediate imperative: to feed his growing family and save his mission from "pecuniary embarrassment."[64] Desperate for income, he accepted a position teaching English at the Shanghai Tongwen Guan, a school established by the Qing government to teach Western language, science, and math.[65] The college, pleased with Allen's instruction, offered him a three-year contract, which he refused, choosing to commit instead for just six months. The Civil War would end soon, he predicted, and then he could launch his cherished itinerant ministry. But Allen had made a severe error based on false hopes. Even after the Civil War ended in 1865, several years would pass before his home mission would resume sending funds. When his short-term contract expired, Allen lost a reliable salary and his students lost their favorite teacher. Fifteen upset students appeared at Allen's residence, with some informing him of their plans to drop out in protest of Allen's replacement. Allen had learned something about himself: he was a gifted communicator of knowledge.[66]

Unfortunately, teaching was the only bright spot in his life. All else was storm and stress. From afar, "it may seem all very fine to be a missionary in a foreign land," an exhausted Allen wrote an Emory alumnus. But "all the romance ... departs immediately on touching the soil of a heathen land." "No one should ever think of becoming a missionary," he admonished, unless they are "thoroughly identified with Christ" and filled with the "spirit of self-denial," because China will "test the material of which the missionary is made." After eight years, Allen had at least acquired sober wisdom. But he had acquired very little else, and as his situation worsened, his mood darkened. By the late 1860s, Mary had given birth to six children, but three had died.[67] Moreover, Allen knew that they had likely died in vain because his evangelical work, the sole reason for their coming, amounted to a paltry seven baptisms.[68] As the years passed, Allen's depression deepened. "Constant embarrassments beset me, annoy me, distract me," he wrote in 1867, citing specific troubles: "no remittances from the Board," "no money in the treasury," "debts due," "my wants pressing," and "Mission work stagnant." "When, Oh when shall deliverance come!"[69] Allen was failing.

Frustration Boils Over

Allen's anguished cry reflected the sense of futility felt by many missionaries. After marching into China supremely confident, many reported that gloom had settled in. It happens frequently now, John Nevius wrote in 1869, that a missionary sees the work as "drudgery," views his decision to come "with regret," "pines for home," and "makes very little progress in gaining ... influence with the people."[70] For the first time, a collection of grim phrases entered into the missionary vernacular: the "horror of heathen darkness," the "cloud of depression," the "stone wall of indifference," and the "dry desert where there is no water."[71] The optimism and zeal that had propelled young men and women to China had all but dissipated.

William Ashmore, previously optimistic, no longer wrote about the "coming dawn." Instead, he laid out step by step how a new missionary gradually slides into despair. To enter China, he wrote, "is to pass from the warmth of a mid-day sun into the shadow of an eclipse, and there to remain." For a while, the "warm fervor of the home-life" sustains the missionary, as he receives "cheering" letters from friends and family. But as time passes, the once steady stream of mail slows to a trickle, and he eventually finds "that brook dried up." As home fades from view, China pummels him with an unrelenting sequence of negatives: "No . . . Sabbath, no sign of a church, no sight of a Christian, no song of praise, no voice of prayer, no joy of the Holy Ghost, no Christ, no God." Instead, the land offers "grimy temples" filled with "hideous idols" and the "ashes of incense offered to devils." To step outside one's mission is to be overwhelmed by human horror. "Everywhere are sores and ulcers and . . . dirt and stench and nastiness and filth" as well as multiple forms of pollution: "pollution of manners, and pollution of speech, and pollution of thought." The missionary's "continuous contact" with loathsome things inevitably takes its toll. He first experiences "lowered vitality" and finally "*numbness* of the spiritual nature." His grand project now seems an "impossible undertaking," a "hopeless chance," and a "useless outlay of time and energy." As frustration sets in, the missionary even wonders if God has forsaken him: "Where is the Lord God of Elijah?"[72]

No matter how committed to the cause one was, years of isolation could wear on a missionary's psyche. One Shandong missionary described what it felt like to be cut off from civilization. "We seemed to be living apart from the rest of the globe," she wrote. "No railroads, no telegraphs, no post offices." She did receive frequent visitors to her home, but they were not of the sort one welcomes: scorpions, lizards, mosquitoes, flying ants, mold, and invisible diseases.[73] A traveler to Shandong visited a band of missionaries who lived in almost complete isolation. "We felt as if it is the loneliest spot in this world," the traveler wrote, while marveling at their ability to prosecute a work that was "so lonesome, so repulsive, so wearing to the body, and so harrowing to the spirit."[74] Not all missionaries could survive such conditions. One gravely ill missionary stationed at a lonely outpost revealed his state of mind in a desperate plea written to his board just prior to his death. "One man cannot live twenty miles from other foreigners in such a climate," he wrote. "We live among a people who call us 'devils' every day, and hate us every hour . . . Help! Help! Help!"[75]

When missionaries died, survivors always attributed the sad event to God's will. If the deceased had labored in China for many years, colleagues would point to the meaningful career of service. But what could one say when a missionary died before getting started? In 1885, Martha Crawford, a missionary in Shandong, took on the unenviable task of reporting to the board the death of Mattie Halcomb, so recently arrived that she had only just begun language study. "You will mourn with us again over the loss of a member of our little circle," Crawford began. "Cut off before being able to enter upon her missionary labors, she doubtless fulfilled her mission to which our Father sent her, for he makes no mistakes." One has to wonder what lurked in the recesses of Crawford's mind as she penned these words. By insisting so emphatically on God's infallibility, was she demonstrating the robust nature of her faith? Or quite the opposite, was she trying to protect her own morale with the reassuring assertion of a divine plan because she found the alternative—that this sad episode was utterly devoid of meaning—too disturbing to contemplate?[76] Indeed, death came with such frequency in Shandong as to prompt one missionary to speak not of the presence of God but rather of a darker entity hovering over them. "It is sad," she wrote, "to see how, one by one, our number is lessened by the death angel."[77]

Many missionaries quit before the "death angel" could swing his scythe. According to Jessie Lutz, who compiled attrition statistics, a startling number left China prior to retirement. Out of all the men and women who started between 1861 and 1876, only about 7 percent retired from the field after full careers. For the other 93 percent, their missions ended prematurely for a host of reasons that included financial trouble and personal conflict. However, the death or illness of either the missionary or a spouse caused the majority of early departures (58 percent). Lutz also found that much of the attrition took place within the first ten years, as nearly half of all missionaries (about 45 percent) failed to last one decade. Almost a quarter exited before reaching the five-year mark, and nearly a tenth either died or departed before marking their first anniversary. When we add to this the fact that proficiency in the Chinese language required on average two years of study, the numbers tell a sad story of missionaries exiting the field before getting started.[78] Mattie Halcomb's case was not uncommon.

Back in the United States, the combination of high attrition rates and low conversion totals attracted attention. In the two decades following the Civil War, support for China missions, as measured by donations and volunteers, ebbed—a decline that caught mission boards by surprise. While understanding that the war must temporarily absorb resources, they had expected that the conflict's end would spark a resurgence of interest in foreign missions. It did not. For some of those lean years, boards could blame low recruiting and fundraising totals on the Depression of 1873.[79] However, discouraging news flowing out of China clearly contributed to the overall mood of apathy that prevailed in the United States. T. D. Woolsey, the former president of Yale and an advocate of missions, summed up the bleak outlook in 1874. "In some respects China seems to be more hopeless . . . than any other part of the world," he observed. It was a "dead, inert mass for the gospel to act upon."[80]

John Nevius experienced the American public's cynicism firsthand while on furlough in the 1860s. Nevius had expected a hero's welcome. That, after all, was the usual treatment that churchgoers gave a returning missionary about whom they had been reading. Missionary magazines wove excerpts from missionary letters into heroic narratives that honored the trials and glorified the exploits of those who labored overseas. Somewhat worried that editors glossed over bad news, Nevius urged them to portray missions realistically. "You seem to wish us to send you only . . . favorable news," he wrote, "while my idea is . . . that we should give the church at home . . . the actual state of things." Magazines should report the "the Bull Run disasters" alongside the "glorious victories." Nevius's call for evenhandedness notwithstanding, the hero's narrative did serve a crucial function. It helped boards recruit volunteers, raise money, and keep congregations focused on the cause. As an unintended byproduct, the narrative ensured that missionaries returning home would feel appreciated.[81]

But this was no hero's welcome that Nevius was receiving. To his shock, Americans had become downright scornful. "No institution," they asserted in his presence, is "more useless than these missionaries." Tired of hearing his life's work slandered, Nevius spoke frequently at churches. He wished to disabuse people of the erroneous impression that missionaries wasted resources. In Brooklyn, a woman thanked him for rekindling her faith in China missions. Previously, she had heard only that "missionary work in China had accomplished nothing, and that missionaries generally led idle, useless, and . . . immoral lives."[82] If Nevius saw the home community as misinformed, Adele Fielde judged it to be truly cruel.

After returning to Swatow in 1873, Fielde complained to her board about the difficult conditions she and others faced. Her pleas accomplishing nothing, Fielde broke an unwritten rule in missionary circles by going public. In a scathing article for *The National Baptist*, she described China as a cesspool, unfit for human life. "The natives live in houses without windows or floors," she wrote, "and eat things to us unclean." "Cholera prevails all summer, small-pox all winter, and unspeakable skin-diseases, vermin, and filth all the year round." Yet instead of addressing the unhealthy conditions, the board continues to send out "young men" to "kill themselves by low diet and overwork." Christ, she claimed, took much better care of his disciples. While blasting her board, Fielde reserved her most potent vitriol for church members. Eschewing the old adage that advises against biting the hand that feeds you, Fielde excoriated donors as sadistic people who gave money not to spread the Gospel but rather to satisfy a "craving appetite for missionary suffering." While "sitting in ease at home," donors took voyeuristic pleasure in watching expendable heroes march inexorably to their doom. They resembled the "Roman spectators in the amphitheater" who "turned down their thumbs for the death" because "the more the blood the grander the spectacle." Like gladiators in the Coliseum, missionaries in China provided the morally perverted donor with a kind of blood-sport entertainment.[83]

Few missionaries shared Fielde's extreme view. That said, many were growing increasingly discontented as they labored in an untenable situation. Missionary frustrations boiled to the surface in 1870 when one of their own questioned the worth of the whole enterprise. In 1870, F. S. Turner, based in Canton, published an essay, "The Missionary Problem," in response to a harsh critique of foreign missions published the previous year. Instead of fighting back, Turner used his essay to take stock of China missions. "For a long time," he observed, "missions have been going on, like a railway train after steam is shut off, by the exhausted impetus of the mighty effort by which our forefathers set them in motion." Missionary work continued to happen, in other words, but only because inertia allowed it to coast with diminishing "velocity" along the "grooves" of "routine": donations flow in, missionaries head out, a few converts are won, hopeful reports are published, new volunteers are recruited, and the cycle repeats itself. Though missions remained in operation, Turner contended that few people paid much attention. "Until recently, who *thought* about missions?" Missionary work had become the background noise of Western civilization. But should Christians continue to allow the train to rumble along? At the crux of his essay, Turner asked the hard question: did the gains, measured in converts, justify the investment of human and monetary capital? Multiple decades of expensive labor in China, he pointed out, had netted between five thousand and six thousand converts—not an insignificant number, to be sure, but also not enough to inspire confidence. Given such meager results, Turner asked, "Have our efforts to convert the Chinese resulted in failure?"[84]

The riders on Turner's train—the missionaries themselves—did not wish to see their vehicle decommissioned. Judging by the outcry Turner provoked in the *Chinese Recorder*, he had struck a nerve. One missionary urged critics to remember the supreme challenge posed by China, the most "anti-foreign" of any "nation under the sun." He described the relationship between Christianity and Confucianism as one of "direct antagonism," and he reminded readers that the missionary's prime objective involved a total overhaul of Chinese religious culture: "to dethrone the ancient sages that have been worshipped as gods for ages" and "to break . . . customs and superstitions" that are "rotten at the core." That was no simple task. Making matters more difficult, saboteurs undermine the effort by concocting "monstrous stories" detailing heinous missionary acts that are "spread from mouth to mouth" and "firmly believed in." "Shall these six thousand then be considered few," he asked, "when we remember the conditions under which they have been gained?"[85]

Conclusion

Of course, this missionary was right: China was hostile to missions. However, in justifying the failure, he implicitly admitted that the failure was real. And if so, missionaries had to confront the hard truth that their current methods were not working, a point Turner made emphatically. "Unless kept alive by perpetual freshness of thought," Turner warned, missions "will slowly stiffen to stagnation." Many missionaries privately conceded that "stagnation" had already set in—that missions work had become "hopeless toil in the face of difficulties apparently insurmountable."[86] Though the current methods had proven themselves ineffective, missionaries had yet to innovate. If they were to escape the crisis, they would have to learn from failure, and not just wallow in it. Innovation—what Turner had called "freshness of thought"—presented the only avenue forward.

Missionaries would also have to admit something else: success would require more help from the Chinese. Most of the men and women described thus far were defined by not just religious faith but individualism. While trusting in God, they believed they could surmount almost any obstacle through the sheer force of will. Indispensable though this trait was, it was not sufficient. Most of the problems that missionaries faced in China lay beyond even a self-reliant person's ability to solve. These problems would require the input of insiders—the Chinese themselves. Only the Chinese knew their own culture well enough to see the hidden openings for a new religion. In short, missionaries could reverse their fortunes only by making two fundamental changes to their approach: they must diversify their methods and they must allow more Chinese influence. That is exactly what some started to do.

3

Christ versus the Demons

Encounters with the Chinese Supernatural

John Nevius received a hint of what he was in for shortly after arriving in Ningbo in 1854. That year, he hired a scholar named Mr. Tu to teach him Chinese. Though Mr. Tu had studied the Confucian canon, Nevius quickly learned that his true interests lay elsewhere. He became animated only when discussing the "supernatural." With "fluency and zest," Tu would regale Nevius with "marvelous stories" of "spiritual manifestations and possessions" by demons. At first, Nevius responded to the fabulous tales with skepticism. "I brought with me to China," he wrote, "a strong conviction that a belief in demons ... belongs exclusively to a barbarous and superstitious age." He even attempted, to no avail, to convince Tu that his beliefs were merely the "combined result of ignorance and imagination." However, Nevius's blanket dismissal of his tutor's occult beliefs did not sit well with Nevius himself. He could not deny the "striking resemblance" between Tu's stories and Biblical passages on "demonology." Though assuring himself that the resemblance was "accidental," the disturbing similarity lingered in his mind. Seven years later, when Nevius started traveling through the Shandong countryside, he "met with many evidences of this same popular belief." Mr. Tu was not the exception. He was the rule.[1]

This chapter explores the spiritual encounter that took place when missionaries first ventured into rural China. In agricultural villages, they confronted a population already in possession of well-established systems of belief. Here the Christian Gospel washed up against local religions populated by gods, ghosts, and demons. What transpired when the two belief systems collided? As Chapter 1 explained, missionaries planned to initiate a spiritual process that we have called "delete and replace": the Chinese were expected to *delete* their old beliefs and *replace* them with Christianity. This plan, however, turned out to be hopelessly naïve; Chinese indigenous beliefs simply were too deeply rooted to be easily eradicated. Interestingly, the opposite scenario did not take place either. The Chinese did not reject Christianity outright. So what did happen?

Chinese villages became spiritual laboratories where Christianity mingled with indigenous supernatural beliefs. Out of this cultural chemistry emerged new spiritual practices, rituals, and stories that neither side expected. When adopting Christianity, converts did not banish the gods, ghosts, and demons from their minds. Rather, they pushed for syncretism: they had God and Jesus co-inhabit the same supernatural landscape as Chinese spiritual entities. Suddenly crowded, this was no peaceable kingdom. That is because the Chinese required that the new Christian deities prove their worth by defeating their indigenous rivals in invisible contests. Some converts claimed that their Christian faith granted them the power to cast out demons by invoking God and Jesus. Before the eyes of bewildered missionaries, converts held exorcisms, a ritual that was mostly anathema to Protestants. One man went further. Hu Yong Mi, a pastor in Foochow, placed demons at the center of his ministry; he attracted followers by recounting his many skirmishes against these enemy spirits. The chapter concludes by discussing the lesson that Nevius learned from his encounters with Chinese supernaturalism. Accepting that Chinese beliefs lay beyond his comprehension, he argued that missionaries must cede more control to converts when trying to integrate Christianity and Chinese culture.

Demon Possession

Nevius Begins Research

In 1879, Protestant missionaries across China received a remarkable circular letter from John Nevius. In it he asked colleagues to fill out a survey, the first question of which got right to the point: "Are cases of supposed demoniacal possession common in your locality or not?"[2] This question did not come wholly out of the blue. Nevius had been contemplating Chinese occult beliefs ever since his sessions with Mr. Tu a quarter century earlier. That being said, his interest spiked in the early 1870s after he attended a gathering in Zhifu. During the winter months, ice rendered steamship travel in and out of the port impossible. To pass the time, idle merchants and missionaries held social and intellectual gatherings. The event Nevius attended featured Timothy Richard, a Welsh missionary, who delivered a paper entitled "Demoniacal Possession in China." Given its sensational topic, the paper attracted a large audience and prompted a vigorous discussion. Foreigners were eager to talk about Chinese demons.[3]

After Richard finished speaking, others related their experiences. Hunter Corbett shared details pertaining to a "haunted house." When a Chinese Christian moved in, the "supposed ghost removed to the next house" where it "gave no peace to the occupants." Wishing the ghost gone, those residents "begged" the Christian "to go over and exorcise it." Obligingly, this man seized his Bible and called on neighbors to join him at the house to pray to God to "protect them from harm." The prayer session worked and "peace was restored to the house."[4] After Corbett finished, others offered their stories. At one point, the group turned to the only doctor present to solicit his "professional opinion" as a man of science. Robert Coltman had, all evening long, "maintained a discreet silence." "I had a stronger opinion than I was willing to give," Coltman recalled, "so I merely said that the cases were very interesting and apparently authentic." What he withheld was his utter shock that "men of good standing" took demons seriously. He was especially appalled that the group gave credence to a theory he rejected as utterly preposterous—that Satan, facing resistance in the Christian West, "had given up" his "persecution there" and shifted his "attention and energy" to China. Occult activity was on the rise in China, in other words, because Satan had relocated. "I went home from the meeting," he wrote, "with the feeling that the Chinese were not the only people who were superstitious."[5]

There is no record of Nevius speaking at the meeting. However, his subsequent actions bespoke his fascination with the topic. "After this memorable evening," Timothy Richard recalled, "Dr. Nevius began to collect evidences of demon possession and demon exorcism from all parts of China." How did Nevius obtain this evidence? He disseminated the aforementioned letter to missions across the country. By soliciting testimony, he was commencing an investigation into Chinese popular religion. Though he had come to China harboring some knowledge of the country's "institutional" religions, Buddhism and Daoism, he remained ignorant of China's vernacular religions. These belief systems featured colorful arrays of gods, ghosts, and demons. Unlike the more theologically defined institutional religions, the vernacular religions could easily evolve to suit local needs. Indeed, it was the adaptability of these popular religions that allowed them to prosper for centuries.[6]

Though Chinese belief systems differed from one locale to the next, they held certain characteristics in common. All of them, according to Richard Von Glahn, provided believers with a "means of invoking supernatural powers to gain some measure of control over" their "mortal existence." Rural Chinese endured a perilous existence, assailed as they were by drought, flood, blight, disease, and bandits. When one burned incense before an idol or engaged a spirit-medium, one did so to propitiate a supernatural being. Through ritual, one hoped to convince a spirit either to bestow good fortune or to cease inflicting misery. The expectation of immediate and direct action on the part of the summoned spirit suggests an interesting facet of this belief system: the Chinese did not imagine supernatural entities as occupying a separate spiritual plane, divorced from the real world. Rather, the "divine and the mundane remained organically connected," in Von Glahn's words, "each subject to powers of change ... inherent in the physical universe."[7] In 1874, a missionary used nonacademic language to make a similar observation. "To the fanciful mind of the Chinese," he wrote, "a numberless host of invisible beings are about him." These entities "soar in the starry regions," "penetrate the darkest abyss," "labor in the patient ox," "scatter the seeds of the wasting pestilence," "travel with the swift and destructive storm," and "vomit the lightning." Spirits were ubiquitous, in other words, which meant that one could attribute all accidents in life—a shipwreck, a collapsed bridge, a drowning man, or a rooster attacking a child—to their agency.[8]

When seeking spiritual aid, the Chinese identified some entities as being more receptive than others. In popular religions, a supernatural being's willingness to intercede in human affairs was inversely proportional to its power. The gods on high, for example, wielded formidable power but maintained their distance from the everyday world of mortals. A supplicant, therefore, could not expect a god to react with helpful alacrity to his ritualized request. In contrast, the spirits of ancestors closely watched the lives of their descendants and exhibited an eager willingness to intervene. Yet given their lack of potency, one could not expect them to alter outcomes dramatically. *Only demons combined power and proximity.* They, according to Von Glahn, constituted the most "potent" of the beings who commonly meddled in human lives. Though these supernatural rogues could inflict multiple forms of torment on their victims, they often chose to unleash plagues or diseases. To rural Chinese, "the scourge of illness" provided physical evidence of an unseen "malefic entity."[9]

It was demons that Nevius heard most about on his circuit. Though he might have maintained a purely academic interest in them, he felt the need to do more because—and this was the strangest part—the families of the supposedly possessed often called upon his converts to intervene. They saw Christians as endowed with the power to cast demons out—to conduct exorcisms. When summoned, Chinese Christians did not scold their fellow villagers for foolishly believing in nonexistent beings. They too treated demons as real. How did the always-rational Nevius respond to the rash of demon possessions? He decided to subject the phenomenon to scientific investigation. He opened a journal and kept a record of each case. He did not know what else to do.[10]

Cases of Demon Possession

His converts always knew exactly what to do. Nevius recorded one incident involving a twelve-year-old boy who started behaving strangely. Inexplicably, he would "cry out with fear" as if "conscious of some unseen presence" before collapsing to the floor "insensible." Was he possessed? The family called in a female "spirit-medium" to rid the boy of the demon. She succeeded temporarily, but the demon soon returned. When a schoolmate was dispatched to fetch her again, he happened to cross paths with Liu Chong-ho, a Christian convert. Liu had not been a Christian for long; in fact, he was at that moment returning from Tengchow where he had received baptism. But Liu did not act like a novice. In self-assured fashion, he instructed the pupil not to bother with the spirit-medium. He would take care of the matter himself. Arriving at the school, Liu calmly asked students to kneel around the afflicted boy. Then, "in almost Scriptural words," he addressed the demon with righteous force: "I command you in the name of Jesus Christ to come out of him." The boy released a "piercing cry" and was "restored to consciousness." "From that day to this," Nevius recorded, the boy never suffered again and his parents joined the church.[11]

It was a happy ending, to be sure, but for Nevius it also raised questions. "Do cases of possession actually exist in China?" If not, what caused the boy's mysterious condition? And where did Liu get the idea to use Christianity in this way? "No Protestant missionary," Nevius wrote, "has ever given native converts instructions as to casting out spirits."[12] Missionaries regarded exorcism as a "magical superstition," a practice that Catholics engaged in but Protestants mostly dismissed.[13] Nevius conjectured that Liu's impromptu exorcism had been "the natural result of reading the Scriptures and applying its teachings." Indeed, both Mark and Luke offer accounts of Jesus casting an evil spirit out of a man in the synagogue (Mark 1:21–28 and Luke 4:33–37). The Chinese were applying Christianity, Nevius discovered, in their own way.[14]

Nevius recorded other fantastic incidents. In the late 1870s, one of his assistants, Leng, visited a village where a woman named Kwo was said to have been possessed for eight years. The village begged Leng to "cast out" the malignant spirit, but he demurred. "I have no power to do anything of myself," he responded. "We must ask God to help us." While Leng led a prayer session in the company of Kwo, the latter spoke, not as herself but as the demon. "God and Christ will not interfere," she said, speaking in rhymes. "You cannot get rid of me." Nothing further transpired and Leng left town. Weeks later, Kwo savagely disrupted a church service by "springing upon the table," howling "wildly," and hurling Bibles and hymnals onto the floor. She also shocked worshippers by announcing that Leng was, at that very moment, approaching the village even though he was not expected. She was right. "No one could have known," Leng later assured Nevius, "that we were coming," at least not in the "ordinary way." Reaching the church, Leng decided to confront the demon. "If you do not leave," he admonished, "we will immediately call upon God to drive you out." Enraged, Kwo hissed back, "I'll not go! I'll stay and be the death of this woman!" His warning unheeded, Leng summoned the power of his faith. While the Christians knelt in prayer, Leng castigated the demon: "You evil, malignant spirit! You have not the power of life and death; and you cannot intimidate us by your vain threats. We will now call upon God to drive you out." When he finished, something miraculous took place. Kwo, "awakening as if from sleep," peacefully joined the others in prayer. Afterward, she greeted Leng "politely" as if nothing had happened.[15]

Leng's story amazed Nevius. To verify it, he traveled to Kwo's village and questioned the people involved. "The statements of Mr. Leng," he recorded, "were confirmed by minute examinations of all the parties concerned." After baptizing Kwo, Nevius heard of another woman, a spirit-medium, who was said to have fallen under the influence of a demon. Villagers told him that she spoke in verses that referred to Nevius explicitly. After making inquiries, Nevius discovered that she was consumed by an inner "struggle": she wished to become Christian but hated to lose her "business as a spirit-medium" (she generated income by telling fortunes and curing illnesses). When Nevius visited her, he found her lying down, so sedate as to appear like a "corpse." He observed that she chanted continuously, rhythmically, and rapidly in a fashion that "could not possibly be counterfeited." While a convert might have tried to cast the demon out, Nevius was reluctant to do so. Presbyterians did not perform exorcisms. Instead, he took her pulse. Normal. He lifted and released her arm. It thumped lifelessly on the floor. Unable or unwilling to do anything more, he left. Months later, she died.[16]

Demon-Possession Narratives and Conversion

Were demons running amok in Shandong? It is impossible for us to know what was really happening in any of these incidents. Perhaps there were acid-tongued spirits who spewed hateful bile on Christianity before capitulating to its superior power. However, we might also speculate that demon possession, at some deeper psychological level, represented attempts by individuals and their families to transition into the Christian faith. We know that the afflicted parties all knew something of Christianity because, in every case, the church had already penetrated the village. We also know that, at this historic moment, family members often applied intense pressure to those flirting with Christianity. Thus, any individuals contemplating conversion engaged in inner struggle as they tried to reconcile their attraction to Christianity with their opposing obligation to their families. Two powerful desires convulsed, like a wrathful demon, within one conflicted self. It follows, then, that persons leaning toward conversion needed assistance convincing others—and, quite possibly, themselves—before making the risky leap.

Demon possession perhaps helped with this crucial persuasion. For centuries, demons had played a vibrant role in Chinese folk culture. Typically, stories involved a spirit-medium who acted as an intermediary between the possessed individual and the supernatural world. In the standard iteration of what we might call the "demon-possession narrative," the suffering would visit a spirit-medium who, while in an altered state, would channel supernatural powers in a way that rid the afflicted person of the evil spirit.[17] How did the introduction of the Gospel affect the dynamic? Initially, missionaries expected converts to jettison their gods, ghosts, and demons to make room for God and Jesus. However, the aforementioned exorcisms conducted by Chinese Christians show how misplaced these hopes were. Instead of delete-and-replace, the Chinese called for the older religion to absorb the new faith through the creation of a variation of the demon-possession narrative. This variation required but a single substitution: *the Christian convert replaced the spirit-medium*. In other words, the family that used a Christian exorcism to deal with a stubborn demon was, in essence, pressing the new and alien religion into an existing folk tradition that already possessed a language, set of symbols, and plot familiar to all.

This variation of the narrative helped all parties involved accept Christianity by breaking down resistance to it. Who could belittle the Christian convert when he has succeeded in exorcising the very demon that had stymied a spirit-medium? Who could question the convert's embrace of Jesus after He had won His showdown with the demon, a representative of the old belief system? The argument here is not that the Chinese staged demonic possessions in a premeditated way to legitimize Christianity. Rather, it is to suggest that the afflicted and their family members were perhaps subconsciously complicit in using the demon-possession narrative to engineer acceptance of Christianity in a society inclined to spurn it.

Women and Demons

Nevius received a letter from Adele Fielde, who shared the details of a remarkable case. Yong, a young woman from a poor family, approached Fielde to describe the terrible physical changes a demon had wrought in her mother: "My mother had violent palpitations of the heart, spasmodic contractions of the muscles, and foaming at the mouth." Yong added that her mother would do or say whatever the demon asked. Though detrimental to the mother's physical health, the demon possession presented certain advantages. It allowed her to perform life-threatening feats without becoming injured; she could walk over fiery coals, bathe in boiling water, or climb a ladder composed of knives. Since her superhuman exploits earned her notoriety, villagers would pay money for a "consultation" with the demon. This extra income aside, the demon was essentially wreaking havoc on the old woman, and she blamed it for a rash of misfortune: her husband died, the two women she had selected as brides for two of her sons also died (mysteriously, within twenty days of one another), and all four of her sons moved out. Her family was destroyed, and the demon was at fault.[18]

Seeking help, Yong took her mother to Adele Fielde. "She seemed such a wreck as a demon might make of a woman," Fielde wrote, and "her mind was completely saturated with heathenism." So too was her body: the old woman had a "forked" tongue because, as a spirit-medium, she had "slashed" it frequently "in her frenzies to draw blood for medicine." Could Christianity save someone who had descended so deeply into the occult? "I wondered whether the rays of Divine light," Fielde confessed, "would ever penetrate the great depth of paganism in which her soul was sunk." To the relief of all, they did. "As the Holy Spirit entered my mother's heart," Yong explained, "the demon went out." Three years later, as Fielde observed the kindly old woman reading the Bible to others, she proclaimed the transformation a "miracle" every bit as wonderful as any exorcism performed by Jesus.[19]

Fielde's account suggests that demon possessions held special meaning for women. A possession conferred some money, power, and influence to women, who typically were denied all three. In the Qing Dynasty, writes religious scholar Xiaofei Kang, elites believed "that women's work should be confined to the domestic arena to maintain social and moral order." They exhorted even "peasant women" to shun any work outside the family home. The role of spirit-medium provided some women with the means "to assume authority outside of family structure" and, by doing so, to escape a circumscribed life.[20] A woman, in other words, could earn income and respect by becoming a healer and prophetess. In this way, women created an alternative pathway to money and influence, outside of the official Confucian social order that excluded them.

Fielde herself seemed to grasp this point. By engaging spirits, Chinese women could evade some of the oppressive customs that restricted them in legitimate society. She observed, for example, that women who were largely confined to their homes used the spirit world as a pretext for gathering. They seized upon the ritual form that, in America, was called a séance: they congregated in groups to contact the dead. These "conclaves are conducted by women alone," Fielde explained, "and are regarded by men with great disfavor." Fielde, who witnessed a session, described what transpired. After the women circled around a table, those who wished to commune with the dead would "throw a black cloth over their heads," hold out "spirit money" (a gift for the dead), and elevate a lit incense stick before their veiled faces. They would then "shut their eyes and remain motionless" as they slipped into a trance. Those who had chosen not to enter an altered state would take bamboo roots, "rap" rhythmically on the table's edge, and "chant invocations" requesting spirits to accept the shrouded women into their "abode." The entranced women, while "trembling violently," would next drop their incense sticks and start to "discourse incoherently." The communication with the dead has begun. Asking the dead about their whereabouts, the entranced women learn that some souls have been reincarnated while others have fallen into realms of horror. They discover that one deceased neighbor is locked in Hell "with nothing to eat but the salted flesh of the infant daughters she destroyed when she was alive." As the women snap out of their trances, they manifest the visible signs of one who has completed an arduous quest: pale faces, "disheveled hair," and looks of "exhaustion."

What was really happening at these séances? Fielde suspected that many Chinese spirit-mediums staged bogus shows to profit from the gullibility of others. However, she dismissed "pecuniary benefit" as the motivation behind the event she had witnessed because no money had exchanged hands. That said, Fielde also doubted that the women had "really been away from home." In support of her skepticism, she noted that the women "bring back no ideas save those which they took with them." But if the event were neither a hoax nor a real communication with the dead, what was going on? Though discerning no evidence of a "conscious deception," Fielde did not rule out self-deception. Animated by a desire to access the forbidden knowledge of the dead, women fool themselves into thinking that their ritual grants them this power. They "see what they expect to see."[21]

By joining séances and becoming spirit-mediums, women claimed the invisible spirit world as a sphere of female authority. Though Fielde favored female empowerment, she did not approve of the occult as a means to achieve it. Her challenge in China would be to locate a similar pathway to female influence that passed through the Christian faith and that left the demons alone. Chapter 5 describes the evangelical model that Fielde devised for this exact purpose.

Exorcisms by Chinese Christians

Nevius received two letters from Chinese Christians that stood out. Wang Wu-Fang, a convert from Shandong, explained that previously, before joining the church, he had dealt with demons using traditional Chinese methods. "Cases of possession by evil-spirits were very common in our village," he wrote, "and my services were in frequent demand." Wang drove off demons by employing a procedure that involved "pricking with needles." After he converted to Christianity, residents from neighboring villages continued to request his services—but he refused. "I could not, as a Christian, follow the former method, so I declined to go." When village elders insisted that he try Christian methods, Wang relented.

In a case involving a young woman, he was summoned by a desperate family that had already hired a spirit-medium and tried needle-pricking. Neither worked. At "wits' end," they turned to Wang in the hope that Christianity could succeed where Chinese methods had failed. As Wang entered the house, a crowd of people promptly opened a pathway to the possessed woman. Very little happened at this first meeting because the demon fled immediately. After the easy victory, the "fame of Christianity rapidly spread" and "there were many accessions to the church." But the celebrations were premature. The demon kept coming back, forcing Wang to make repeated visits. At his final meeting, the woman presented a cadaverous appearance: "her face was purple, her body rigid, her skin cold, her respiration difficult, and her life almost extinct." She looked "dead." After a round of vigorous prayer, the demon left—this time for good. Impressed by Wang's power, the family asked him for Christian books. This, in fact, was his point in recounting the episode to Nevius. "In our preaching," he explained, "to be able to tell people that in our holy religion there is the power to cast out demons . . . is certainly a great help to the spread of the Gospel." On his own, Wang had conceived of a strategy to win converts by pitting God against Chinese demons. He was not alone. Chen Sin Ling also endorsed exorcism after witnessing similar cases. "If cases of possession are met with," he advised, "and Christians are able . . . to cast out the demons, the effect would certainly be favorable to Christianity." Christians, in other words, could exploit the demon phenomenon through the strategic use of exorcisms.[22]

Chen, who was a resident of Foochow, reported that cases within the city were rare. "They are more numerous," he informed, "in the villages."[23] In 1883, one of those outlying regions, the Kucheng District, played host to a dramatic demon-related event. Occurring four years after Nevius's letter, the case did not enter the missionary's study. If it had, it would have provided the advocates of exorcism with a cautionary tale. The incident in Kucheng caught the Christian community by surprise; missionaries had seen opium, not demons, as the district's biggest problem. In fact, the church tried to attract new members by helping to wean addicts off the drug. "Many of our members," Nathan Sites wrote in 1881, wished "to be saved from the slavish and impoverishing habit of using opium."[24] In 1883, the district fell under the oversight of Frank Ohlinger, a missionary from Ohio, and Yek Ing Kwang, a Chinese minister. Neither man expected anything untoward to happen. After all, the previous year Sites had forecasted that a "sure and glorious harvest awaits the faithful laborers of this vineyard."[25]

That was before a supernatural visitor induced mass hysteria. A "remarkable case of demoniacal possession," Ohlinger wrote, "threatened a rupture between our people and their heathen neighbors." The event caught Chinese Christians off guard. They had never before witnessed a demon possession and had acquired, in Ohlinger's judgment, a dismissive attitude toward such phenomena. Many had "imbibed" a rational way of thinking, he observed, "that boastfully denies the existence of demons." But even those who believed in evil spirits probably felt they had little to fear should they encounter one. All the anecdotal evidence, after all, suggested that a Christian could simply invoke God to banish a demon and, with this show of divine power, attract people to the church. One could even regard demon cases as beneficial—when, that is, they conformed to convention.

But this case did not. In fact, it reversed the traditional roles: instead of Christ scaring away a demon, it was the demon who spooked the followers of Christ. As the Chinese preachers initiated the exorcism, they believed they had the upper hand. But the "unwelcome visitor" surprised them by listing each "by name" and presenting "a minute account of their former and present spiritual condition." Inexplicably, the demon had obtained knowledge of "their secret faults" and gleefully "mocked" them with it. Their hidden insecurities exposed, the Christians became flustered; they lost their nerve and retreated from the exorcism in disarray. In the end, the demon did vacate its host. However, it did so not after bowing to superior power but rather after succeeding in "negotiations." In a quid pro quo, the demon agreed to "abandon his present abode on condition that pastoral labor and care were withdrawn from certain lukewarm Christians." The demon would, in other words, take his malice elsewhere if the preachers consented to back away from those Christians still harboring spiritual doubt. The standoff ended when the preachers gave up those individuals. It was like a hostage negotiation.[26]

The immediate crisis was over but the aftershocks reverberated through the community. In painful fashion, the case taught Christians that a demon possession presented a double-edged sword. Of course, a Christian victory could yield easy conversions among those who viewed a successful exorcism as persuasive. But losses were devastating. By appearing weaker than the demon, the church lost face in its community, impairing its ability to recruit. Potentially more damaging still, though, was the effect of defeat on the fragile psychologies of the vanquished Christians. One account of the occurrence portrayed the entire church as gripped with terror: "Fear came on the whole Church, and deep heart searching and contrition were manifest."[27] Ohlinger himself corroborated this assessment, observing that the demon "brought preachers and people in great contrition to their knees." The demon, whether real or imagined, provoked a crisis of faith that made it difficult for church members to resume normal activities. Even if they did work up the courage to persevere, they faced diminished prospects. For this reason, nobody likened Kucheng to a "vineyard" anymore. The following year brought a new metaphor: "hard stony soil in which to cast the seed."[28]

Hu Yong Mi

A Troubled Youth

One Chinese minister in Foochow knew better than to underestimate demons or to see them only strategically as entities the church could exploit to recruit new members. Throughout his youth, Hu Yong Mi feared demons and respected their power. After converting to Christianity, he did not abandon his belief in demons but instead integrated these beings into his ministry. Hu's preoccupation with the supernatural helped him relate to rural Chinese, because he shared their beliefs, and explain to them the advantages of the Gospel.

This ability to connect with people did not manifest itself early in his life. In his autobiography, Hu describes a childhood in Fujian Province spent mostly in solitude. Instead of interacting with others, he remained aloof. On a typical day, he might climb a hill, locate a "shady retreat," and read works of Buddhism. "I was inclined to be quiet and meditative," Hu wrote. "I seldom spoke." Hu's parents, alarmed by his antisocial behavior, feared something must be terribly wrong. Desperate for answers, they consulted the one authority they trusted: the temple idols. Despite their attempt to find a spirit-based solution, Hu remained isolated. Mistaking his silence for low intelligence, people called him "stupid."[29]

Hu was anything but. In fact, he suffered not from an inactive mind but from a hyperactive one. Hu projected onto the material world a fantastical spiritual overlay of ghosts and demons. "I was greatly afraid of devils," he recalled of his youth, "and troubled about spirits." Indeed, the spirit world bore down hard upon Hu. For him, a demon was not a metaphor for something else, such as a proclivity for strong drink. A demon was an actual demon. And the constant fear of incurring a demon's wrath placed Hu in a perpetual state of heightened anxiety that precluded normal social behavior. Unfortunately, evil spirits not only added stress to everyday life, they also wrecked one's chances for a peaceful afterlife. Hu dreaded that inevitable time when "our bodies [are] given to worms" and our souls are "dragged by wicked spirits into a region of darkness."[30] "I dreaded ghosts and feared death," Hu recalled, and "my heart was constantly disturbed."[31] Though his mind churned with supernatural horror, Hu told no one, choosing to suffer alone. "Day and night, in secret, I shed tears" and "at night, wherever I went, I feared evil spirits." Hu lived in a phantasmagoria of terror, a frightening mental landscape inhabited by beings of wanton malice. He was a troubled young man.[32]

Believing that demons used vice to ensnare mortal man, Hu fixated on sin. "Sin was like a river," wrote Hu, and "danger" lurked "everywhere." In his autobiography, Hu told of several encounters with sin. His father, hoping to increase his reclusive son's contact with reality, arranged for Hu to work in a relative's store. "He feared that I was too much immersed in solitude," Hu wrote, "and desired that I should learn something of the business and social customs of the outside world." The store did bring human interaction, but working there only exacerbated Hu's anxiety. That is because the shop sold opium, which fed Hu's obsession with sin. Though he resisted temptation ("the pipe never came to my mouth"), he made himself miserable agonizing over the possibility that he might succumb. "Each day seemed like a year," he wrote of the six-month emotional strain. When the owner tried to engage him permanently, Hu declined: "I told him that as soon as the term of engagement expired I would go home." Hu confronted temptation a second time while working at the wine shop of his stepbrother. This relation pressured Hu unsuccessfully to join him in various forms of "dissipation"—alcohol, opium, and prostitutes. The stepbrother's vice-ridden life ended sadly with his early death, but Hu avoided self-destruction and lived on.[33]

Games of chance also beckoned. Coaxed one day into playing cards for money with family friends, Hu found himself in a bizarre situation: he could not lose. "From noon till night I won every game," he wrote. "All the company in turn lost, I alone won." While the other players were "surprised" by the freakish winning streak, Hu discerned paranormal forces at work. Something malevolent, he thought, must be employing good fortune to lure him down a path to sin. Hu quit the game, but his perilous good luck returned later when he played the lottery. The lottery worked like this. Players who purchased a chance would reach into a revolving urn containing thirty-six marked bamboo slips and try to select the one winning piece. Determined to prevail, Hu's cousin consulted "diviners"—but to no avail. She lost repeatedly. Seeing her disappointment, Hu gave the game a try. Against staggering odds, he pulled out the winning piece three consecutive times. "All regarded it as strange," but Hu saw much more than that—nefarious forces were at work. When Hu contemplated these episodes, he identified a pattern: evil spirits wished to seduce him into a life of sin. But the pattern included more than just temptation. A mysterious counterforce—something of greater power—always intervened to help him resist opium, alcohol, prostitutes, and games of chance. Who or what was offering aid remained a mystery.[34]

Conversion to Christianity

Christianity allowed Hu to decode the strange occurrences. When he first learned of Christianity through his older brother, he did not take to the new faith. That, in fact, is an understatement. After his older brother disposed of his idols, Hu urged family members to "with one heart... beat the drum and drive him from the house." Hu also tore up his father's Bible after finding it on the shelf.[35] Hu, in short, engaged in the familial resistance that missionaries complained about. But Hu's opposition eventually abated. Around 1860, he followed his father and two brothers, Hu Po Mi and Hu Sing Mi, in joining the Methodist Episcopal Church. "The Hu family is really remarkable," a missionary noted, to have produced so many "men of God."[36] Looking retrospectively, Hu applied a Christian gloss to the sequence of temptations that had bewildered him in youth. And when he did, he discerned an underlying spiritual reality: these were "baits" that "Satan used... to catch me." How had Hu fended off so many attacks from the arch tempter? The "Spirit of God" had "outstretched his saving arm to assist me out of all pitfalls." Had he lacked this divine aid, Hu believed he would have "entered the dark region" before receiving the Gospel.[37]

Though conversion was a family affair, we would be mistaken in suggesting that Hu did so merely to conform to the wishes of parents and siblings. Rather, Christianity alleviated the crippling anxiety of a young man who felt besieged by maleficent forces. After his conversion, Hu did not stop believing in his demon cosmology. The old demons remained in Hu's mind, though he started identifying some as Satan and his horde. However, to this supernatural catalog, Hu added two new entities: God and Jesus. And just as the demons inhabited the same physical space as Hu, so too were the new Christian deities close at hand. In fact, Hu claimed he could speak directly to God. "Lord, where art thou?" Hu once asked while sick. "I am on thy left side, and I am on thy right," the calming answer came.[38]

With God and Jesus in Hu's life, the once dominant demons had to reckon with a superior power—and this diminished the threat they posed. After conversion, the heavy gloom abruptly lifted and a new emotion replaced Hu's debilitating fear:

> I recognized that the Holy Spirit helped me and filled my heart with sighs and tears of *joy*. I wished to sing continually. Everything in which I engaged seemed to excite me to *joy* and to tears. I very much wished to tell of my *joy*, but was unable to express it.... Each day was a new day. With this *joy* the most glorious things in the world, the most exceeding precious, were incomparable, because the *joy* proceeded not from aught earthly, but welled up from the soul. If the world and all therein were destroyed, this *joy* would remain.... My soul alone knew this great *joy*. (italics added)

Seldom does a writer use the word *joy* seven times in a single paragraph. Through repetition, Hu expressed the euphoria that he carried into his post-conversion life. Wishing to spread the faith to others, the former introvert "could not endure not to preach." Releasing charisma that had been bottled up for years, Hu carried the Gospel into the streets by day. At night, he would visit the homes of neighbors to invite them to "walk in the way to heaven." Hu's abrupt change in behavior surprised those who had previously viewed him as odd, reclusive, or stupid. "This man, when young, never wished to speak a word," he heard them comment. "Now, suddenly, he has great courage, and speaks in a loud voice, without ceasing." Hu had found his purpose.[39]

The Role of Demons in Hu's Ministry

In his early years as a Christian, Hu trained under the missionaries. After his tutelage ended in the 1860s, he ventured out into the countryside where he discovered within himself the ability to connect with rural Chinese. He had discovered his voice. How could someone who had previously shunned society now relate so well to ordinary people? Throughout his life, Hu had felt like an outsider, someone whose obsession with the supernatural precluded normal interaction with society. Preaching had the effect of converting his worst handicap into his greatest asset. The cause of his social isolation—his occult beliefs—was in fact *not* unusual in the Chinese countryside. As we have already seen, rural Chinese often attributed their misfortunes to the work of invisible spirits. They too felt harassed by demons and yearned for relief. In other words, Hu had been an outsider among the Chinese not because he was different *from them* but rather because he was an intensified version *of them*. He grasped intuitively how they thought, and this understanding allowed him to package Christianity in a way that spoke to their deepest need—to achieve a sense of control over their unpredictable environment. And since ordinary Chinese saw demons as the root cause of their troubles, these beings figured prominently in Hu's ministry.

Hu would, for example, perform exorcisms. On more than one occasion, he claimed to have battled a malicious entity called the "fox demon." In Hu's telling, he first encountered the fox demon when a concerned husband invited him to see his troubled wife. The husband explained that, when the demon first entered his wife, she "committed self-injuries and mutilations" and "would lie ten days or more without eating" but then eat "voraciously" all of a sudden. If she spoke, it was to utter not her own words but those of the demon, which "were of secret, abstruse meaning, or prophetic." Before commencing his exorcism, Hu introduced the husband to "the doctrine of faith," and "told him that if he had faith," prayer would compel the demon to "flee from his house." By setting faith in God as a precondition for success, Hu increased the likelihood that his efforts would yield new church members. "I believe," the man confirmed, allowing Hu to commence a prayer session. At the conclusion, the husband "found his wife already risen from her bed, well." Though the exorcism was successful, Hu had not vanquished his foe. The fox demon located a new host, this time one of Hu's neighbors. After Hu's wife cast the demon out of this body, it leapt immediately into a different neighbor's daughter. "I have been cast out by the Christians," the fox demon said to the girl, "and have no place to dwell. I happen to meet you" and "now come to you."[40] Hu had more work to do against his mercurial foe.

Who or what was the fox demon? For centuries, the Chinese had viewed foxes as liminal animals that crossed boundaries between the material and spirit worlds. "The dead and living walk different roads," wrote a Qing scholar, "but foxes are between the dead and the living." According to a vernacular expression, one who wished to "talk of foxes and speak of ghosts" was signaling a desire to discuss "supernatural" topics. The fox demon, far from obscure, had achieved fame in China. It has a storied history in Chinese folklore, appearing in sources dating back two millennia to the Han Dynasty, though its popularity spiked during the Qing.[41] Xiaofei Kang, who has studied the cults surrounding this particular entity, describes its typical behavior. "Using the art of metamorphosis and magic," she writes, "the fox often engaged in spiritual possession of people" by creating "illusionary visions," causing them to "go mad, talk nonsense, and laugh and wail uncontrollably."[42] In China's crowded spirit world, the fox demon rose above others. It was a supernatural celebrity.

By declaring his foe to be the much-chronicled fox demon, Hu raised the stakes of his contest. This was no obscure spirit he was contending with but a notorious spirit outlaw, one that established religions and the state had pursued for centuries. According to Kang, Buddhist monks, Daoist priests, and Confucian officials "took the major responsibility for destroying fox dens, exorcising fox demons, and expelling their malignant influence on the community."[43] By engaging with this particular adversary, Hu could join company with leaders within China's official religions and institutions. In this way, the fox demon conferred a degree of legitimacy to the Christian faith.

Stories drawn from Hu's own experience, such as his skirmishes with the fox demon, contributed to his evangelical efforts. When out on the circuit, he would supplement Bible stories with narratives of his personal encounters with Chinese gods and spirits. In one such narrative, Hu told of his arrival in Lek Tu, a village that had seen scarcely a drop of rain since his previous visit two months earlier. "Heaven, earth, send rain!" the people cried, "We starve." Hu promptly summoned all Christians to the chapel to pray for rain. The Christians were not alone in soliciting supernatural aid. Outside the chapel, villagers paraded down the streets hoisting an idol in the air. Hearing their noisy procession clang by, Hu recognized the high stakes. If rain were to fall after the idol procession, villagers would celebrate the "great power" of the god represented by the idol—not the Lord. With the followers of two separate belief systems making simultaneous calls for rain, Lek Tu had become an arena of competing gods.

To win, Hu needed divine assistance. And that is exactly what he got, at least according to his retelling. While deep in prayer, he claimed that a voice, inaudible to others, communicated a clear message: "To-morrow at this time rain." God had spoken directly to Hu. Relieved, Hu shared the divine promise with his group and ended the prayer session. Before returning home, some of his more confident parishioners "published the matter" about the village, announcing on God's authority the precise timing of the rains. Hearing the bold forecast, non-Christians viewed the next day's weather as a test of Christianity. "If this heaven sends rain to-morrow," they said, "then we must all join with the Christians." When Hu awoke the next morning, "not the least cloud appeared in the sky" and the "sun was hotter than before." As villagers ridiculed Hu, he knelt down and prayed for rain. Looking up, he discerned no change in the skies. He prayed a second time. Again, only silence from above. The third time he prayed, he felt his soul soaring through the air, "grasping the clouds, and drawing them over the face of the sky and the sun." While still bent over in prayer, he heard the rumble of thunder and felt the winds pick up. Soon, a "very great rain poured down" and "from every house" came "sounds of joy." God had won again.[44]

Before audiences, Hu could recount Christianity's other decisive victories over Chinese gods. In the town of Ngu Kang, Hu's evangelical success drew the ire of those who despised Christianity. Wishing to quell the Christian movement, Hu's opponents tried different forms of persecution. Within families, spouses beat their Christian partners, deprived them of food, and expelled them from the home. Out in the town, anti-Christians engaged in a concerted effort to intimidate anyone who refused to donate money for idols. While officials turned a blind eye, anti-Christians stole animals from Hu's converts, denied them well water, and refused to let them pass in the streets. Though the Christians buckled under so many "oppressions," they maintained their composure. Their refusal to respond to provocation either by quitting the church or by fighting back vexed their antagonists.

Frustrated by this passivity, the anti-Christians escalated the conflict by resorting to supernatural bullying. "They beat drums," Hu remembered, "calling upon the 'five rulers,'" also called the Ngu-ta, "to come and seize us."[45] Who were the Ngu-ta? According to a Foochow missionary, they were among the most prominent gods worshipped in the province. Each was associated with one of the five elements (metal, wood, water, fire, and earth), the five colors (yellow, green, red, black, and white), and the five directions (North, East, South, West, and Middle). Devotees would fashion fearsome statues for use in street processions, giving the gods "hideous faces" with animalistic features.⁴⁶ After conjuring up the fearsome Ngu-ta, the anti-Christians called upon them to cast a plague upon the Christians.

Hu believed that his antagonists had bet heavily on the wrong gods—and he was right (at least in his version of the story). The Ngu-ta, learning that the Christians were their target, withheld their wrath. "Their god is very great," the Five Rulers communicated through a spirit-medium, and so "we dare not approach them." Undeterred, the anti-Christians next "called upon the demons of cattle and dogs," whose "priests" introduced "into our drinking-water" a "charm" intended to afflict Christians with "grievous maladies." The plan backfired. While Hu and his followers maintained their health, those who had concocted the scheme were "seized with very serious illness." Why had the plan gone horribly awry? The dog-and-cattle demons themselves explained the reversal. Lacking physical forms, the demons took possession of the people stricken with disease and, in an act of ventriloquism, used them as unwilling mouthpieces. "You sent us to beat the Christians," they said, but "we did not dare to go into them" and so "we have come to you, and now are about to carry you off."⁴⁷ In Hu's narratives, Christians won all spiritual contests because they could summon the superior power.

A Struggle with Satan

Hu's evangelical arsenal included multiple accounts of battles with demonic foes. His most powerful story, however, featured his personal struggle with Satan himself, which he claimed took place after he had started preaching. Confident that he had vanquished sin, Hu admitted to being lulled into a false sense of security. Though evil spirits still lurked about to menace others, he viewed his own mind and soul as inviolable. What is more, his success as a minister had inflated his pride. "I became vain," he recalled, "and fancied I was a superior preacher." He was not prepared for the surprise attack when it came.⁴⁸

"One day I was alone in my study," he recalled, when "suddenly I saw in the room a light, like a flash from a heavy cloud." Though he did not at first regard the light as threatening, he soon realized that Satan, not God, loomed behind the pyrotechnic show. "I now discerned," Hu soberly wrote, that the light carried a "limitless mechanism of torture." As Satan proceeded to strip away all Christian "blessings," Hu experienced agony. He felt as if he were "a fish alive upon the spit" or "as if the poisonous fangs of a great serpent . . . were thrust into my flesh." As Satan twisted the knife in Hu's side, "a multitude of noisy devils" appeared before him in a vengeful mood. In his preaching, Hu had frequently maligned them without suffering any consequences. Now it was their turn to inflict pain. "You have courage in every place to slander and blaspheme us, because we have not contended against you," they gloated. "Now we only stretch out one finger, and you find it intolerable. If we exert our strength, what will you do?" Hu tried to find God in the scriptures, but to no avail.

If anything, the Bible itself had become a "mechanism of torture." Hu described several months of torment during which he "passed through all the experiences of Adam, Saul, David, Samson," and "Job." In his disturbed state of mind, he was somehow transported to the scene of the crucifixion where—to his horror—he beheld himself nailing Jesus to the cross. As guilt and regret flooded Hu's mind, his body broke down and his hair turned gray. He had reached a spiritual nadir. It was at this point, however, that his recovery began. He realized that God had not abandoned him but rather was using Satan to test and purify him. Hu likened himself to a "piece of clod" that, after much grinding, becomes as "polished as a precious stone." Hu emerged from his spiritual crisis stronger and more resolute than before.[49]

As we read the story today, we find it simultaneously innovative and derivative. Concerning the latter, the story fuses together familiar Bible episodes, namely Satan's torturing of Job (with God's approval) and his temptation of Jesus in the desert. Yet the story also innovates by presenting Christianity as highly private and personal. Unlike Hu's other stories, which promoted Christianity's power to uplift an entire community, this one shifted the focus to the human interior: the solitary individual's quest to conquer sin and achieve salvation under a benevolent God's caring eye. What peasant farmer wouldn't find Hu's personal story comforting?

Marketing Christianity

For all of Hu's stories about Satan and demons, we can never know what truly happened. Perhaps events did transpire in the sensational fashion he described. It is far more likely, however, that Hu collected experiences from his life and circuit that he later revised and embellished. By doing so, he converted these experiences into evangelical commodities—compelling stories that could be told and retold. Though the stories may be of dubious factual merit, from them we can infer Hu's strategy for marketing Christianity. The stories suggest that Hu focused far less on scripture than the missionaries who trained him. He likely surmised that Chinese peasants could not easily relate to ancient stories from a distant land. While he did share some Bible stories, he bolstered them with personal narratives that were of more immediate interest to his audience. Though not scriptural, his stories shared some of the Bible's plot lines and conventions. For example, God communicates directly to Hu Yong Mi, as He does with Moses in the Old Testament. God also responds directly and with alacrity to crises faced by Chinese Christians, as He does with the children of Israel. And Satan devotes special attention to Hu, as he does with Jesus and Job. Last, Hu's contests of gods, as Ryan Dunch has noted, have an Old Testament antecedent: the prophet Elijah competed with local gods to see which one could bring rain.⁵⁰ The point is that a Chinese farmer did not have to trust that, long ago in another part of the world, someone named Elijah ended a drought. The same story was taking place in Chinese villages in the present day. In this way, Hu presented rural China as a new Holy Land and cast himself in the role of Old Testament prophet. By doing so, he brought Christian theology to life and infused it with immediacy and relevance for ordinary people.

Hu also seems to have crafted his stories to meet a Chinese peasant's greatest psychological need: to achieve a sense of control over his environment. For centuries, rural Chinese had tried to gain a modicum of control by currying favor with spirits and demons. They would present burnt offerings to idols in temples or make humble requests through spirit-mediums. Despite these efforts to placate a cruel universe, infants still died, droughts still punished, bandits still pillaged, and locusts still ravaged. What was going wrong? The Chinese, as was stated earlier, understood their unfortunate plight as the result of a tragic misalignment of power and proximity in the spirit world: the potent gods who could provide help kept themselves distant; the ancestral spirits, though sympathetic and close at hand, lacked the power to effect desirable outcomes. Chinese peasants, in sum, found themselves in a centuries-old predicament for which there appeared to be no solution. Enter Hu Yong Mi. He dangled before long-suffering peasants an irresistible idea. If they embraced God and Jesus, they could enjoy access to divine beings who *combined supreme power with loving care*! This tantalizing proposition glowed behind many of Hu's stories.

Still, peasants required convincing. God and Jesus, in order to attract converts, needed to defeat a foe. For this reason, Hu chose not to wipe clean China's roster of supernatural entities. Demons, after all, proved useful as foils. They also helped Hu simplify the decision-making process for anyone considering Christianity. Hu did not ask prospective converts to learn Christian theology because, realistically, most peasant farmers possessed neither the time nor the necessary literacy to take on such intellectual labor. In one farming village, Hu described the "pitiable" condition of the people: "Not a chair was there to sit upon. All went out to work in the fields. They had no leisure to comb hair or wash faces."⁵¹ To render the choice simple for these people, Hu reduced the matter to a basic contest of strength. Who do you wish to worship, he implicitly asked, a stronger power or a weaker one? If audiences believed his stories, the decision was easy.

Finally, by leaving China's spirit catalog intact, Hu prevented conversion from becoming an all-or-nothing proposition. He did not ask of anyone the wholesale rejection of one belief system and the complete adoption of another. To convert, one only needed to add two deities—God and Christ—to the existing spirit ecosystem. By presenting Christianity less as something drastically new and more as an upgrade, Hu rendered conversion less daunting. Attuned to the needs of ordinary Chinese, Hu enjoyed decades of success as an evangelist. Ordinary people would invite him to preach in their villages and would travel miles to hear his sermons.[52]

Conclusion

In the final analysis, how did Nevius regard the demon phenomenon? At first, he embraced the current academic theory, which held that "primitive" peoples understood certain physical symptoms as "spirit possession" because they lacked the modern scientific terminology with which to properly label a physiological disorder. But after witnessing actual cases, Nevius came to view this theory as unconvincing. How was it that an inarticulate person could, without training, speak eloquently and poetically like a "professional orator"? How could an individual communicate "accurately and fluently" in a language he had never studied? How could a person acquire the clairvoyance to "foretell" future events—and later be proved right? Academic theory, in sum, failed to make sense of the astonishing behavior he had documented.[53] Letters from other missionaries poured in, but they failed to solve the riddle. Though most had witnessed similar episodes, opinion was divided as to the underlying cause. A few dismissed demon possessions as mere "delusion," a "larger number believe them to be real," and a "still larger proportion" dwelled in a "state of uncertainty." In the end, Nevius could not claim to understand the phenomenon at all. It remained a total mystery.[54]

But this was a mystery that yielded enlightenment. Throughout his prolonged interest in demons, Nevius was struck by the confidence of the converts and the ease with which they inserted themselves into complex demon-possession dramas. The Chinese understood their own culture intuitively, Nevius realized, and so could expertly manage situations that baffled foreigners like himself. This insight—which applied not just to demons but to all things—prompted Nevius to question the primacy of the foreign missionary in the larger evangelical project. Since the integration of Chinese culture and Christianity was proving to be more difficult than any missionary had imagined, Nevius decided that it was time to slide the missionary out of the central position. He began experimenting with a new approach to missions that handed responsibility and ceded control to the Chinese.

4

Cutting the Cord

Chinese Ministers Out on Their Own

When Hu Yong Mi started his preaching career, he trained under the watchful gaze of missionaries. Hu respected these teachers and appreciated their oversight. But it is hard to develop a self-confident ministerial voice when one's supervisor is constantly watching. Hu found that the mere presence of foreign missionaries inhibited expression and stifled creativity. When one of his mentors invited him to preach before a congregation, Hu initially felt excited and "stirred with many thoughts to preach." But before long, self-consciousness set in, and Hu thought less about inspiring the audience and more about making mistakes in front of his mentor. "I was timid about taking a text of Scripture to expound," he wrote, "lest the exposition and the text might not accord." The situation changed dramatically when Hu was on his own. "If missionaries were not present I had boldness in preaching." Alone before a congregation, Hu felt free and unfettered—and the words flowed.[1]

In response to challenges, a handful of missionaries experimented with a somewhat counterintuitive evangelical model. Instead of providing Chinese ministers like Hu with *more* resources and *more* supervision, missionaries would supply *less*. By removing responsibility from the missionary, the new model transferred agency to the Chinese. In Foochow, Nathan Sites and others spearheaded their version of this hands-off approach—the "self-support" program. Up north in Shandong, John Nevius developed his "Nevius Plan." Though self-support differed from the Nevius Plan in the details, the two overlapped with regard to their basic features. In both, the missionary saw himself less as a permanent fixture in China and more as a catalyst; he would enter a locale, spark religious interest, set up a chapel, and identify native leaders. For the latter, he would provide guidance, oversight, and Biblical training. Then, as soon as it was feasible, he would withdraw himself, allowing the fledgling church to manage on its own. Though some churches might fail, others would survive, lay down roots in their communities, achieve self-sufficiency, and avoid protracted dependency on missions. Crucially, these would be indigenous churches—not foreign institutions imposed on the Chinese and run by white clergy.

How did the Chinese respond to their expanded role? This chapter focuses on the first Chinese preachers to work under the new evangelical model: Zia Ying-tong, Sia Sek Ong, Ling Ching Ting, and Hu Yong Mi. These men all saw Christianity as a powerful force that could transform individual lives, communities, and even China itself. They recognized that one could use Christianity to escape self-destructive debauchery and then secure converts by showing others the pathway to personal reform. They also figured out that the Christian church afforded someone with charisma and organizational ability the opportunity to head an institution. Indeed, these men all possessed untapped reservoirs of leadership potential that the Confucian system, which rewarded memorization and test-taking skills, failed to identify. This chance to become dynamic community leaders attracted them. So too did Christianity's subversive power. They understood that, in any locale, the church presented an alternative source of authority that could empower ordinary people, allowing them to challenge a Confucian order that advantaged the educated elite. In sum, when missionaries loosened their grip, Chinese Christians discovered on their own the opportunities and rewards of the new faith.

Zia Ying-tong and the Nevius Plan

Calvin Mateer frequently accused Chinese officials of sabotaging missionary work. Though John Nevius did not disagree, he also did not view officials as the chief threat. In his opinion, a more corrosive force was undermining foreign missions. Nevius attributed much of Christianity's failure in China not to obstructionist officials but to missionary ignorance. A "greater hindrance exists," he observed, "in the foreigner's comparative ignorance of native ideas, customs, and habits of thought." In contrast to the bumbling and benighted foreigner, the native knows his culture "intuitively" and is thus "better fitted to approach his own people," "detect the undercurrent of their thoughts," and "sympathize with them in their trials."[2] Simply put, Nevius had reached the conclusion that the Chinese knew far better than the foreigner how to harmonize Christianity and Chinese culture. For someone who had journeyed across the ocean to impose his religion on others, this was a humbling thought. But it was also a liberating one. Indeed, it meant that the missionary did not have to do everything himself. Instead, he could step back and allow the Chinese to evangelize their own country mostly in their own way.

It took several years for Nevius to codify this insight into a coherent method. However, an early experience taught him to respect Chinese agency. In the 1860s, Nevius wrote extensively about San-poh, a district in Zhejiang Province comprising seven villages that he had visited from his home base of Ningbo. So remote was San-poh that when Nevius first arrived, the people peppered him with questions ("Does the sun shine in your country, as it does here?") while touching his clothes and commenting on the whiteness of his skin and the length of his nose. Nevius rated the district "encouraging." At the same time, he was becoming acquainted with Zia Ying-tong, a young man who wanted to convert but faced intense pressure from his mother. To prevent her son from attending church, she would tie him up, beat him with a stick, and threaten to disown him. Amazingly, Zia not only stuck with Christianity, he volunteered his services to a British missionary running a nearby school. Not needing his help, she sent him to proselytize in San-poh.[3]

Nevius viewed her assignment as reckless. The mission, he wrote, had "adopted the principle of not sending our native assistants away from us to labour by themselves, but kept them with us . . . under our constant watch and supervision." Expected to struggle, Zia surprised Nevius by sending back a favorable report. "There is a great interest in Christianity here," Zia wrote, "and every night large numbers of the villagers assemble at my stopping-place, and I talk to them till a late hour." Adding that he was "imperfectly fitted to do his work," Zia asked Nevius to send his friend Lu Sin-sang to help. Nevius dispatched Lu, who also enjoyed success. "The number of interested persons is increasing," Lu reported. "I have talked till I am hoarse."[4] After Lu asked Nevius to send two friends, the missionary again obliged and more good news followed. According to Zia, people were walking miles to meet them, conversing with them late into the night, and discarding their idols. A Christian church was being born in San-poh.[5]

The awakening did not take place in a vacuum. Like a chemistry experiment, Christianity reacted in combustible fashion, inflaming many people's long-simmering resentment toward the Confucian ruling class. It started when the poor recognized Christianity's power as a leveler of social hierarchy. Indeed, the new faith allowed those occupying the bottom rung on the Confucian ladder to claim spiritual supremacy over those above them. *They, after all, had embraced the one true religion and the Confucian elites had not.* Their confidence surging, ordinary Chinese began to challenge their former superiors. "The converts, even those of the humbler classes," an astonished Nevius wrote, "acquired great boldness" as they "found that with truth and Christ on their side they could stand before learned men." The "educated men," he continued, "were afraid to enter into controversy with these defenders of the new faith" who seemed to possess "special wisdom."[6] Christianity had upset the applecart in San-poh. The last had become first, and the first were now last.

But the Christian craze proved ephemeral. The situation in San-poh was highly volatile, and change was not long in coming. After interest in Christianity ebbed, the energy shifted to the countermovement, and a wave of persecution followed. The Christians, Nevius reported, "met with opposition, abuse and annoyance from their neighbours and relatives." Doors previously thrown open to Zia now slammed shut, as no one wanted to be caught assisting "preachers of corrupt doctrines and disturbers of the peace." Worse still, the "zeal of many grew cold," crowds no longer gathered to hear the Gospel preached, and "one after another," the Chinese who had identified "with the religion of Jesus withdrew." In this dark hour, Nevius would not have been surprised had Zia and his friends quit. Perhaps he even expected it.

Instead, something remarkable took place. Zia and his small band persevered. They kept their church from dissolving, weathered the storm of persecution, and then quietly returned to their evangelical work. "The Lord's Supper is now celebrated in rotation in the seven villages," Zia reported to Nevius, adding that the number of church members stood at eighty. Though eighty was not a big number, most of the members seemed committed to staying. As further encouragement, church events started generating excitement again among nonmembers. After a period of tumult, Christianity in San-poh had reached a state of equilibrium. Though the initial exuberance surrounding its introduction had dissipated, the church had stabilized itself and appeared likely to endure.[7]

What role did Nevius play throughout the great drama? As it turns out, a very small one. From Ningbo, he monitored the rising and falling fortunes of Zia's group, offering them advice in letters. Crucially, he resisted the temptation to travel to San-poh to extend a helping hand. "I determined not to visit," he wrote, "but to leave the work in the hands of the natives ... giving them counsel and direction as they needed it."[8] He wanted to see if Zia and his helpers could find a way to make Christianity work without staging a missionary intervention. They passed the test.

As the years rolled by, Nevius formalized what had begun as an impromptu experiment into a deliberate method. By 1870, Chinese agency glowed at the core of his new strategy for missionaries—the "Nevius Plan." What exactly was the Nevius Plan and what method did it replace? Before this innovation, Nevius had followed the same hands-on approach to missions as the vast majority of his colleagues. In abandoning this "Old System," Nevius stated that his "change in opinion" had been "brought about by a long and painful experience" filled with "personal error."[9] Under the Nevius Plan, missionaries would continue to travel to remote rural areas to open outstations, establish churches, and install "native" pastors. At this point, however, the old and new plans diverged. Under the Old System, the missionary would maintain an active presence for many years. In contrast, the Nevius Plan called for the foreign missionary to cede control to the Chinese as soon as possible. On this point, Nevius understood that, for many missionaries, letting go would be hard. If so, they must remember that their chief objective was "training native Christians to rely upon themselves and Christ rather than the foreign missionary." Furthermore, the missionary who refused to release his grip risked "inflicting a positive injury" upon those he aspired to uplift. He will "cramp their intellectual and spiritual development," Nevius wrote, "dwarf their manhood, and make them permanently dependent." In short, the controlling missionary could stunt the growth of a promising Chinese minister and, by doing so, smother the indigenous movement he had dedicated his life to sparking.[10]

To illustrate his philosophy, Nevius likened the Christian church metaphorically to plants and trees. "In the spiritual as well as vegetable kingdom," he explained, there is a "law of life and development": a "plant" will "thrive best" when "contending with all the forces of its environment." For example, a "pine tree" will "tower heavenward as the king of the forest" if it is "subjected to the . . . adverse influences of scorching sun, biting frost, and surging tempest." However, should the overprotective gardener deprive a plant of tough conditions, he will inadvertently produce not a hardy survivor but a "feeble exotic" that "can only live when nursed and sheltered." Excessive care is "injurious," Nevius insisted, "and may be fatal to the life which it is intended to promote." The lesson for foreign missions was obvious: missionaries needed to step back and let Chinese churches learn to survive on their own, even if the process involved storm and stress.[11]

If foreign missionaries were no longer to preach at outstations, in what sort of activity should they engage? Under the Nevius Plan, they would operate theological schools in the cities. For two months, Chinese pastors like Zia would attend these institutions for Bible training and periodic review.[12] Missionaries, in sum, would play an important role in the "raising up, training, and superintending of native laborers," but the latter would spread the Gospel by themselves.[13] With this plan, Nevius had found a possible solution to the missionary crisis. He had a new model to share with colleagues.

Sia Sek Ong and Self-Support

Nevius was not alone in handing responsibility to the Chinese. At roughly the same time, a similar idea gained traction with missionaries in Foochow. The missionary's function, they were coming to believe, was to locate, inspire, and train a native pastorate who would start churches at promising sites. Once a Chinese pastor founded a church, the missionary would commence doling out tough love: he would withhold monetary support as a way to compel self-sufficiency on the part of the fledgling church. They called this strategy "self-support." Like the Nevius Plan, self-support did not materialize out of thin air. Rather, it was borne out of experience, emerging in the 1860s only after the mission began working with a handful of extraordinary Chinese preachers. This talented cohort convinced missionaries to place their trust in self-support. The first to succeed on his own was Sia Sek Ong.

Sia grew up in a village thirty miles outside of Foochow. One day at school, he happened upon a Chinese morality book. The book, which employed scare tactics to inculcate good behavior, offered graphic depictions of demons torturing sinners in a gruesome vision of the afterlife. Sia reacted viscerally to the disturbing images, some of which continued to haunt his mind in adulthood. One evildoer was "snatched up at death by the Prince of Devils and sawn asunder," he wrote later in life, "while others were roasted at a copper-pipe to which they were chained." Though the book was not Christian, it left Sia receptive to the Christian themes of sin and retribution that he would encounter as a young man.[14]

In the early 1860s, Sia accepted a teaching position at a school located near a Christian chapel. There he met Nathan Sites, then a relatively new missionary, who hired him as his language tutor. Like most well-educated Chinese, Sia was an ardent Confucianist; he accepted Sites's offer only because his family relied on him for financial support. Since his tutoring brought him into close proximity with Chinese Christians, his belief system clashed unavoidably with theirs. One day, while Sia tried to study inside the chapel, the smallness of the building forced him to listen to the blustery sermon of Li Yu Mi, a blacksmith whom Sites was training. "There is but one name that can save," Li exhorted the gathering, and "that is the name of Jesus." Unable to concentrate amid so much Jesus talk, an exasperated Sia rose from his desk and slammed the door. "How does this blacksmith," he muttered to himself, "who can scarcely read his own language, dare to tell us that there is only one name that can save?" Though nothing of significance transpired here, the anecdote encapsulates the larger story of social and ideological friction caused by the introduction of Christianity. Before Christianity's arrival, an unchallenged Confucian hierarchy ordered society, teaching all people their proper place. An uneducated artisan like Li Yu Mi would never have been so audacious as to present himself as an authority on anything other than blacksmithing. On moral or philosophical matters, he would have deferred to Sia, a scholar well-versed in the Confucian classics. But Christianity changed the social dynamic. The lowly blacksmith was holding forth as if he knew something—much to Sia's irritation.[15]

If the chapel walls were too thin to allow for a separation of Christianity and Confucianism, the partitions within Sia's mind were more porous still. Through frequent exchanges with Sites, Sia found Christianity gradually seeping into his thoughts, where it clashed with Confucianism. Sia was a conflicted young man. The breakthrough came when Sia's first-born child, a son, fell ill. A wicked spirit, relatives and neighbors felt sure, had inflicted the sickness on the boy. To the shock of all, Sia refused to appease the spirit by making offerings at the local altar, choosing instead to let God handle the crisis as He saw fit. The child died. Instead of offering condolences, the community turned abusive, cruelly mocking Sia for failing to perform the rituals that would have saved his son. "Everybody laughed at my folly," he recalled, "in not appealing to the idols." Interestingly, this agonizing experience strengthened rather than weakened Sia's Christian faith. Even though God had elected not to save the child, the incident cast Sia's family and neighbors in a clarifying light: they came across as merciless, vindictive, and unsympathetic. Their behavior, in short, was decidedly *unchristian*. Sia also resented a community that deigned to tell him, during a crisis, how to act, who to worship, and what to believe. In this way, society's insistence that he forsake Christianity compelled him to desire the faith all the more.[16]

Emboldened by this incident, Sia began to teach the Gospel with new-found vigor. By doing so, he inadvertently caused a schism to open in his village. Attracted to his passion and charisma, some people flocked to Sia; a local dealer in religious idols even destroyed his entire stock in a bonfire. But Sia reported others who became "violent and threatened to tear down [Sia's] building" and "expel me from the village." Late one night after the furor died down, a restless Sia, unable to sleep, realized in the dim candlelight that his great inner conflict was resolved. "The two giants within me had stopped fighting." He was a committed Christian.[17]

For a period Sia apprenticed under Nathan Sites, who took him on his travels and provided him with opportunities to preach on his own.[18] In 1869, Sia's tutelage ended when he was ordained as a minister and Sites assigned him to a remote district where Sites had previously established a church. Alone at his outpost, Sia confronted a serious problem, the solution to which would define his career. Tasked with the job of building up the church, Sia expected to work easily with the Chinese Christians who had maintained the station in Sites's absence. Naively assuming that all converts shared his passion and integrity, Sia discovered to his dismay that some had joined the church solely for the salary. When he tried to weed out the insincere, he found himself in a life-threatening situation. After Sia fired an older employee who depended on the church's wages, the man resolved to retaliate with murder. "Five or six times," Sia recalled, "he came to chapel with a knife hid in his sleeve intending to take my life." The man planned first to provoke a fight with

Sia and then to stab him in the heat of battle. This way, Sia's death would not appear like premeditated murder. Spying the concealed blade, Sia survived by maintaining his composure and never allowing any disagreement to escalate.[19] This and other incidents convinced Sia that foreign money was polluting something that must remain pure—the individual's Christian faith. As long as the Chinese remained on mission payrolls, Christianity's detractors could easily undermine the legitimacy of the movement. They could say, with some accuracy, that Chinese "preachers ate the foreigners' rice and therefore spoke the foreigners' words." If allowed to remain, these "rice Christians" threatened to prevent the church from gaining traction in the community. After all, who would join a church if the preacher's integrity was in doubt?[20]

In 1870, Sia took decisive action: he severed financial ties with the mission. "I withdrew from the mission's pay-list," he wrote, "and began to lead the members to support their preachers." The umbilical cord severed, Sia was on his own. Before long, anxiety crept into his thoughts. What if he lacked the physical and mental fortitude to succeed? On the eve of a major church service, Sia awoke at 3 A.M., listened to the torrential rain outside, and experienced a panic attack. Should the rain continue, the poorly ventilated church would fill with people, many of whom would smoke. "With a weak body like mine," Sia fretted, it would be "torture to be shut up . . . with a crowd of smoking, noisy people." As worries flooded his consciousness, Sia heard an otherworldly voice. "Sia Sek Ong! How do you know there is such a thing as a human soul? If there is no soul, then you are very foolish to trouble yourself so about going to that meeting." The mysterious message triggered massive doubt in Sia. *If there was no such thing as a soul, then his career in Christianity was a fraudulent waste of time.* The next day, Sia abruptly canceled the service and resolved to pull out of the village altogether. However, the following night he received a second communication. Lying in the dark, he claimed that "suddenly a bright light filled the room and the cross of Jesus shone in indescribable splendor before my eyes." He realized instantly that the previous night's voice had come from the "enemy" who had used the "fear of hardship to tempt" him to abandon the mission. His sagging faith restored, Sia stuck to his post.[21]

Through hard work, Sia created a permanent church. He did so, crucially, without requesting any financial aid from the mission. Previously, missionaries had spoken of self-support as theoretically possible; however, it was Sia who quietly proved the method's viability. "During the first few years," he later recalled, "I never spoke to any one of my affairs and no one knew how I was getting on financially." When a Chinese Christian accused Sia of secretly accepting money from missionaries, Sia proudly disabused the man: "Since 1870 my hand had not handled a foreign dollar." Sites, the catalyst who had provided the initial spark, was no longer necessary. This was truly a church by the Chinese for the Chinese: Sia provided spiritual guidance and his congregation compensated him with a living wage. "I could leave the matter of salary," Sia wrote, "to the judgment and good will of the native Christians."[22] Sia's example proved instrumental in convincing the Foochow mission to commit to the self-support model during its annual meeting in 1870. And other Chinese Christians, inspired by his model, started self-supporting churches of their own.[23] Among the most famous was Ling Ching Ting. Though a contemporary of Sia's, Ling possessed a background that differed dramatically from that of the Confucian scholar. He was a pirate.

Ling Ching Ting

When Samuel Binkley of Ohio arrived in China in 1861, his heart burned with ardor. In 1852, when only sixteen years of age, Binkley had had a religious experience. Near midnight on the day that he joined the Methodist Church, he approached the altar to pray. When he did, he received his "call." In the mystical night air, he discerned "clear evidence" of God's plan for his life. In ensuing years, Binkley set the divine plan in motion: he completed college, graduated from seminary, found a wife, and embarked for Foochow. Though missionaries typically required two years of intensive language study before preaching, the eager Binkley rushed straight into the field. Unable to speak Chinese, he hired an interpreter to translate while he preached in the street.[24] Though most Chinese passed by without showing interest, one observer watched him keenly. "His zeal and perseverance were wonderful," the stranger said of Binkley. "In all kinds of weather he was at his post."[25]

One day in 1863, Binkley delivered a sermon in a chapel outside of Foochow. In staccato fashion, he would utter a phrase and then wait for the interpreter's translation before advancing to the next line. Though it was a slow-moving sermon, the stranger was spellbound by the message of personal redemption. At the end of the service, as the congregation flowed out of the chapel, that man worked his way to the front where Binkley stood. The chapel doors had been left open, he informed Binkley, and so he had wandered in on a whim. The stranger sought clarification on one crucial point. He wished to know if Jesus, with whom he was unfamiliar, "can save me from all my sins." Binkley unhesitatingly answered in the affirmative; the entire religion, after all, was based on this concept. The stranger next issued an ominous warning: "You didn't know me when you said that." He then proceeded to rattle off the highlights of his lifetime of sin. Along with being a disturbingly "licentious" man, he had gambled, engaged in sorcery, and smoked opium for twenty years.[26] He was also a notorious pirate.

As the stranger reached the end of his list, he perhaps expected Binkley to back off. This Jesus might be forgiving, but even he had to draw the line somewhere. However, Binkley did not turn the stranger away. Instead, he reiterated the lesson of Christ's infinite power to wash away sin. He later escorted the man to Nathan Sites, who started to work with him. Months later, after Binkley's wife fell gravely ill, he prepared to depart China forever. His missionary career, which had begun with so much zeal, was ending after just two years. As disappointing as this abortive experience must have been, Binkley could claim one noteworthy achievement: he had attracted, won over, and baptized Ling Ching Ting.[27]

If the lyrical, rhyming name "Ling Ching Ting" sounds too good to be true, that's because it was. At the time of his baptism, the reformed pirate fabricated a new name for himself by combining the written characters he saw on three storefront signs.[28] With this small but deliberate act, Ling Ching Ting revealed his thinking about what one of Christianity's greatest advantages was: the new faith afforded the individual a chance to reinvent himself. By changing his name, Ling Ching Ting signaled to friends, family, associates, and—most importantly—*himself* that he was a new man. But personal reinvention was not as simple as changing a name; one could not assume a Christian identity without first ridding oneself of sin. Since Ling could not serve both God and opium, he needed to break his addiction. "This was a struggle almost to the point of despair," Sarah Sites recalled. However, "by unceasing prayer, daily encouragement, nourishing food and helpful surroundings... his victory was complete."[29] Ling vanquished his inner demons.

Wasting little time, Ling announced bold plans for his ministry. He would carry the Gospel into the Hok-chiang district, which is where he was from. Though missionaries appreciated Ling's eagerness to get started, they identified a problem: itinerant preachers were supposed to undergo theological training first. And while Ling had embraced the Gospel and conquered his opium addiction, he had not undertaken rigorous study of the scriptures. But Ling—much like Binkley—refused to accept delay. According to Stephen Baldwin, Ling skipped his theological education entirely. "There was no time... for theological training," Baldwin wrote, so Ling embarked with only "the Word of God in his hand."[30]

Along with making a rash decision, Ling also courted danger. Though missionaries viewed Ling's lack of preparedness as problematic in any setting, it was especially troubling given his choice of Hok-chiang, a district notorious for having a feisty population that treated evangelists roughly. In fact, when Ling's own family learned of the plan, they cautioned him strongly not to go. "They will soon take your head off," they admonished before stating the obvious about headless evangelists—"and that will stop your preaching." Eschewing all dire warnings, Ling marched into the lion's den armed with only a rudimentary knowledge of the Bible and a narrative of personal salvation. "Jesus can save you from all your sins," Ling hollered in the streets.

"I know it, for he has saved me from mine!" The people showed no mercy. Ling was "stoned in one place, pelted with mud in another," and "beaten in another." Undeterred, "he pressed on with indomitable energy" and—miraculously—started to make progress. Ling, it turned out, had charisma in abundance. He spoke with a powerful conviction that gave him the ability to persuade.[31]

His unexpected success infuriated Christianity's opponents, and this group plotted to silence him. According to Baldwin, Ling's enemies brought spurious charges against him, delivered him to the district magistrate, and lined up "false witnesses" to testify against him. After hearing the case, the magistrate ruled against Ling and ordered a severe punishment—two thousand lashes with a bamboo switch. When friends carried the bleeding evangelist back to the mission in Foochow, Baldwin described him as "almost dead." "I don't think we can save him," the physician informed Baldwin. "I never saw such terrible injuries from beating. The flesh on his back is like quivering jelly." Sitting at Ling's bedside, Baldwin was about to comfort Ling with soothing words when the latter surprised him by speaking first. "Teacher, this poor body is in great pain just now," Ling said with great effort, "but if I get up from this, you'll let me go back to Hok-chiang, won't you?" Pleased to see the "old fire flashing" in Ling's eyes, Baldwin either agreed to allow Ling to return or at least did not take measures to stop him. Either way, Ling returned to Hok-chiang, where he enjoyed considerable success.[32]

Ling proved that he could flourish on his own, even in the face of adversity. Though Nathan Sites did check on Ling periodically, the latter primarily "worked single-handed," Sarah Sites wrote, "wholly without the help of any missionary."[33] Not surprisingly, the exuberant but untrained Ling was prone to error. "He was very impulsive," a missionary noted, "and sometimes made mistakes." However, these mistakes flowed out of virtue, not vice: his "zeal for the success of the church" sometimes "over-ruled his judgment" and "led him into error."[34] But that same passion and charisma were what ultimately contributed to his success. Before his death in 1877, Ling had brought hundreds into the church and recruited twenty native ministers.[35] Ling, in sum, embodied the self-support model: he was a Chinese pastor working independently within a church structure that was American.

Hu Yong Mi and the East Street Riot

Two years after Ling's death, Hu Yong Mi had a dream. "I saw Ling Ching Ting dressed in very white clothes, and riding on a beautiful white horse." After Hu asked the deceased evangelist why he had come, the latter answered, "To invite you to go with me." Hu demurred, indicating that night had already fallen. Ling did not accept this excuse. "The way upward is very urgent," he commanded, "you must go immediately." Though choosing not to join Ling, Hu did promise to follow in the morning. Then he woke up. Convinced that vivid dreams always carried portentous meanings, Hu ruminated over this one before settling on an interpretation: Ling must be a messenger from the beyond come to inform him of his own impending death. Later at a conference, Hu had the strange experience of observing himself inexplicably requesting an assignment to Hok-chiang. He could not fathom why he had volunteered to preach in a place filled with "many troublesome things." When he arrived at Hok-chiang, he shared both his dream and his interpretation with Ling's sons. Without hesitation, they reassured Hu that his death was not imminent. Their father had merely wished for Hu to assume leadership of his old self-supporting church.[36]

Though supernaturalism is key to understanding Hu's ministry, so too is the self-support model. Excessive missionary oversight, Hu believed, could inhibit the self-expression of a Chinese minister. In fact, that was the least harm it could do. In areas prone to xenophobia, foreign missionaries who hovered over a Chinese minister-in-training could act as lightning rods for violence. Early in his career, Hu learned in agonizing fashion how a foreign missionary, despite good intentions, could endanger the lives of a Chinese minister, his family, and his congregation.

In 1863, the mission installed Hu, not yet ordained, in the East Street Church in Foochow. It assigned Carlos Martin, a young missionary from Vermont, to mentor Hu and provide oversight. More specifically, Martin's job was to secure a building to serve as a church, guide Hu in making renovations, help Hu with the theological points in his sermons, and assist him with the practical aspects of church management. To fulfill this role, Martin leased a residence for his family on Black Rock Hill overlooking the city. The choice of location was strategic: it was close but not too close. From this position, he could supervise Hu (whom he referred to as "Tong Mi" in his journal) without appearing excessively involved. So while Hu led religious services in the unfinished church, it was Martin who pulled the strings from behind the scenes. "Today Tong Mi was sent for," Martin recorded in his journal, "and I went with him to the Chapel" to instruct him "to repair the dwelling part" and "to call the carpenter." On another day, he dispatched a convert "to tell Tong Mi to preach at Chapel tomorrow." "Looked over and criticized a written sermon by Hu Tong Mi," Martin wrote in a third entry.[37] Martin may have viewed his supervision as inconspicuous, but dangerous elements within the community were watching.

On January 17, 1864, Martin's plan appeared to be going smoothly as it entered a crucial stage. The church was finally ready, and Hu was to preside over the official dedication, a joyous occasion that would feature singing, prayer, and entertainment. Though Martin had tried to maintain a low profile, Christianity's opponents knew who he was, where he lived, and why he had come. Nor were they fooled by this new church that tried hard to present itself as an indigenous institution—not a foreign one. It might appear Chinese on the surface with its native pastor, but they knew better: behind the Chinese façade lurked an instrument of foreign intrusion. As Hu spoke inside the church, a noisy crowd gathered outside. "Their voices were raised in such tumult," Hu remembered, "that it was impossible to preach." After Hu locked the doors, the boisterous crowd "raised a louder clamor, using insulting language, and beating the doors." Leaving his seat, Martin ventured outside and "seized a man in the act of beating the door." While opting not to turn the disruptive man in to authorities, Martin did solicit the district magistrate's help when he learned that the crowd was assaulting Hu's guests as they exited the church. Constables arrived on the scene and started making arrests.

They could not keep the peace. At nightfall, the angry crowd started to organize itself. "The mob was to separate in three companies," Hu later wrote, with each one given its special target. One phalanx would destroy Martin's residence, another would "lay waste" to the nearby American Board Mission, while a third would attack the East Street Church. Though the mission was spared, one mob did ascend Black Rock Hill in search of the Martin family. "Soon we heard yells and screams," Carlos's wife Mary wrote in her diary. At this point, Carlos ominously noted that "they were coming." Anticipating trouble, Carlos had earlier carved out a small hole between his home and the adjoining property, a Daoist temple. Seizing their two children, the couple escaped through the aperture and into the temple, where the Daoists granted them refuge. The mob meanwhile hacked its way into the Martin residence with an ax and tore the structure down. Another phalanx laid siege to the East Street Church where Hu, his wife and children, and his sister and her children huddled inside behind locked doors. Outside, a rabble of forty or fifty men hurled stones and ceramic shards at the building. Then they shifted tactics. A group of men hoisted a stone pillar onto their shoulders and used it as a battering ram to smash the front door. In a back room, Hu and his family cringed in terror as they heard the final crash of the wooden door breaking. The mob was inside.

Hu would never forget the horrifying events that transpired next. After wrecking the chapel's furniture, the mob headed to the back rooms. Now in imminent danger, Hu scooped up his young son and instructed the two women to take hold of the other children and follow him. As Hu attempted to escape amid the darkness and confusion, he tripped over broken furniture and fell hard to the floor. As he recovered, he called back to the others, "but no answer was returned." Why had they failed to follow? Outside, Hu handed his son to his brother before returning to the church to locate his family. He plunged into the mob, but the force of it carried him back out to the street. Hearing "weeping," Hu homed in on the source and found his family. He was too late. The mob had "struck" his wife and sister "with missiles of wood and iron," "burnt the face and side of one of them" with fire, "stripped them of their clothing, and grossly violated them." So disturbed was Hu by the atrocity that he opted to leave the most shocking parts out of his account. We know about the violation only from Mary Martin's diary.

Had Hu abandoned this church—or Christianity altogether—no one would have faulted him. But Hu Yong Mi did not quit. Instead, he grew stronger. "Through these troublous times," he wrote, "my soul experienced comfort and strength from the Lord." Somehow, Hu managed to hold his church together, losing not a single member in the riot's aftermath. He also turned the tide as far as the local community was concerned. Members of the mob, feeling remorseful, started to seek him out. "As I sat quiet at home," Hu wrote, "neighbors led men into my presence to confess their wrong." He even became, according to missionaries, "widely known and respected, not only in Christian circles, but among his heathen countrymen."[38]

In the months following the riot, missionaries tried to comprehend the howling rage at the East Street Church. What had been the cause? "It is doubtless in some way," they determined correctly, "a development of the deep-rooted hostility to foreigners."[39] They also endeavored to rebuild and repair their operation. The U.S. Consul, at Carlos Martin's request, successfully sued the Chinese government for damages. When Martin presented Hu with financial compensation, the latter recoiled in fear. "I knew," he wrote, "that wealth devoured peace of mind like a serpent."[40] In his view, money from foreign sources or unequal treaties was highly problematic, if not polluting. "Such prosperity is not genuine," he would later say. "It is like the house built on the sand." When a church accepts ill-gotten money, "the house falls." The only pure money flowed out of Chinese people wishing to support their church. "It is a shame for us to be always looking to foreign countries for money," Hu wrote, when "we must help ourselves."[41]

Hu's belief in self-supporting churches went even deeper. He argued that a church, through the elimination of mission funds, could disarm critics and remove all foreignness, leaving only a Chinese institution. "Ignorant or malicious people say that the native preachers are hired by foreigners to labor for their benefit," Hu declaimed before a Christian audience. "But *you*, members of the Church, know better; you know we are not hired by foreigners to labor for their benefit. The words we speak to you are not foreign, the doctrines we preach are not foreign; we toil for *your* benefit, and for the benefit of all China."[42] Despising foreign money, Hu at first refused to accept compensation for the losses sustained during the riot. After Martin indicated that Hu had no choice, the latter reluctantly channeled the money into a construction project: the erection of a new church to replace the one destroyed by the mob.[43]

The start of construction marked the beginning of the end for Martin. As he had done before, Martin stepped in to assist Hu. When he did, tragedy struck. During the summer of 1864, Foochow's missionary community saw multiple cases of cholera and dysentery, some of which proved fatal. In September, Mary and Carlos's infant son, Lucius, showed symptoms. Leaving his son in his wife's care, Carlos departed from home on a hot morning to meet Hu at the construction site. After returning home, Carlos showed signs of illness and took to his bed. He would not leave it alive. For the next two days, Mary tried in vain to nurse her husband and baby back to health, but the sickness overpowered both. "How shall I find language to express my terrible experience of the last two days?" she wrote on the day both perished. "It is a dreadful blow to me." Six months later, Mary boarded a ship bound for San Francisco with her surviving son. She would never return.[44] The loss of Martin also affected Hu. "Although the Heavenly Father gave him everlasting rest," Hu wrote of Martin, "that could not prevent us from mourning unspeakably."[45]

Conclusion

Partly in response to failure, a handful of missionaries in the 1860s adopted a rather radical approach. Instead of orchestrating all aspects of the missionary enterprise themselves, they ceded control to the native preachers whom they trained. With either light supervision or none at all, these young men carried the Gospel into towns and villages. This was, in every sense of the word, an experiment. Since there was no precedent, the missionaries did not know how the village receiving the native preacher would react to the novelty of one of their own peddling Christianity by himself. Would they greet the man warmly? Would they ignore him? Or would they murder him? All these scenarios loomed as possible outcomes.

None predicted what eventually did transpire. Though some villages rallied their residents against the Chinese preachers, the latter held their ground and eventually established churches. The success of native preachers played a crucial role in the development of American institutions in China. Were these Chinese pastors to fail, the setback might have proved almost fatal to China missions, which were already reeling from fierce resistance, sickness and death, and low conversion tallies. Had the Chinese proved unable to master theology, explain it to their countrymen, operate churches, and attract and hold members, their collective failure would have sent the devastating message to Americans that China and Christianity did not mix. Why should any churchgoer in the United States continue to send donations toward a hopeless cause? Yet the success of these courageous Chinese preachers emboldened supporters of China missions. It proved that Christianity could take hold in China and that the Chinese could supply churches with capable leadership. After all, there were hundreds of Sia Sek Ongs out there, supporters believed, if only an expanding missionary presence could locate them.

5

Crisis Breeds Invention

The Emergence of New Missionary Models

Hunter Corbett collected odd things. In Zhifu, he enjoyed showing his stuffed birds, colorful rocks, and mechanical devices to the Chinese, who manifested great curiosity in the strange objects from the outside world. At first, he gave scarcely a thought to his hobby and the eager onlookers it attracted. He, after all, was an itinerant preacher. However, as his career in China entered its second decade, he acknowledged the difficulty inherent in his form of evangelism—difficulty punctuated by the harrowing ordeal of 1873, when angry villagers had nearly taken his life. He also understood how hard it was to make progress when so many Chinese felt apprehensive about revealing interest in the Gospel. Jesus, after all, was a touchy subject. In contrast, Corbett noted that the Chinese showed no hesitation whatsoever in inquiring about his curiosities. These objects, unlike Jesus, were safe to talk about because they played absolutely no role in the high-stakes ideological war between Confucianism and Christianity. For this reason, Corbett found them useful in generating "good will." Other than that, he saw them as of little consequence.[1]

One day Corbett had an epiphany. What if he were to expand his collection, converting it into a museum that could teach visitors about the outside world? Though primarily educational, the hypothetical museum might also be made to advance the Gospel: those who came to see the exhibit would also hear a sermon. That would be the price of admission. When Corbett returned to America in 1875 on furlough, he located benefactors willing to make contributions. Returning to Zhifu, he lacked only a building in which to install his growing collection. Once again, fortune favored him. A wealthy Chinese merchant both donated money and agreed to sell a row of buildings he owned at below market value. After Corbett moved in, his "Museum and Gospel Hall," as the complex was called, dominated an entire city block.[2]

The museum earned far-reaching fame. Outside the doorway, Corbett would stand like a carnival barker, beckoning people to step inside to see the wonders of the world. The people came in large numbers. Helping Corbett was his doorman, a Chinese dwarf whom he had adopted during one of his itinerancies. Once his chapel was filled to capacity (seventy people), Corbett would shut the door and commence his half-hour sermon. He would then direct the crowd to the museum, where the dwarf would present one marvel after another. "It is a wonderful place to the Chinese," commented Arthur Judson Brown, a visiting American clergyman, "who never weary of watching the stuffed tiger, the model railway and the . . . specimens that Dr. Corbett has collected from various lands."[3] Corbett himself described the impact of the stuffed tiger after he placed it on a "high platform." "It looks so lifelike," he wrote, that many guests reflexively "start back" upon seeing it, "fearing it might spring upon them." After just four days of the tiger exhibition, "the rush of visitors" was so great as to compel Corbett "to call in two extra preachers . . . to assist."[4]

The museum boasted impressive attendance figures, drawing close to 100,000 visitors each year. But did it generate many conversions? It's hard to say. Corbett believed the museum granted him access to populations who might otherwise have been unreachable. "We have had visits from officials," he wrote, and "also from women and children, people whom we could not [otherwise] reach." Some of these became "Christian workers."[5] Though Brown was less sanguine, he insisted nevertheless that the museum accomplished much good. "Friendships are gained, doors of opportunity opened, tracts distributed," and "men led to think."[6] And when preaching along his circuit, Corbett discovered that "prejudice has given way" and that "we are now greeted on the streets, and treated as friends." The famous museum proprietor now met with hearty welcomes—not showers of stones.[7]

Corbett's museum formed part of a larger turn toward experimentation in China missions. The hardships and failures of the 1860s and 1870s convinced many missionaries to discard a cherished idea they had previously accepted as an article of faith: that itinerant missionaries, with God at their backs, could Christianize China with dogged perseverance alone. The problem with this mode of thinking, and its fatal flaw, was that it assumed triumph to be divinely foreordained: God Himself had guaranteed the success of the enterprise. Believing victory inevitable, a missionary had no incentive to exhibit flexibility, creativity, or sensitivity to the needs of Chinese people. He needed only to impose his righteous will. A Christian battering ram, he could pound his message relentlessly against the wall of Chinese intransigence, certain the latter would crumble. It held firm. After years of failure, missionaries began experimenting with alternative models that departed from conventional itinerant preaching. These models are the subject of this chapter. Make no mistake: the missionaries had neither softened their views nor abandoned their goals. They remained committed to subverting Confucianism and spreading their faith. However, they were starting to construct more nuanced delivery vehicles for the Gospel. Though these models appear here in embryonic form, some would evolve into full-fledged institutions, as later chapters show.

These new models, like the Nevius Plan and self-support, all involved a high degree of Chinese agency. Repeated failure had taught missionaries a crucial lesson: one could not simply impose one's religion onto the Chinese and expect them to adopt it. To ensure Chinese acceptance, a missionary needed to include the Chinese and become receptive to their needs. Finally, a group of missionaries did exactly that. John Kerr, Adele Fielde, Young J. Allen, and the Mateers built institutions geared toward meeting Chinese wants, not just their own evangelical objectives.

Adele Fielde's Bible-Women

In 1873, Adele Fielde returned to Swatow with a clear purpose. She would use her mission to rescue Chinese women from their deplorable condition. What was the cause of their oppression? In her opinion, the Confucian social order was to blame. When delivering recruiting speeches in the United States, Fielde would explain how a Chinese woman progressed through a series of life stages, starting from infancy and advancing to old age. Each stage, Fielde claimed, imperiled the woman with a new danger—physical pain, male tyranny, or premature death. After a girl is born, her parents might decide to drown her, either because they cannot afford another mouth to feed or because they prefer boys. "The first question that comes to a girl," Fielde sadly noted, "is whether she will be allowed to live at all. Very many girls are murdered by their mothers." Should the girl survive infancy, her reward in youth is to undergo the painful procedure of foot-binding. Through the daily wrapping of tight bandages, her parents force her feet to grow not outwardly in a healthy direction but inwardly upon themselves. Though rendered more marriageable, the girl is left with deformed feet and curtailed mobility. "The next horror," Fielde continued, arrives with marriage, when the young woman is "forced to wed men who were cruel and worthless." Through her adult years, the pitiable woman must survive her husband's beatings, her mother-in-law's tyranny, her own depression, and the temptation to commit "suicide." That, according to Fielde, was the life of a Chinese woman. It was one of "gloom and darkness."[8]

Chinese women desperately needed the kind of empowerment that Christianity could supply. This was the idea that resurrected the career of Adele Fielde. But what form would the empowerment take? Fielde scrutinized the training regimen that Ashmore used to prepare Chinese preachers for the field. Before a gathering of trainees, he would read aloud a Bible story, like the "raising of Lazarus." He would then ask each man to retell the story "in his own words" and to keep doing so until he "knew the story by heart."[9] Fielde saw no reason why Chinese women could not undergo similar training. Her innovation lay, in other words, not in the devising of an original system but rather in the application of an existing system to women. Once she had worked out the kinks, Fielde unveiled her model before her colleagues. After this group approved, Fielde got busy.[10] "Miss Fielde . . . has taken hold of the work not only with interest but with enthusiasm," a missionary wrote. "She is training Bible-women."[11] Fielde's missionary model—the Bible-women—was designed to empower Chinese women and rescue them from a cruel fate. It would also rescue Fielde by infusing her sagging career with fresh purpose. In its simplest form, the plan required that she train a small cadre of Chinese women who would bring the Gospel to hundreds more. Though we cannot credit Fielde alone for the idea (other missionaries were experimenting with essentially the same idea), she was the first to systematize the training and oversight of an all-female evangelical unit.[12]

Before her system could be operational, Fielde had to build the necessary infrastructure. First, she arranged for the construction of a large house in Swatow that included classrooms and lodging to accommodate thirty women at a time. She also visited numerous Baptist outstations within a sixty-mile radius of Swatow; in each village, she either rented or built residencies that could provide shelter for her Bible-women when they traveled. Second, she produced a textbook that retold key Bible stories in "the simplest terms" using the "popular language."[13] Third, she traveled again to many villages to recruit. Rather than taking all who volunteered, she handpicked women of intelligence, character, and good health whom she believed could handle the physical and emotional strain of the peripatetic life. She chose mostly women who were middle-aged or older because, in her words, "native social customs permit elderly women to go freely from house to house and from village to village." Older women, in short, threatened no one and so enjoyed almost unlimited access.[14] Typically, the women she chose had endured hard lives. The majority had either lost their husbands through death or become "grass widows," women whose husbands had left China to work in Thailand, Singapore, or Sumatra and never returned. Some women had escaped domestic abuse at the hands of a husband or mother-in-law. Regardless of their individual stories, the recruits were all free from male control when Fielde found them.[15] Fourth, Fielde invited cohorts to her headquarters in Swatow—the Mingdao Women's School—to participate in two-month training sessions.[16]

The model's success hinged on Mingdao. It was here that Fielde turned thirty illiterate women into articulate Bible-women who could inspire others. She accomplished this feat by eliminating all but the most practical essentials from her lessons. She began by giving the women an oral text to master, such as one of Aesop's fables. If a woman could repeat the fable in her own words, she was ready to move to Bible stories.[17] With the Bible, Fielde maintained realistic expectations. Whereas a theological school would expect students to master the scriptures, Fielde presented her trainees with a stripped-down curriculum featuring only a handful of Bible stories. "They learn the Bible stories," she wrote, "with great rapidity," first by listening to them and then by retelling them in their own words with "vivacity." If a student could tell a story from memory in class, she could do so out in the field. Fielde boasted that previously illiterate women could now "read the four Gospels" and "tell from memory in detail the whole life of Christ."[18] To prove their readiness, students were required to pass a two-hour examination proctored by William Ashmore and Fielde. "The women had gone to the chapel with reluctance and trembling," Ashmore wrote of exam day, "but they had done so well that they felt completely re-assured."[19] Despite Ashmore's sunny account, not all trainees marched out as Bible-women; some failed the test, Fielde weeded out others, and a few quit.[20] However, her system did yield a corps of capable storytellers who could "hold an audience of untaught village women motionless" late into the night with "sleeping children in their laps."[21]

Like self-support and the Nevius Plan, Fielde's model removed the foreigner from direct evangelism and shifted that responsibility to Chinese women. They became the agents of spiritual change. "The selection, training, and superintendence of native Christian women," she wrote, "is probably the way in which the foreign missionary lady can effect most in the work of evangelizing Asia."[22] In pairs, the Bible-women ventured out to villages vetted by Fielde. In all cases, these were villages that male missionaries had been visiting for some time; highly conspicuous, those male missionaries had triggered resistance, preached mostly to men, and failed to penetrate the home, where women resided. In contrast, the Bible-women moved by stealth, slipping in and out of villages undetected while gaining access to homes.[23] Suspecting that women would speak their minds only if men were absent, Fielde instructed her Bible-women to hold sessions that prohibited men. When they did, Chinese women would "come pouring in from the doorways." It turned out that there was a hunger for female-to-female association that Fielde's operation tapped into.[24]

The Bible-women embraced their new role as the bringers of spiritual change. They ventured out bearing inspirational sobriquets, such as "Speed," "Tolerance," "Guide," "Rectitude," and "Innocence."[25] It is unclear whether they chose the names themselves or Fielde assigned them. Either way, each name—by representing a woman's identity or finest character trait—carried an implicit message of empowerment. No one had treated these women as individuals before, and many blossomed under Fielde's supervision. "Could you discern, as do I," Fielde wrote, "the blessed changes that the touch of Christ has produced in these women, their furrowed faces would be as beautiful in your eyes as they are in mine."[26] Ashmore also commented favorably on the experiment. "Miss Fielde's success has gone far beyond my most sanguine expectations," he wrote. The "'old folks' have done remarkably well."[27]

Along with running the program, Fielde documented the life stories of individual Bible-women. She understood the value of these portraits in generating publicity for her model in the United States. In the 1870s, she incorporated their stories into articles appearing in the *Baptist Missionary Magazine*. Missionary magazines played a crucial role in the larger evangelical ecosystem. By inundating churchgoing readers with articles about the wretched lives of "heathens" and the heroic exploits of missionaries, these magazines prevented missions from receding to the background of American life and thus ensured continued donations. They kept, in other words, the money pump primed. After her success with the magazine, Fielde repackaged the stories into a book designed to reach an even broader readership. A bestseller, *Pagoda Shadows* (published in 1884) featured the personal stories of Chinese women, dictated to Fielde by the women themselves.[28]

Indeed, *story* was the key to the book's success. Fielde shared unforgettable narratives of flesh-and-blood Chinese women transformed by Christianity. Readers read about Silver Flower, who had been sold into three difficult marriages. Her first husband, she recounted, "hated me as soon as he saw me." Every night, he carried a knife into bed so that he could "kill me if he felt the desire." Her second husband was an incorrigible gambler who beat Silver Flower and lost the family's money, leaving his wife and children to starve. Her third husband did not have a self-destructive vice, but with him she bore nine children. Unable to feed so many, the parents suffocated four girls and threw the corpses into the river. This was the life of Silver Flower before she became a Bible-woman. It was a story that surely caused American readers both to gasp in horror and to pledge monetary support for Fielde's program. After all, it offered Chinese women a better life through Christianity.[29]

American readers also enjoyed meeting Speed, whose father left the farm when she was thirteen to join the Christian church in Swatow. Speed agonized over her father's decision because villagers had told her that "he would have his heart and eye balls taken out" by the missionaries. Returning unharmed, her father urged Speed not to bind her feet, and she agreed (had she decided otherwise, she would likely have taken a different name). In recounting her life story, Speed shared an anecdote that symbolized Christianity's liberating power. One day her village received a strange visitor. A "hideous" bamboo dragon "painted in gorgeous colors" and bearing "glaring eyes" drifted down the river and got caught in the bank. Horror-stricken, superstitious villagers ascribed vast powers to the bamboo construction, with some auguring that it would "breed pestilence." When a few villagers did become sick, that fact prompted the healthy ones to make daily offerings of food in an effort to placate the dragon. The village had become paralyzed, in thrall to the people's belief that an inanimate object possessed malevolent power. Speed, now a Bible-woman, knew better. "There is but one true God," Speed later recounted to Fielde, "who keeps those who serve Him from the power of all dragons." Before a crowd of onlookers, Speed prayed to God, approached the river bank, "punched holes in the dragon" with her umbrella, and "pushed it off the shore." As the defeated foe floated harmlessly downstream, amazed villagers flocked around Speed, eager "to have me tell them about the God who protected me."[30] Liberated by her faith from oppressive superstitions, Speed had become an agent of good on the Chinese landscape. Stories like this one, by speaking to Christianity's transformative power, left a deep impression on American readers.

In 1876, three years after the launch of her experiment, Fielde reflected on her astounding reversal. "To me personally," she wrote, "they have been years of perfect physical health, and profound spiritual joy." They were also years of achievement. Her effort had yielded a corps of sturdy women, about thirty in number, which had touched profoundly the lives of another 150 women.[31] Both numbers promised to grow in the future. Fielde, in sum, had rejuvenated her missionary career by empowering a group that had historically languished in the margins of Chinese society. The trial period now complete, Fielde had a model to share with other missionaries. In 1877, she traveled to Foochow to consult with Sarah Sites and other female missionaries, her goal being to help them establish a Bible-women program of their own. "Miss Fielde ... made a visit," they reported, and "hearing of her success and her methods ... gives us more faith in the woman's work."[32] Two years later, those same missionaries expressed their wish "to take the very successful work of Miss Field [sic] ... as a model."[33]

Young J. Allen's Magazine

Through hard work and self-sacrifice, Sia Sek Ong successfully founded his mission's first self-supporting church. That being said, he barely scraped by in the early years. In 1871, Sia raised 60,000 cash in donations from his congregation at a time when a Chinese pastor required a minimum of 72,000 to run a church and support his family.[34] As Sia wondered how he would make up the 12,000 shortfall, a missionary approached to convey congratulations and a packet of money.[35] Months earlier, Young J. Allen had announced a contest in the pages of *The Church News*, a Chinese-language periodical he had recently started. A cash prize would go to the Chinese Christian submitting the best essay discussing the nature of Christ. After evaluating all entries, Allen selected Sia's essay, "Who is Jesus?" Though we do not know what made Sia's submission stand out, quite possibly his stylistically innovative decision to write from the perspective of Jesus had impressed Allen. "Though originally without a body, yet I have a body," Sia wrote in Jesus's voice. "I was exalted, but for your sakes humbled myself and condescended to become a man."[36] The prize, by enabling Sia's ministry to remain afloat, allowed the self-support model to survive its crucial first test.

But what exactly was *The Church News*? Recall that Allen had come to China to preach but that a dearth of funds had forced him, somewhat grudgingly, to accept secular work outside the scope of missions. In 1868, after losing his teaching position at the Tongwen Guan, a desperate Allen reluctantly accepted a part-time editorship at the *Shanghai Daily News*, a Chinese-language newspaper published by the British *North China Herald*. Though he took the job purely out of financial necessity, something unexpected happened after he started working. Not only did Allen learn how to operate a printing press, he also came to view publishing as a possible solution to some of the problems that had vexed him personally and foreign missions generally. He realized that a newspaper could spark his personal reinvention and, more broadly, help rescue Protestant missions from their malaise.[37]

One could sum up Allen's diagnosis of the missionary problem in three words: *missions lacked reach*. Every Sunday, Allen held a service in Shanghai where he made contact with only about a dozen Chinese. Every year, his mission reported paltry numbers of converts (twenty-five joined between 1868 and 1869). Missions, therefore, needed to find a way to *reach* deeper into the Chinese population to touch more lives. More specifically, Allen believed, missions must *reach* two groups: women and the literati. Women held great influence in society because they raised children; yet since they lived, in his view, in intellectual and spiritual darkness, they perpetuated the very superstitions that missionaries wished to eradicate. If women could be turned to Christianity, so too might all of China. As for the literati, Allen knew that they were orchestrating much of the anti-Christian violence in defense of their Confucian system. Thus, the missionary needed to *reach* into their minds to "supplant the ... system of Confucius." "While ... female society remains ... the nursery of superstition," Allen summarized, "and Confucianism dominates the ruling classes, there is no hope of permanently converting China." Finally, Allen faulted missionaries for focusing excessively on narrow church dogma when their message ought to *reach* "the whole man." At Emory, Allen had benefited from the secular as well as the religious parts of the curriculum. Would not Chinese minds also profit from history, science, and literature? Missionaries, therefore, must teach not just the Bible but also Western Civilization. How could a missionary extend his *reach* in the ways outlined above? To influence Chinese females, Allen would found a school for girls (see Chapter 8). To obtain the other forms of reach, Allen started a newspaper.[38]

In 1868, Allen launched the Chinese-language *Church News* using the Presbyterian Mission's movable type. At the outset, the organ's purpose was merely to connect the geographically spread-out Chinese Christian population by providing them with a common source of mission news and Christian content. But as time passed, the paper acquired a secular focus that belied its title. Allen tried to spark readers' interest in the natural world (articles described scorpions, alligators, and flying fish) and in scientific fields like Astronomy, Biology, and Chemistry. He even published serially a Chemistry textbook written by a fellow missionary. The paper also documented marvels of engineering and technology such as the Suez Canal, the transatlantic telegraph, and North America's transcontinental railroad. Finally, Allen wrote favorable articles on forward-looking Chinese institutions, such as the nearby Kiangnan Arsenal, which had built a modern steamship.[39]

Why did Allen focus on science and technology? In his view, the implicit assumption of the Confucian elite was that all valuable wisdom resided in the hoary past. A society could achieve perfection, in other words, not through innovation but rather by heeding the wisdom of the sages uttered two thousand years earlier. Allen used his paper to posit a counter idea—*that transformative knowledge capable of improving Chinese lives was being generated right now.* This single idea undergirded every issue of *The Church News*, which became a de facto user's manual to Western civilization. Yet one chore remained. Since the paper had clearly deviated from its original purpose, it required a new name. In 1874, Allen settled on *The Globe Magazine*.[40]

The paper possessed one other crucial feature: it was interactive. It provided Chinese readers with a forum in which they could share ideas, experiences, and opinions and engage in debate. Indeed, the contributions of Chinese readers constituted a major thrust of the paper. After thorough analysis, Adrian Bennett, Allen's biographer, found that Chinese submissions outnumbered those of foreigners by a wide margin.[41] Additionally, the paper neither privileged foreign authors nor suggested that Chinese authors, who were new to Christianity and Western thought, were less qualified to offer commentary. In this way, the paper amounted to an intellectual space of racial equality.⁴² What topics did Chinese authors explore? Allen gave Chinese contributors latitude, allowing them to write on whatever interested them. They could even criticize foreign missionaries. One writer, for instance, urged missionaries to be more considerate of Chinese customs. Contributors also discussed topics that hit close to home, such as whether a prospective convert was obligated, out of filial piety, to obtain permission from parents before joining the church.⁴³ That said, Allen would often steer the conversation toward topics that advanced his other objective—to break down resistance to Western thought among the literati. Toward this end, he had Chinese discussants locate zones of overlap between Christianity and Confucianism. "Although Confucianism is correct," wrote a Chinese Baptist, "the way of Jesus is even better."⁴⁴

While the *Globe Magazine* kept many readers informed, for a few it accomplished much more. It changed the direction of their lives. We have already seen how Sia Sek Ong's timely victory in Allen's contest saved his church from a financial shortfall. The magazine had an even greater impact on Sia's young associate at the Foochow mission—Huang Naishang. As a boy, Huang did something unusual: he read the Confucian classics critically. Instead of accepting the texts as unassailable repositories of truth, he faulted them for leaving important "metaphysical" questions unanswered. How did creation take place? And what was the relationship between man, nature, and the divine?⁴⁵ People claiming to have answers soon materialized. In 1866, when Huang was seventeen, Nathan Sites and Sia Sek Ong stopped in his village to preach. Huang gravitated toward Sites and his "sincere, humble and unassuming" manner. When Sia and Sites returned each month, Huang would seek them out to debate the big questions knocking about in his mind. Before long, he joined the church with the intention of following in Sia's footsteps.

The mission initially had Huang shadow Hu Yong Mi, who characterized his young charge as "diligent in study" and "helpful in evangelizing." Huang even preached for a brief stint at the East Street Church, the once hostile neighborhood having been pacified by Hu. But Huang would not become a preacher. Recognizing his intellectual gifts, Sites reassigned him to the mission's publishing operation in 1872 to assist with composition, editing, and translating. It was there that Allen's newspapers fell into his possession, and the insatiably curious Huang consumed their content. But he did more than just read. In 1874, Huang worked with Frank Ohlinger to publish *Zion's Herald*, which, according to Anne Pi-Yau Pang, closely resembled Allen's magazine. Like Allen, Huang covered a wide array of topics specifically chosen to help Chinese readers acquire a modern point of view: international news, religious discussions, reform theories, and Western learning. Huang had imitated Allen's model.⁴⁶

Huang and Allen eventually became, in Ohlinger's words, "most esteemed friends." Though each man possessed an intellect the other could appreciate, they also agreed on the important issues. This was no coincidence. Having accessed Allen's ideas through the print medium when his mind was in its formative stage, Huang unsurprisingly adopted many of Allen's opinions. When he later met Allen in person, the two discovered a happy alignment in their views. In particular, Allen felt, and Huang agreed, that China could not thrive in the modern world unless it underwent a complete overhaul of its political and intellectual culture. The country is "physically helpless," Allen wrote, "her mental forces abated and her morals decayed." Huang too believed that the magnitude of China's problems required an infusion of fresh thinking that only Christianity could effect. "Our countrymen lack public morality," Huang wrote, sounding much like Allen himself. "Only Christianity is able to inspire and motivate the people." In an effort to reform government from within, Huang studied for the civil service examination. He was successful, receiving a low-ranking degree in 1877. Through his newspaper, Allen had influenced a young man who had succeeded in penetrating the scholarly ranks and who would later become a reform-minded intellectual.[47]

Since 1860, when Allen arrived in China, his career had evolved in a way he could not have predicted. Though he had come to preach the Gospel, he found himself in the 1870s running a newspaper with an annual circulation approaching 100,000 copies. The Chinese clearly appreciated a paper that provided them with an intellectual space in which they could figure out, on their own, exactly what Christianity and Western civilization were and how they might help China. The Chinese, in other words, appreciated Allen because he presented solutions to China's problems and conceded space in each issue to their viewpoints. This, Allen believed, was as it should be. He even predicted that the Chinese would one day take over the publication altogether.[48] Allen had developed a new model for missions.

Calvin and Julia Mateer's School

The 1860s brought one humiliation after another for Calvin Mateer. If there was a silver lining, it was that, through painful trial and error, he had absorbed two lessons. First, a missionary paid a steep price whenever he invoked his treaty rights. Irwin Hyatt has speculated that Mateer was driven to prove that he was smarter than the Chinese officials who tried to block him.[49] If so, it must have frustrated him to no end that he had lost, in embarrassing fashion, his showdowns with officials when he turned to consuls and gunboats for help. This lesson, though solving one problem, raised a difficult question. If a missionary were to remove the legal option from his arsenal, what should he do when a violent mob attacked? Mateer had no answer. The sad case of Miao delivered a second sobering lesson: Christianity would fail to take permanent hold even in promising candidates if they were not intellectually prepared to receive it.[50] But this lesson too prompted a tough question. Itinerant preaching, in that it involved brief stops along a circuit, prevented the missionary from giving converts sustained attention. How could the peripatetic missionary reorganize a Chinese mind according to Christian concepts if he were always on the move? Again, Mateer had no answer.

The implications of the two lessons shook the foundations of Mateer's beliefs. Thus far, he had operated under the assumption that straight preaching was the best way to propagate the Gospel. In this regard, he fell into perfect alignment with the missionary establishment. For decades, mission boards had elevated this method above others as the purest and best evangelical method. This bedrock principle informed the long career of Rufus Anderson, who oversaw all overseas assignments for the American Board of Commissioners for Foreign Missions (ABCFM) between 1832 and 1866. "The proper test of success in missions," Anderson asserted in a lecture following his retirement, "is not the progress of civilization, but the evidence of a religious life." Focus on the "Gospel alone," he advised, and never become sidetracked teaching the "languages, literature, science, and manners of Western civilization."[51] Yet in the 1870s, Mateer reassessed this hallowed principle. He now sought a new missionary model that would eliminate wasteful friction with officials and allow for the rigorous training of the Chinese mind. Only then could it receive the Gospel. But what would his new model look like? Mateer turned with fresh eyes to his wife's struggling school.

In the early 1870s, Calvin Mateer altered his trajectory in China. "The first years I was in China I traveled a good deal," he wrote in 1875, "and preached and sold books in the streets. I have not done so much of it the last two or three years, having been more closely engaged in my school."[52] Electing to stay home, Calvin worked with Julia to reorganize the school. The single biggest change involved classroom instruction. When the Mateers founded the school, they insisted upon Chinese—not English—as the medium of instruction, even though the latter would have allowed them to teach the classes themselves instead of hiring Chinese instructors. We can only understand this policy, which makes little practical sense, in the context of Calvin Mateer's larger evangelical project in China. He had learned the hard way how difficult it was to introduce Christianity to a mind patterned according to Confucian precepts. For Christianity to take hold, Chinese minds must receive Western learning first; the acquisition of Western knowledge was thus a precondition to the spread of the Gospel. But how could Western learning penetrate China? As long as that knowledge remained locked in the English language, its influence would be confined geographically to the treaty ports where English was spoken. If, however, the school could teach Western knowledge in the Chinese language, graduates could carry it *anywhere* in China. There was no limit to its reach.[53]

While this thinking seemed sound in theory, the Mateers faced the practical problem of finding suitable Chinese teachers. At first, they insisted that all teachers be church members. By hiring Christians only, they hoped to quarantine the school from the corrupting influence of Confucianism. The Confucian education, Calvin wrote scathingly, is a "wretched system" that is "as destitute of ideas as a jellyfish is of bones."[54] Though the Mateers' policy could keep Confucianism out, it also shrank the candidate pool: they could hire only from Tengchow's church members. Some of these teachers proved to be so deficient that they had to be fired. The most disastrous teacher, Chou Wen-yuan, had seemed promising at first because he possessed a strong education. However, after he passed the state examination, he quit the church and started acting like a member of the literati. He taught Confucianism in the classroom and slandered the school in front of the students. He departed in 1871 after inflicting five years of damage.[55]

Faced with crisis, the Mateers made two concessions that saved the school. First, they eliminated church membership as a prerequisite for employment. Here they followed the credo that "heathen teachers are far less hindrance spiritually than inconsistent Christians." It was better to have a strong Confucian educator, in other words, than a weak Christian one. Hiring out of an expanded applicant pool, they selected capable classroom instructors who were also Confucianists.[56]

Second, the Mateers removed the pedagogical handcuffs they had previously imposed upon their instructors. Up until this point, the Mateers had demanded that teachers deliver the curriculum—including Chinese lessons—using Western methods. They forbade teachers from employing the traditional Chinese pedagogy based on rote memorization. During drill sessions, a Chinese teacher would recite lines from a text, and students would commit each line to memory by shouting the line, as many as a hundred times, back to the teacher. A comical eighteenth-century poem described the cacophony emanating from a village school: "The night breeze is disturbed by the cries of the crows. / Those pupils altogether showing off the strength of their throats."[57] Education in China was truly a noisy affair. When the Chinese method entered the Mateers' school, Calvin struggled to comprehend the "uproarious studying." The students commit the classics to memory, he observed, "by chanting . . . rhythmically at the top of their voices." Though he found the "din" quite "distracting," he noted that "the Chinese teacher seems to enjoy it." Mastery, as far as he could tell, happened in two phases. First, the boys memorize an entire book verbatim without understanding it. When a student demonstrates he can recite a book "from beginning to end," phase two begins: "the teacher commences to explain it to him." Comprehension, in short, followed memorization.[58] Though the shouting gave Julia headaches, she agreed the "Chinese method was best for Chinese children."[59]

Calvin Mateer's about-face was stunning. The unapologetic hater of all things Confucian now presided with his wife over a school in which Confucian teachers taught Confucian texts using a traditional pedagogy practiced for centuries by Confucian scholars-in-training. Given what we have seen of Calvin Mateer thus far, these concessions perhaps seem out of character. It is hard for us to fathom how a man with an iron personality now appeared to be backing down from his ideological opponent. A missionary whom Hunter Corbett once described as having never failed at anything had ostensibly admitted defeat.[60]

Or had he? Mateer had something up his sleeve. He had recognized that the school, as it was formerly constituted, remained true to his core beliefs but did not meet the needs of Chinese parents. For them, it had stood as an alien institution, too strange to gamble on. Though the prospect of a free education enticed parents, the school's potential downside was, in the final calculation, too great: its religious emphasis, Christian teachers, and Western pedagogy were likely to diminish, not enhance, their sons' prospects for a good life. Even worse, their boys might become social outcasts. Better to have no education, parents reasoned, than a risky education. However, by making concessions, the Mateers allayed these fears and, in doing so, eliminated the local opposition. The school now gave Chinese parents something they had desperately sought but, until now, could not receive from Chinese institutions: a free education for their sons that would not preclude a normal life.

The Mateers, in other words, had exploited a gap in the Chinese educational system. During the Qing period, Chinese boys could receive an education in a variety of ways. Affluent families hired private tutors, clans set up exclusive schools, and villagers pooled their resources to hire a teacher. But what option did parents have if they lacked access to a clan school and were too poor to hire a tutor or contribute to a teacher's salary? The Qing government did establish charitable schools to educate poor children, but its coverage left massive gaps. By the 1870s, population growth had exceeded school capacity to the point where most boys had no chance to receive any education at all. "It is far from being the fact that every Chinese village has its school," wrote the missionary Arthur Smith, "but it is doubtless true that every village would like to have one." Statistics, though not perfectly reliable, support Smith's observation: in Shandong Province, the government's charitable schools served only 1.1 percent of school-age boys. In short, when it came to free education, demand outstripped supply.[61] The Mateers' school carved out a niche by catering to Chinese families who had fallen through the cracks.

For any Chinese school, the civil service examination provided the ultimate measure of the school's quality. Since "success in the examinations opened the way to the most lucrative and prestigious of occupations" and "state service," writes Jessie Lutz, "most Chinese considered passing the civil service examinations the real goal of education."[62] Student success on exams would also reflect favorably upon the institution that had trained the student. In 1873, the Mateers felt confident enough to roll the dice. They convinced their top student, Chou Li-wen, to take the qualifying examination for a low-ranking academic degree. He passed. Even more satisfying, the two sons of Chou Wen-yuan failed the same exam. With this victory, a powerful message rippled through the community: the Mateer school could equip a student for a conventional career track in Chinese society. Over the next decade, seventeen other students would take the exam, and sixteen of them would pass. Once a strange foreign institution, the school had earned the trust of the community.[63]

With that trust, Calvin Mateer had his Trojan Horse: he could now smuggle Western learning into China, and even into its government, cloaked in the Chinese language. As the school gained momentum, Mateer worked to strengthen the Western part of the curriculum—especially math, science, and engineering. In 1873, he somewhat nervously entered the classroom himself as Algebra instructor. His apprehension stemmed from the fact that he had written the textbook himself in Chinese and was uncertain whether his method would work with Chinese students. After the experiment succeeded, he added Geometry, Trigonometry, Astronomy, and Chemistry to the curriculum, composing textbooks for each.[64] By 1874, he had also begun to exhibit all sorts of scientific wizardry in the classroom, as his journal entry makes clear:

> I practically gave all my time to the business of teaching and experimenting, and getting apparatus.... I got up most of the things needed for illustrating mechanics, and a number in optics; also completed my set of fixtures for frictional electricity, and added a good number of articles to my set of galvanic apparatus. With my new battery I showed the electrical light ... I had an exhibition of two nights with the magic lantern.... In chemistry I made all the gases and more than are described in the book, and experimented on them fully.... The students ... appreciated very much what they saw.[65]

With such displays, Calvin Mateer and Chou Li-wen, who stayed on to teach Chemistry, dazzled the students with the wonders of science. No Confucian scholar could possibly inspire this much awe—and that was precisely the point. Science allowed Mateer to reinvent his missionary identity. No longer the bedraggled missionary atop a mule, he now presented himself as the authority on a body of knowledge that explained the secrets of the universe better than Confucianism could. Whereas the Chinese had once pelted Mateer with rocks, they now enrolled their sons in his school.

John Kerr's Chinese Colleague and Medical School

Death and misfortune plagued John Kerr's early years in Canton. His mission was severely threatened when his hospital burned down during the Second Opium War. He also sustained personal loss; following the passing of his first wife, the three children of his second wife also died. But Kerr recovered. After securing a new location, he reopened the hospital and threw himself into his work.[66] He opened a vaccination department that he linked up with the city's existing vaccination establishment, providing Cantonese practitioners with supply.[67] Known to rise before the sun to make his rounds,[68] he would then turn to the usual packed slate of surgeries. In a single day, he sometimes performed as many as seven surgeries, as his log for July 1, 1875 demonstrates:

> 1st—Two operations for extraction of Cataract.
> 2nd—One operation for Lithotomy.
> 3rd—Exsection of eyeball for cancerous tumor.
> 4th—One operation for Fistula in ano.
> 5th—One case of circumcision for phymosis.
> 6th—One operation for soft Cataract.
> 7th—One operation for removal of necrosed bone from thigh.[69]

Indefatigable, Kerr also carried his work outside the hospital. Twice each week, he would depart after midnight to travel to neighboring towns, dispensing medicine and Christian literature.[70] He made house calls when patients were too infirm to walk to the hospital. During these excursions, he often encountered people in need. "If he found sick children, beggars or helpless people who were diseased," a former student recalled, "he would try to have them carried to the hospital." Kerr also visited society's outcasts. "I had never known a foreigner," the student added, "who was so humble as to be such a friend to lepers and prisoners."[71]

Wong Fun

When Kerr was away, the hospital had to function shorthanded. Kwan Ato was not enough; Kerr desperately needed more doctors. Unexpectedly, help arrived in the form of an extraordinary young Chinese man with unique credentials. Born in Canton in 1829, Wong Fun attended the missionary-run Morrison School in the 1840s. In 1845, Samuel Brown, one of his teachers, announced that he was returning to New England and was willing to take several boys along. Bravely, Wong Fun and two other boys—Wong Shing and Yung Wing—volunteered (Yung is described in Chapter 7). In America, Wong Fun studied for two years at the Monson Academy in Massachusetts before moving to Scotland to study medicine at the University of Edinburgh.[72]

It did not take long for the precocious Wong to distinguish himself. "We have much pleasure in recording an interesting fact," wrote Edinburgh's *Monthly Journal of Medical Science* in 1852. "Wong Fun . . . has gained the highest prize in the botanical class." Wong's talent in medicine was beginning to manifest itself.[73] In 1855, he made history, becoming the first Chinese to complete his medical training in the West. At commencement ceremonies, Dr. James Young Simpson, a leading physician in obstetrics, focused on Wong's achievement and future prospects in his address. Wong, he hoped, would return to his "distant home" not as a "Physician merely" but also as a "Christian medical Missionary." In this way, Wong could "scatter among his three hundred millions of countrymen" not just "modern European medical science" but also "glad tidings of great joy."[74] Just as Simpson had hoped, Wong volunteered with the London Mission Society and sailed for Hong Kong in 1857. One year later, he moved to Canton to practice medicine at the Kam-li-Fau Hospital, which was run by his mission.[75]

It was there that he met John Kerr. Though attached to different hospitals, the two physicians assisted one another when circumstances demanded. Wong, writing his hospital's annual report, described a case in which Kerr had taken his place (Wong was away) for a difficult surgery that involved removing a tumor from a woman's jaw.[76] Their partnership grew after 1860 when Wong, upset by the "fraudulent and commercial" behavior of some of the converts, resigned from his hospital.[77] In the 1860s, Wong practiced mainly with Kerr at the Canton Hospital, and the latter recognized his technical skill in annual reports. "The assistance of Dr. Wong has been cheerfully rendered," Kerr wrote in 1869, "and many of the capital operations were performed by him."[78] Though Wong treated a wide array of medical problems, he made his greatest contribution in childbirth.

Childbirth was one area where Western medicine enjoyed an advantage over Chinese medicine. According to historian Yi-li Wu, the Chinese approach to childbirth involved a division of labor that split along gender lines. Female midwives "managed the physical aspects of birth" while the male physician "would be called only in an emergency," where he "was primarily responsible for administering drugs." Why would he prescribe medicine rather than take invasive action in challenging cases? Chinese doctors, Wu explains, cultivated a "gentlemanly identity" and held "disdain for manual techniques." Their general preference for pharmaceutical solutions intensified in cases involving reproduction because "prevailing norms of gender segregation" situated childbirth solidly within the "female sphere." In the interests of preserving "female modesty," doctors conceded the birth room to midwives and shied away from going inside the female body even in dire circumstances.[79]

China was not unique in this regard. For much of American and European history, the same gender division characterized childbirthing practice. Before 1800, "childbirth was almost exclusively a women's event," writes Judith Walzer Leavitt. "When a woman went into labor, she summoned her women friends and relatives to aid her."[80] In the West, however, the once firm gender barrier started to fracture in the nineteenth century as male medical authority encroached upon the traditionally female space. The career of Dr. James Simpson, Wong Fun's mentor in Edinburgh, exemplified the shift. Thus, John Kerr and Wong Fun had training in handling difficult childbirths, and this gave them an advantage over Chinese doctors. In tough cases where midwives did not know what to do and Chinese doctors insisted on physical detachment, some families—as a last resort—summoned Western physicians. They were willing to take invasive action.

These cases seldom ended with a smiling mother holding a healthy baby. With midwives handling all "normal deliveries," a family contacted the Canton Hospital only when complications imperiled the lives of mother and child or when the midwife had made a catastrophic error.[81] Sadly, Wong and Kerr often found themselves operating solely to preserve the life of the mother, having already pronounced the fetus dead or unsavable. For example, when Kerr was summoned to the home of a pregnant woman in 1874, he discovered that midwives had already "torn away the head of the child." With the child lost, Kerr acted to save the mother. Reaching into the birth canal, "I plunged my finger into the mutilated . . . chest of the child" and "immediately the body was born," which revealed itself to be a "curiously deformed monstrosity." The delivery was awful, but Kerr's action saved the mother.[82]

In 1860, one extremely difficult case solidified the two doctors' bond of mutual respect. After inspecting a pregnant woman, Kerr discovered that the "head of the child was bent backward, and rested between its shoulders."[83] Starting in the 1890s, physicians confronting a complication like this might perform a Cesarean section (the Canton Hospital's first Cesarean took place in 1892). This option was not available in 1860.[84] After "all our efforts failed," the two physicians accepted that they must "destroy the child as the only chance of saving the mother." But how to remove a fetus so awkwardly positioned? Wong decided to perform an "embryotomy," a gruesome operation that Kerr described:

With a pair of cutting forceps, Dr. Wong pierced the head, and reduced its size by crushing the bones and removing the brain; after which, with a pair of straight forceps, the delivery was readily accomplished, and the patient soon recovered her usual health. The necessity of resorting to so dreadful an operation, may be judged of by considering that the head and chest of the child were so situated that they had to be forced through a passage which was barely large enough to receive the head alone. This is the first case, so far as is known, in which embryotomy has been performed for the delivery of a Chinese female.[85]

In an embryotomy, the surgeon cuts part of the fetus into pieces while it is lodged in the womb so that it can be safely removed. Wong's surgery marked the first time this specific operation had been performed in China.[86]

New Facility and New School

In 1865, Kerr expanded his operation. He purchased a plot of land adjacent to the Pearl River and laid plans to "erect buildings in the Chinese style."[87] Along with a much larger hospital, the new complex would include a patient ward, supply area, chapel, and physicians' residence. In design, Kerr eschewed ostentation, opting instead for a utilitarian structure. "The building lays claim to no display of architectural adornment," Kerr wrote. "It is simple in construction" and built to produce "strength, ventilation and dryness." To pay for the new complex, Kerr solicited contributions from the Chinese community. Chinese donors responded, delivering the majority of the $6,400 required. As this construction project illustrates, Chinese financial support played a crucial role in Kerr's vision. Along with helping to defray expenses, Chinese philanthropy bonded the community to the hospital. For example, when the hospital found itself in dire need of money in the 1880s, Kerr disseminated a call for funds to city residents. "The Canton Hospital, a charitable institution, provides modern Western medicine to the Chinese," Kerr began. "I am not Chinese and live in a country thousands of miles from China, but I volunteer to offer medical assistance to the Cantonese in order to show God's compassion." He went on to urge the "prosperous and wealthy" to "contribute money to help your brothers and sisters." They did, but they were not the only ones—government officials also donated funds. The same class of men who had orchestrated attacks on missionaries generously allocated money toward keeping the hospital afloat. By the 1890s, Kerr could report that "the larger part of the funds comes . . . from the Chinese."[88]

As the new facility was being built, Kerr entertained a bold idea that would redirect the trajectory of his career: a medical school. "It is of the utmost importance," he declared, "that a thoroughly equipped school of medicine should be established for the vast multitudes of the empire."[89] Foreigners, Kerr recognized, could not oversee the advance of Western medicine across China on their own; there simply were not enough of them. Only Chinese educated in medical schools could spread the knowledge. "If you opened an office for private practice," Kerr reasoned, "one man's work" would present "benefit . . . to a few only." However, "if you were the dean of the Canton Medical School," then "you could confer degrees on 40 students a year." When these young men "went out into the world . . . your labours would be multiplied forty fold." At the heart of his medical school lay the same principle that had animated his fundraising: foreigners could not, by themselves, effect change in China. Change required active Chinese participation and monetary investment. That the Chinese appreciated Kerr's practice became apparent in 1871 when the Shan Sin Fan scare incited mass hysteria in Canton (Chapter 2). After a rumor alleged that missionaries were orchestrating a mass-poisoning campaign, a wave of antiforeign violence pulsated through Guangdong Province. Amid all the destruction, one foreign institution remained unscathed: the Canton Hospital. That the hospital was spared, in Kerr's opinion, implied the "tacit acknowledgement" of its value on the part of the Cantonese. After all, "nothing would have been easier than to invent stories" that the hospital was dispensing poison to Chinese patients.[90]

The South China Medical School opened in 1866 with eight male students. John Kerr, Wong Fun, and Kwan Ato kept cohorts small because hospital operations and patient care remained their primary obligations. In any given year over the ensuing three decades, one would find between twelve and twenty students training at the school, though that number would rise to almost forty by 1900.[91] The program required three intensive years of study. Instructors taught in Chinese and at night to allow physicians to spend the day treating patients.[92] As far as the curriculum was concerned, Wong Fun handled Anatomy, Physiology, and Surgery; John Kerr covered Chemistry and *Materia Medica*, the medicinal properties of plants and herbs; and Kwan Ato taught Practical Medicine.[93]

Though Kerr had launched a medical school, two major problems undermined the institution's effectiveness. "The want of textbooks," Kerr wrote in 1875, addressing the first problem, "is still felt."[94] To solve the problem, Kerr launched a multiyear effort to translate existing works into Chinese and compose new texts. He was nothing short of prolific. Seizing the spare hours of the day, the indefatigable Kerr completed on average one book every year between 1871 and 1884: *The Principles of Chemistry* (1871), *Manual of Materia Medica* (1871), *Essentials of Bandaging* (1872), *Chemical Terms* (1872), *Cutaneous Diseases* (1874), *Symptomology* (1874), *Syphilis* (1875), *Eye Diseases* (1880), *Operative Surgery* (1881), *Inflammation* (1881), *Fevers* (1881), *Lungs,*

Liver, Heart, Kidneys, and Spleen (1882), *Hygiene* (1883), *Anatomical Atlas* (1883), and *Physiology* (1884).[95] Confronting a curricular void, Kerr had willed a medical library into existence. To make sure his books were read, Kerr was known to awaken medical students at 5 A.M. to remind them to study.[96]

The second problem also involved a shortage. As important as textbooks were, medical students also required hands-on experience with the human body: to peer inside the body, examine organs, and practice using surgical tools. Unfortunately, the school lacked cadavers and had no way to procure them. "The want of opportunities for dissection has been much felt," Kerr wrote, "and the superstitious regard of the Chinese for the dead would seem to be an insurmountable obstacle." Along with superstition, cultural and legal taboos prevented the school from obtaining corpses. Even if a dying individual wished to donate his body, his approval was not sufficient. No less of an authority than Confucius had asserted that the individual does not own his own body—his parents do.[97] Chinese law presented another obstacle. The legal code viewed the dismemberment of a corpse as a felony; in terms of punishment, authorities treated the crime like a murder, "reduced one degree." If one mutilated the corpse of one's own relative, the crime increased in severity in the eyes of the law.[98] Kerr hoped that, over time, the Chinese might become "gradually familiarized with dissection as an essential part of medical education." However, he could not afford to wait for Chinese law and culture to shift in his favor. The school needed cadavers immediately.[99]

Kerr improvised. When "patients without friends" died in the hospital, Kerr would arrange for students to observe his "post mortem examinations." During these autopsies, Kerr would "dissect an arm or a leg" to reveal their underlying anatomies even when the deceased's limbs bore no relation to the cause of death.[100] Kerr also exploited those rare occurrences when an unsavable patient entered the hospital unattended by family. On a frigid day in 1865, Kerr learned that an infant with a "congenital deformity" on his head had been abandoned in the street. Hoping to save the baby, Kerr dispatched a staff member to locate it, but the baby died in the hospital after two hours.[101] Though the circumstances were sad, Kerr made the most of any cadaver that fell into his hands. "The fact that the Chinese have little or no regard for the corpse of a child," he wrote, "has been taken advantage of."[102] In order to reuse the few specimens in his possession, in 1876 Kerr opened a medical museum for his students.[103]

A Year Without Kerr

John Kerr held that Western medicine would never penetrate the nation in a thorough way as long as it remained the exclusive domain of foreigners. Thus, he believed in training the Chinese so that they could spread medical knowledge themselves. In 1867, this principle received its first major test. Kerr departed for the United States, leaving Wong Fun in charge of the hospital and medical school. "Dr. Kerr being compelled to be absent from China on account of the health of his family," Wong wrote, his "Hospital was placed under my care."[104] For the better part of a year, the hospital would be run entirely by Chinese physicians and staff.

In his annual report for that year, Wong described the trickier operations. He devoted a large amount of space to coverage of "Urinary Calculi"—mineral accretions blocking the urinary tract that cause pain and inflammation ("Cystitis"). When presented with these cases, doctors had two options: Lithotomy and Lithotrity. In a Lithotomy, the operating physician opens up the urinary tract and surgically removes the stone. In the less invasive Lithotrity, the physician uses a surgical tool called a lithotrite to break the stone into smaller pieces. More specifically, he inserts the lithotrite through the urethra and proceeds to crush the stone, with the small fragments exiting the body through the normal flow of urine.[105] Over the years, the hospital removed hundreds of stones from patients, with the largest weighing nearly half a pound. Leung Kin Cho, a former student, recalled "two large baskets, weighing about 130 pounds," in which the faculty deposited the stones.[106]

With Kerr on leave, Wong had to make executive decisions about numerous patients, including those who had started under Kerr's care. Wong's analysis of operations for "Urinary Calculi" provides us with a window into hospital operations during this crucial year:

> *Urinary Calculi.* A large number, 20 cases, have been operated on during the year . . . 18 by Lithotomy, and 2 by Lithotrity. . . . In case 93 the crushing was commenced by Dr. Kerr, and completed by . . . Achung the Senior pupil; who also performed Lithotrity on case 110. Case 90 was operated on several times by Dr. Kerr; but on account of the unfavorable prospects of the patient, I determined to perform Lithotomy, which was successful. All the other cases, 17 in number, were operated on by me. . . . All recovered but two.
>
> *Lithotomy after Lithotrity.* This is Case 90 already referred to. The patient, a farmer, aged 37 years, was admitted into the Hospital last year for stone. Lithotrity was performed on him 5 times by Dr. Kerr, and a great deal of powder from the crushed stone was removed. But Cystitis was excited, and the man was brought very low. I determined to perform Lithotomy as soon as the irritation had somewhat subsided. This was done five months after his admission into the Hospital, and a stone weighing 2 oz was extracted. . . . 34 days after the operation the patient left the Hospital quite cured. It seems

therefore that in some constitutions, Lithotomy is safer than Lithotrity, although the latter may in future time come to supersede the former, when longer experience shall have rendered the operation more perfect.[107]

From these passages, we can draw two conclusions. First, though the medical school had entered only its third year, instructors did not shy away from giving trainees experience at the operating table. Indeed, at least one student (Achung) had progressed to the point where Wong felt comfortable delegating cases to him. Second, Wong clearly viewed himself as a medical authority every bit the equal of John Kerr. In Case 90, which Wong inherited from Kerr, Wong observed that his colleague's treatment regimen, which had subjected the patient to repeated Lithotrities, was failing to cure the patient and relieve him of pain (the man was "brought very low"). Reversing course, Wong decided to operate. Several weeks after removing the stone through Lithotomy, Wong discharged the "cured" patient.

Wong's report impressed Kerr when he returned. "The Hospital," Kerr observed, was "during nine months, conducted entirely by Chinese, and the number of surgical operations during that time was perhaps greater than in any equal period of time before." The hospital could function well, he discovered, in the absence of a foreign doctor. Wong's report, Kerr claimed, "gives abundant evidence of the acquirements of the pupils, and of the confidence of the people in their countrymen who have been educated in the Foreign art of Medicine and Surgery."[108]

Conclusion

In the 1860s, John Kerr developed a missionary model involving a medical school that trained Chinese and a hospital that the Chinese could run on their own. In 1871, Hunter Corbett witnessed Kerr's model firsthand upon visiting Canton. Greatly impressed, Corbett described a hospital functioning at peak efficiency. Each day, ten Chinese physicians would meet and process the two hundred patients who arrived at the door. Trained by John Kerr, the ten doctors all owned nearby practices of their own. In exchange for free tuition to medical school, they had "pledged themselves to return" on certain days to "give their services free" for three years. How skilled were the doctors? They "were able to deal with the great majority of the patients" on their own, Corbett observed, while referring "only the most difficult cases" to Kerr. In all facets of hospital operations, Corbett was struck by the fact that "all the native physicians and nurses seemed to know just what to do." But did Kerr's medical operation bear evangelical fruit? On Sunday morning, Corbett accompanied Kerr to a large chapel where he beheld five hundred former patients and family members streaming into the pews. "They felt that the doctor was their true friend," Corbett reflected, "and would not deceive them." Though a few joined the church, most did not. Nevertheless, Corbett's account suggests that Kerr's hospital—like Corbett's own museum—had broken down a barrier.[109]

Corbett had recognized the value of John Kerr's missionary model, but would other missionaries agree? In the 1870s, it remained to be seen whether missionary innovators like Kerr, Fielde, Nevius, Corbett, Sites, Allen, and the Mateers would earn the acceptance of their colleagues. Though all sought this approval, Calvin and Julia Mateer needed it to survive. Their mission board had grown upset with them for funneling into their school funds earmarked for itinerant preaching.[110] What the Mateers and the others needed was a platform upon which to present their models to the missionary community. Without such a stage, their successful experiments might languish in obscurity while the less-effective itinerant preaching was allowed to enjoy more time as the uncontested method. In 1877, they received the hearing they sought, in the form of a major conference that would change missions forever.

6

The Spirit of Debate

The Missionary Conference of 1877 and Aftermath

In the summer of 1874, Presbyterian missionaries from multiple provinces gathered in Zhifu for their synod. During meetings, the group listened to reports from the various Presbyterian missions and discussed "questions of common interest connected with the mission work." The meetings were constructive, so much so as to prompt the group to entertain a question: Why limit the conversation to Presbyterians? "It was during these meetings," Calvin Mateer recalled, "that the subject of a General Conference of all the Protestant Missionaries in China came up." The next step was to gauge the interest of other denominations. A committee sent out a circular letter to all missionaries, soliciting their opinion. Though some opposed the idea as being too costly and time-consuming, the majority expressed support.[1] John Nevius took the lead in planning a two-week conference that would be held in Shanghai in 1877. After a year, he handed the reins to Mateer, who excelled at logistics. The methodical Mateer proceeded to create an agenda, select speakers for each topic, and arrange for steamship companies to offer reduced rates. He also agreed to publish the proceedings after the event concluded.[2]

In May of 1877, the historic event took place in Shanghai. From across China, one hundred twenty-six missionaries hailing from ten provinces and representing twenty-one different Protestant organizations converged on the city. For two weeks, the seventy-four men and fifty-two women gathered in the lecture hall of the Temperance Society. Together they took stock of their collective effort, reflected on their experiences, and debated—sometimes contentiously—almost every aspect of their work.[3] Importantly, most of the new evangelical models found a forum: Bible-women, secular publishing, self-support, medical missions, and schools. Only Hunter Corbett's museum, which was only just opening, did not receive a hearing. Nathan Sites, Young J. Allen, Adele Fielde, and Calvin Mateer all spoke at the conference. John Kerr, away on furlough, shared a paper in absentia, as did Hunter Corbett. John Nevius missed the conference even though he had served as organizer and had a promising model to share. Why did he fail to show? He was detained by a horrific event in the Shandong countryside.

Famine Relief

As the conference got underway, John Nevius was conspicuously absent. In the official record, Calvin Mateer noted cryptically that his colleague was "providentially prevented from attending."[4] What kept the missionary away? In February of 1877, when Nevius set out on a routine itinerating tour, he had every intention of attending the conference in May. But out in the countryside, he beheld a shocking scene. In what had always been a rich agricultural region, Nevius encountered a wasteland. Across the dry, desolate landscape, gaunt people drifted listlessly about, their cheeks hollowed out and their ribs protruding. "Nine out of ten of the persons you meet," he recorded, "have pinched faces and sunken eyes, and some are tottering skeletons."[5] Nevius had stepped inside of Psalm 23. This was the Valley of the Shadow of Death.

The Northern Chinese Famine of 1876–1879 was a natural disaster of mammoth proportions. The famine affected a vast swath of land that covered five provinces and was home to 100 million people. For three years, the near total absence of rain produced drought conditions that caused a succession of failed harvests. Making matters worse, the people had cut down entire forests to obtain wood to burn for heat and cooking. When the heavy winds, unblocked by trees, started to blow unimpeded through the plains, they kicked up dust and dirt, which buried the already struggling crops of corn, wheat, millet, and sorghum. The missionary Timothy Richard watched in horror as the food supply dwindled and the desperate people started consuming inedible things to avoid starvation: grain husks, potato and buckwheat stalks, turnip leaves, roots, grass seeds, and elm bark. When these were all devoured, they would pull down their houses, sell the wood, and eat the rotten reeds out of which roofs were made. Some ate dried leaves usually burned for fuel, while others swallowed clay from the earth. Fathers sold their daughters for a pittance. As the people died faster than the weakened living could bury them, villages resorted to digging mass graves called "ten thousand men holes." Most frightening of all, some villages descended into cannibalism. At first, people ate what little flesh hung on the skeletons of dead; however, as the months wore on, they resorted to killing the living. The stories Richard heard and the chilling scenes he witnessed were so "fearful as to make one shudder."[6]

The Qing government did have a famine relief program in place. During ordinary years farmers contributed grain to granaries, which officials could tap into should a harvest fail. Unfortunately, during the Taiping Rebellion, the government had neglected to maintain not just the granaries but the roads that were vital to the logistics of this plan. As a result, the government could not effectively transport to famine-stricken areas what little grain reserves it had. Exacerbating the problem, the absence of rain left water levels in canals too low for boats to transport food cargoes to devastated areas. Even if the Qing's system had been fully operational, the colossal scope of this natural disaster would likely have overwhelmed it. While conservative estimates place the death toll at nearly 10 million, Timothy Richard conjectured that the number was twice as high.[7]

As Nevius surveyed the ravaged landscape, he felt certain that God had placed him there for a reason. Putting other projects on hold, he devoted his full attention to relief work. A believer in organization, Nevius promptly devised a system that would distribute money rather than food to the suffering, since food was difficult to acquire and harder to transport. After establishing a headquarters in the town of Kao-yai, Nevius organized the thousands of aid-seekers into groups, such as villages or clans. Every five days, each group of sufferers would send a single representative to Nevius, who would provide an allowance just sufficient to ensure the group's survival. The amount "seems very small," Nevius wrote, "but added to what they can get in other ways, it will keep them alive." To aid him with this operation, Nevius employed a handful of his most trusted converts. "Sung is doling out cash," he wrote, "my old scribe is copying names in the record-book," "Leng, Sue, and Kiang are stacking cash," and "Tsao, Li, Tan, and Chang" are "out in the villages enrolling names." All await the return of "old Kiang and Chang the fisherman," whom he expected to arrive with more cash to distribute.[8]

Where did that money come from? For Nevius's system to succeed, it required the continuous replenishment of its money stores. He acquired a reliable stream of funding by connecting his local system to Timothy Richard's larger famine relief program—the China Famine Relief Fund. Having observed the woeful inadequacy of the government's response, Richard had developed a plan of his own. "The Government is far too careless (or rather helpless)," Richard wrote. "Let us foreigners show a better example and help our fellow-men." Richard's plan, which Nevius plugged into, also involved sending money rather than food into afflicted areas. Richard raised money from the foreign residents in the treaty ports and then sent this money to thirty distributors, eleven of whom were American, stationed in the famine-stricken areas. The distributors handed out money using essentially the same system employed by Nevius.⁹

The greatest test of his missionary career, the famine pushed Nevius to the brink of physical exhaustion and psychological collapse. As he rode through the countryside on horseback, the hungry would approach him seeking money or food. One man, whom Nevius described as "an animated skeleton, with glaring eyes," refused to let the missionary pass. After Nevius declined to offer a handout, the desperate man beseeched him, "You don't know how hungry I am!" In denying the man, Nevius was not insensitive to his plight. Rather, he understood that if he offered aid outside his system, he would undermine the system itself. Who, after all, would patiently register in Kao-yai and accept the five-day waiting period if one could instead accost the missionary? Nevius also knew that handouts could spark violence. "Should I give whenever importuned to," he noted, "thousands would collect" and "a mob might ensue." As hard as it was, Nevius stuck to his system. "My greatest trial," he confided to Helen Nevius in letters, "is that I cannot help such people." But this was not his only trial: he was also breaking down. Nevius reported that he had "never before had such a tax on my nerves and strength." As his body started to fail, he wondered if he would see his wife again. "I sometimes think that perhaps this is the last work which God has for me to do."[10]

Finally, relief came. A successful wheat crop signaled that the worst had passed. As Nevius prepared to depart the region, he learned to his astonishment that the people planned to throw in his honor—of all things—a banquet. When Nevius arrived home in the summer of 1877, he brought with him a handful of children whom he had rescued from starvation. Helen noticed immediately how much the daily strain had aged her husband in just four months.[11] Though the ordeal had taken its toll on his health, his achievement was staggering. Nevius and his assistants had distributed aid to 32,539 sufferers living in 383 villages.[12]

The relief effort also delivered one unexpected benefit. Previously, the Chinese in these areas had looked upon missionaries with suspicion. But missionaries, by engaging in famine relief, proved their good intentions and, in the process, disabused the people of their negative perceptions, which had impeded Christianity's progress. "The famine relief presented us to the people in a new and favorable light," Nevius wrote, and "gave a fresh impulse to our work of evangelization."[13] Evangelical rewards started to appear almost immediately. When Hunter Corbett headed out to a region that had received relief, he achieved success easily. It was the "open sesame" moment for his traveling ministry.[14] Nevius soon followed, as did the English Baptists. Combined, this group reaped an unprecedented evangelical harvest: they established 150 stations and secured nearly 3,500 new converts.[15] "The providence of God," Calvin Mateer concluded, "was in it all."[16]

The Missionary Conference

Calvin Mateer on Schools

In 1877, Calvin Mateer found himself in need of divine aid. When the Shanghai conference began, he had the most to gain or to lose. With his own sponsor threatening to cut off funding, he arrived in Shanghai needing not only to defend his school but also to give legitimacy to the larger education model. Indeed, when the *Chinese Recorder* listed the priorities of missions, education did not merit inclusion in the top three.[17] If Mateer's career were to remain viable, he would need to convince his colleagues to graft education onto the body of accepted missionary practice. In this endeavor, he faced a stiff challenge. Reflecting the views of many, D. N. Lyon argued that "of a hundred ordained missionaries, ninety-eight should devote their whole strength to the direct preaching of the Gospel." Of the two remaining, he allowed that one might become a "school teacher."[18]

In preparing his address, Mateer knew that he could not win without defusing his opposition's most powerful weapon. That weapon, ironically, was the Bible. More specifically, it was the Acts of the Apostles, which narrates the founding of the Christian Church and its early spread through the Roman Empire. Since the apostles were the first Christian missionaries, Griffith John, a Welsh missionary, could refer to Acts as "that great missionary journal" and giver of "guidance." Like John, missionaries treated Acts like a handbook to evangelism—and an infallible one at that. Why did the apostles present Mateer with an obstacle? As a matter of principle, many missionaries insisted upon limiting themselves to practices employed by the apostles. "We are here," John declaimed before the gathering, "not for the mere promotion of civilization" but "to do battle with the powers of darkness" and "conquer China for Christ."[19] Emulating the apostles, John traveled thousands of miles through China's interior, preaching sermons and founding churches.[20] Mateer, who had failed at itinerant preaching, believed exactly the opposite—that Christianity could thrive only if erected on a foundation of Western learning. But how could he convince a group that refused to deviate from a method dating back to the first century A.D.?

In his paper, Mateer acknowledged the contentious nature of the debate. "While some advocate schools," he said, "others oppose them, and even go so far as to denounce them as a misuse of consecrated funds" and a "degrading of the ministerial office." Of the critics, he continued, many cite the "Apostolic example," "reminding us that the apostles did not open Schools to teach science" but only "preached the Gospel." While that was all true, Mateer slyly inserted that the apostles did use "the means which God put in their hands" which included "the power to work miracles." Why did God grant the apostles the power to heal lameness or cure blindness when such miracles did not directly save souls? These special abilities, Mateer asserted, lent the apostles spiritual credibility in the eyes of those whom they wished to convert and thus "indirectly" brought about "the salvation of souls." What did miracles have to do with teaching? Mateer delivered his coup de grâce: "God has not given to his church in this day the power to work miracles," but He has compensated by giving missionaries "a true science . . . to use in the same way." Science, in other words, could ably substitute for miracles because the Chinese regard the "wonders which modern science has wrought" as "akin to the miraculous." Of all evangelical models, schools could most effectively deploy the miracle of science. "I argue hence that Protestant missionaries are not only authorized to open schools for the teaching of science, but that Providence calls them so to do." The Lord Himself, Mateer claimed, backed his educational model.[21]

Having made his case, Mateer awaited the response of colleagues. The verdict, though mixed, tilted negative. Of the six who lodged comments, only two favored education. However, missionary leaders saw enough promise in the model to form a special committee on textbooks and to place Mateer and Young J. Allen on it.[22] Over the ensuing thirteen years, the textbooks committee would become a powerhouse in Chinese education. It would oversee the publication of hundreds of instructional books, maps, and charts. During that same period, the number of Chinese enrolled in schools would nearly triple, surging from 6,000 to 17,000. The textbook committee would also contribute directly to China's military modernization by establishing a relationship with the Kiangnan Arsenal, which would underwrite the publication of textbooks in science, math, and technology.[23] In this way, the textbooks committee became arguably the most important offshoot of the entire conference.

Young J. Allen and Secular Publications

Young J. Allen's magazine also included scientific content. Like Mateer's school, Allen's model attracted praise and criticism during a session devoted to secular literature. Griffith John, though not dismissive of Allen's effort, suggested that most missionaries should pass on his model. "Mr. Allen has shown himself thoroughly qualified for this line of work," John observed, so "let him persevere in it." Other missionaries, however, should stop "dabbling" in publishing projects, because they could more profitably spend their time fulfilling "the higher calling" of direct evangelism. Allen, in sum, could continue to publish but others should not follow: he must remain an outlier. D. N. Lyon was even less sanguine. He evaluated Allen's publication unfavorably against his single criterion: its success in generating conversions. "Mr. Allen's paper," he pointed out, "is taken almost exclusively by Christians" and has "very few heathen subscribers." Thus, the issues reach "very few of those whom they are intended to benefit."[24]

Though Allen absorbed several blows, he also had his defenders. Calvin Mateer, discerning a natural alignment between schools and magazines, argued that Allen's publications "open the door" for Christianity. To illustrate his point, he described an occurrence he had experienced "hundreds of times." "I am stopping in an inn," he began, and some "respectable men" approach to talk. Is their purpose to "ask about religion? Not at all, but to ask about the science and civilization of the West." If the missionary ignores these questions and launches into a sermon on "sin and repentance," the inquirers will walk away in disgust. If, however, he uses his scientific expertise to answer their questions, he places himself in an "advantageous position for teaching them the Gospel." Science, in other words, allowed a missionary to get his foot in the door. Joseph Edkins, a British missionary, agreed. "Journals like that of Mr. Allen," he offered, "will open the native mind to the facts of Western civilization" and "pave the way for the Gospel." When Allen himself rose to speak, he painted a bleak picture of a China descending into darkness without the light of secular literature. "If missionaries neglect secular literature," Allen warned, "religion will decline, and the darkness of the dark ages be repeated."[25] In the end, Allen did not receive unanimous endorsement for his model. However, most acknowledged the value of the *Globe Magazine*.

Adele Fielde's Bible-Women

Adele Fielde also had a model in need of promotion. Unfortunately, the conference program, dominated by male speakers, did not include her (though it did include the papers of two women). To give Fielde some publicity, S. B. Partridge, her colleague in Swatow, praised her work during a session devoted to female missionaries. "The Bible women, employed by Miss Fielde," he informed the gathering, "reach those whom we ourselves could not reach." Though grateful to Partridge, Fielde felt an irrepressible desire to explain the model herself. To achieve this goal, she made the bold decision to disrupt the proceedings. She rose to her feet and announced that, though she had not planned to speak, her duty to the Lord compelled her to "relate her personal experience in teaching Bible-women."[26] In a conference otherwise devoid of spontaneity, Fielde's intrusion stood as an unprecedented and even shocking event. The "impromptu address," Arthur Smith recalled, "created a flutter." Yet her gamble seems to have paid off. Smith described the audience, once it had recovered from her breach in decorum, as captivated by her "commanding presence" and "poised" oratory.[27]

Speaking without notes, Fielde made her case with force. After recounting the origin story of the Bible-women ("I began with five old, wrinkled, ignorant women"), she laid out in detail the structure of her organization. Next, she expressed her gratitude to men like William Ashmore, without whose support the Bible-women would not have succeeded. On this point, she could not resist uttering a provocative line that surely caught many off guard: "And if any of my sisters finds this help wanting, I think she should stop her work and devote herself to praying for the conversion of her male associates!" We do not know how the men in attendance reacted to Fielde's barb about male chauvinism. Likely, it elicited nervous laughter from some and disgust from others. Or perhaps there was an awkward silence. Regardless, the unexpected remark ensured that Fielde would hold the audience's attention as she reached her conclusion—a conclusion intended to fire imaginations with the promise of the Bible-women. "Chinese women," Fielde asserted, "are eminently fitted for being trained as evangelists." "They are of the stuff," she said in closing, "of which martyrs have . . . been made, and they are destined to become a great power in the future evangelization of China."[28]

The impromptu nature of Fielde's speech precluded her from receiving formal feedback (responses to addresses were scheduled in advance just like the addresses themselves). Informally, however, a colleague from Swatow shared that he was "often congratulated on having so efficient a co-laborer."[29] And elsewhere in the conference, other speakers endorsed her Bible-women. Andrew Happer, a missionary in Canton, stressed the significance of the new model in his address. "One of the most important labors," he said, "for those who come from Christian lands will be the training of Bible women."[30]

Nathan Sites and Self-Supporting Churches

Fielde was not the only one to arouse the gathering. Nathan Sites wrote one of two essays for a controversial session devoted to the advantages and disadvantages of employing Chinese for missions work. It was not Sites, however, but the other essayist—T. P. Crawford—who sparked the uproar. A Baptist from Kentucky working in Shandong, Crawford was known to be eccentric. Hoping to look and sound like an Old Testament prophet, he sported a long beard, strode about with a shepherd's cane, and solemnly uttered fateful prophecies that, though sounding Biblical in cadence, were usually made up. He had also earned a reputation as a provocateur. He carried pistols, initiated poisonous rivalries with other missionaries, antagonized Chinese officials, and entered into shady business deals with foreign and Chinese merchants. In one such scheme, he hired laborers to dig up a plot of land he had rented so he could study its geologic content. In fact, he was hoping to find coal to sell, but Chinese officials accused him of disrupting graves and a major furor followed. Crawford was the black sheep of the missionary community. He may have been insane.[31]

Crawford began innocently enough by noting the lack of a Biblical precedent for the paying of Chinese workers. "Did Christ send forth his Apostles," Crawford asked rhetorically, "with gold and silver to hire . . . preachers?" While missions ought to "encourage a spirit of self-denial, sincerity and zeal," Crawford contended that foreign money "begets a spirit of the opposite kind"—corruption. Making points that Sites mostly agreed with, Crawford explained how the Chinese see money dangled "before their eyes" and hear it "clinking in their ears." Irresistible, the money seduces them and they succumb, becoming Christian purely for financial gain. Crawford guessed, based on anecdotal evidence, that only "one in four" of all paid Chinese assistants were "zealous, efficient men." If true, that meant that most of the money sent in good faith by home institutions went to waste.

What should home institutions do? At this point, Crawford dropped his bombshell: *he urged home institutions to turn off the spigot.* They should abort their practice of bankrolling missionary operations while trusting the disbursement of these funds to the discretion of the missionaries. Instead, home institutions should channel all of their resources toward sending as many missionaries as possible to China. This policy would purify the missionaries themselves because, relieved of their roles as employers, they would only preach the Gospel (and presumably lead austere lives since they lacked incomes). As for the Chinese churches, they would become self-supporting out of dire necessity, cut off as they were from a foreign money stream.[32] It was, to say the least, a radical plan.

After Crawford took his seat, Nathan Sites faced the unenviable task of going next. Doing his best, Sites repeated the basic arguments favoring self-support. He explained how congregations look with distrust upon Chinese ministers in the employ of foreigners. "It is very easy for you, on your ready silver-dollar-pay," Chinese detractors say to paid pastors, "to make fine speeches to us about forbearance and obedience to church requirements." What was worse, in Sites's opinion, was that the honest Chinese minister might internalize his critics' suspicions, unfounded though they were. That the minister "is suspected of making a false profession" and "that he is looked upon as serving foreigners for his rice, lessens his courage and unnerves him." In the end, the Chinese minister receiving foreign money sustains a "conscious loss of moral power."[33]

Though Sites made his points clearly, the bitterly negative comments that followed suggested that missionaries failed to distinguish his views from those of the firebrand Crawford. "I am unable to see the example of our Lord in the same light as that of the essayists," wrote one missionary. "I am sorry the writers have drawn such illogical conclusions," declared another, because "their arguments" would seem "to overthrow the whole work" of foreign missions. Calvin Mateer, who was all too familiar with Crawford's ill-advised schemes, pointed out the ramifications of his colleague's plan. Missionaries, if left adrift in China bereft of funding, would all have to subsist at the Chinese level "both in food and dress" and "depend for these things simply on the converts we make." Preoccupied with Crawford, Mateer neglected to comment on Sites's essay, as did Samuel Dodd, who fixated on Crawford's "destructive" paper. Though Dodd would not go so far as to demand leaving the paper out of the conference proceedings, he feared the implications of inclusion: a reader might mistakenly assume the assembly had endorsed Crawford's outrageous plan. Dodd insisted that the editor (Calvin Mateer) place an "earnest dissent and protest" alongside it. In the end, Crawford's essay was accompanied by a disclaimer: "It is not to be inferred from the fact that both of the essayists took the same side of this subject, that the majority of the Conference holds the same views."[34]

If Sites read these words, he must have been apoplectic. Though he, as a self-support advocate, joined Crawford in opposing the payment of Chinese employees, he had never voiced support for Crawford's controversial proposal. Likely, Sites left the session wondering what sort of reception he would have enjoyed had his views not been tethered to those of the radioactive Crawford. Fortunately, the self-support model did receive a fair hearing at the conference. On a different day, Stephen Baldwin argued that "the native church ought to become self-supporting at the earliest possible moment." He even devoted several minutes to the example of Sia Sek Ong, whose heroic story of self-sacrifice he recounted.[35]

John Kerr's Medical Missionary

John Kerr missed the conference because he was on furlough in California.[36] In San Francisco, Kerr witnessed the anti-Chinese immigrant movement that had been building throughout the decade. Disturbed by it, he delivered a speech at the YMCA defending Chinese immigrants, excoriating their opponents, and urging Americans to defend the unjustly vilified minority.[37] Kerr participated at the Shanghai conference by proxy, submitting a paper that another missionary read. Kerr clearly had much to boast of; he, after all, had built an impressive hospital and medical school. Interestingly, the success of his model seems to have diminished the power of his essay. Unlike other missionaries, he did not have to introduce a new model or defend it with argumentation. Though not everyone in attendance recognized the value in teaching science, training Bible-women, or publishing magazines, they all respected the medical missionary. Kerr, in short, operated within a zone of consensus. With nothing to prove, he composed an essay that lacked a driving rhetorical purpose. Instead of showcasing his medical school or hospital, Kerr stressed the urgent need for more medical missionaries by describing the poor state of health care in China. Chinese physicians, Kerr explained, worked without knowledge of modern science, misunderstood the fundamental cause of disease, and lacked surgical ability. Chinese midwifery also presented problems. "Hundreds of cases occur every year," he pointed out, "in which both mother and child are sacrificed for the want of that knowledge and skill." Medical missionaries, in short, were sorely needed to rescue the Chinese people from their own doctors and midwives.[38]

Had Kerr attended the conference, he would have discovered that medical missionaries were not monolithic in their views. A wide gap separated Kerr from some of his colleagues on one key issue—Chinese participation. Shortly after Kerr's paper was read, William Gauld, a British doctor, presented his vision of medical missions. On the question of Chinese involvement in hospital work, Gauld diverged sharply from Kerr. Kerr had confidence in the ability of his Chinese doctors and nurses to execute important tasks; he trusted them to screen and treat incoming patients and even to run the hospital in his absence. In contrast, Gauld had far less faith in the Chinese. When screening, Gauld insisted, "the medical missionary should direct the treatment of all new patients himself, rather than leave it to his native assistants." Gauld also warned foreign doctors to keep a close watch on the Chinese—even those he had trained himself—when "dispensing" medicine, "performing operations," or "dressing wounds." The Chinese "need to be closely superintended," he stated, because "they are apt to . . . do their work in a perfunctory way." He also questioned their compassion. The "Chinaman," Gauld insisted, "does not show the same practical interest in his fellow countrymen as the Christian foreigner."[39] Having little faith in the Chinese, Gauld saw them as unfit custodians of their own medical future. His opinion, when juxtaposed with that of Kerr, allows us to see how progressive the Canton Hospital really was.

Conference Aftermath

After two weeks, the Shanghai conference drew to a close. In the immediate aftermath, it was not clear what, if any, long-term changes would result from the event. Indeed, the missionary community had debated much but resolved little. Nevertheless, the conference remains a watershed moment in the history of China missions. It is certainly true that the body had not officially endorsed any of the new models—schools, secular publishing, Biblewomen, or self-support. But it had not repudiated them either. What is more, the spirited nature of the discussions showed that missionaries were at least open to learning about alternative models, even if they could not agree to back any one in particular. In the end, almost every missionary departed Shanghai feeling at least moderately satisfied. The itinerant preachers left the conference feeling reassured that their apostolic method would hold onto its dominant position a while longer. However, advocates of the new models could also feel emboldened. After stating their cases and withstanding criticism, they found themselves still standing. They could return to their stations inspired to develop their innovative models further.

Many did exactly that. In Swatow, Adele Fielde continued to build and promote her Bible-women program. Her success, which was becoming widely known in the United States, strengthened the case for the single woman missionary. Though just a handful of recruits fitting this profile had started careers in China, their numbers would increase dramatically in the 1880s. Many of them would run schools (Chapter 8), a model that Calvin Mateer had ably defended. In medicine, John Kerr would innovate again after he returned to Canton. He would make crucial additions to his hospital and medical school that would enable Western medicine to more easily reach Chinese women (Chapter 9). And in Foochow and Tengchow, missions would launch Christian colleges just a few years after the conference (Chapter 12). The new colleges were made possible by remarkable changes occurring in Foochow and Tengchow mere months after the conference. The remainder of this chapter is devoted to these developments.

Empowered Pastors in Foochow

Not a single Chinese Christian attended the conference in Shanghai. Their absence allows us to make a key inference with regard to missionary attitudes: most missionaries did not value Chinese voices on matters relating to evangelism. But change was afoot. When Nathan Sites returned from Shanghai, his mission underwent a startling metamorphosis. The self-support initiative had released into evangelical work a powerful new energy—Chinese agency. Sites and other advocates of the model had empowered men like Hu Yong Mi and Sia Sek Ong to become self-confident pastors. These capable men now led thriving churches where substantial congregations met to worship. Chinese agency, however, did not remain confined to preaching—it extended into church governance. By leading successful churches, the Chinese pastors earned for themselves increased influence within the church structure. How did they acquire this influence and what did it allow them to do?

In December of 1877, Bishop Isaac Wiley of the Methodist Episcopal Church presided over the ceremony that conferred real power upon the Chinese pastors. This was not Wiley's first visit to the city. Back in 1851, he had sailed to Foochow to serve as one of the city's first foreign missionaries. His term there, though pioneering, lasted just three years. "I had left the city with but very little encouragement," he recalled, citing opium trafficking and the closed nature of China as insurmountable obstacles to progress. Now an ordained bishop, Wiley was making a return visit to his former station as a part of a larger tour of Asia. He saw immediately that the tide had turned. He was most struck by the remarkable changes wrought by the self-support model. "I now see before me eighty native Chinese preachers," he wrote, "and between two and three hundred native Chinese Christians, representing a Church membership of more than two thousand." The thriving mission, Wiley announced emphatically, was "ready to be organized into an annual conference!" In creating a "conference," Wiley was formalizing a major change to church governance in Foochow. He was, essentially, shifting control of Chinese churches from the foreign mission to the conference, a new governing body composed of fifteen Chinese pastors and five missionaries.[40] Since each conference member possessed one vote and all votes were equal, the church had effectively transferred governing power to the Chinese preachers. After all, they outnumbered missionaries by a ratio of three to one.[41]

The Chinese handled their new authority with aplomb. In the opinion of Frank Ohlinger, the native leadership performed so well as to obviate the need for missionary guidance. An advocate of self-support, Ohlinger had been appointed to the newly constituted conference along with Nathan Sites. At conference meetings, he observed the Chinese in their new roles. "I was amazed," he wrote, "to see the native brethren take up the business of the last conf[erence]." More than just amazed, Ohlinger started to feel "insignificant and superfluous" after witnessing their rapid progress. He even began to question his own relevance. "They preached, argued and voted," he noted, "until I was ready to believe myself of use anywhere but at Foochow." Ohlinger cited translation projects as the only form of work where foreigners still surpassed the Chinese. Describing himself as little more than "foreign ballast," Ohlinger questioned his own purpose: "What are we here for?!" In 1878, he requested a transfer to a new station on the grounds that Chinese competency had rendered him obsolete.[42]

Obsolescence was, of course, a good problem to have. Had not a self-sufficient native church been the goal all along? For this reason, Ohlinger, like Nathan Sites, welcomed the change. He did so fully understanding that, in any institution, power was a zero-sum game: the rise of Chinese power must effect a concomitant decline in missionary authority. Indeed, the conference's voting membership, lopsided in favor of Chinese ministers, must necessarily usher in a new reality to Foochow in which the Chinese made the important policy decisions—decisions that missionaries would have to accept. Not all missionaries so readily accepted the new status quo. When a Chinese call for a new direction impinged upon the established ways of older missionaries, conflict was the inevitable result. In later chapters, we examine the Chinese pastors' demand for curricular changes to a girls' school (Chapter 8) and the establishment of a college (Chapter 12).

Calvin Mateer's Furlough

No one derived more momentum from the Shanghai conference than Calvin Mateer. The event propelled him into the next phase of his career, one that would feature math, science, and engineering as much as Christianity. Since Mateer was already earning a reputation in these fields, John Nevius traveled to Tengchow to observe his colleague in the classroom. "I was very much delighted with what I saw," Nevius wrote to his board in 1879. He was pleased that the "advanced class" in math had finished "analytical geometry" and was "about to commence conic sections." But it was the sciences that impressed Nevius most. He made the astonishing observation that instruction in Chemistry and Astronomy "correspond very nearly to *a full college course*" (emphasis added). With these words, Nevius communicated his most important finding: Mateer was elevating science education in China to a higher plane. But Nevius did not visit the school merely to satisfy his curiosity. He had an ulterior motive. "I hope that if you are obliged to cut ... in the future," he advised the board, "you will at least make an exception of that school." The pioneering school was breaking ground in math and science and must not be terminated.[43]

Back in the United States, the mission board performed an about-face. The Mateers received the welcome news that the board would not only continue to fund the school, it would pay for an expansion. This reversal had a profound effect on Calvin Mateer: he shifted his mental energy away from defending a controversial institution and toward realizing a promising vision. In 1879, the Mateers departed China on furlough; it would be their first trip home after sixteen hard years. In the United States, Calvin relentlessly pursued support for the school. To aid his promotional effort, he shrewdly referred to the school as a "college" even though it was not one—at least not yet. In "an age of pretentious titles," he reasoned, donors were more likely to support "Tengchow College." He also boasted that his institution maintained a "higher standard of scholarship than any similar school in China."[44]

While pursuing financial support for the school generally, Mateer specifically sought resources that could bolster its science and technology offerings. He persuaded the manager of the Baldwin Locomotive Works in Philadelphia to grant him access to the factory floor and the company's team of engineers. No mere tourist indulging his curiosity, Mateer intended to master the assembly of these engines so that he could replicate the process on a smaller scale in his workshop in Tengchow. He imagined that, one day, his Chinese students would gaze upon a miniature locomotive and learn about the forces propelling it along the track. To improve Astronomy, Mateer convinced two benefactors to buy the school a "ten-inch reflecting telescope."⁴⁵ After returning to campus, Mateer would build an observatory to house the expensive new instrument. "The observatory for the new telescope is finished," he reported in 1882, "and I expect to mount the telescope in its place to-morrow."⁴⁶ In a stroke of serendipity, Mateer crossed paths with Cyrus Field, the business magnate who had financed the first successful transatlantic telegraph cable in 1866. Mateer did not allow this chance encounter to go to waste. After returning to China in 1881, Mateer wrote to Field to request an electric dynamo for the school. The dynamo, Mateer reasoned, would yield two benefits: along with helping him teach the principles of electricity, it could generate the power to illuminate a building. Field obligingly shipped a new dynamo to Tengchow.⁴⁷

In 1881, Calvin Mateer returned from furlough with mechanical knowledge, industrial machines, and scientific equipment. Though students and colleagues understood vaguely that these acquisitions were somehow intended for classroom use, Mateer's larger purpose remained mysterious. In a letter to a prospective teacher later that decade, he explained the vision behind his apparatus:

> The things most likely to be needed in China, are first, electrical engineering, especially telegraphy, and second, civil engineering, especially surveying and laying out of railroads. Special preparation in one or both of these things would be very valuable. But what is more necessary for immediate use . . . is a practical knowledge of scientific apparatus,—how to make and how to use it. I have myself picked it up from books, without any instructor, but only at a great expense of time and labor.⁴⁸

With this letter, Mateer connected his school to the needs of the nation. Modernization in China, he explained, would demand expertise in fields such as electrical and civil engineering. However, before a student could master these fields, he must first acquire "practical knowledge of scientific apparatus." He needed, in other words, to become adept at using tools, assembling machines, and fixing them. Mateer, autodidact that he was, had picked up these skills the hard way—by reading manuals and tinkering on his own. For his students, he imagined an easier path. They could learn through his textbooks, his classroom demonstrations, and his hands-on instruction in the workshop. In this way, Mateer used his furlough to upgrade the school, preparing it to give students the technical education that would allow them to participate in China's coming modernization.

Conclusion

As Mateer's quest for machines and instruments makes clear, the newer models often demanded resources above and beyond what itinerant preaching required. If missionaries were to revise the essential purpose underpinning foreign missions—shifting it away from pure soul-saving and toward institution-building—they would need to convince supporters in America of the wisdom of investing in costly hospitals and schools. Those donors, after all, had thus far agreed only to fund missions in the conventional sense: missionaries would spread the Gospel but leave the rest of Chinese civilization alone. Donors had not signed up for the far more ambitious project of renovating the Chinese mind through education and medical training. How could anyone even be sure that the Chinese would take instruction from Americans?

Indeed, a long-standing stereotype stood in the way of anyone contemplating major institution-building in China. The stereotype, harbored by many Americans, held that a singular character flaw rendered the entire Chinese race incapable of progress—pride. The Chinese resisted Western influence before the First Opium War, critics claimed, and after the war they had obstinately refused to absorb the lesson implicit in Britain's victory: namely, that their own ideas, technology, and culture were woefully out of date. The Chinese were simply too proud, stubborn, and conservative to change.[49] Though the stereotype was cruel and inaccurate, it nevertheless polluted the popular view of China in America. It presented an obvious obstacle to institution-building missionaries, who based their entire effort on the premise that the Chinese were adaptable. Those missionaries needed somehow to combat the stereotype by presenting clear evidence that the Chinese would flourish in American institutions, if they were built.

What form would that evidence take? Of course, Mateer and Kerr could report the size of graduating classes at their schools, Fielde could divulge the number of women who had passed basic training, and Corbett could share the annual attendance at his museum. However, statistics failed to change many minds. They were too abstract. What missionaries needed was to showcase some kind of "Exhibit A." They required a flesh-and-blood Chinese person whose fortified mind and evolved identity presented living proof of the transformative power of American institutions. But where would such an individual come from?

On rare occasions, missions had sponsored the educations of Chinese boys in American schools and colleges. Though few in number, these young men had returned to China and become quite accomplished both inside and outside of the church. Could not one or more of these men serve as Exhibit A?

7

A New Kind of Man

Experiments in Hybrid Identity

In 1878, a writer for the *Phrenological Journal* published a scientific study, if we may call it that. In it, the author claimed he could draw hidden meanings from the anatomical features of a Chinese man's face by employing the tools of Physiognomy, a popular "science" conceived in the 1700s by Johann Lavater. Physiognomy was closely related to its sister science, Phrenology, which held that the elements comprising the human interior—one's traits, talents, and tendencies—manifested themselves physically on one's head. Thus, Phrenologists could, by interpreting the tangible contours of a skull, reveal that person's intangible mind. In much the same way, practitioners of Physiognomy believed they could access a person's inner self by taking precise measurements of a subject's facial features and "reading" the underlying geometry.[1]

The Chinese subject being analyzed was far from ordinary. His life had followed a unique arc that added intrigue to the examination. He had attended missionary schools in China as a boy, become a Christian, and completed his education in New England. In all, he had spent eight years in America and even graduated from college. Having lived abroad for so long, the subject could no longer be classified as a typical Chinese. He was, in the author's phrasing, "a modified type of the Chinaman." To the Physiognomist, the length of the Chinese man's American experience raised a profound question. He already knew that the subject's prolonged exposure to the country's people, culture, and institutions had repatterned his thoughts. But had his facial features undergone a parallel and commensurate change? If they had changed, the results would carry great consequence for two reasons. First, they would legitimize Physiognomy by demonstrating that one's outer facial geometry always reflected one's inner mind. Second, they would prove that the educational experiment, that of passing a Chinese boy through American institutions, had bequeathed to the world a stunning creation—*a new kind of man.*

The author of the journal article got to work by analyzing a photograph of the Chinese man. Since the subject spoke Chinese and English, enhanced linguistic ability should appear in his facial anatomy. It did: "The eye is full and indicative . . . of unusual facility in language." Other distinctly American traits had also assumed physical form. "The development of the orbitar ridges, especially toward the outer angles of the eyes, shows a nice appreciation of system, order, and precision." The features also revealed that the subject is "steadfast in opinion," like any good American, and "zealous," as a Christian convert ought to be. The subject is, in sum, "a frank and sincere man, holding firmly to his moral convictions." What conclusion did the author draw from the empirical data? "Upon his Oriental stock has been grafted the better elements of modern civilization," he wrote, with the result being a "higher form of the Asiatic organism." The subject, a man named Yung Wing, had developed in a way that left him superior to other Chinese mentally, physically, and morally. He was a new form of humanity never before witnessed on earth—a Chinese superspecies.[2]

The science may have been fraudulent, but Yung Wing most certainly was not. He truly did shine in America. By thriving, he provided convincing evidence for those who, later in the century, would advocate for the building of American institutions in China. Indeed, Yung amounted to a de facto Exhibit A: a living, breathing, walking embodiment of the essential idea that American institutions could transform the Chinese. Promoters of this idea could point to the Yung Wing experiment to persuade others that American systems successfully improved Chinese people. Though someone like Yung Wing was rare, there were a few others like him. This chapter also examines Wong Kong-chai and Yen Yung Kiung.

The three men did more than support a theory with their successful lives. Believing in the transformative power of their American educations, they adopted two strategies to bestow these benefits upon other Chinese: they sent Chinese students, including their own kin, to study in America, and they founded, administered, and taught in schools and colleges in China. The three viewed their efforts as highly significant. They even went so far as to envision American-style institutions as playing a major role in the national rejuvenation they believed a weakened China sorely needed. But none of the men entertained such lofty ideas when, as mere boys, they first embarked for America. Indeed, it was often chance or whim, not a forward-looking plan, that launched their American odysseys.

Wong Kong-chai

New Frontiers

In 1842, the missionary William Boone could wait no longer. An Episcopal from South Carolina, Boone had chosen China as his mission field because he believed that the "spiritual necessities" of 360 million "civilized and intelligent" Chinese demanded his sacrifice.[3] Arriving with his family in Macao during the First Opium War, Boone confronted a China that was still closed. However, he sensed that the war could change things. In Macao, Boone sat restlessly on the edge of the Chinese Empire, anxiously awaiting the opportunity to carry the Gospel to new cities. As the war began to wind down, Boone spied his chance. A British vessel heading to Gulangyu, an island off the coast of Xiamen, offered him passage. With his wife and two small children at his side, Boone joined David Abeel at the first American mission to be established outside of Canton. It was a historic moment, and one not lost on the island's Chinese population. As Boone and his family walked about, they attracted crowds of people who wondered about the intentions of these unwarlike white people. Sensing their curiosity, Boone decided to address the onlookers. "Elders and brothers, I have this day brought my family to live among you," Boone orated. "Please come to our humble home at any time and you will be welcome." When Boone finished his salutation, the Chinese smiled and dispersed. Boone had begun what he expected would be a long and productive mission in Gulangyu.[4]

It was anything but. Every day, Sally Boone would manage their living quarters and watch their children, Henry and Mary, while William and David Abeel distributed Christian tracts. Needing help, Sally asked Mr. Wong, the caretaker of the property, if she might hire his wife. In declining, Wong offered instead the services of his fifteen-year-old son, Wong Kong-chai. Upon meeting "Chai," Sally noted his "eager, intelligent air." He also had a way with children, playfully carrying them on his back. Sensing his intellectual potential, Sally began to tutor him daily in math and English. William Boone, who believed the "church of the future should have educated . . . native leaders," taught Wong the written Chinese language. Just as the Boones were becoming settled, tragedy struck. Sally ate a bad piece of watermelon and fell violently ill. After days of diarrhea and vomiting, she died. Having arrived with the "brightest prospects," a disconsolate Boone wrote, "My house is left unto me desolate." Fearful that the children would also contract the disease, Boone decided to remove them to America. Observing Boone's predicament, Abeel offered a suggestion: why not take Chai with you? He could help take care of the children during the long sea passage and then continue his education in America. To Boone's astonishment, Chai's father agreed to the plan, so strong was his desire to have his son educated. In 1843, they sailed for America.⁵

Wong Kong-chai's American experience had a profound effect on him. On a personal level, the two long sea passages bookending a short residence in South Carolina cemented a bond with the Boone family that would endure for decades. On a philosophical level, the experience sparked in Wong an insight that would shape the rest of his life. As the Chinese teenager walked about in the American South, he was struck by the contentment and prosperity he witnessed.⁶ This was nothing like China. At some point, either during his American sojourn or just after, Wong experienced an epiphany. If Christianity and Western education could generate happiness in America, then these two things could uplift China as well—if only China would receive them. Wong knew exactly what he must do: *he would be the deliverer.* In sharing this idea with the Boones, the ebullient Wong could not contain his emotions. "Oh! American people all seem so happy, and everything so good," he exclaimed, while "China people are so poor, and they have so many bad things—quarrel and lie." Why was there such a difference? "I think it because America have Christ's religion," while in China "the Gods they pray to cannot help them." "Oh!" he continued, "I feel I want to go to every part and tell them Christ."⁷ William Boone's prospects also improved in America. The Episcopal Church consecrated him Bishop to China,⁸ and he found a second wife.⁹

Tests and Trials

During the voyage to China, Phoebe Boone took an instant liking to Wong. Converting the ship into a classroom, she worked with Wong on his English and introduced him to the scriptures, which seemed to take hold of him.¹⁰ "He was an indefatigable student," William Boone wrote. "I often saw him sitting for hours in his state-room poring over an English Bible."¹¹ Arriving in Hong Kong, the Boones hoped that Wong would join them in Shanghai, the site of the new Episcopal mission. China needed native pastors, William Boone believed, and Wong might "prove to be such a leader." To the Boones' disappointment, Wong parted company with them, choosing to return to Gulangyu to ascertain the wishes of his parents. The Boones later learned from a missionary that Wong's father objected to his son's plan to move to Shanghai. Wong appeared to be lost.¹²

A second tragedy would return Wong to the Boones' orbit. In 1845, he appeared unexpectedly at the Shanghai mission looking tired, frail, and distraught. "He looked so poor and weak I could hardly keep from tears," Phoebe recalled. The Boones learned the cause of Wong's pitiable condition when he recounted the horror story that had been his family reunion. Upon returning home, Wong discovered that his father had been stricken by an epidemic then ravaging the area. As he attempted to nurse his father back to health, his mother contracted the same disease. Responsible for two sick parents and two younger siblings, ages three and seven, Wong became overwhelmed. Then his loved ones proceeded to die. His mother was the first to succumb to illness; she was followed by his father and youngest brother, who perished on the same day. When the seven-year-old expired too, the carnage was complete. In the end, Wong managed to save only his teenage brother who had received treatment from a foreign doctor. Bereft of money and feeling feverish himself, Wong was in desperate circumstances. With nowhere else to turn, he secured passage on a boat bound for Shanghai.[13]

Whereas the Boones had once needed Wong, now he needed them. He joined the family, becoming an older brother to Henry. Phoebe worked hard to educate Wong, teaching him and Henry simultaneously. "Chai is now in the next room with Henry," Phoebe wrote, "and I am hearing their sage speculations about the planets." On Easter Day in 1846, William Boone baptized Wong in what he described as "the most intensely interesting service in which I have ever engaged." Choked up with emotion, Boone could barely utter his lines.[14] After his baptism, Wong ascended rapidly through the ranks of the Episcopal Church, becoming one of the most prominent Chinese Protestants in China. In 1851, the church promoted him to deacon in a ceremony. "To see a Chinese in a surplice," rhapsodized the missionary Caroline Tenney, "once a heathen, now a Christian, and his excellent character well known to us all—it was indeed a happy sight!" Deploying an astronomical metaphor, Tenney described Wong as "the star that preceded the dawn of a gospel daylight in this great empire!"[15] In 1863, Wong's career culminated with his ordination as priest.[16] But the first Chinese Episcopal priest would not enjoy his achievement for long. A storm was brewing.

In 1864, crisis struck the mission: William Boone died of illness just months after the death of Phoebe. At the memorial service, Wong delivered an impassioned address, and Yen Yung Kiung, a promising young convert (covered later in this chapter), also spoke.[17] As the mission struggled to recover, it drifted into a period of grave uncertainty. Boone had been a figure of massive importance, and his passing left a gaping leadership void. "The death of Bishop Boone," observed one missionary, has opened a "vacancy in our missionary force."[18] With disappointing yields in terms of converts and now the death of the patriarch, Wong sensed that the mission verged on collapse. "O dear friends! try to strengthen this mission," Wong pleaded in a letter to American churches. "Send us another Bishop, and more clergymen, for the harvest truly is plenteous, and the laborers are few."[19] But with the Civil War raging, reinforcements were unlikely to come. Out of options, Wong accepted an increased workload that tested his stamina. "Mr. Wong-Chai has carried on his work at the city church with great regularity," reported the missionary Elliott Thomson, who then listed his other responsibilities: he headed two boys' schools in Shanghai, held regular church services in the city, and preached in the countryside. Thomson's next line revealed that Wong, already under stress, was also coping with a personal tragedy: "He had a very sore trial in the loss of his only son."[20] Close to his breaking point, Wong persevered, guiding the mission through the rocky decade. "The progress was very slow at the beginning," he reported in 1872, "but now is much easier."[21]

Throughout his trials, Wong maintained a special fondness for schools. Education, after all, had transformed him, and he wished to spread its benefits to other Chinese. Toward this end, he taught classes at the several schools operating under the auspices of the mission.[22] When the church opened new schools, it would place them under Wong's supervision.[23] By 1879 Wong was superintending eight schools, and by 1884 that number had risen to fourteen. His "happiest hours and efforts," wrote the younger William Boone, whom Wong had helped raise from infancy, "were in our day-schools."[24] The role of education was expanding in the Episcopal mission, and Wong was the chief reason why.

A Hybrid Identity

For Episcopalians, Wong presented an important symbol. The author of a history of the church in China explained how the "story of Wong Kong" gave hope to those who had invested in missions but suspected that China's "hyper-conservatism" might prove insurmountable. Old customs and beliefs, they feared, had become so ingrained in Chinese culture as to block the Gospel. For them, Wong provided living proof that Christianity could overcome an entrenched culture. The author reminded readers that Wong's family and culture put forward the usual obstacles to Christianity. Indeed, when Wong finally accepted baptism, the ceremony was for him tantamount to "giving up family and friends," "outraging . . . one's ancestors," and "insulting China's incomparable past." Viewing Wong as a microcosm of China itself, the author indicated that Wong's case explained why "our converts are counted by the hundreds rather than by the tens of thousands." However, that Wong had overcome formidable impediments proved that others could too. For this reason, the author counted Easter Day in 1846, the day of Wong's baptism, as "a day of great moment in the history of our work." Wong's story, in sum, reminded Christians that victory in China was possible.[25]

In Shanghai, missionaries marveled at the new kind of human being evolving before their eyes. Though strongly Christian, Wong remained Chinese in other ways. The Americanization process, while changing Wong profoundly, eventually struck an impenetrable iron core of Chinese values. In terms of his identity, Wong could no longer call himself Chinese. But neither was he fully American. He was somewhere in between—a hybrid. Aware that there was no one else remotely like Wong, one missionary called him "a young man" in an "isolated position."[26] His unique identity posed a challenge when it came time to locate a spouse. Since "there was no Christian woman within his reach," wrote the missionary Caroline Jones, the "only way for him to procure a fit help-meet, was to select a nice girl, and have her placed under Christian instruction." Wong, in short, needed to put a young woman through an abbreviated version of the process that had produced him. After choosing a girl named Kiung-Kiung, Wong enrolled her in a school under Jones's supervision. His hope was that she would become an American-educated Christian just like him.[27]

But this story of courtship has another side. Caroline Jones's initial reaction to Wong's selection of Kiung-Kiung was shock: the girl had bound feet. From this single fact, Jones drew deep meaning. "You see," Jones concluded, "that even our excellent Mr. Wong was not proof against the attraction of this celestial [referring to a native or inhabitant of China] custom, which we Westerners deem so cruel and disfiguring." Older Chinese ways, Jones maintained, clung tenaciously to Wong; no amount of Christianity or American schooling could completely extirpate them. The Chinese side of Wong's hybrid identity expressed itself in other ways. Wong resorted to both Western and Chinese medicine when, prior to the wedding, an eye disease robbed Kiung-Kiung of her vision. The Western doctor failed; the Chinese treatment succeeded. Finally, in 1851, the wedding service followed a bicultural format in which Bishop Boone presided over a ceremony that preserved Chinese customs.[28]

In the 1880s, an older Wong reflected on the interplay of Christianity and Confucianism in both himself and China. "I am nearly sixty now," he said, and "I have seen much suffering for myself and my country." What was the source of the pain? "As boys we all learned the words of the classics," he wrote, referring to the Confucian canon that taught one to "choose the virtuous," "advocate sincerity," "cultivate peace," and shun "idleness." To adhere to these principles was to follow "the Great Way." Unfortunately, China had, in Wong's view, deviated from this worthy path. "Instead of holding to the great precepts of the ancients," the Chinese "have been clinging to rotten branches" and not to the "sturdy green tree" of good values. As examples of rot, Wong cited popular "customs and superstitions." As the rot spread throughout China, the noble "seed" planted long ago by the sages had died. How could China return to its former higher state? The seed, Wong asserted, could "rise into life" again through "our Lord Jesus Christ." Wong imagined a Chinese fall from grace that bore some resemblance to the Biblical story of the Garden of Eden. To return to paradise ("the Great Way"), society required an infusion of moral and spiritual power that only "the word of God" could deliver. In this way, Wong did not envision Christianity replacing Confucianism. Rather, he saw the new faith as helping his people reclaim a fallen ideal—Christian means used to achieve a Confucian outcome. Only a hybrid intelligence could formulate a salvation scheme like this.[29]

Yung Wing

Standing Up

In 1856, an extraordinary visitor appeared unannounced twice at the Episcopal mission in Shanghai where Wong Kong-chai worked. A Chinese Christian educated in America, this mysterious visitor was one of the few people on earth with a profile similar to Wong's. Like Wong, the young man was animated by the lofty ambition to regenerate China with American institutions. If anything, his passion burned even hotter. But what form would his desired change take? The visitor did not yet know; his plan remained nebulous. In fact, at the time of this visit, he was still casting out lines hoping to hook a salaried position that would, in some way, clear the fog that cloaked his destiny. He did know one thing, however. Missionary work would *not* figure into his grand plan. "He called on me this evening," the missionary Edward Syle wrote, "and I perceived . . . that his drawings of heart were not to the ministry." Syle nevertheless believed that the visitor—like Wong Kong-chai—presented a template for a new Chinese identity. He would be accomplishing "*a very great work indeed*," Syle commented, by serving as "the example of a truly upright, honorable, Christian man of business."[30] A few months later, the visitor returned, this time approaching Caroline Jones. After greeting her with what she called "an American air," the young man got to the point. "Ah-Wing told me he had been wishing to visit the school," Jones wrote, "and asked if I would take him over to it." Ah-Wing was Yung Wing, and he had Western education on his mind.[31]

In 1845, Yung Wing stood up and his life changed forever. How could the simple act of leaving one's seat alter one's life trajectory? To understand this moment's pivotal significance, we must first review Yung's early years. Born in 1828 near Macao, Yung was sent by his parents in 1835 to attend a boarding school run by Mary Gutzlaff. Since his older brother studied in a standard Confucian school, Yung later speculated as to why his parents had made this unorthodox choice for him. His theory was that they were prescient. Though the foreign influence in China amounted to hardly a ripple in 1835, his parents "predicted" that it might swell into a "tidal wave." Should the Western tsunami wash over China, his parents would have proactively placed one of their sons in an "advantageous position" with regard to the "business and diplomatic world." They had, in other words, bet on a certain vision of the future—and history would prove them correct.

Yet when his father dropped him off at school, the small boy comprehended neither the vast historical currents in play nor his parents' long-term strategy. He knew only that he was being separated from his family against his will. What was worse, there was a strange pale-faced lady dressed entirely in white gliding toward him. Though Mary Gutzlaff meant to be welcoming, her ghostly appearance terrified Yung. Clinging to his father, Yung "trembled all over with fear" as his life at boarding school began. Fortunately, Yung came to love Gutzlaff, and the feeling was mutual. In 1840, when she closed her school, she extracted a promise from a friend before sailing for America: he must locate Yung when the Morrison School, then being planned, opened.[32] At about this time, the death of Yung's father in the First Opium War left the family in precarious financial straits.[33] For a period, Yung used his English to earn a small income assisting a Catholic priest. In 1841, he matriculated at the Morrison School, studying under Samuel Brown, a Yale graduate from Connecticut. It was here that Yung made his fateful choice to stand up.[34]

In 1845, Samuel Brown announced to students that, due to health concerns, he would be sailing home. He next dropped a bombshell. Students wishing to finish their educations in America could accompany him, and they should "signify" their intention "by rising."[35] One can only imagine the thoughts that must have swirled about in Yung's mind. Likely, he contemplated the loneliness he would experience in a strange land. He may also have wondered how America might affect his future. By attending missionary schools, he had already veered off the conventional educational track. If he were to stand, he would be committing himself to a far more radical course. Before Yung, only seven Chinese had traveled to America for their educations.[36] Would the American experience enhance his career prospects—or destroy them? Somehow Yung rapidly processed these concerns and made his fateful choice: "I was the first one on my feet." Two other classmates, Wong Shing and Wong Fun (Chapter 5), soon followed.[37] His tearful mother provided her reluctant consent on the condition that he return after two or three years. Yung gave his word and embarked for America.[38]

Metamorphosis

Brown and the three boys arrived in New York in 1847. A New Englander, he moved the boys north to Massachusetts and enrolled them in the Monson Academy. As they walked about town, the three stood out as oddities. Most Americans, even those living out west, had never seen a Chinese person before (the Gold Rush of 1848, which would attract thousands of Chinese to California, was a year off). In addition, the boys tied their hair in single long braids called "queues" that appeared feminine to Americans. They did not dare to snip them off because the Qing government regarded queue-cutting as an act of rebellion punishable by death.[39] "Of course they have been great objects of curiosity," Samuel Brown wrote, "and it has been annoying to them to be gazed at."[40]

The Monson headmaster, Charles Hammond, paid close attention to the boys' development. He did so, according to Yung, out of his remarkable farsightedness: he foresaw "the possible good" for China "that might come out of our education." A lover of literature, Hammond exposed Yung to the great authors of the English language. In teaching writing, Hammond placed "greater stress on pointing out the beauties of a sentence," Yung remembered, than "on grammatical rules." Finishing Monson in 1849, the boys had a decision to make: should they return to China or continue their educations in America? Wong Shing, suffering from poor health, opted to sail home. Wong Fun, wishing to be a doctor, embarked for Scotland to study medicine in Edinburgh. Only Yung elected to attend college in the United States.[41]

Before he could do so, he would need his family's approval. He wrote a long letter to Samuel Wells Williams, a missionary he had befriended in Macao, asking Williams to secure permission from his uncle. Yung also explained his rationale for staying:

> The reason why I made these requests of you is perhaps obvious, for I have a great inclination to get a liberal education, and there is a great probability so much so that it amounts to almost certainty that I am going to stay, and of course you are aware that my feelings would not allow me to have my mother and the brothers & sisters since I promised them all when I left China to return in two or three years and you know full well the prejudice of the Chinese, how they misrepresent things and that they are not able to see as you or any enlightened minds do, the object, the advantage, and the value of being educated. Ignorance and superstition have sealed up the noble faculties of their minds.... I beg you to talk to my uncle... to persuade... him of the object of my stay in this country for 6 years more, and the results which arise from education, in short tell as good a story as you can, how knowledge increases happiness.

The letter tells us two important things. First, Yung's rambling prose, which included a sentence of 121 words, suggests Hammond should have taught grammar. Second, and more importantly, the letter offers a snapshot of Yung's mind two years into his American experience. In one sense, Yung remained quite Confucian: he sought permission not from his mother but from his uncle, the family's ranking male in the absence of Yung's deceased father. In other respects, the letter reveals a mind in transition. Yung had become critical of Chinese thinking, referring both to the "prejudice" of the Chinese and to the pernicious influences of "ignorance and superstition" in bottling up humanity's "noble faculties." In contrast, he respected the "liberal education" he was receiving in America; it generated the "knowledge" that "enlightened minds" use to "increase happiness."[42] The Americanization process, in sum, was underway. After receiving permission, Yung made plans to attend Yale, the alma mater of Samuel Brown and Charles Hammond.

Deciding to attend Yale was easy. Paying tuition was hard. After Brown and Hammond informed him of a "fund for indigent students," Yung met with the fund's trustees. The money was his, they informed him, provided he "sign a pledge" to return to China as a missionary after graduation. As Yung listened to the conditions, he must have realized that, once again, he stood at a crossroads: the decision he made would dictate his life's trajectory. While thanking the trustees for their generosity, Yung turned down the scholarship. His reasoning offers additional insight into the changing landscape of his mind. Though Yung had, by this time, formed a vague desire to uplift China, he remained unsure as to the specifics. Perhaps China needed him to bring Christianity, but perhaps it did not. What if he could better serve his people in some other capacity? "The calling of a missionary," he told the trustees, "is not the only sphere in life where one can do the most good in China." If the letter to Williams revealed Yung's diminishing respect for Chinese thinking, then this decision sheds light on his evolving view of Christianity. Christianity possessed real value to be sure, but it did not, in Yung's opinion, provide a panacea for China's problems. By declining the money, Yung signaled his determination to keep his options open. Of course, the problem of tuition lingered. With Brown's help, Yung cobbled together enough money by accepting charitable donations and taking jobs on campus.[43]

Far more worrisome than finances were his academics. Yung arrived ill-prepared to handle the rigorous Yale curriculum. "As compared with the college preparations of nine-tenths of my class-mates," he recalled, "I was far behind." Playing catch-up, "I used to sweat over my studies till twelve o'clock every night the whole Freshman year."[44] Writing to Williams on Christmas day in 1850, Yung reported that he had "no time to think of any [thing] else, except study." Along with schoolwork, Yung coped with the "mortifying news," conveyed in a letter from Williams, that his older brother had died.[45] Yung felt overwhelmed, and his health started to fail him. He did survive the year—but just barely. He finished his first semester with a 2.12 grade point average, which he managed to raise to 2.45 the following spring.[46] More than other subjects, math gave him fits. "I used to fizzle and flunk so often" in Calculus, Yung wrote, "that I really thought I was going to be ... dismissed from college." But Yung persevered, gutting it out in the tough classes and finding other places to shine. He became quite accomplished in Composition, even winning awards for essays.[47] He also, after noting the robust constitutions of peers, embraced physical fitness and participated in a football game.[48]

When Yung graduated in 1854, the achievement did not go unnoticed. "Being the first Chinaman ... to go through a first-class American college," Yung remembered, "I naturally attracted ... attention."[49] Traveling from "considerable distances," people came in droves to catch a glimpse of what one newspaper would call the "wonderful Chinaman" whose "tastes, feelings" and "habits of life and thought" had been "Americanized."[50] "The education of a young Chinaman of talent and piety in ... one of our principal colleges," wrote another newspaper, "is an incident of no small moment."[51] One writer recalling the scene years later described Yung's manner as "reserved," which is what one should expect from "a man somewhat out of place ... *who is looked upon as an experiment*" (emphasis added). Indeed, Americans who had watched Yung's academic career unfold saw him as a laboratory test that had gone smoothly.[52]

Yung had his degree. But what should he do with it? And did his individual achievement hold any meaning for other Chinese? Prior to graduation, Yung experienced an epiphany in which he saw these two questions as inextricably linked. In answering the second question, he determined that his educational experience was transferable to other Chinese. If Western education could improve one man, it could transform an entire nation. When it did, the falling fortunes of China could be reversed. "I was determined that the rising generation of China," he idealistically wrote, "should enjoy the same educational advantages that I had enjoyed" because "through western education China might be regenerated." But who or what would serve as the delivery vehicle for the education miracle? Yung addressed the first question—*what should he do with his education?*—by envisioning himself as the deliverer. He would become the instrument that would modernize China through education. "To accomplish that object," he announced to himself, "became the guiding star of my ambition."[53]

Seeking Purpose in China

Later in 1854, Yung sailed for China to reunite with family before launching his career. In Macao he visited his mother, who had not seen him for eight years. Dressed in Western clothes and sporting a mustache (which in China was reserved for married men), he appeared highly Americanized. After he described his college degree, his mother "naively" asked him "how much money it conferred." The degree, he opined, offered something far more valuable than money. "Knowledge... is power, and power is greater than riches." He then launched into a grandiloquent speech intended to impress her: "I am the first Chinese to graduate from Yale College, and that being the case, you have the honor of being the first and only mother out of the countless millions of mothers in China... who can claim the honor of having a son who is the first Chinese graduate of a first-class American college." She smiled affectionately and urged him to shave his mustache.[54]

Yung's self-confidence evaporated when he started hunting for a job. No longer fully Chinese, he felt an acute sense of difference from others. "China was like a strange land to him," an American friend explained. He had "almost entirely forgotten his native tongue," "had no friends," and had "nothing to give him any standing." He was an "exile" in his native land, and a "cheerless, forbidding prospect lay before him." Yung would later describe himself as an alien, "a being coming from a different world."[55] Though he felt out of place, his grand dream impelled him forward. He wished to find some way to convert his abstract vision into a concrete plan. But when one's goal was to uplift all of China, where exactly did one begin? "He longed to devise some plan," Samuel Brown wrote of this trying time, "by which the educational advantages he had enjoyed might be given to other Chinese young men." Unfortunately, his lack of both "rank" and "influential friends" meant the obstacles looming before him were almost "insurmountable."[56] In under a year, he started and quit three different positions, prompting him to wonder if he would ever achieve his aspiration. "I myself began to think," he recalled, "that I was too dreamy to be practical."[57]

Refusing to quit, Yung landed a position with an English tea firm. Though the firm failed, an incident related to its closure would lift Yung out of obscurity. The drama unfolded at the auction where the dissolved tea firm was selling off assets to bidders. While observing the proceedings, Yung felt a tug on his queue. Turning around to ascertain the cause of the annoyance, he discovered a "stalwart six-footer of a Scotchman" tying cotton balls to his braided hair "simply for a lark." This was not good-natured joking. This was malice.[58] What had led the Scotsman to believe that he could, with impunity, humiliate a Chinese man in China purely for sport?

After China sustained losses in the First Opium War, the foreign powers severely downgraded the nation. China had lost the respect of the West. Exacerbating the problem, China's treaties with Europe and America included articles of extraterritoriality that allowed a foreigner accused of a crime against a Chinese civilian to be tried not in a Chinese court but in a tribunal convened by the foreigner's own country. China, in short, had lost the ability to prosecute foreign wrongdoers on its own soil. Shanghai, in its architecture and culture, reflected China's descent to semicolonial status. With distinct Chinese and foreign sections, it was a segregated city. An "observer would have been aware of two separate urban enclaves," writes historian Linda Johnson. "To the south, there was the traditional walled Chinese city" with a government office, temples, gardens, crowds, and narrow city streets. "To the north... was the small, modern European town, with neatly laid out, rectilinear streets and European dwellings, the Race Course and Park, and... impressive mercantile buildings lining" the waterfront.[59] To many foreign residents, separate did not mean equal. Indeed, a clear racial hierarchy structured their minds. According to Stella Dong, many Westerners adopted a "patronizing attitude" toward the Chinese and kept interactions with "natives" to a minimum.[60] Empowered by notions of superiority, the Scotsman felt certain he could bully Yung without suffering repercussions.

But he had targeted the wrong Chinese man. Looking first for a peaceful resolution, Yung politely asked the practical joker to desist. But the Scotsman only defiantly "folded his arms" and glared down upon Yung with "disdain and scorn." Yung repeated his demand, only to feel seconds later the Scotsman's fist crashing into his jaw. Stunned by the blow, Yung had good reason to back down. Along with the brawn of his antagonist, there was the implied racial hierarchy that Yung was expected to respect. Yet if Yung contemplated these points during this blurry moment, it was only to dismiss them. He swung his fist hard, landing a "stinger" on his assailant's face. As the blood flowed "in great profusion" from the lips and nose of the Scotsman, the latter seized Yung's wrists to prevent another punch. Just as Yung prepared to kick his foe's genitalia, the tea firm's head intervened to break up the fight. The Scotsman, embarrassed to be bleeding, took flight into the crowd. When someone asked Yung if he had wanted to fight, he responded that he was "only defending myself" against the provocations of a "blackguard."

In the ensuing days, the fight caused a "sensation" in Shanghai, dominating conversation in both foreign and Chinese communities. From foreigners, Yung learned that the Scotsman had hid to avoid public scrutiny. "He did not care to show himself," Yung wrote, "on account of being whipped by a little Chinaman." The Chinese regarded Yung as a hero. "I was looked upon with great respect," Yung recalled, because no Chinese in the treaty port "had ever been known to have the courage and pluck to defend his rights, point blank, when they had been violated... by a foreigner." Why were the Chinese reluctant to stand up for themselves? The extraterritoriality of the treaty-port system, Yung believed, had had a pernicious effect on their character, robbing them of "moral courage." Left with a "meek and mild disposition," the Chinese "allowed personal insults and affronts to pass... unchallenged." The incident also compelled Yung to reflect upon his own evolving identity. Why had he chosen to retaliate when other Chinese had backed down in comparable situations? The answer, as he understood it, was that he was no longer fully Chinese. He was a hybrid—a new kind of man. The incident brought Yung fame, and lucrative opportunities in the tea trade followed. He was no closer, however, to realizing his dream.[61]

Self-Strengthening

After the sensational fight, Yung's life pivoted. Word of the remarkable hybrid man got out, and the Chinese became aware of his unique life story. "My name began to be known among the Chinese," Yung wrote, "not as a fighter this time, but as a Chinese student educated in America."[62] Crucially, he attracted the attention of Zeng Guofan, a high-ranking Chinese official and advocate of Self-Strengthening, a new governmental initiative intended to forestall China's slide into chaos. In the early 1860s, the Qing Dynasty verged on collapse. Westerners and Chinese observed the stunning success of rebel armies during the Taiping Rebellion of the 1850s, the ease with which small European forces demolished Qing armies in the Opium Wars, and the humiliating burning of the Summer Palace at the hands of Anglo-French soldiers in 1860. As entropy seemed to be taking hold of China, observers saw the dynasty's demise as imminent. "The old foundations of government are thoroughly rotten," noted the *North China Herald*, "its ranks and orders are broken." Unless the Qing could find some way to save itself, anarchy loomed.[63]

In the 1860s, a group of reform-minded Qing officials met the challenge. To stave off destruction, this cohort initiated a sweeping "self-strengthening" program. They identified key sectors where they could, through the application of Western thinking, either modernize old institutions or create new ones. Though self-strengthening required that China learn from the West, supporters did not abandon the Confucian philosophy that had guided China's statecraft for centuries. Self-strengtheners sought preservation, not revolution. They imagined Western technology as forming a protective shell around a superior yet vulnerable Confucian essence, shielding it from threats from within (rebellions) and from without (foreign powers). "If we wish to find a method of self-strengthening," Zeng Guofan wrote in 1862, "we should ... regard learning to make explosive shells and steamships and other instruments as the work of first importance." To revamp the military, reformers founded arsenals, shipyards, and technical schools. They based the Yangtze Navy on the Western model; to equip that navy with a modern fleet, they founded the Foochow Shipyard and hired French engineers to oversee operations. Similarly, they tasked the new Kiangnan Arsenal in Shanghai with manufacturing modern artillery. The Qing also opened a government school, Tongwen Guan, which employed foreign teachers (including Young J. Allen) to deliver a curriculum in Western science, math, and technology.[64]

In 1863, Zeng Guofan sent for Yung Wing. Though aware that Zeng had his own reasons for the summons, Yung recognized the value of a private audience with China's most powerful official. He hoped to sell his bold plan to reform China through education to a man who possessed the power to make it happen. After reaching Zeng's headquarters, Yung learned of the leader's wishes: Yung was to use his American connections to purchase mechanical equipment for a machine shop. Aware of Yung's unique background, Zeng also used the meeting to pick his brain. "He asked me what . . . was the best thing to do for China at that time." Though sorely tempted to share his education-centered plan, Yung decided that the timing was not right. He merely suggested that, rather than building a machine shop that could manufacture one thing only, such as a rifle, Zeng might broaden its scope. Why not assemble one that could manufacture the equipment for additional machine shops, each one capable of producing armaments? Yung, in short, sold Zeng on a plan for a machine shop that could reproduce itself.[65] Of course, what Yung really sought was a program that would replicate not machinery but Yung Wing himself.

To Zeng's delight, Yung accomplished his mission. Purchasing machinery in America did not turn out to be easy, since the Civil War was raging and most factories were occupied with military contracts. While Yung waited for his order to be filled, he volunteered to enlist in the Union Army, but was told he was not needed. After the cargo of machinery reached China in 1865, Yung had it installed in the Kiangnan Arsenal and led Zeng on a private tour. "He went through the arsenal with undisguised interest," Yung recalled. "He stood and watched its automatic movement with unabated delight, for this was the first time he had seen machinery." As a pleased Zeng stood mesmerized by modernity, Yung recognized the propitious nature of the moment. It was time to introduce his educational scheme.[66]

The Educational Mission

Buoyed by his triumph, Yung sent Beijing a set of four proposals designed to advance self-strengthening objectives. Why did he submit four proposals instead of just the one calling for American-style education? It was pure strategy. Proposals one, three, and four recommended the sorts of projects self-strengtheners salivate over—steamships, railroads, and mineral mining. Into this attractive package, Yung tucked the magical proposal number two. "Of the four proposals," Yung wrote, "the first, third and fourth were put in to chaperone the second, in which my whole heart was enlisted." The second proposal recommended that, every year, the Chinese government send thirty teenage boys to the United States for schooling. Yung was attempting to recreate his own educational experience—with one exception.

He inserted a clause attaching Chinese teachers to the initiative so that the boys could "keep up their knowledge of Chinese." This clause reveals Yung's savvy and self-awareness. While his agenda overlapped with that of the self-strengtheners, he understood that he was not one of them. They had not studied abroad and so their inner natures had not evolved. They maintained an unquestioning faith in Confucianism and had only reluctantly turned to Western learning in response to crisis. In contrast, Yung's American education had changed him to his core, a process he called a "metamorphosis in his inward nature."[67] His worldview transformed, Yung saw Western learning not as a mere expedient but as valuable in its own right. For him, the self-strengthener's protective shell exceeded in worth the Confucianism it safeguarded. All that said, he knew also that a proposal that appeared radical was sure to fail. By including classical Chinese instruction, he hoped to increase the proposal's chances for approval in the halls of power.

Though cleverly crafted, the proposal languished in Beijing until a tragic incident demonstrated its relevance. In 1870, an antiforeign mob in Tianjin murdered twenty-one French nuns and burned down a cathedral (Chapter 1). In the Tianjin Massacre's aftermath, Yung was called to Tianjin to translate for Zeng in his negotiations with foreign leaders. Since the atrocity, in Yung's view, arose out of "gross ignorance and superstition," it demonstrated China's urgent need for better knowledge of the outside world. That was Yung's opening: "I seized the opportunity to press [for] my educational scheme." Late one night, word reached Yung that Zeng intended to recommend the plan to the emperor. The news electrified him. "While lying on my bed, as wakeful as an owl," he wrote, "I felt as though I were treading on clouds and walking in air." Yung returned to America in advance of the first student cohort to make preparations.[68]

In 1872, the first detachment of thirty boys, ages ten to sixteen, reached Hartford, Connecticut, the chosen headquarters for the Chinese Educational Mission (CEM).[69] So as to accelerate their adoption of English, B. G. Northrup, Connecticut's commissioner of education, convinced Yung to assign the boys to host families. "The present movement is an experiment," Northrop stated candidly in his call for volunteers. "If wisely conducted at the outset, it will be a grand success."[70] Northrop received responses mostly from families, but one single woman also replied. By hosting two boys, Mary Kellogg came into contact with Yung Wing, and a love affair followed. In 1875, they got married.[71]

In managing the CEM, Yung was assisted by Chen Lanbin, a classically trained official who did not speak English. According to historian Edward Rhoads, the Chinese government intended the Confucian-minded Chen to provide a counterweight to the Americanized Yung. The CEM was designed, after all, to train a cadre of young men who, while at ease in Western civilization, could serve in the Chinese government. Its purpose was decidedly not to strip the boys of their language, culture, and heritage. With this goal in mind, the two commissioners asked host families to mandate one hour of Chinese study each day. In addition, all boys would congregate in Hartford once each year for several weeks of rigorous Chinese instruction. Though the boys enjoyed reconnecting with one another, they despised these boot camps. Every student "made his annual pilgrimage to Hartford with great reluctance," one boy recalled, "and looked upon it as one of the evils of life." A blunt student referred to Hartford as "the Hell House."[72]

Cultural Alloys

Once the boys started school, Americanization proved irresistible. They wished to fit in with peers and acquired a fondness for American dress, sports, religion, music, dancing, and girls. At first, the boys walked around town wearing long Chinese gowns and queues. According to Wen Bingzhong, one of the students, they attracted mockery because their appearance "made them look like girls." Though their superiors allowed the boys to adopt American dress, they were forbidden from cutting their queues. Most solved the problem by hiding the braid under a shirt or coiling it inconspicuously beneath a hat. Looking less like outsiders, they plunged with eagerness into sports: rowing, hunting, bicycling, baseball, and football. The students fielded a baseball team that they humorously called "the Orientals."[73] William Phelps, a classmate of some CEM boys, recalled their athletic prowess. "In baseball," he recollected, "Tsang was a great pitcher, impossible to hit." In football games, the player both sides wanted was Se Chung, "a short-thick-set boy . . . who ran like a hound and dodged like a cat." Phelps described another boy, Kong, as possessing "bull strength," which allowed him to "cross the goal line, carrying four or five Americans." Enthusiastic participants in sports, the boys did not hold back at social gatherings either. Phelps recalled that, at dances, the "most sought-out belles" chose the Chinese boys.[74] "Showered with fragrant blossoms by the fair ones," a Chinese official later observed, the boys "have found the country of superb happiness" and "are too happy to think of their fatherland."[75]

Sports and dances were one thing, but religion was another. Most host families and school friends attended Protestant churches. Not surprisingly, many boys became curious about Christianity and wished to know more. Some sought out private conversations with the Reverend Joseph Twichell, Yung's close friend. In 1878, Twichell arranged for Dwight Moody, America's foremost evangelist, to meet the students in Hartford. The affable Moody won them over there before traveling north to Springfield where, according to Edward Rhoads, he had a "similarly electrifying effect." "I did not take to

Christianity kindly at first," Li Enfu wrote. But when the "grand man of God, Mr. Moody, came to proclaim the Gospel in Springfield," Li was taken in. He "had a personal interview with Mr. Moody" that "strengthened . . . my resolution to be a Christian." Though adopting the faith, Li held back from officially joining a church. He did so in accordance with Yung Wing's wishes. Though a Christian himself, Yung understood that church membership, should his superiors in Beijing learn of it, could jeopardize the CEM. Walking a fine line, he permitted students to read scriptures in private but asked that they avoid "public professions" of faith. But religious feeling can be hard to contain. After Moody's galvanizing visit, eight students founded a Christian organization, the Chinese Christian Home Mission, whose purpose was to guide "fellow-students to the foot of Jesus' Cross" and then to carry the Gospel to their "benighted countrymen" in China. The more the students Americanized, the more Yung Wing fretted—even if he tacitly approved of the subversive behavior.[76]

While Yung had cause for concern, Americans marveled at the stunning transformation wrought in the boys. "They have become to all appearances," a journalist wrote, "except in the facial marks of their race, American young gentlemen."[77] "They have attracted much attention," observed another, "by their intelligence, their probity, their fluent command of the English tongue," and their "American notions and Yankee airs." They had become, in his word, "Americanized."[78] One writer, noting some boys' matriculation at scientific schools, labeled "successful" the "experiment in America."[79] "It is gratifying to Americans," summed up one writer with pride, "to see the tendency of . . . China . . . to model after us."[80] Americans, as they had with Yung twenty years earlier, fully embraced the new cultural alloy emerging from the CEM laboratory.

More than just being passing curiosities, Yung Wing and his boys figured prominently in a contentious political issue—the so-called Chinese Question. In the 1870s, Americans debated the future status of the Chinese in their country. Should the nation welcome immigrants from China or should it expel them and lock the gates? Speaking at a congressional hearing in 1877, Augustus Loomis, pastor at a Chinese church in San Francisco, argued in favor of Chinese immigrants. After a senator asked Loomis to comment on the "intellectual capacities" of the Chinese, Loomis pointed to Yung Wing and the CEM. With his Yale degree, Yung offered proof of the Chinese intellect, as did "the rapid progress" of "the Chinese students in our eastern institutions." In response to a separate question, Loomis asserted that the Chinese were "capable of becoming citizens." "When a Chinaman becomes christianized," he elaborated, "I think he has capacities equal to any people I ever knew." Searching for an example, Loomis again extolled Yung Wing. "There is not a grander man on the face of this earth than this same Yung

Wing," Loomis gushed. "He is a noble fellow" with "a grand head—a Daniel Webster head."[81] Since Daniel Webster's legendary cerebral powers had always been linked to his massive forehead, this was lofty praise indeed.

The Dream Collapses

In the early 1880s, the experiment appeared to be flourishing. By 1881, at least 60 of the 120 boys had reached college at a time when few Americans did. Unfortunately, three developments plunged the CEM into a state of crisis from which it could not recover. First, in what was a major disappointment to China's self-strengthening faction, the United States denied the students entrance to West Point and the Naval Academy. Second, the Chinese government, aware of Yung's utility as a diplomat, started deploying him on assignments that drew him away from Hartford. He was absent when his program needed him most. Third, the Chinese government dispatched a new commissioner in 1880 who was intensely conservative in outlook.[82]

When Wu Zideng reached Hartford, he was outraged by what he found. The students had adopted, in his view, the worst aspects of American society. "The customs of the foreign land have numerous vices," he reported back to China, and the boys "are already susceptible to its evil habits." With this unfortunate Americanization came a concomitant diminishment of Chinese learning and values. The students were "forgetting the roots," he fulminated, while he also bemoaned their lackadaisical approach to "Confucian books."[83] According to Yung Shang Him, one of the students, Wu charged the boys with being "Americanized and denationalized," and he predicted "they would do no good, but positive harm, to China, if they were allowed to finish their studies." Yung called Wu "a bigoted and fanatical conservative."[84]

Wu responded swiftly to the backsliding. He tripled the length of the Hartford boot camps and demanded additional hours of daily Chinese study. He also dealt harshly with those students who had strayed the furthest. Wu ordered Rong Kui, converted under Moody, to recant his faith. When Rong resisted, Wu had him "shut up" and forced to "live on bread and water." Wu also summoned Tan Yaoxun, a Yale student, back to Hartford. A founding member of the Chinese Christian Home Mission, Tan refused to bow before the tablet of Confucius.[85] One CEM official called Tan and other disrespectful students "runaway horses."[86] Though Rong and Tan ultimately surrendered to Wu's wishes, he nevertheless ordered their return to China. Determined to remain in America, the two absconded while changing trains in Springfield. Edward Rhoads suspects that Yung Wing "played a behind-the-scenes role in the defection." When the two fugitives emerged from hiding, they had cut their queues and joined churches.[87]

In 1881, all CEM students were forced to pack their trunks when the government terminated the program. Even a letter from Ulysses S. Grant to Li Hongzhang, the deceased Zeng Guofan's protégé, could not forestall the closure. Recalled to China, the students were placed on trains to San Francisco, where they awaited their steamship. During the layover, a baseball team from Oakland challenged "the Orientals" to a game. "The Chinese walloped them," Wen Bingzhong fondly recalled, before departing for Shanghai.[88]

The dissolution of the CEM vaporized Yung's dream. It "scattered my life work to the four winds," he wrote, and was "enough to crush my spirit."[89] As Yung bemoaned the premature ending of his grand experiment, he perhaps took some solace in the fact that its long-term effects remained unknown. The students, after all, had absorbed the American education he so passionately coveted. Some of them might find a way to release it into China. Capturing this sentiment, the *Connecticut Courant* printed a portentous message:

> The Educational Mission, though now in ruins, has not utterly perished from the earth. Its influence survives; no imperial decree can abolish that. The bright lads who are unwillingly going back to China carry ideas among their own luggage. And an idea is more dangerous . . . than a cargo of dynamite.[90]

But when would the explosives go off? Yung could only watch and wait.

Yen Yung Kiung

Off the Confucian Track

In Shanghai, the CEM students faced a severe reentry crisis owing to their association with a bold experiment that the government had labeled a dismal failure. They were treated with contempt, eyed with suspicion, and placed in poor living conditions. Huang Kaijia decried the "shabby and mean treatment we received at the hands of our paternal government" and likened their housing to Andersonville, the notorious Confederate prisoner-of-war camp. "We were . . . disgraced prisoners," wrote Rong Shangqian. "A guard or soldier was placed at the gate."[91] In addition to the unpleasant distrust, the students also found themselves poorly equipped for employment. Though they were required to work for the state, the government passed them over for all good positions, favoring civil servants who had mastered the Confucian classics. If such men could be described as hyperliterate, then the CEM students were semiliterate, their command of Mandarin having atrophied after so many years abroad. Unsure what to do with them, the government placed them in training positions[92] with minuscule salaries that one student described as "atomical."[93]

One man watched their travails closely and empathetically. When the students struggled, he intervened, becoming a benefactor to many.[94] Who was the kind stranger and why did he care about their plight? Born in 1838, Yen Yung Kiung flashed signs of brilliance at a young age. Like all Chinese parents blessed with a precocious son, Yen's father and mother first sought to place him on a conventional track: they enrolled him in a private school in Shanghai that drilled students in the Confucian canon. One day, they dreamed, he would pass the state examinations and become a scholar-official. Unfortunately, the elder Yen, an assistant to a shopkeeper, lacked the resources to sustain this plan. The parents scrimped and saved for a while before reluctantly withdrawing their son in 1848. At this point, they found themselves in a quandary: how could they nurture their child's intellect without access to a school? As a last resort, the family explored an alternative educational pathway. In 1846, William Boone had opened a school in Shanghai that attracted pupils by promising much for free: tuition, uniforms, textbooks, and lunch. The Boone school, though not ideal, presented promise enough and so the parents enrolled Yen in 1848. He was nine years old.[95]

The youngest boy in the school, Yen made the largest impact. Since his slight frame left him susceptible to bullying, another student served as his protector. Yen was "younger and smaller than myself," his friend recalled. Should "any bad boys go for him, I [was] always on his side."[96] However, Yen was fully capable of standing up for himself. On one occasion, a teacher who had grown irritated by disruptions pulled out a yardstick and announced his intention to beat all the students. Yen, who had not misbehaved, argued that the innocent should be spared the rod. Receiving a beating anyway, Yen stormed out of the room, tears streaming down his cheeks. Minutes later, students noticed water mysteriously "cascading down from the ceiling." On the floor above, Yen had dumped a bucket of water to protest the injustice to which he had been subjected.[97]

Yen's talent did not escape his missionary teachers. When only fourteen, he rose to the top of a class composed of many students over age twenty.[98] According to Yen's son, the missionary John T. Points became "especially interested in the progress . . . of my father."[99] In a letter to his board written in 1854, Points singled out Yen and one other student, Yang He-ding, as "by far the most clever" and "most advanced" pupils in the school's history. More importantly, Points shared that the two boys were heading to America to continue their educations. The school's decision to send Yen and Yang abroad may seem remarkable, and perhaps it was. However, this mission, located in the busiest of all Chinese ports, accepted that Chinese boys, excited by the constant arrivals and departures of ships, were growing curious about the outside world. The mission also viewed the case of Wong Kong-chai as strong evidence in favor of overseas experience. And so when former students sought positions as cabin boys, the mission saw little harm in approving these adventures. "Even if they should not do much in America," Points reflected, "their increased knowledge of English and their enlarged ideas will give them a better chance" in life.[100]

There was one boy for whom Points reserved special affection—Hong Niok Woo. Though both Yen and Woo would later play prominent roles in the mission, they would follow remarkably different trajectories. As a child, Woo studied alongside Yen, enjoying especially the classes of Lydia Fay. When a strict new teacher took over both the school and Fay's class, Woo floundered academically and lost his confidence. As the situation became unbearable, he decided to quit. Fay recalled one day finding a message from Woo written on a piece of slate: "I run away like other boys. Superintendent say I am dunce. I think I stupid. I go." Woo vanished, and for years Fay heard nothing as to his whereabouts.[101] One day, however, he not only resurfaced but expressed an earnest wish to receive baptism. Points took an "especial interest" in the mission's prodigal son who, while lacking Yen's academic gifts, clearly possessed character. Though the mission declined to invest further in Woo's education, Points did place Woo on the *Susquehanna*, a vessel bound for Philadelphia having completed its role in Commodore Matthew Perry's expedition to Japan.[102] So while Yen and Woo were both voyaging to America, they did so under different circumstances. Seeing Yen as its prize pupil, the mission planned to enroll him in excellent schools to cultivate his mind for a missionary career. Woo would have to fend for himself in the school of hard knocks.

A New Archetype

Coincidentally, Yen's arrival in America coincided with Yung Wing's graduation from Yale. Education, as it had for Yung, would dominate Yen's experience. When Yen and Yang He-ding were not in school, the Episcopal Church featured them at events promoting the China mission. Like show ponies, the two boys were trotted out before audiences and presented as living proof that a Christian education improved the Chinese race. "It is difficult for us in a Christian land," wrote an author covering one such event, "to imagine the degradation and ignorance which are to be found in China." Having established the bleakness of "heathen" China, he then shared verbatim the speech delivered by Yang He-ding. The contrast was stark. Yang began by reminding the gathering that the Shanghai mission school had taught him English. "We cannot speak as well as you," he said in flawless English, "so I beg you to excuse me, when you find any mistake or deficiency in my speech."

Of course, there were none, and that was precisely the point: the school ably converted ignorant "heathens" into eloquent Christians. "But when we were enjoying all the privileges and happiness in that school," Yang continued, "we never could forget our native children" whom we wished could "enjoy the same privilege." How might the congregation spread the blessing of American education to more Chinese children? They could support the opening of "more Mission-schools." Yang also described his extreme homesickness. Thankfully, he assured the audience, the "bitter moment" had passed.[103]

It hadn't. Shortly after delivering this speech, Yang sailed for China.[104] Yen would stay in America. In 1858, William Boone took Yen to Ohio and enrolled him in Kenyon College.[105] Unlike Yung Wing, Yen encountered little difficulty adjusting to college life. More than merely surviving, he maximized his Kenyon experience. Yen earned consistently high grades, acing even Calculus, the course Yung had barely passed.[106] While excelling academically, Yen took full advantage of the collegiate experience. He participated on the debate team, wrote for the *Kenyon Collegian*,[107] and learned to swim, play baseball, and ice-skate.[108] He also joined a fraternity[109] and a secret society that required him at initiation to intone an "iron clad oath of secrecy."[110] Named valedictorian for the class of 1861, Yen delivered an address at commencement. In quieter moments, Yen must have reflected on the impact college had had on him. Yes, he had collected high marks, honors, and a degree. But for him, college was about so much more: it had intrinsically changed him. He now valued free thought and expression, believed in math and science, embraced sports and physical culture, and saw merit in social organization. Had his parents managed to keep him in the Confucian academy, he would have committed classical texts to memory but missed out on everything else. Yen emerged from college, in the words of scholar Seiji Kodama, a "very new type of Chinese."[111]

Years later, Yen's son tried to explain his father's metamorphosis. "It has been asserted," he wrote, that a Chinese man "denationalizes" himself when he adopts Western culture. This process, critics contend, "degrades" the man, making him less than his countrymen. While agreeing that his father had evolved "mentally, morally, and a little socially," the son refused to view his father's story as one of loss. On the contrary, his father "stands out prominently as an archetype" of a new "class of man," one who is "externally Chinese but endowed with a westernized mind and soul." This new entity, whom he called "the Reformed Chinese," could use his "voice or pen" to "defend his native country" and speak out against the "corruptness and wickedness" within the government. For this reason, Yen Yung Kiung, and others like him, remained "the only hope and salvation of China."[112]

The younger Yen's term *archetype* could also apply to Yung Wing, who had graduated from Yale seven years earlier. Like Yung, Yen wished to confer the blessings of his American experience upon other Chinese. Though pursuing the same end, Yen parted company with Yung as to the means. Yung had refused to accept funding that would have locked him into a missionary career. Yen, in contrast, allowed the Episcopal Church to cover tuition and expenses, committing himself in the process to the missionary's life.[113] Far from viewing the church as restrictive, Yen believed he could express his intellect through its channels. And so when he embarked for China in 1861, he fully intended to work as a missionary. During the voyage, he dazzled the captain by applying high-level mathematics to the vessel's navigation.[114] Yen was not prepared for the news that awaited him in Shanghai.

Yen's Mission

His family had suffered greatly during his seven-year absence. Yen's aging father, unable to support the family, had assumed large debts. Desperate for money, he had sold his daughter—Yen's sister—into servitude.[115] Realizing that his first obligation lay with his family, Yen made a formal request to William Boone to delay the start of his missionary career. Boone agreed. In fact, with mission funds suspended during the Civil War, Boone likely could not have paid Yen anyway. Seeking employment, the bilingual Yen ventured into Shanghai's foreign district, where he easily found lucrative employment. He worked as an interpreter first for the British Consulate, then for a British trading firm, and finally for the Municipal Council of the International Settlement. In just a few years, he earned enough money to purchase his sister and send his younger brother to Kenyon. He then returned to the Episcopal mission, this despite entreaties from the Municipal Council urging him to stay.[116]

After Yen had restored his family to sound financial footing, he confronted a second problem that, deeply psychological in nature, proved less easy to solve. In 1865, he began preaching in Shanghai as a minister-in-training. He submitted a report to the mission that politely questioned the logic of training him in "abstruse theology" instead of in "Chinese literature and idolatrous tenets." In Yen's view, it was foolish to master esoteric theology while remaining ignorant of the beliefs of the people he sought to convert. But this slightly subversive comment was just the tip of the iceberg; beneath it loomed growing discontent. In the same letter, Yen revealed the submerged ice. "Perhaps you ask me whether I still think of America?" he began, though no one had asked. "Yes, every day," he answered himself. And then the floodgates opened:

> And when I do, I feel more gloomy than pleased, because being absent from its shores, I am absent from all my friends. After the novelty of a few months, I became alive to the fact that China is no

longer a home to me. The pleasures of enlightened society, and the friendship of tried and genial friends, are gone, as well as the enjoyment of means of grace and Christian sympathies. These, to me, are greater trials than even the discouragements which a missionary here meets with. Perhaps you may call this feeling weakness, but it is a weakness common to all of the same situation. Had I no labor to interest me, this loneliness ... would have overcome me, and probably long ago decided me to sail back to the western hemisphere. But a higher duty detains me here.

Yen was depressed. Having spent so many years abroad, he affiliated more with America than with China. He had discovered the painful truth that "China is no longer home to me." Yen missed not just America but its people. With most of his friends living across the Pacific, he experienced intense "loneliness" though living in a crowded city. What kept him at his post? Only his "higher duty" to God. Yen was learning the hard way that one could not study overseas without paying a stiff price.[117]

If there was a bright side to Yen's life, it was that his intellect enabled a rapid climb through the Episcopal hierarchy. Robert Nelson, who oversaw Yen's theological study, marveled at his student's "quick and inquiring mind." "His prospect for usefulness" exceeds "that of any other assistant we have ever had," Nelson observed, because his "talents are so much better cultivated."[118] Wong Kong-chai, now an ordained priest, also recognized Yen's utility. In 1868, he traveled with Yen to Soochow to scout possible sites for a new station.[119] One month later, Wong and Nelson presided over the ceremony promoting Yen to deacon.[120] In 1870, Yen and William Boone Jr. obtained priesthood in the same ceremony.[121]

During Yen's excursion to Soochow with Wong, a minor incident yielded an insight that would alter the direction of Yen's missionary career. As Yen watched, Wong approached two "respectable" men and handed one a Christian tract. The other, becoming irate, "snatched it out of his hands" and "threw" it at Yen. "We know only Confucius," he said with disgust, "we do not know Jesus." In Yen's mind, the incident raised important questions. Why had these men, clearly of the learned class, rejected Wong's book without giving it a look? Was not the purpose of an education to spark curiosity and original thought in an individual? It dawned on Yen that, in China, this was decidedly *not* the purpose of an education. Conceiving of education narrowly as an "avenue to office," the Chinese system "trained" students to "revere and adopt the views of the ancients ... without any independent opinion." Indeed, the system actively discouraged one from thinking for oneself. The Chinese education system, unless it changed, would continue to bend "the Chinese mind to a shape unfit to receive the Gospel."¹²² With this insight, Yen moved education to the foreground of his mind.

Yen carried this idea into the Chinese interior. In 1868, the mission asked him to establish a new station five hundred miles up the Yangtze River in Wuchang and Hankow. He would remain there for eleven years.¹²³ In 1871, he sent a report sharing dismal returns: just twenty-one new Christians in three years. "Alas!" he exclaimed, "our progress is slow." In logical fashion, Yen proceeded to lay out the reasons behind the failure, most of which had to do with the entrenched nature of Chinese beliefs.¹²⁴ Instead of becoming disheartened, Yen innovated. Later that year, he founded two boarding schools, one in each city. In Wuchang, Yen oversaw the construction of a simple two-story building; classes met and meals were served on the bottom floor while the upper floor became the dormitory.¹²⁵ He named the institution the Bishop Boone Memorial School in honor of his benefactor. The school would evolve as the century wore on, becoming first a high school, then a college, and finally a university after 1900.¹²⁶ By teaching and administrating in these schools, Yen learned the skills that would allow him to make his largest contribution to Chinese education—the founding of St. John's College (Chapter 12).

Home Life and Causes

The paradox of Yen's life was that he was an expatriate in his homeland. Intellectually and culturally, he aligned himself more closely to the West than to China. Thus, the only way he could remain content in China was to Americanize portions of life. For his wife, he chose a woman who had attended schools in his mission. A lover of Western classical music, Mrs. Yen taught her children to play the piano.¹²⁷ Music constituted just one of many foreign influences in the Yen household. "To the end of his days," his son W. W. Yen recalled, "he retained his American training and habits." The younger Yen described the decor of their home as "foreignized." The family celebrated Christmas "after the American fashion" with a "decorated and candle-lit tree."¹²⁸ At meals, the Yens ate both Western and Chinese dishes with knives and forks, not chopsticks. With regard to child-rearing, the affectionate Yen eschewed the Confucian model of the strict but distant father, respected but not loved. "He was more than a father," his son wrote, "he was our mentor and friend." Not surprisingly, Yen prized education as "the noblest heritage he could leave to his children." Toward this end, he sent his children and nephews to American schools and colleges.¹²⁹

In describing Yen as affiliating with the West, we must be careful. While it is true that he preferred *Western culture*, he did not view *Western people* as superior. Like Yung Wing, Yen harbored a fierce passion for China and its people that he mostly expressed through his teaching. However, that passion could also manifest itself through his pursuit of justice. When Yen saw Chinese people subjected to abuse or exclusion, the sight ignited his righteous anger and moved him to action. He would contact authorities whenever he saw police officers "brutally assaulting wheelbarrow coolies and aged beggars." Yen also bristled at the tendency of Shanghai's foreign population to treat the Chinese as second-class citizens. Noting the exclusion of Chinese people from a public garden, Yen lodged a vigorous protest with city officials. Though his efforts failed to win Chinese access to the garden, the Municipal Council (his former employer) opened a new garden for Chinese residents.[130] Finally, Yen spoke vehemently in the American press against the Chinese Exclusion Act (1882). "We condemn the Exclusion Bill," he wrote in *The Forum*, "because it ... degrades us." "What America has to fear is not from China," he continued, "but from the fact that she stands before the world convicted of injustice toward a weak nation."[131] Though no longer the small boy protesting an unfair teacher, Yen had not lost his fervor for justice.

Conclusion

In the late 1870s, two CEM students inadvertently set in motion a sequence of events that would change China forever. In Boston, Wen Bingzhong and Niu Shangzhou would periodically visit the tea store of a Chinese merchant. One day, they struck up a conversation with the owner's twelve-year-old assistant. They described "their life at school," which they adored, and urged the boy to pursue an education himself. For Wen and Niu, this was mere idle banter, quickly forgotten. But the impressionable boy drank in every word. Suddenly dissatisfied with his position, he quit the store and went to sea.[132] That boy would later acquire the name Charlie Soong.

We do not need to repeat here every fact from Charlie Soong's biography. It suffices to say that he surfaced in North Carolina and, under the oversight of the Methodist Church and a tobacco magnate, studied at Trinity College (later Duke) before transferring to Vanderbilt.[133] The plan was to prepare Soong for a career as an evangelist in Young J. Allen's Shanghai mission. He would be for Allen what Yen was to Boone: a prototype for a bicultural missionary endowed with unique abilities. That was the hope, but this experiment would go awry. Soong struggled academically and Allen lost faith in him. Though missionaries had embraced the hybridity of Wong and Yen, Allen regarded Soong not as an asset but as a "*denationalized* Chinaman," a botched human being of little use. When Soong returned to China, Allen treated him coldly and shirked his mentorship role. He seemed content to sweep the failed experiment under the rug.[134] Angry and disaffected, Soong quit the mission.¹³⁵ When he did, he discovered his latent talent as an entrepreneur and went on to earn a fortune in the printing business. He also formed ties with secret societies and befriended Sun Yat-sen, whose successful overthrow of the Qing Dynasty in 1911 he would bankroll.¹³⁶

Charlie Soong's impact on twentieth-century China was seismic. Without him the 1911 Chinese Revolution probably would still have happened, but it would have occurred at a different time, assumed a different form, and involved different leaders. Soong affected Chinese history in other ways. Some of the most influential Chinese figures were either enabled by him (Sun Yat-sen), fathered by him (Soong Ai-ling, Soong Ching-ling, T. V. Soong, and Soong Mei-ling), or married to one of his daughters (Sun Yat-sen, Chiang Kai-shek, and H. H. Kung). Indeed, it is no exaggeration to claim that, without Charlie Soong, China would have looked dramatically different after 1900. He provided much of the source material—capital, connections, and DNA—out of which twentieth-century China emerged. What was it about Charlie Soong's formative years that allowed him to wield such influence? Though it is impossible to know for sure, Soong would likely have remained obscure had he never met Wen and Niu in Boston. It was that chance encounter, after all, that planted in him the desire for an American education. Had that education gone smoothly, he probably would not have secretly undermined the Qing government. He might instead have spent his life, much like Wong, dutifully running mission schools in Shanghai. It required a failed educational experiment to generate the creativity, drive, and rage that Soong channeled into the 1911 Revolution.

If anyone had just cause to spurn Christian schools it was Charlie Soong. After all, Allen and others had severely mishandled his education. But Soong's subsequent actions suggest that he did not view these institutions in a negative light. In the 1890s, Soong started enrolling his children in mission schools before sending them to American colleges. By doing so, he followed a pattern established earlier by Yen, who sent his kin overseas to study, and Yung Wing, who launched the CEM. The decision shows that Soong, despite his trials in America, ultimately credited the experience with transforming his identity in a positive way. The hybrid Chinese individual, Soong came to believe, could think in a way that no one else on earth could. He truly was a new kind of man. It was a remarkable discovery, and one that Yung, the CEM students, Wong, Yen, and Yen's children made as well. "We are to be the interpreters . . . of America to our own people," wrote W. W. Yen. "We are able to bring to our own people a knowledge of the American people that no amount of explaining . . . by Americans themselves could accomplish. We constitute a bridge across the Pacific Ocean."¹³⁷

8

Challenging Convention

Single Women Enter Missions

In 1869 a missionary couple from India, Edwin and Lois Parker, returned home to Boston on furlough. After Sunday services at the Tremont Street Methodist Episcopal Church, the couple shared their overseas experiences with a group of female church members. The gathering discussed "the condition of women in India" and the "powerlessness of the missionaries" to "alleviate their state on account of their isolation." How could Indian women be helped? The situation would remain utterly hopeless, Lois Parker contended, unless "Christian women took up this work as a special and separate duty." "Women alone," she asserted, "could have access to women there." Parker's message galvanized the group, which proceeded to act upon it with lightning speed. Two days later, female church members met to explore the possibility of establishing a new missionary society intended solely for women. Shortly after that, a second meeting resulted in the founding of the Woman's Foreign Missionary Society (WFMS). Two weeks later, the ambitious new society met to discuss China as a destination for new recruits.[1] Though the WFMS remained the most visible organization of its type, others that followed added to the movement.[2] The transformation in missions was stark. Just a few years earlier, a clear consensus *against* sending single women abroad had reigned in missionary circles. Now multiple organizations existed for this sole purpose. It had all happened very fast.

In the 1870s and 1880s, a new kind of missionary—the single woman—appeared on the Chinese landscape. This chapter examines four of them:

Gertrude Howe, Elizabeth Fisher, Laura Haygood, and Adaline Kelsey. Most of the new female recruits chose the educational model so ably defended by Calvin Mateer in 1877. That said, they diverged from Mateer in one crucial respect: while he focused on educating boys, they operated schools for girls. To their institutions, the young women brought fresh ideas, modern priorities, and novel forms of behavior. Not surprisingly, these women met with resistance from some veteran missionaries who resented the brash newcomers and their eschewal of established methods. The Chinese too pushed back against female missionaries who did not show proper respect to traditional gender roles. But resistance represents only half of the story. In some missions, the young women met with Chinese communities and missionaries who welcomed both them and the innovation they brought.

The WFMS

Back in 1866, Adele Fielde had made the hard choice to remain in Asia after the death of her fiancé. As a single female, she was an outlier in a profession that strongly favored married women. Once rare, the single female missionary became increasingly common in the 1870s and 1880s. What caused the shift? According to Dana Robert, the Civil War transformed foreign missions in two ways. First, the prolonged conflict drastically depleted the number of able-bodied young men who might have served overseas. Single women stepped into the demographic void. Second, women had, during the war, organized themselves into voluntary associations to address the needs of soldiers. After the war ended, many chose to maintain their high level of organization while transferring their energies to a new cause—the "heathen."[3]

In doing so, these women heeded calls from missionary wives, already out in the field, who reported an urgent need for more women. "It seems to me there must be work enough for ten ladies," wrote Harriet Baldwin, the wife of Caleb Baldwin, of Foochow. "If one could be found who felt that she could . . . keep house by herself," Baldwin continued, "I think she could make herself useful." "If" was the key word in Baldwin's statement. *If* a single woman failed to take care of herself, she would only place additional burden upon the missionary wives, who already supported their husbands. But *if* a single woman could achieve self-sufficiency, she could immerse herself in missions work and accomplish far more than the mostly housebound missionary wives.[4] She could also address the glaring problem that male missionaries had failed to solve—the sad plight of Chinese women. Missionary wives frequently described Chinese women as oppressed by "heathen" religious traditions and cruel patriarchal customs. Yet sequestered from society, they remained inaccessible. In Shandong, Arthur Smith described the Chinese female as living in forlorn isolation—"a frog in a well."[5] How could missionaries usher in Christianity while failing to reach half of the population? Only female missionaries could save these millions of souls.[6]

In the United States, new institutions emerged specifically to address the tragic condition of native women. Founded in 1869, the WFMS was among the first to capture and direct this surging evangelical energy. To promote its agenda, the WFMS launched a magazine, *The Heathen Woman's Friend*, shortly after its inception.[7] Every movement needs a symbol, and this one was no different. Most female missionaries regarded Mary Lyon as their patron saint. In 1837, Mary Lyon founded Mount Holyoke Female Seminary in Massachusetts. Along with educating young women, Lyon energetically promoted missions as a viable career for women. After she died in 1849, her name rose in stature and her movement gathered strength. In 1887, Mount Holyoke alumnae accounted for one-fifth of all women sent abroad by the ABCFM.[8] For inspiration, single women consumed biographies of Mary Lyon authored by former students.[9]

Lyon's belief in the power of education to uplift women fired the minds of the young women venturing overseas. Though intending to save *souls*, they would simultaneously educate the *minds* of indigenous women so as to elevate their status within their own societies.[10] This focus on schools placed the WFMS in opposition to the missionary establishment, which maintained its bias in favor of itinerant preaching into the 1880s. Sometimes, these competing visions generated friction. In 1876, the ABCFM released a report that reinforced the primacy of "direct evangelizing" as the best way to promulgate the Gospel. Going further, it actually condemned the education model as "likely to intrench heathenism" instead of "subdue it." Schools, in short, undermined the Christian cause overseas. The WFMS responded swiftly. Since women ran the majority of mission schools, the WFMS interpreted the report as a direct attack on its operations. The WFMS turned to its publishing arm, *The Heathen Woman's Friend*, to issue its response. The magazine blasted any "theory of missions" that harbored "misgivings" about education as "pitifully narrow and practically mischievous." To achieve God's object, the magazine went on, the Lord employs not only preaching but "almost every namable human force," a list that included "the press," "organizations of reform," and—most importantly—"the school." Missions should value education's contribution to evangelical work, the magazine insisted, not disrespect it.[11]

The Woolston School Controversy

Though the exchange with the ABCFM was contentious, the WFMS had no difficulty deciding upon an appropriate response. After all, the principles upon which the WFMS was founded had demanded a vigorous defense of schools run by women. But in 1879, a controversy erupting in Foochow presented a far greater challenge. Unlike the skirmish with the ABCFM, this ugly debate—which centered on a school for girls—did not pit female missionaries against a male establishment. It was not so straightforward. In fact, both sides worked under the WFMS umbrella, favored education for Chinese girls, and agreed that female missionaries should be the ones to teach them. So what exactly was the nature of the dispute? The two sides disagreed— quite vehemently—on the *kind of young woman* a school should produce. This controversy, in sum, revolved around competing visions of womanhood. Making matters worse, what started as an intramural affair among female missionaries acquired a layer of racial tension when Chinese pastors, newly powerful within the church, entered the fray.

Since 1859, Sarah and Beulah Woolston had operated a boarding school for girls in Foochow. Though single females, the sisters did not provoke concern in the missionary community because, like a married couple, there were two of them and they always worked in tandem. Through their school, the Woolstons aspired to uplift Chinese females, whom they saw as oppressed by forced ignorance and cruel customs (Sarah assailed foot-binding at the Shanghai conference of 1877).[12] To improve conditions, the Woolstons imported to China the kind of education that, in their view, had helped women achieve their relatively high status in American society. They delivered a curriculum that aligned with the norms of Victorian-era domesticity. Though the school taught basic literacy, math, the Bible, and some science, it focused squarely on household arts.[13] "Their great aim," wrote Esther Baldwin, was to make the girls "useful Christian women in their own homes" by teaching them "to cook, wash," and sew their own clothes. Conspicuously absent from the classroom was "anything that could be of no possible use to them in the future."[14]

Though the school seems utterly unthreatening in its traditional approach, that it taught girls at all prompted some Chinese men to view it as dangerous. "Whoever heard of a girl learning to read?" some asked disparagingly when the notion of female education was broached. "You might as well hold a book before a cow and ask her to read."[15] Given this degree of prejudice, the Woolstons encountered difficulty attracting students when the school opened. Opponents undermined the school, one missionary recalled, by spreading the "vilest slander" in the community. After several "fruitless" months, the Woolstons finally found one family willing to register their daughter—but only on one condition. The parents insisted on attending school with the child to "guard against her having her eyes gouged out."[16] With so few applicants, the Woolstons taught mainly orphans at first. Though community distrust ran high, the sisters eventually won over enough families to render their school viable, though low enrollment persisted as a problem.[17] In 1871, the school found a new sponsor when the WFMS agreed to fund it. For the WFMS, this was an easy decision. A school run by women that provided Chinese girls with a Christian education aligned perfectly with its values. The WFMS could not possibly have predicted the controversy that lay ahead.[18]

When the sisters departed on furlough in 1879, temporary leadership devolved to Sarah Sites. This was not her first experience heading the school, as the Woolstons had gone on furlough before. This time, however, Sites did something different out of respect to the newly empowered Chinese pastors (Chapter 6). In order "to know what the preachers were thinking," she invited them to observe closing exercises. As the Chinese looked on, the demonstration of knowledge captivated them. "Great were their wonder and delight," Sarah recalled, "to see the girls point out on wall maps the various nations of the strange barbarian world."[19] Had these men observed the same spectacle a decade earlier, it likely would have elicited only apathetic approval if not outright opposition. That is because, for much of their lives, their views on female education had reflected those of society. But recent experiences had prompted them to revise their positions. Hu Yong Mi had his epiphany in 1870. That year, the mission received funding earmarked for the training of female evangelists, and Nathan Sites tapped Hu for the job.[20] Though Hu acquiesced, he questioned the training on the grounds that women "should keep silence in the churches." However, when the young woman placed in his charge impressed him, Hu reversed his stance. "If only men preach, only men will be converted," Hu reasoned before his colleagues, and "only half the people will be preached to."[21] Newly enlightened, Hu enrolled his daughter in the Woolston School. He also stopped binding her feet.[22]

Once inclined to follow custom blindly, Chinese pastors now wished to see the potential of girls unleashed. In fact, they progressed so rapidly in their thinking that their "ideals," Sarah Sites discovered, "had outrun" those of the Woolston School. They told Sites as much after viewing closing exercises. "Geography and numbers and the Bible" were all fine, was their comment, "yes, so far so good." But the school ought to make additional advances in English, music, and the Confucian classics. To oblige, Sarah set about changing the school's curriculum. She dispatched Nathan Sites to Hong Kong to purchase classical Chinese textbooks and hired a Confucian scholar to handle instruction. When the Woolston sisters returned from furlough, they were apoplectic. It was as if a new school had replaced theirs entirely. Anticipating trouble, Nathan Sites tried to convince the sisters that the continued growth of the native church depended on a modernized curriculum.[23] But to no avail. The outraged Woolstons opposed the changes and a nasty power struggle ensued. The explicit purpose of the school, they insisted, was to prepare Chinese girls to be Christian wives and mothers. The new curriculum would undermine this purpose, rendering women "unfit" for the homelife that awaited them.[24]

The sisters also railed against the addition of English classes. Interestingly, English instruction was a touchy subject not just in Foochow but in missions across China. Whenever it was brought up, missionaries took sides and tempers flared. Some argued in support of English on the grounds that literacy allowed Chinese students to read the books that encapsulated Western knowledge—knowledge that China sorely needed, in their view. This faction pointed also to the fact that Chinese Christians, like Foochow's Chinese pastors, almost always favored English instruction. How could anything that granted access to enriching knowledge, Chinese Christians wondered, possibly provoke controversy? Critics of English cried foul. Missionaries, they asserted, had been sent to China to spread the Gospel. Period. Since English did not advance this primary objective, schools that taught it were engaging in an unauthorized reinvention of the entire missionary enterprise. "The use of English as a medium of instruction," writes historian Dana Robert, "implied that teaching secular subjects for their own sakes was a worthy goal of missions . . . alongside church planting." With so much at stake, the Woolstons refused to back down. Back in charge, they dismantled the curricular apparatus erected in their absence and restored the school to its former state.[25]

The Chinese pastors retaliated swiftly and decisively. First, they removed several girls, damaging already precarious enrollments. Second, they used their annual conference, where they enjoyed a voting majority, to confer official sanction to the idea that girls deserve a broad curriculum.[26] Third, they went over the heads of the Woolstons by sending a letter directly to the WFMS. When the letter arrived, the WFMS was baffled, unaccustomed as it was to receiving mail like this. "One of the most remarkable documents received by our Society," the WFMS recorded, "is one from the native preachers, asking for the higher education of the females."[27] Fourth, the Chinese pastors inflicted a massive insult upon Sarah Woolston by conspicuously passing over her during Holy Communion. Though they subsequently apologized for this slight, the Woolstons were too hurt to make amends. Embittered, they resigned from the mission in 1883 and left China.[28] Sia Sek Ong assumed control of the school until a new head could be found.[29]

In its annual report, the WFMS faced the awkward task of explaining the sudden withdrawal of the Woolstons. Readers were probably surprised to see an account of outright dissension in a report that almost exclusively printed good news:

> It is with regret that we receive this as probably the last report from these time-honored veterans of our work—the Misses Woolston, the

pioneers of our distinctive woman's work for women in foreign lands. New Educational methods, including the study of English, the Chinese classics, music and other accomplishments, are being introduced into China, which they do not approve, and, therefore, will not adopt; but, in retiring from this work, these sisters bring with them the highest appreciation and esteem of the oldest missionaries.... In two respects our work in Foochow is passing through a transition state, and is practically seeking the solution of two problems—one the advisability of giving English and advanced education to Chinese girls; the other, how far the native church should regulate the affairs of a mission. Let us hope the solution may prove the wisdom of the experiment.[30]

In crafting its statement, the WFMS walked a tightrope. On the one hand, it needed to laud the Woolstons for twenty-five years of selfless labor. Toward this end, it described the sisters as "pioneers" who had earned the "esteem" of the "oldest missionaries." The inclusion of the superlative adjective "oldest," far from being accidental, allowed the WFMS to frame the dispute as a generational conflict, which it partly was. While expressing gratitude to the Woolstons, the society wished to avoid offending younger female readers who espoused a more progressive vision of womanhood and who constituted the majority of new recruits. The society handled this delicate rhetorical challenge by sharing the facts concerning the curriculum battle without passing judgment: "New Educational methods . . . are being introduced into China, which [the Woolstons] do not approve, and, therefore, will not adopt." Finally, the society noted that the education of Chinese women was not the only point of contention. A second potential controversy loomed, and it involved the "experiment" of Chinese authority: to what degree should the "native church" be allowed to "regulate the affairs of a mission"? To this question, the society conspicuously avoided taking a side. One powder keg was enough for this annual report.

The Woolston incident, though ugly, was revealing. At the personal level, it showed how territorial missionaries could be and how rancorous they could become when detecting the encroachment of a rival. The incident also shed light on a previously hidden fault line separating tradition-minded missionaries from the younger and more progressive ones. Specifically, the two groups diverged on three key questions: How much education should Chinese girls receive? Should mission schools emphasize English and secular subjects? And how much power should Chinese pastors wield? Indeed, the Woolston incident exposed a missionary community struggling with the ascendant Chinese power it had nurtured through self-support. As the Chinese asserted more influence, American missionaries could no longer dictate the terms. Nor could they achieve their objectives without Chinese help. "If you carefully look into the circumstances of things," the Chinese pastors reminded missionaries in 1883, "you will see that it is very difficult for foreigners in China to accomplish good in any work without faithful native assistants."[31] They were right. Chinese ministers now possessed leverage, and missionaries would need to tailor their institutions to match Chinese priorities.

Gertrude Howe

Gertrude Howe, one of the WFMS's first recruits, tilted strongly to the progressive side of the debate. Growing up in Michigan, Howe imbibed constant encouragement from her mother, who herself had not received an education. "Gertrude," her mother said repeatedly, "I want you *to be something* and *to do something* when you grow up."[32] Trying to do just that, Howe was one of the first women to attend medical school at the University of Michigan, which became coeducational in 1870.[33] In 1872, without completing the program, she joined the WFMS, which sent her and Lucy Hoag to Jiujiang in Jiangxi Province. Howe journeyed to China animated by a singular ambition: to uplift girls by running a boarding school. To her dismay, the Chinese community withheld its children from her school; Howe received only a handful of day students and no boarders at all. As she strolled about the city with Hoag, Howe lamented the "cruel prejudice" to which girls were subjected in China. But Chinese girls were not the only ones with problems. The disastrous start to her missionary career pushed Howe into a state of crisis. She found herself far from home and unable to consummate the plan that had been her sole reason for coming.[34]

Then chance dangled a fresh possibility before her eyes. During a language tutorial, Howe asked her teacher to locate a child in need of care. Though Howe later claimed to have made the request in jest, the tutor missed the joke. He surprised Howe by informing her of an unwanted baby girl.[35] Why was the girl available? After the infant's birth, her parents had hired a blind old fortune-teller to reveal "her fate." The girl "should be killed," he said, "or sent away to another family." A second fortune-teller delivered more bad news from the heavens: the child was born under the wrong star. Not wanting to destroy their child, the parents sought a surrogate parent to raise her.[36] Howe believed deeply in adoption. To "take little children, save them from heathenism, teach them, and let them grow up Christians," she maintained, accomplishes more good than proselytizing among adults. If local opposition prevented Howe from uplifting girls through schooling, she could achieve similar goals, though on a smaller scale, through adoption. The child's name was Kang Aide. Her English name became Ida Kahn.[37]

There is a reason why, in the history of Protestant missions, we see so few adoptions. Howe, by taking the infant, had violated an unwritten rule. According to Connie Shemo, missionaries placed great credence in the idea that Chinese children must retain their native culture. A boy or girl could best contribute to the growth of Christianity, missionaries believed, by growing up fully Chinese, by finding a Chinese spouse, and by keeping a Christian home. Missionaries discouraged adoption because it placed this desirable outcome in jeopardy. The child raised by a white mother in an American-style household would grow up caught between two cultures. Alienated from her own people, she would become a foreigner in her own land and hold no influence in her community. In 1900, long after Howe had made her radical decision, the WFMS formalized its opposition by banning adoption.[38]

After Kahn, Howe adopted three more Chinese girls. "Had I not taken them," Howe insisted in the *Heathen Woman's Friend*, "they would all be dead, without doubt."[39] Actually, there was some doubt. Perhaps to justify her controversial adoptions, Howe overstated the risk of death faced by one girl. Shih Mei-yu entered Howe's home at the age of seven after her father asked the missionary to train his daughter to be a doctor. Specifically, he requested that Howe prepare her academically for future study in an American medical school.[40] It was an astounding proposition, one made by a man whose vision of female potential lay far ahead of his time.[41] Mr. Shih's unexpected request prompted soul-searching in Howe. Giving girls a loving home and saving them from foot-binding was one thing. Providing them with an overseas education was another. Before answering, Howe prayed to God for guidance. She also studied the example of Yung Wing's boys. Did education in American schools "tend to make them unhappy" later in life? Did it spoil their good natures, leaving them "stuck up"? Did "contact with American life" create a new kind of person who was "worse than heathenized"?[42] After much deliberation, Howe agreed to the proposition. Over the ensuing years, her household became a laboratory of hybridization where Chinese girls received rigorous instruction in English, Mathematics, Chemistry, Physics, and Latin.[43] "My schoolgirls are progressing finely," she reported in 1882. "I look to the future of my babies."[44] Quite possibly, Howe headed the most unusual home in all of China. If the Chinese thought her unorthodox, they were not alone—so too did missionaries. Shih Mei-yu, who took the name Mary Stone, recalled that the missionary community subjected her mother to "ostracism."[45]

Though focused on her daughters, Howe did not give up on her school. The same fiercely independent streak that led to Howe's unique family formation also shaped her small school. Intent upon running it her own way, she did not hesitate to defy missionary convention, even if that meant ruffling feathers—which it did. Ahead of its time, her school required its girls to take a full complement of courses in math, science, religion, and the Confucian classics.[46] The challenging curriculum, however, was not what precipitated her conflict with other missionaries. Controversy erupted in 1883 when John Hykes invited Howe to bring her students to services in the mission's chapel. Howe stunned her male colleague by refusing on the grounds that marching her girls through the streets would offend the local population. Respectable families, she lectured Hykes, insisted that young girls be kept out of public view. In addition, some of the girls had bound feet, which further complicated his proposed promenade. His simple request rebuffed, Hykes became indignant. Gertrude Howe had already trampled on the rules and customs of *both* Chinese and missionaries by adopting girls. Why had she, all of a sudden, become highly sensitive to Chinese notions of feminine propriety that he knew she disagreed with? Her stance, in short, defied credulity. Hykes had a point, but Howe stood firm. "Miss Howe does not attend our services herself and does not bring the school-girls," an infuriated Hykes wrote. "If the ladies of the W.F.M.S. will not work in harmony with us, then our wives must do the work among the women themselves."[47] One of them did. The mission removed Howe as school head, replacing her with a missionary's wife. Seeing her ousting as a cue to leave, Howe and her girls traveled eight hundred miles up the Yangtze River to Chongqing. There they joined Francis Wheeler, another WFMS recruit, who had courageously founded a small station in the distant western city.[48]

Gertrude Howe had stirred the pot. She had entered a mission dominated by males and their wives and caused a major disruption. Her radical decisions in regard to school curriculum and adoption, as well as her standoff with Hykes, illustrate how the WFMS could change the dynamic. By deploying young women like Howe, the WFMS brought to China new ways of thinking and forms of behavior that some established missionaries welcomed and others did not. Sensing that she could achieve her purpose only by remaining single, Howe declined several marriage proposals. "My work is laid out for me," she wrote. "I cannot do my work if I marry."[49] Gertrude Howe was not the only single female missionary to flout convention. Others followed in her footsteps.

Elizabeth Fisher

In 1884, Elizabeth Fisher headed to Foochow to run a school. This was not just any school, however. The WFMS assigned her to the same institution that, the previous year, had descended into bitter acrimony. In 1883, following their ugly dispute with the Chinese pastors, Sarah and Beulah Woolston had resigned in anger from the school they had founded. Though the departure of the sisters alleviated tensions, the fundamental disagreements at the root of the conflict simmered beneath the surface. Compounding the difficulty, Fisher faced problems of a purely practical nature. She was inheriting leadership of an institution with dangerously low enrollments. The position, in short, presented nothing but problems. If ever a missionary appeared set up to fail, it was Elizabeth Fisher. And she was only twenty-two years old.

Though young and inexperienced, Fisher brought to China a determination to succeed. She possessed a redoubtable independent streak that had manifested itself in childhood. "I had a fierce will," she said later in her life. "I wanted to be King of my own life without yielding to anyone." Aware of her strong will, her parents tried repeatedly to curb it with discipline. On one occasion, she embarrassed her father, a Methodist minister, by throwing a tantrum in front of church members when she did not get her way. Since her petulance had been visible to the church community, her father insisted upon an equally conspicuous punishment. "I could whip you," he said, but "I have a responsibility to the children who heard you" and who "must know that we are terribly ashamed." He decided upon solitary confinement on the most fun day of the year. During the annual church picnic, he sequestered his temperamental daughter in her bedroom, allowing her only bread and water. While other children partook of the festivities, Elizabeth sat alone in her hot room watching a buzzing fly knock against the window pane. "I was not easy to live with," Elizabeth conceded.[50]

Elizabeth did not remain headstrong for long. At the age of ten, she had a spiritual experience that turned her greatest negative—her stubborn willfulness—into a positive trait: implacable self-confidence. She emerged with an unconquerable belief in herself as God's obedient servant. The pivotal experience happened on the day that her father, always physically frail, died at the age of thirty-six. That morning, Elizabeth stood with other family members around her father's bed. As she looked on, the "light faded from his face" and "death crept" into the room. He was gone. Or was he? Elizabeth's aunt, overcome by grief, began to "sob uncontrollably" and call out his name. To the startlement of all, the eyes of the assumed-to-be-dead man abruptly opened. Visibly annoyed, he asked his sister "reproachfully" why she had summoned him back. He then proceeded to explain before his "awestricken" family that, during his visit to the "Beyond," he had reunited with his deceased brother and witnessed many "wonders." At dusk, he sank into death a second and final time.

To Elizabeth, the experience was transformative. Her father had seemingly returned from the dead bearing both a credible report on the afterlife and a "smile" so serene and reassuring that she would never forget it. "As a child I had seen father die happy and unafraid," she explained, "and that had left me unafraid, too." Elizabeth converted this revelation into a bold philosophy of life. Released from the human tendency to worry about dying,

Fisher concentrated on living: she marched through life supremely confident and willing to take risks. With her new outlook, she entered a state of perpetual optimism. "I always expected wonderful things to happen, and they always did."[51]

At the age of eighteen, she gave her life to God after experiencing an awakening in church. While kneeling at the altar, she felt God's presence for the first time. "God had put His arms around me," she recalled, "and made me His own." But what exactly did God want her to do? He did not say, at least not immediately. For four years, Elizabeth taught school while she awaited divine instructions. Finally, what she interpreted as God's call came at last. The WFMS requested that Elizabeth and another young woman, Carrie Jewell, run a school in Foochow. Though she felt relieved, Elizabeth discovered to her chagrin that her family members all disapproved, and so did the community. A woman so young, all admonished, must not leave the safe confines of home "to face the terrors of unknown China." But Elizabeth had long ago rejected any approach to life predicated on fear. So she forged ahead with her preparations alone and in "silence." In 1884, as she boarded a train bound for San Francisco, her anxious family members saw her off at the station. She was the only one who believed in what she was doing.[52]

To a country where missionaries famously went to fail or die, Fisher brought buoyancy and optimism. "That first year in China was wonderful," she recalled, stressing the excitement of the "new": "a new country—a new home—a new language—new work." In Foochow, she described herself as "always ready for fun and adventure." In characterizing her mood in such positive terms, Fisher differed dramatically from most missionaries, who spoke somberly of sacrifice and hardship while making no mention of (and perhaps scrupulously avoiding) the word "fun."[53] But to Elizabeth, *China was fun*. She set about her primary task with optimism: to revive the Woolston School and infuse it with fresh purpose.

Fisher reimagined the school as a training center for future teachers. After graduating, her students would open schools in the villages they were from; by doing so, they would spread female education from the port city to the interior. The plan, though inspired, presented one major challenge: it required Fisher to travel to faraway villages to recruit students. Without any apprehension, Elizabeth set out on her adventures. In the "biting chill of winter" and "steaming heat of summer," she traveled by sampan up and down the Min River, the province's major waterway, recruiting girls.[54] On one junket, she trekked five hundred miles in forty days.[55] In some villages, the people had never before seen a female missionary—only men had visited. Most of them would, after arriving, retire to the chapel to rest and eat in privacy. Fisher, in contrast, took her meals outdoors. "What a strange people these Americans are," she overheard a villager say. "Their strong men come to visit us and hide inside" but "this young little woman eats out in the open and talks to us. She isn't afraid at all." Fisher never forgot this stray comment. A perceptive stranger had identified the trait of which she was most proud. She had no fear.[56]

Fisher tackled school leadership with the same fearlessness. She advanced a bold plan to elevate the curriculum above even the level called for by the Chinese pastors during the Woolston imbroglio. Starting in 1885, Fisher held regular examinations that tested the girls on their knowledge of the scripture, Chinese classics, and English language. Aware of her institution's troubled history, she wisely included the Chinese pastors in the process. "These exams were conducted by our most able Chinese preachers," she wrote, "who highly commend" the students. As the year drew to a close, Fisher submitted a self-confident report to the WFMS. "While others were expressing surprise at the success of our first year," she wrote with evident pride, "we wondered not, for we knew from whence it came."[57]

Though Fisher could run an empowering school for girls, she wielded little influence elsewhere. Gender inequality in Chinese society bothered her greatly. In church, she railed against the strange practice of using large screens to separate male and female worshippers. "The partitions in many of our chapels are a bane to the women," she wrote. Women sit "at the back" or in "a little side room" where "they cannot see the minister" and where they feel as a consequence "that they are not a part of the congregation."[58] What may not have occurred to Fisher was that there was a causal relationship linking gender segregation in Chinese society and her position at the school. Indeed, it was Chinese society's insistence upon separating the sexes that forced missions to create all-girls schools requiring female heads. Men, after all, were forbidden from working closely with the opposite sex. For some female missionaries, writes Jane Hunter, "the gender stratification of Chinese society worked to their benefit."[59] So while the segregated church offended Fisher, the underlying sexism paradoxically provided her with the opportunity to shape an institution with her vision.

In 1886, Fisher got the chance to articulate that vision before an audience. The mission asked her to deliver at its annual conference a paper that answered the single question that had been the source of so much controversy: "How Much Education Shall We Give Our Girls?" Hoping to impress, Fisher worked diligently on her speech. Unfortunately, her placement in the program reflected her lack of seniority: she would give the concluding paper in the last session of the conference's final day. Dead last, she had the "poorest spot on the program." When the session began, Fisher sat on the platform anxiously "clutching my manuscript" as she awaited her turn. But when she scanned the audience, she beheld a discouraging sight. The Chinese pastors had all "dropped off to sleep." "I believed so strongly in my answer to the question," she recalled, that "I was ready to cry." When her turn came, Fisher abandoned her script, choosing to speak spontaneously. "Please all wake up," she commanded, "as I have something important to say." As the "weary ministers" emerged from slumber, each looked "virtuously" around the room as if to ascertain who the inconsiderate offenders were. Once she held everyone's attention, Fisher announced that there would be no speech. "I have prepared a long speech," but "I shall not give it now." She then dropped her "bombshell." In answer to the question "How much education for your girls," Fisher uttered a single phrase: "Exactly as much as you plan for your boys." As the stunned audience tried to process the shocking performance, Fisher took her seat.[60]

Laura Haygood

Fisher and Howe both brought strong wills to their schools. The difference was that Fisher, though always bluntly speaking her mind, also worked well with Chinese pastors and other missionaries. This allowed her to head a school that she called "revolutionary" without facing resistance.[61] Howe, in contrast, clashed with established missionaries and eventually lost control of her school. A third single woman, Laura Haygood, glided with frictionless ease into the plans of an older missionary—Young J. Allen. The near perfect fit was not the result of chance. Allen had studied Haygood from afar and hand-picked her to lead his new school.

Laura Haygood was precocious. Born in 1845 in rural Georgia, she learned to read at the age of four and required only two years to graduate from Wesleyan Female College in 1864. "Everyone knew she had performed a feat," a college friend wrote, "but it seemed perfectly natural that she should do so, for her power was felt." After college, Haygood turned her formidable intellect toward her career ambition—the founding of a school for girls in Atlanta. At this point, however, historical forces intervened: General Sherman's army swept through the state, destroying her family's Atlanta home. What would have been a life-altering calamity for others only delayed Haygood. In 1866, she sold off some of her father's property and used the money to build her school. Haygood ran the school until 1872, when she transferred to a new girls' high school opening in the city. She remained there, both teaching and serving as headmaster, until 1884. That was the year she left for China, having been recruited by Young J. Allen.[62]

Why would a missionary in China notice an obscure educator in Atlanta? For years, Allen had urged missions to develop an effective strategy to target Chinese women. "The degrading systems of the East," Allen wrote, "are based mainly on the condition of woman." If missionaries were to "make any permanent impress on society," they must have access to Chinese women, a task that only female missionaries can accomplish. They alone, he insisted, "can reach the source of evil."[63] But where could Allen locate women capable of advancing his vision? Allen, who hailed from Georgia, enjoyed strong ties with the Southern chapter of the WFMS (SWFMS). Founded in 1878, the SWFMS was led by Mrs. Willie Harding McGavock. Under her leadership, the organization attracted 70,000 members and supported numerous missionaries.[64] Working through McGavock, Allen learned about Haygood, who along with owning an impressive record of school leadership also supported her church's effort to send female missionaries abroad. Haygood did so because she saw missions as advancing two kinds of good: while saving "heathen" souls, missions simultaneously uplifted American women. In 1884, Haygood explained her philosophy in an essay urging young women to put their educations to work in foreign missions. "Do we not too often in our schools shut our girls *out* from the real world with its real needs," Haygood asked, "and shut them *in* to the narrow ways of self and selfish aims?" American society, she argued, shielded young women from the world when it might instead ask them to improve it. "Can we not show women," she continued, "that their refinement and culture are never so resplendent as when they shine in the darkened homes of the poor and the sorrowful?" Haygood, in sum, possessed the right credentials and experience while also espousing a philosophy of female engagement with the world. For Allen's purposes, she was perfect. In 1884, she boarded a steamship with Allen's wife and children and traveled to China under the SWFMS. Before she arrived, Allen found her a living space and even had it whitewashed.[65]

In Shanghai, Haygood had "long conferences" with Allen in which he unveiled his plan. He wished her to open a school—that part she expected—but not the typical missionary school. This one would possess a novel profile. In her essay, Haygood had stressed the noble obligation to care for the "poor and the sorrowful." Ironically, that was *not* the group that Allen's proposed school would serve. The strategically minded Allen believed that missions could not afford to neglect China's wealthy and powerful. His logic went like this. In a hierarchical society like China's, those on top exerted influence over those below. Therefore, if missionaries could convert the wealthy and powerful, Christianity would cascade downward, permeating all social strata. Allen asked Haygood to found a school that would wed the two sides of his vision—Chinese females and elites—by catering to the daughters of Shanghai's upper-class families. Since all other mission schools served the poor, this institution would be unique. "There are no schools now for Chinese girls save those connected with the various Missions," Haygood wrote, "and none of these . . . invite the girls of the higher classes." Haygood fully embraced Allen's model and thought it was viable. "We have every reason to believe," she wrote McGavock, that "there will be a sufficient number of pupils to commence a High School for girls of the better classes . . . whose parents are able and willing to pay."⁶⁶

Why was Haygood so sanguine about the prospects for a tuition-charging institution when, elsewhere, free missionary schools struggled to attract students? Haygood predicted that a model that would likely fail elsewhere would succeed in Shanghai. She explained her theory in a letter to the SWFMS intended to elicit support for the proposed school. "Chinese parents at Shanghai are more willing," she wrote, "than those of any other city in China to have their children taught in foreign schools" because "their prejudices have been to some extent overcome" through "frequent contact with foreigners." Haygood had a point. By the 1880s, Shanghai's Chinese residents had coexisted with foreigners for over three decades. Accustomed to foreigners, they were far less likely to manifest the same aversion to Western institutions that missionaries had witnessed elsewhere. Along with familiarity, Haygood offered one other reason why the novel plan would work. Shanghai parents, "dimly suspecting that schools have something to do with the power that foreigners possess," wish to give their children access to that same power. The SWFMS approved the plan and assisted with fundraising. When the school opened in 1892, it carried the name "McTyeire" in honor of a recently deceased bishop.⁶⁷

What would the school's identity be? This simple question invites a complex answer. What Haygood privately wanted was a school that could unleash the latent potential in girls, producing graduates who harbored a burning social obligation to uplift the less fortunate. Shanghai, after all, needed strong women every bit as much as Atlanta. Her personal wishes notwithstanding, Haygood sensed correctly that, if she were to promote this vision too aggressively, she might appear radical in the eyes of the parents she hoped to attract. They might pass on McTyeire, choosing educational options that presented less risk. Of course, Haygood could also go in the opposite direction by organizing the school around the conservative values of elite families. However, she viewed this option as unsatisfactory for a different reason. Operating with conservative values, McTyeire would enjoy robust enrollment, but would forfeit its mission of female empowerment. Her school would fail to rescue girls from "an aimless life" by helping them "develop a strong, true womanhood."⁶⁸ For Haygood personally, it would mean she had traveled all the way to China to open a finishing school for rich girls. Where was the personal satisfaction in that?

Between these two poles, Haygood tried to find middle ground. She discovered, however, that even a moderate course presented challenges. Some situations required her, for the good of the institution, to tolerate rather than contest Chinese customs grounded in conservative gender roles. She faced exactly this kind of situation right at the school's beginning—the opening reception. Given the school's plan to attract elite families, it made sense to invite Shanghai's wealthy and powerful to the event. Their imprimatur could put the school immediately on the right track. The problem was that Chinese custom allowed only men to attend ceremonial events. This being the case, Haygood had to decide whether to flout custom not just by allowing women to attend *but by being present herself!* Opting to go ahead with the all-male reception, Haygood invited the city's leading citizens, a group that included Nie Qigui, daotai of the Shanghai circuit.[69] Missing from Haygood's list of attendees was Haygood herself. Though absent from her own reception, Haygood remained on the premises and even made an unplanned appearance. After taking a tour, the men retired to the dining hall for refreshments. At this point, Nie Qigui asked to be introduced to the headmaster. To accommodate him while still obeying protocols, Haygood had to think creatively. She slipped into the parlor as her male guests sipped tea in the adjacent dining room. When the double doors separating the two rooms opened, the men rose to their feet and beheld Haygood across the threshold in the neighboring room. She had found a way to be simultaneously with the men and apart from them. Nie Qigui approached her, offered "complimentary remarks," and returned to his "tea and cake." The guests left the reception impressed, and newspapers printed favorable reviews of McTyeire.[70]

There is no record of Haygood commenting on this event. However, she likely viewed it as absurd. If so, the anecdote presents us with a window into her leadership style. That she opted not to protest—choosing instead to smile politely in the face of gender segregation—reveals her remarkable self-control. It is doubtful that Gertrude Howe could have summoned this much restraint. But Haygood tolerated the bizarre custom because she saw that the fortunes of McTyeire hung in the balance. Her calculated decision to suppress her own views paid off: she impressed Shanghai's prominent male citizens, earned favorable press coverage, and ensured the school's successful launch. But by acquiescing to an all-male reception, did Haygood veer too far in the direction of accommodating sexism? Not exactly. The very next day, she held another event—a second opening reception—exclusively for women. This was "the real opening day," a friend observed, "when pupils were received."[71] The pragmatic Haygood, in other words, had chosen a course of action that allowed her to remain mostly true to her principles without sacrificing the needs of the school. This was the sort of delicate balancing act that Haygood performed at McTyeire.

The Chinese families of Shanghai accepted the McTyeire School. When it opened its doors, only seven girls matriculated. Within weeks, a couple more arrived. In ensuing years, enrollments grew to the point where, by 1896, the school had achieved maximum capacity.[72] It was during these early years that Charlie Soong sent the first of three daughters to the school (after graduating from McTyeire, all three studied at Wesleyan, Haygood's alma mater).[73] Having met her enrollment benchmark, Haygood requested funds from the SWFMS to build a new structure. She also asked repeatedly, and ultimately successfully, for more teachers.[74] In 1900, the school moved into a three-story building, spacious enough to handle seventy-five boarders and twenty-five day students. The fathers of many of the girls held influential positions in and around the city.[75] That had been the plan all along. Laura Haygood had brought Young J. Allen's vision to fruition.

Adaline Kelsey

That was how it was supposed to work when an older male missionary worked with a younger female. Unfortunately, not all missionary veterans embraced the mentorship role, or even knew they were supposed to. Calvin Mateer failed to make the accommodations that might have helped Adaline Kelsey succeed. He was at least partly responsible for driving her out of China. Though her career ended prematurely, it started with great promise. Indeed, one would be hard-pressed to imagine a recruit with superior credentials. Originally from upstate New York, Kelsey matriculated at Mount Holyoke where she imbibed Mary Lyon's zeal for Christianity and education. After graduating in 1867, Kelsey stayed on an additional year to teach. Moving next to New York City, she studied at the Woman's Medical College of the New York Infirmary, earning her degree in 1875. A loyal alumna, Dr. Kelsey returned to her alma mater in 1876 to work as resident physician. In 1878, she joined Mount Holyoke's proud tradition by accepting an assignment in Shandong.[76]

Like many Mount Holyoke graduates, Kelsey maintained a deep and abiding affection for her beloved institution. In China, she kept an active correspondence with the college, sending descriptive letters written to be shared with students. In doing so, Kelsey pursued several objectives. First, she used the letters as a recruiting tool. She provided aspiring young women who were contemplating missionary careers with accurate information about life in China.[77] In addition to letters, Kelsey shipped artifacts for display in the campus museum. In this way, the students would receive not just a word picture but also an object lesson in Chinese life.[78] Second, the letters helped her financially. Kelsey urged her "sisters" to raise money so that she "may not be crippled for . . . support" as she labored among the "wretched, sick, and ignorant." By collecting donations, Mount Holyoke supplemented the salary Kelsey received from her board.[79] Third, and perhaps most importantly, the unmarried Kelsey wrote letters because she saw Mount Holyoke as her family. "I have had great comfort in all my wanderings," she wrote, "in knowing that so many & so fervent prayers were going up for me in the dear Holyoke home."[80] In short, strong emotional ties bonded Adaline Kelsey to the school.

The friction between Calvin Mateer and Kelsey did not start immediately. In a stroke of good fortune, the Mateers' departure for America on furlough coincided with Kelsey's arrival. For this reason, she was able to send Mount Holyoke an enthusiastic early report of her new colleagues. "I have found such good friends," she wrote, and "I like all the missionaries here." Though generally favorable, this letter included one curious comment. "The missionaries of Tung Chow are <u>workers</u> not <u>idlers</u>," she wrote, adding underlining for amplification. "They work so enthusiastically that foreign residents in other places say they are quite 'crazy.'" Kelsey had made a discovery: Calvin and Julia Mateer had created a highly pressurized zone of work of such intensity that it could survive in their absence.[81]

Kelsey did not oppose hard work at all. A letter she wrote recounting an itinerating tour in the Shandong interior showed exactly how physically demanding her work could be. In March of 1880, Kelsey headed out with Margaret Capp, a Chinese helper, and several mules. Margaret Capp, formerly Margaret Brown, was the younger sister of Julia Brown Mateer. Like Kelsey, she had come to China as a single woman before marrying Edward Capp. Later widowed, Capp took an immediate liking to Kelsey.[82] As traveling companions, the pair functioned well together partly because Kelsey's medical ability complemented Capp's evangelical skills. After spending four days in a village, Kelsey reported that "125 patients have been healed." She also described Capp's prayer sessions as "well attended" with "many standing in the yard who cannot get in."[83] Through the agency of Capp and Kelsey, Chinese villagers saw modern medicine and Christianity as interlocking parts of the same whole.

Though the letter is sometimes uplifting, it is most remarkable for its gritty realism. For instance, Kelsey was alarmed by the Chinese villagers' disregard for her privacy. She described how they "swarmed" into her room, "crowd around us," "gaze upon us," "comment upon our dress" and "our features," "try on our gloves & our hats," and "explore our pockets." She had not expected such invasive behavior and struggled to countenance it. "They are ... brought up in herds," she wrote with disgust, and "do not know what it means when one wants to be left alone." Kelsey also expressed skepticism as far as conversions were concerned. Though Kelsey saw Capp "surrounded" by "gazers & listeners," she doubted that the Christian faith was making any real progress. She noted that Capp had to wield a bamboo stick during prayer sessions because the "noisy" women and girls would not pay attention unless they received "a little rap on the head." Conversions were hard to obtain when people refused to listen. Kelsey did hold out hope for one promising individual—an educated woman who was "friendly to missionaries" and "influential" in the community. Initially, Kelsey viewed the village matriarch as a prime candidate for conversion. Her hopes were summarily dashed, however, when, one by one, her possessions started disappearing, and she caught the lady in the act of stealing. "As far as can be seen," Kelsey concluded, "the Word has not yet taken any deep root in their hearts."[84]

Kelsey's letter also made one point abundantly clear: insufficient rest, unremitting work, and the strain of travel were wearing her down. Partway into the trip, she described herself as "utterly exhausted, mind, body & spirit." Later, when Capp was away visiting another village, Kelsey's health collapsed. "I am left alone" in a "dark, damp & dismal" room "laid up with a sore throat and neuralgia of head and face." As sharp pain shot through her head, Kelsey urgently required rest. She barred the door and drew the curtain so as "to keep their peering black eyes from looking in." Despite her efforts to attain privacy, the Chinese continued to seek her out for medical attention. Grudgingly, Kelsey reopened her temporary clinic and, after treating an additional fifty patients, headed back to Tengchow.[85]

It was after returning to the mission that Kelsey wrote Mount Holyoke. The letter she produced was a strikingly ambivalent one in which competing narratives coexisted in a state of tension. On the one hand, she described missionary work optimistically as offering young women the chance to perform God's work. However, she also saw fit—given her own exhaustion and sickness—to admonish readers about the danger to health posed by the strenuous lifestyle. Sadly, she informed them, a missionary might not realize she is "breaking down" until "it is too late to mend." Kelsey complained of so much hardship in the letter that the young readers must have collectively scratched their heads. Did the author truly intend, as was Kelsey's ostensible purpose, to inspire other Holyoke women to join her in China? Or did she really mean to dissuade them from missionary careers by conveying the grueling nature of the work? Or perhaps a third possibility more closely approximated the truth. The letter may simply have reflected the struggling author's need for compassion and sympathy.[86]

She would receive neither from Calvin Mateer. The trouble began after he returned from furlough in 1881. By this time, Kelsey had started to break down. As she descended into depression, she needed the helping hand of a veteran in the field. Calvin Mateer offered no support. Instead, he and Julia accused Kelsey of being "lazy" and of refusing to execute her share of duties. How can one explain his callous response to her plight? Calvin Mateer was one of those indefatigable people who derived all satisfaction in life from work. As such, he could neither understand nor tolerate an associate who could not maintain his relentless pace. He also existed as something of a medical anomaly. In Shandong, where disease sent many missionaries to early graves, Calvin Mateer lived over four decades without once becoming seriously ill. The man of iron had trouble empathizing with someone of a weaker constitution.[87]

Calvin Mateer also worked poorly with single women. That, according to Irwin Hyatt, was the unavoidable interpretation of Kelsey herself. Unlike Gertrude Howe, who insisted on doing things her own way, Kelsey showed a willingness to work within a system put in place by others. But she was still a single female, a missionary category looked upon with suspicion by Mateer and other members of the old guard. When Kelsey showed signs of frailty, that old guard did not hesitate to make her life unbearable. In a letter to her board, Kelsey complained of "overt acts of tyranny and oppression" committed by her colleagues, singling out the men in particular. "The gentlemen here," she wrote indignantly, "act as though they hold as a *principle* the idea that a lady and *most especially* a *single* lady has no right which a *white* man or a *yellow* man either is bound to respect." In her view, the men of the Shandong mission, Chinese and American alike, fostered a culture of hostility to single women. As Kelsey made her exit, she urged the board to "never again send an unprotected lady to this place."[88] If the stories of Fisher, Howe, and Haygood show how single women could change missions from within, Adaline Kelsey's experience exists in counterbalance as a cautionary tale. The rigors of the work and the opposition of older missionaries could overwhelm even someone as earnest and well-trained as her.

Conclusion

With Adaline Kelsey, Calvin Mateer revealed himself to be coldly unsympathetic to a single woman. He was at least consistent. He did not relax his standards when dealing with his own kin. Lillian Mateer, his younger sister by over two decades, learned this lesson the hard way. After graduating from Mount Holyoke, Lillian taught school for several years before deciding to venture to China as a single woman with her brother Robert. Though she had flirted with marriage twice prior to her departure, both engagements had fallen through. The two siblings planned on long careers in their older brother's Shandong mission. That was the expectation. For Lillian, the reality turned out differently. While many single women flourished in missions, Lilian was not one of them. Her emotional instability brought drama to the mission—and drama was what Calvin Mateer despised most. Missions were all about work, he believed, and an individual's inability to control her emotions created a distraction that pulled others away from their work. Thus, one person's dysfunction had the potential to disrupt the efficiency of the entire group. Lillian, in short, lacked that interior gyroscope that brother Calvin deemed essential to a productive missionary career. In Shandong, Lillian tried to convince herself that she was content to remain single, but she was only deluding herself. She impulsively rushed into marriage with a Baptist missionary despite receiving the stern and unequivocal disapproval of Calvin.[89] Calvin declared Lillian to be a "failure" of whom he was "thoroughly ashamed." How did the sad saga end? After the newlyweds moved to Shanghai, Lillian's husband lost his mind, thus forcing the couple to leave China forever. Calvin paid their fare to America before forwarding the bill to the Baptist Mission.[90]

Though Adaline Kelsey and Lillian Mateer left China prematurely, many single women enjoyed long careers. After its inception in 1869, the WFMS expanded rapidly. By the mid-1890s, nearly 600,000 American women belonged to either the WFMS or societies like it, more than had joined either suffrage or temperance societies.[91] The addition of these women's boards succeeded in tipping the overall gender balance in foreign missions. Jane Hunter points out that, by 1890, the number of single and married women accounted for 60 percent of all missionaries in the field. There was, in her words, a "feminization of the force."[92] Many of the young female recruits—like Howe, Fisher, and Haygood—ran schools for girls. That said, Dr. Adaline Kelsey was not an outlier. As the next chapter shows, single female doctors also came to China to serve Christ and humanity.

9

Transforming Health

Female Doctors Enter Medical Missions

In 1884, Adele Fielde and two other women sat in an auditorium at Blockley Hospital in Philadelphia waiting to hear a lecture on medical science from a professor who was nowhere to be seen. Surrounding the three women were 150 male medical students—who were starting to get impatient. As the minutes ticked by, the increasingly restless young men entertained themselves by making a "noisy demonstration" aimed at the "delinquent teacher." When this source of amusement lost its appeal, they shifted their "playful" ridicule to a new target—away from the overdue lecturer and toward the women. The three females, the hecklers reasoned, would not dare fight back. They did not reckon with Adele Fielde.

Fielde rose to her feet to address her mockers. "Gentlemen," she began politely but with evident force. "I have for eighteen years been a missionary in China. The Chinese have no medical science, and superstitious rites are chiefly relied on in the treatment of disease." As the men sat in stunned silence, Fielde expounded upon the dire medical situation in China. She explained how Chinese women lived in desperate need of gynecological attention since custom forbade male physicians from treating "any disease peculiar to her sex." Family members would rather let an ailing woman live in "agony" or "die" than allow a male doctor to treat her. What did the grave situation in China have to do with her attendance at this lecture? She hoped to find in "our great medical schools" some "self-sacrificing young women" willing to enlist in a "work of mercy in Asia." As Fielde took her seat, the men erupted in cheers. One man, speaking for the others, promised that his peers would never again "annoy" women seeking medical careers. The latter had won their "respect and sympathy."[1]

In Philadelphia, Fielde was preparing for the next phase of her missionary career. Like the previous phase, this one would involve innovation. She aspired to equip Chinese women not just with Bible stories but with medical know-how—specifically obstetrics. Her plan, though inspired, would be only partially successful. As this chapter details, health problems and personal turmoil overwhelmed her attempt to reimagine women's missionary work along medical lines. Her stumble, however, did not extinguish this idea, because she was not its lone torchbearer. John Kerr also played a pioneering role in advancing women's medicine. He started admitting female students to his medical school and recruited two women doctors from the United States to treat female patients in the Canton Hospital. These two women, Mary Niles and Mary Fulton, would follow Kerr's example by establishing institutions of their own in Canton.

Adele Fielde's New Horizons

After the 1877 conference, Adele Fielde experienced two epiphanies that compelled her to remap her career. First, her extensive experience with Chinese women taught her that this group required far more medical attention than they were receiving. While stateside on furlough in 1883, Fielde endeavored to recruit women doctors for missions. She also sought training for herself. Given the high death rates of Chinese mothers and infants during childbirth, Fielde identified obstetrics as the area of most urgent need. To address that need, she took courses at the Woman's Medical College of Pennsylvania with one goal in mind: to receive the knowledge that would allow her to train the Bible-women to be midwives as well as evangelists. If her female army could offer this vital service, missions could save lives and further ingratiate themselves with the population.[2]

As her second epiphany, Fielde discovered Charles Darwin. Her reading of *The Origin of Species* forced her to question the Biblical account of Creation. Throughout her life, she had accepted the Garden of Eden story as factually accurate, going so far as to translate a simplified version for her Bible-women.[3] Yet exposure to Darwinism shook the foundations of her beliefs. She came to view the Book of Genesis as "poetic but not true." More shockingly (for a missionary), she described the entire Bible as offering "great wisdom but imperfect knowledge." In contrast to her colleagues in Swatow, who regarded Darwin as sacrilege, Fielde described herself as possessing "a great intellectual hunger" to know more of Biology and Evolution. To satisfy her craving, Fielde approached the men of science affiliated with Philadelphia's Academy of Natural Sciences. While describing her "quest," she impressed them with her conviction. "My talks with these scientists," Fielde recalled, forced them to confront the embarrassing fact that a woman interested in biology "had no place in which to study . . . in Philadelphia."[4] The city's medical community, averse to the concept of women in medicine, had not welcomed women into its institutions.[5] To rectify the problem, the Academy agreed to establish a biology department at the University of Pennsylvania open to women. In the meantime, the scientists granted Fielde unrestricted access to their library and laboratory. "I studied and dissected twenty-six classes of animals from amoeba to mammals," she wrote, and had "help whenever I needed" from the scientists. "I got a new mental horizon." This was not your typical missionary furlough.[6]

The furlough was typical in one way: her missionary society put her to work. In America, Fielde found that her reputation preceded her. Baptists knew all about the dynamic lady who had, on her own initiative, trained an army of fearless Bible-women. They wished to meet her in the flesh, and her board happily obliged. It set up an extensive lecture tour that included visits to major cities. Following a grueling itinerary, Fielde slogged across the country, delivering presentations in one city after another. In each venue, she would educate and entertain the eager audience by sharing her personal experiences among the Chinese. Though the attention was flattering, audiences wanted more of Fielde than she was physically and emotionally able to give. They siphoned off her strength. Fame, she learned the hard way, was a double-edged sword. In all, she made 150 appearances over a five-month period, logging thousands of miles of travel. The experience broke her. Unable to continue, Fielde directed her manager to accept no further engagements[7] and proceeded to suffer a "nervous breakdown."[8]

When Fielde returned to Swatow in 1885, she no longer possessed the passion, drive, and energy that had previously fueled her work. While she did train some Bible-women in obstetrics, she had lost all motivation for evangelical work. In her mind, Darwinism eclipsed the Bible as the intellectual authority, and she found herself more interested in collecting specimens of rocks, plants, and bugs than in spreading the Gospel.[9] Other problems, some of her own making, contributed further to her discontent. Her aging body began to ache, and she complained often and loudly about her colleagues, creating discord in the mission. After Eliza Ashmore, her closest friend, departed China terminally ill, the lonely Fielde struggled "to fill the void."[10] Unfortunately, she filled the vacuum with conflict, entering into an ugly feud with a missionary wife that gave her anxiety attacks. "If you knew the terror I suffer when I think of going to missionary meetings," she informed the board, "you would remember the nervous breakdown" that had caused her to cut short her American tour. A similar collapse, she implied, was imminent.[11] To make matters worse, her health was slowly deteriorating. For months she suffered from a nagging throat infection. A missionary doctor diagnosed her also as having edema in the legs, which caused them to swell, and cardiac troubles, which gave her chest pains and shortness of breath. Adele Fielde was breaking down.[12]

The final straw came in 1888 when Fielde published an article in a medical journal. Newly connected to the scientific community, Fielde wished to make her own contribution to medical knowledge. Though her ambition may have been noble, she selected a topic that could only stir up controversy: an account of her experiment smoking hashish in Thailand in 1868. "In the midst of this radiance and beauty I was infinitely joyous," Fielde wrote rhapsodically in the article. "Every atom in me quivered in unspeakable spiritual bliss," as she realized, "I am now in heaven." Baptists were not fond of articles, especially written by one of their own, describing spiritual experiences achieved through hallucinogenic substances. Though the board had tolerated Fielde's eccentricities until now, this breach in decorum was more than it could bear. It had had enough of Adele Fielde, and the feeling was mutual. In 1889, Fielde tendered her resignation in a conciliatory letter to her board. "Ever since . . . I found myself in appalling desolation alone on the shore of Asia," she wrote, you have "tried to be a kind husband to me."[13]

For her valedictory, Fielde traveled to Shanghai in 1890 to attend the General Conference of the Protestant Missionaries of China. A sequel to the pivotal 1877 meeting, the conference attracted over four hundred missionaries from across China. On the first day, attendees gathered for a group photograph intended to commemorate the event while also signifying the spirit of unity animating the denominationally diverse group. That was the plan, anyway. But when hundreds of missionaries climbed onto a makeshift platform supported by bamboo scaffolding, the rickety structure started to sway ominously under their collective weight. And then, disaster. The "whole structure doubled up like a fan," one missionary wrote, "piling men and women, young and old, in one mass . . . seven or eight deep." In assessing the damage, he found that many had "received cuts, bruises or sprains," and "a few wounds were serious," though none so grave as to "endanger life."[14]

The conference delivered other unscripted moments, though none as visually spectacular. Fielde flummoxed her colleagues by sharing a baffling essay on Bible-women, a subject that had earned her accolades in 1877. But Fielde had changed in the intervening thirteen years. In 1877, a self-confident Fielde had boldly thrust her new evangelical model before an unexpecting body; in 1890, missionaries beheld a jaded woman retrospectively assessing her work before bowing out. Fielde's essay joined a session that also included a contribution from Laura Haygood, then planning her school. If Haygood's star was rising, then Fielde's showing left no doubt she had entered rapid decline. No longer interested in promoting Bible-women, Fielde candidly conveyed the results of her once hopeful experiment. Though acknowledging the admirable effort put forth by the Chinese women, Fielde reached the conclusion that, after "many years," there has been "no marked increase of church-membership that could be traced directly to [their] labors." If these dismal findings were not surprising enough, her next words stunned the gathering: "Were I now beginning a similar enterprise, I would pay no native for evangelistic work."[15]

Conference attendees were taken aback. Had Adele Fielde conceded failure? Was she advising missionaries *not* to follow her model? One by one, confused missionaries sought clarity. "I wish to call attention to the last point in Miss Fielde's paper," spoke John Nevius, who proceeded to read aloud the paragraph from Fielde's paper that had bewildered him. She "advises others against the plan she herself followed," Calvin Mateer interjected, but "her advice carries very little weight." Mateer explained that he refused to accept guidance from anyone who takes up a "line of work," promotes it "vigorously," makes it a "hobby," and then, "when it seems to fail," instructs "others not to follow their example." "Let us hear" instead, he insisted, from those who have "employed Bible-women and made their employment a success." Mateer's harsh critique, especially his use of the word "hobby," struck a nerve in William Ashmore. "We do not consider Miss Fielde's work as a hobby," he snapped back, and "intend to keep it up." While fending off Mateer, Ashmore could not hide his own alarm. To mitigate the damage, he attempted to explain away the perplexing paper by offering context: Fielde had composed it in an unhealthy mental state. "Miss Fielde's essay was written when she was unwell," he revealed, "and she has done injustice to herself." As final acts go, this was a sad one. In 1890, Fielde departed China never to return.[16]

In making her exit Fielde strayed from established norms, as she had done consistently throughout her career. However, her idea to deploy female medical practitioners aligned with a new imperative shaping China missions: to send women trained in medicine into Chinese homes. No one understood this need better than John Kerr, who launched two important initiatives designed to give his hospital greater access to female patients.

Female Medical Students in Canton

In the spring of 1878, the sky above Canton turned ashen gray as the city bore witness to a meteorological event that was rare for this part of the world—a tornado. For two minutes, wrote a missionary, the churning and howling twister cut a swath of destruction three hundred yards wide, demolishing "everything in its way" and "burying thousands of people in ruins." "The appearance of the whirlwind in the distance," he wrote in language recalling the Old Testament, "was like a great pillar of smoke reaching from the earth to the sky." The Chinese also dipped into their storehouse of myths to explain the unruly visitor. To them, the serpentine funnel cloud, with its "twisting and writhing" movement, "resembled a dragon" that was "taking his flight across the country." In the end, parts of the city were turned upside down. To help with the humanitarian crisis, a benevolent institution asked one of Kerr's first medical students to open a temporary hospital.[17]

The next year, Canton experienced a second upheaval of sorts, this one occurring in the medical profession. A family summoned John Kerr for a routine house call—a woman was experiencing pain in her urinary tract. Kerr's handling of the call, however, was anything but routine. Instead of going himself or sending a male doctor, Kerr dispatched a new kind of medical practitioner, one never before seen in China:

> I sent one of the female medical pupils to relieve her, as it would be more in accordance with Chinese ideas of propriety to have a female attendant in such a case. This female pupil had become familiar with the operation in attending to one of the ovariotomy cases. This is doubtless the first instance in which an operation so easy and so necessary in many cases, was ever performed by a Chinese Woman.[18]

In his records, Kerr adopted a matter-of-fact, even nonchalant, tone that belied the stunning nature of the case. After all, he was reporting what we might call a "first"—the first known surgical operation in history performed by a Chinese woman. Who was this female pupil, and how did she enter Kerr's orbit?

The young woman came from a nearby school for girls founded in 1872 by Harriet Noyes. Noyes was a Presbyterian from Ohio who sailed for China in 1868. On the vessel, she met John Kerr, then returning from furlough.[19] Four years later, she opened the True Light Seminary, a school for girls situated in close proximity to the Canton Hospital. One year later, Martha Noyes, her sister, joined her at the school.[20] In 1879, two students approached Harriet with a novel proposition. Studying in the shadow of the Canton Hospital, they had become, according to Noyes, "imbued with the desire to study medicine." They wished to matriculate at Kerr's South China Medical School.[21]

One of the students had arrived at this juncture after enduring a life of hardship. Mui Ah-Kwai was the daughter of her father's third wife. After losing his money gambling, her father sent his wives and sons away because he could no longer afford to care for them. He sold his daughters for cash. Two years after her initial sale, Mui was purchased once again, this time by a man who took her to Canton. In the city, he promptly sold her to another man seeking a wife. This man—her third owner—left her in Canton while he embarked for California to seek his fortune. In America, instead of gold he found death. Though the story becomes murky at this point, Mui ended up at True

Light, where she converted to Christianity. She also appears to have imbibed the school's vision—that women could, through education, achieve independence and lead accomplished lives. Though Mui had never seen a female doctor (because there weren't any), she somehow got the idea to become one herself.[22] It was at this point that she and a friend approached Noyes with the radical proposition. Since "this was an entirely new idea for a Chinese woman," Noyes weighed the "pros and cons" before broaching the idea with Kerr. Taking no time to deliberate, Kerr placed the two in medical classes, "promising them the same advantages . . . that the young men received."[23]

That Kerr agreed to the proposal so quickly suggests he had considered the idea before. Having practiced in China for twenty-five years, Kerr knew that Chinese men benefited from far more medical care than Chinese women. Indeed, if we examine his records for 1879, we note a substantial disparity. For those Kerr categorized as "out-patient," the hospital treated 14,226 men and 2,683 women, with female patients accounting for 16 percent of all cases. For those he classified as "in-patient," the hospital treated 832 men and 308 women, with female patients constituting 27 percent of the total.[24] Why did the ratios skew so heavily toward male patients? According to historian Guangqiu Xu, social mores prevented Chinese women from easily seeing male doctors. A Chinese woman "was not supposed to meet men not in her family," Xu writes, thus rendering it difficult for her to be "thoroughly examined—even touched—by a general practitioner."[25] How could a physician overcome this social obstacle? The answer, Kerr realized, was to train Chinese women to treat female patients. "Two of the female students," Kerr remarked, "give promise of being very useful . . . in the Hospital."[26] Three more True Light students enrolled shortly after the first two, and a steady flow continued.[27]

Though excited by the advantages afforded by female practitioners, Kerr was not blind to the explosive potential of his experiment in the community. Conservative Chinese might easily view female medical students as a violation of societal gender roles. Wishing to avoid trouble, Kerr adopted two policies intended to show proper sensitivity. First, he divided his classroom by sex and installed a heavy curtain between male and female students. Second, he forbade male students from participating in the clinical side of gynecology and from inspecting the female body up close. By draping his radical admissions policy in the familiar garb of conservative gender propriety, Kerr hoped to placate potential critics. For several years, the school adhered to these rules and avoided protest.[28]

In 1886, Kerr abruptly changed course. He did so, interestingly, after hearing the arguments of a new student who had come to him seeking more than medical knowledge. Physicians like Kerr, with their powers of healing, could appear incandescent on the Chinese landscape. As sources of light, they attracted the occasional moth fluttering about in the darkness. In 1886, a young man named Sun Wen appeared at the Canton Hospital searching for answers to big questions. *What kind of knowledge can enable China's rise? What career should I personally pursue?* To Sun Wen, the two questions were linked: he understood his own life as inextricably tied to the fortunes of his nation. Convinced that Western doctors possessed answers, Sun enrolled in Kerr's medical school. He would later go by a different name—Sun Yat-sen.

Up until this juncture, Sun Yat-sen had struggled to find his purpose in life. He yearned vaguely to help China return to its former status but was unsure what form his contribution would assume. In this respect, he resembled Yung Wing, whom he would come to admire. After the 1911 Revolution, Sun would even reach out to Yung and ask him to assist in building a new republic.[29] But in 1886, Sun had not committed himself to revolution or, for that matter, to any specific solution to China's ills. He was a seeker. He felt certain that part of China's problem was that its adherence to the past—to old traditions, bodies of knowledge, and bureaucratic structures—blocked the modernization the nation sorely needed. However, he did not always express this view constructively. For example, in 1883, while still a teenager, he returned to the village of his birth with a friend, Lu Haodong. This was no social call. The two vandalized a temple, smashing all of its idols. Two years later in Hong Kong, Sun struck up a friendship with Charles Hager, an American missionary. Hager baptized Sun and brought him along when he preached. Though Hager hoped Sun would become a minister, Sun recognized—as Yung Wing had earlier—that Christianity alone could not save China. He was drawn instead to medicine, which seemed to offer a more direct conduit to the West's power. In 1886, Hager provided Sun with the reference letter that secured his admission to Kerr's medical school.[30]

Sun would study there for only one year. However, his decision to depart was not precipitated by any dissatisfaction with the school.[31] Sun respected the "venerable Dr. Kerr" and enjoyed the latter's medical lectures. He left in order to seize an opportunity to study at a new medical school opening in Hong Kong.[32] Before his departure, Sun approached Kerr to discuss gender segregation at the school. He contended that Kerr should not try to accommodate or placate the Confucianists because they discriminated against women. To this argument, he added a practical consideration. Since male doctors would eventually have to treat female patients, did it make sense professionally to deny them training in gynecology? Kerr recognized the merit of these points. The curtain came down.[33]

Mary Niles

Kerr's new focus on the underserved female population also brought a personnel change to the hospital. The "seclusion and modesty of the female,"

Kerr observed, had opened "an unlimited field in China for the Lady Physician."[34] Hoping to secure one, he urged his board to send female doctors.[35] The board obligingly dispatched Mary Niles, an unmarried woman from Wisconsin who had recently graduated from the Woman's Medical College of the New York Infirmary. After reaching Canton in 1882, Niles took up residence at True Light and immediately commenced assisting Kerr in the hospital.[36]

Why did Mary Niles pursue overseas missions instead of practicing at home? Though we must not discount Niles's spiritual motivation, compelling professional reasons likely influenced her decision. In the latter half of the nineteenth century, medical education in the United States underwent a transformation, becoming more systematic, credential-based, and institutionalized within universities. Women, according to Regina Morantz-Sanchez, did not figure in the new paradigm. "When universities took charge ... and legal standards of qualification were established," she writes, "women were excluded" because "no one thought of them as either able or willing to submit to the new conditions imposed." But women were willing. In fact, most of them strongly preferred joining men in coeducational schools to separating in single-sex institutions. They wished to study alongside men, enjoy access to the same resources, and be judged according to the same standards. Elizabeth Blackwell, the first woman to receive a medical degree from an American institution, held this view. She and others feared that the forced segregation of the sexes would result in women attending inferior institutions. "Isolated groups of women," wrote Blackwell's colleague Mary Putnam Jacobi, "cannot maintain the same intellectual standards as are established and maintained by men."[37]

When most universities decided to deny admission to women, Blackwell had no choice but to establish a separate institution. In 1868, she founded the Woman's Medical College as a part of the New York Infirmary for Women and Children. Though harboring doubts about their school's viability, Blackwell and Jacobi proved their own fears to be unfounded. They oversaw an institution that offered an education equivalent to what the men were receiving. They achieved this goal by forcing their institution to meet the highest standards of their profession. Blackwell even arranged for a board of examiners, composed of New York's most respected physicians, to evaluate and approve each student before she could graduate. Mary Niles, in short, completed a program every bit as rigorous as those undertaken by men.[38]

Though trained as thoroughly as men, Niles and other female doctors did not enjoy comparable professional opportunities. As women tried to launch private practices or secure hospital positions, they lacked the connections of their male counterparts. Indeed, until the 1870s, most professional associations barred women from membership. The American Medical Association, the organization most responsible for regulating medicine in the country, did not allow female members until 1915. Nor was the discrimination limited to their profession. Women doctors also faced a society biased in favor of male practitioners; when presented with a choice, prospective patients often expressed a preference for men. Given the challenging landscape, most women expected to take between two and five years to establish themselves. Simply put, it was difficult to gain a foothold in a profession dominated by men.[39]

By choosing foreign missions, Mary Niles bypassed this difficult early stage. Not only did the mission defray the cost of education, it also placed her in a position where she could immediately enjoy relevance and command respect. That was because China possessed a vast female population that male doctors were unable to serve consistently. Since the "need was obvious," writes Jessie Lutz, female doctors "gained general acceptance in China before they did in the West."[40] "The missionary enterprise offered adventurous women the opportunity to practice a far wider range of skills than at home," agrees Michelle Renshaw. "They were more likely to be able to work as equals with men... rather than as handmaidens."[41] Though neither foreign missions nor Chinese society was immune to sexism, the glaring demand for female physicians tended to overpower prejudice. In China, Mary Niles could achieve a status that would have been tough to obtain in the United States—that of a medical authority.

John Kerr seems to have treated her as such. He welcomed Niles to the hospital and commented favorably on her impact. "The patients," Kerr wrote in his annual report for 1883, "appreciated the advantage of having a physician of their own sex." Specifically, Kerr cited Niles's invaluable assistance in three difficult childbirths and two removals of cancerous tumors from ovaries. Since Kerr had not received patients with ovarian tumors before, these cases provided clear evidence of Niles's utility: she could attract a type of patient who, previously, would have stayed away, choosing "suffering" over "modern medical science."[42]

In the ensuing years Niles's role only expanded—sometimes out of necessity. At the end of 1883, Kerr announced sad news to the hospital staff: "My health broke down."[43] Taking temporary leave, he departed Canton with his wife, Isabella. After the couple reached America, Kerr recovered but Isabella fell ill and died.[44] In Kerr's absence, Niles took on greater responsibility. She earned the title Lady Physician to the Canton Hospital and opened a dispensary for women and children. In the 1885 annual report, which Niles authored in Kerr's absence, she described the highlights of her practice. "Thirteen times during the year," she recorded, "I have been implored to perform instrumental delivery in obstetrical cases." By "instrumental," she meant that the difficulty of the cases had required her to use surgical tools to extract the fetus. The thirteen cases included one embryotomy, the challenging operation Wong Fun had performed twenty-five years earlier. Niles also removed a twenty-three-pound tumor from a woman's back.[45]

In 1886, John Kerr returned to China a widower. He did not hold that marital status for long, marrying Martha Noyes later that year.[46] Even with Kerr present, Niles's role did not diminish. Since Chinese women preferred to receive a female physician in the privacy of their homes, Niles made house calls. "Attending patients at their homes is becoming an important part of our work," read the report for 1889, "and as these calls are for the most part for females the larger part are attended to by Dr. Niles." That year, Niles made 247 house calls, 47 for difficult child births and 200 for "other cases of sickness."[47] Starting in 1887, she coauthored annual reports with John Kerr.[48] To help supporters back home understand her work, she described a typical week in a letter to a women's missionary magazine. Amid the tumor and cyst removals, cataract surgeries, breast amputations, and house calls, readers could not miss the letter's main point: Mary Niles was far busier in China than she would have been if she had remained in America. Given the incredible demand for women doctors, Niles fittingly ended her letter by referencing a request she had made to her board: send "another lady physician."[49]

Mary Fulton

Two years after Niles started in Canton, the Presbyterian Board sent a second female doctor to join her. In 1884, Mary Fulton graduated from the Woman's Medical College of Pennsylvania before embarking for China with her brother Albert and his wife and child. In Canton, Fulton sought out Mary Niles. "As Dr. Mary Niles is the only other lady physician in this province," Fulton wrote, "I was keenly anxious to meet her." Niles did not lose any time helping her new colleague become oriented; she invited Fulton to observe operations at the hospital and took her along on house calls.[50] Had Fulton come to China alone, she probably would have remained in Canton and become, in a sense, a second Mary Niles. As it was, she was attached to her brother, and he harbored a burning desire to proselytize in the interior.

But where in the interior? To answer that question, the Fultons gathered around a map and discussed the tactical advantages of various sites. While studying the locations of existing Christian outposts, they made a key observation. Guangxi Province, situated to the west of Guangdong, possessed a population of eight million but, so far, had not received a single missionary. "As there is not a missionary in the province," Mary Fulton wrote, "we think we should try to start work there." It was a logical choice but, for Fulton, a somewhat ominous one. "I hesitated about going," she recalled, because the province was "notoriously hostile" to foreigners. Undaunted, Albert ventured out alone on a reconnaissance expedition. After returning, he announced that he had rented rooms in Guiping, a city two hundred miles west of Canton. "With the aid of medicine," Mary Fulton wrote, Albert "thinks we may gain a foothold in the city." This, in other words, would be a brother-sister operation: he would provide the Gospel while she handled the healing.[51]

In 1885, John Kerr escorted the Fultons on their long journey to the remote city they would call home. As the party departed, Harriet Noyes expressed skepticism about the venture. "No one excepting themselves," she wrote, "has much faith in their success."[52] The Fultons were joined by two of Kerr's graduates—Mui Ah-Kwai and Leung Kin Cho, a young man of twenty-two years. While packing his trunk, Leung curiously stowed away a human skull—a remnant from Kerr's Anatomy class. He would later regret this decision. Arriving in Guiping by the Xi River, Mary Fulton stepped off the boat with trepidation. "Never before had a white woman, nor a white baby been there," she said, referring to herself, Albert's wife Florence, and the infant Edith. The home base Albert had rented fell well short of minimum standards for a medical practice. "The floors are mud," she recorded, "and there are no windows" and "no ceilings," just the clay tiles of the roof overhead. Once Fulton had established her rudimentary hospital, John Kerr prepared to depart. During this poignant farewell, Fulton felt a powerful foreboding—"our bridges were burned." But since there was no turning back and "much land to be possessed" for Christ, Fulton and the others "threw" themselves "whole-heartedly into the work." As Albert preached to anyone who would listen, Florence mainly cared for Edith. Dr. Leung treated male patients in the makeshift hospital while also preaching. Mui Ah-Kwai, trained as both a Bible-woman and a physician, assisted Fulton with female patients. "She knew just how to talk to the unlettered women," Fulton said of Mui. While Mui could tend to both medical and evangelical matters, Fulton, who was still learning the language, practiced medicine exclusively.[53]

Experiencing the "real" China for the first time, Fulton tried hard to adjust to the local culture. Sensing that a single misunderstanding could spark violence, she made a point of treading cautiously around popular superstitions. "We have to be careful of every word and movement," she wrote. "Should we stop to read the inscription on a gravestone we would be accused of wanting to rob graves." She added that here, as elsewhere, some Chinese "believe we take children's eyes for medicine." Guiping was full of dangerous trip wires. Fulton also made an effort to respect customs, even those with which she disagreed. For example, though she did not wish to receive gifts from grateful patients, she knew it was impolite to refuse. The best thing to do was simply to accept graciously whatever showed up at the door, whether that be a duck, a chicken, a goat, or a pig. One thankful patient sent a water buffalo that, Fulton was told, had to be taken indoors at night since wild cats roamed about. Presumably, it joined the missionaries during the evenings. Other aspects of the local culture filled her with shock and horror. Fulton was appalled that people would eat reptiles and mammals under the assumption that they would absorb a creature's powers; a "serpent" increased one's wisdom, they believed, and a "tiger" could "make one brave." She also encountered infanticide. After delivering one newborn girl, Fulton returned the next day to check on the mother and child. "When I inquired for the little girl," the mother replied that she "had thrown 'it' in the river." That woman confessed she had "disposed of" four other girls in this fashion, lacking the rice to feed them.[54]

Fulton also had experiences that lifted her spirits. One day, a poor shoemaker who had gone blind visited the hospital. Fulton informed him that she could restore his vision, so long as he agreed to cataract surgery. After he consented, she cleaned her "tiny mud hospital" as best she could. Along with the challenge of creating a sterile space, Fulton faced one other problem: she had never performed cataract surgery. "I had seen it skillfully performed in Philadelphia," she recollected, "but to do it alone, hundreds of miles from another doctor, was different." Though caution dictated against the risky operation, Fulton went ahead. Her gamble paid off. When the bandages came off, the man could see—much to his elation and Fulton's relief. As he spread word of the miracle, the blind started lining up outside the hospital, as did people with other maladies. By 1886, Fulton guessed that she had seen four thousand patients. "Medicine seems to be the key," she offered, "that is opening all the doors to high and low, rich and poor."[55]

Her practice flourishing and her outlook brightening, Fulton elected to move her practice to a more suitable facility. "I greatly feel the need of a hospital," she wrote. "Without it I can undertake no serious operations." Fulton purchased a plot on a hill surrounded by bamboo, and construction on a new building began. This was a big step, and one a missionary would take only if she felt assured of her long-term safety. Thanks to the good will she was earning through her practice, her fears with regard to the region's reputation for xenophobia had largely subsided. "Our immediate environment is now friendly," she wrote optimistically, "hostility and suspicion being slowly disarmed."[56]

Fulton had spoken too soon. A piece of terrible luck aroused the dormant antiforeign sentiment. As the new hospital facility neared completion, the magistrate raised taxes on local gambling houses, prompting many to close their doors. With nowhere to go, "multitudes" of gamblers, men Fulton described as "fellows of the baser sort," flowed out into the streets "ready for any diversion." They mingled with a group of high-minded literati who happened to be in town to take the civil service examination. Out of this mixing, a combustible synergy resulted. The "proud students" convinced the disgruntled gamblers to "drive out" the "foreign devils." When Albert noticed that some Chinese were behaving in a "radically different" manner toward him, he knew something nefarious was brewing. After instructing Mary and the others to shut themselves in the new hospital, he set off with Leung for the magistrate's office to request armed protection.

That was when trouble began. While en route, Albert walked into a hailstorm of rocks. "The stones struck him on feet, legs, back and head," Mary wrote. "They were hurled with such force that he would have been killed" had his hat not absorbed some of the impact. Though wounded by the bombardment, Albert managed to reach the magistrate's office where "he was dragged in" by a staff that had to "beat back the rabble with the bamboo rods." After Albert explained that he must return to the hospital to help his family, the magistrate "utterly refused." Albert, he insisted, would meet with "certain death" were he to venture out. Instead, the magistrate assigned an armed guard to escort Leung back to the hospital to rescue the others.[57]

Rescuing was exactly what this group needed. Huddled inside the new facility, the missionaries waited nervously. Unbeknownst to them, the students had posted signs around the city directing everyone, at an appointed time, "to carry a bundle of straw" to the "House of Ghosts," meaning the new hospital. They planned to "set fire" to it. In response to the signs, a large crowd massed, in Leung's words, like "ants on a lump of sugar."[58] It did not take long for the crowd to devolve into a mob. When Mary Fulton heard a loud "crash" outside the building, she knew the mob had broken through the bamboo encircling the compound. The siege had begun. The unruly group next "hurled" onto the roof "heavy stones" causing clay tiles to fall in crumbled pieces over the beleaguered missionaries. The mob also tried to force open the front door but failed; Fulton had alertly spied a pile of unused iron rods and used them to buttress the door. Failing to break in, the mob shifted strategies, electing to smoke the foreigners out. At each entrance, men lit piles of dry straw on fire. Unable to breathe, the missionaries had no recourse except to surrender. The "roar of the flames and the smoke," Fulton wrote, "at last forced us to walk out in their midst." Resigning herself to her fate, Fulton took Albert's infant daughter in her arms and exited the building. "Now, in a moment or two," she thought to herself, "we will be in heaven."[59]

Outside, the four defenseless females confronted the crazed mob. "Kill them!" cried the enraged men. "Butcher them!" "Cut them open!" But Fulton's group would escape unharmed, saved, oddly enough, by human greed: the mob's desire to loot exceeded its lust for murder. As the men ransacked the hospital looking for valuables, Fulton's party snuck off to the nearby river, hoping to find a boat to convey them to safety. Though all boatmen refused them passage, Leung arrived with a complement of soldiers that escorted the group to the magistrate's office where Albert waited. Hoping to save their lives, the magistrate placed them in the most inaccessible place he could think of—a room built on stilts over a mosquito-infested frog pond. Back at the hospital, the mob set the structure ablaze. All of Fulton's belongings—books, medical instruments, and medicines—"went up in smoke."[60]

Though in the magistrate's custody, the missionaries were not out of trouble. Around town, placards appeared promising rewards for the severed heads of Mary and Albert who, the signs claimed, were guilty of murder. *Murder?* While plundering the hospital, Mary Fulton later explained, the looters had found two items they believed were the bodily remnants of "the person we had murdered." The first piece of evidence, a jar containing a mysterious white substance, was said to be the liquefied flesh of the deceased (it was a jar of "soft soap"). Though the missionaries could explain the "flesh" to the magistrate, far more damning was the mob's second piece of evidence—a skull discovered in a locked trunk. When the magistrate shared the news, Mary was at a loss. How did a skull find its way into the hospital? It was at this point that the group learned of Leung's unfortunate souvenir. With a bounty on her head, Mary and the others spent two anxious nights in the elevated dwelling conscious of the fact that they were being watched. "When we dared glance out," she wrote, "it was to see dark faces peering from out the foliage." Though Fulton feared that the mob would eventually overwhelm the magistrate's defenses, that scenario did not take place. On the third day, the magistrate secreted the party away to a waiting boat. Five days later, they reached Canton.[61]

New Medical Institutions in Canton

Though antiforeign violence forced Mary Fulton to abandon her hospital in Guiping, the harrowing experience did not dampen her faith in institution-building. In the years that followed, she would establish three pathfinding institutions. In 1901, her conviction that Chinese women were well-suited for medical careers convinced her to open a medical school. "I can testify," she wrote, that "Chinese girls become almost ideal doctors." Intellectually, they "learn quickly and have good memories"; physically, they possess "small hands . . . adapted for delicate surgical work"; and emotionally, they evince a "calm, dignified and self-possessed" demeanor. Their traits, in short, matched the profession's needs. To locate students, Fulton recruited at True Light, which acted as a feeder institution.[62] During her medical school's first year, she lacked an appropriate facility and so improvised by teaching in a church. In 1902, she moved the school into her second institution, the David Gregg Hospital for Women and Children. Later that year, construction finished on the three-story Hackett Medical College for Women.[63] It was, Fulton claimed, "the only college in the empire distinctively for women."[64] Also in 1902, Fulton opened a third institution, the Julia M. Turner Training School for Nurses, which she lodged in the David Gregg Hospital.[65] Though

Fulton sparked the founding of these institutions, the Chinese eventually assumed control over their management. According to Connie Shemo, by 1915 Hackett graduates were largely running both the hospital and the medical school.[66]

Mary Niles also launched an institution after a chance occurrence prompted an epiphany. In 1889, a blind girl was rescued from the street and dropped off at the Canton Hospital. The child was a "singsong girl," a homeless waif who begged for money by singing. When Niles heard the child's story, she was appalled. She reacted by taking into her care not only this child but several more and placing them in a small school run by Martha Noyes Kerr. It was at best a temporary solution. Niles recognized that these children, and others like them, required a school designed to meet their unique needs. After her board declined funding, Niles made a direct appeal to Christians back home. In a women's missionary magazine, she published a moving article, "The Blind Girls of Canton," which triggered an outpouring of support for her proposed school. The strategy worked. Her board experienced a sudden change of heart, and the school opened in 1896, occupying a space within True Light. In 1897, Niles named her institution "Mingxin," which means "understanding heart." After 1900, Mingxin was moved to a large plot outside the city, filled with trees and trails. Recognizing the value of the school, Canton's citizens and government supplied the funds to erect a classroom building and dormitory.[67] Mingxin had won acceptance from the Chinese, who did not view it as an alien institution.

As Niles and Fulton built their institutions, John Kerr made the hard choice to leave his. In 1899 Kerr stepped down from the Canton Hospital in order to found China's first mental health institution. This idea did not materialize out of the blue; it had been gestating in Kerr's mind for three decades. He had first presented the novel idea to his board back in 1872 but was rebuffed. Care for the insane, the board contended, lay outside the scope of missions and was a burden the Chinese must bear themselves. That burden, as Peter Szto explains, had historically fallen on relatives, as one would expect in a family-centered Confucian culture.[68] But were kin still meeting this obligation? Kerr and other missionaries had their doubts after observing rising numbers of "homeless insane."[69] In 1891, Kerr decided to establish his own facility. Using his life savings, he purchased a plot outside of Canton, deliberately selecting bucolic land, replete with hills, trees, and a nearby river.[70] After receiving a gift from a mysterious donor, he started construction on the site. "I do not know where the money is coming from," wrote a colleague, "but God does, and that is enough." In 1897, Kerr's Refuge for the Insane received its first patients.[71]

Two larger philosophies guided Kerr's design for the Refuge. First, he wished to emulate the Friends Hospital in Philadelphia, an asylum founded by Quakers in 1817. Kerr first learned about the Friends Hospital while studying at Jefferson Medical College in the 1840s; he later scrutinized its design and methods on his furloughs. The Friends model, Szto writes, endeavored to treat patients by placing them in pastoral settings that "re-created the intimacy of a small farming village." While embracing this model, Kerr eschewed the more institutional American asylums that, as Szto explains, practiced the "warehousing" of large numbers of patients in a "single elongated building." Rather than confining patients in cells, Kerr allowed them to stroll freely on the Refuge's picturesque grounds. The combination of "kind and careful attention, comfortable surroundings, good food and out-door exercise," Kerr wrote, may "result in cure."[72]

Second, Kerr designed the Refuge to blend into its surroundings. He had his architect draw up plans that fused Chinese and European styles. He favored European features that rendered life hospitable in the warm and humid climate of southern China. On each floor, verandas with handrails surrounded the building, allowing patients to walk freely about. The spacious rooms had high ceilings and large windows to let in natural light and prevent feelings of confinement. On top of this European-style edifice, Kerr placed a distinctly Chinese roof. With its upturned ceramic shingles, the roof could both block heat and, in the Chinese view, deflect evil spirits. Inside the building, Kerr instructed his Chinese staff to preserve local customs with regard to diet and hygiene. By taking these measures, Kerr hoped to convince the Chinese to view the Refuge as a useful institution within their community and not, as Szto writes, "a symbol of foreign imposition."[73]

But did he achieve this goal? The answer came, but only after Kerr's death in 1901. In 1904, the Cantonese police arrived at the Refuge with an insane man and inquired if the institution would accept him at the police department's expense. When the Refuge agreed, a relationship was born. In the years that followed, police would routinely drop off patients. According to Guangqiu Xu, this development showed that Cantonese officials viewed the Refuge not as an alien Christian operation but rather as an "important part of the welfare system in the Cantonese society."[74]

Conclusion

This chapter has explored women doctors who established practices in China. By founding institutions, they formed part of a larger medical expansion in China missions that is reflected in statistics. In 1881, only thirty-four missionary physicians, from several different countries, were active in China. By 1890, that number had tripled to one hundred. Similarly, hospitals nearly quadrupled in number between 1877 and 1890. The proliferation of medical missionaries, though exciting, did present a problem. They had become so numerous and geographically dispersed as to convince Kerr of the efficacy of centralization.

He was not alone in holding this opinion. Dr. Henry Boone, who had grown up alongside Wong Kong-chai and ran a hospital in Shanghai, also saw the need for coordination. In 1885, Boone conceived of the idea, which Kerr supported, to bring all medical missions under a single umbrella organization. The next year at a conference in Shanghai, medical missionaries not only discussed Boone's idea, they formally approved it. The China Medical Missionary Association (CMMA) was born. For the CMMA's first president, the gathering elected John Kerr by a unanimous vote, he being the doctor with the most seniority and stature.[75] In its first years, the CMMA outlined several objectives. Along with promoting Western medicine in China, it endeavored to bring uniformity to medical nomenclature. Up until this point, missionary doctors translating Western texts into Mandarin had used a variety of Chinese words to refer to the same thing. In an initiative spearheaded by Kerr, the CMMA standardized medical terminology.[76]

It also launched a journal in 1887 and appointed Kerr editor. For the inaugural issue of the *China Medical Missionary Journal*, Henry Boone composed the lead article. "Our union will give us that *esprit de corps*," he wrote of the CMMA, "without which . . . our best efforts would be scattered." Boone and Kerr imagined the fledgling journal as a place where doctors could not only share knowledge but also advance a glorious vision. Toward this end, Boone posed a "burning question" to all CMMA members and requested their response: "What have you found to be the best method of gaining the respect, the attention, and the power to influence the Chinese around you, so that you may lead them to higher thinking and living than they have ever had any opportunity of attempting before?" The question, though very long, was intended to remind doctors not to lose sight of the bigger picture—why they had come. With it, Boone captured the lofty aspiration of the CMMA: to uplift the Chinese through medicine.[77]

That aspiration was not lost on the Chinese, who increasingly placed their trust in missionary physicians. Between 1877 and 1890, the annual number of patients rose from 41,000 to 350,000.[78] Some Chinese gravitated toward these doctors even when healthy. Indeed, there was something about the optimistic message of progress that attracted them. In Foochow, Hu Yong Mi had a brilliant daughter, Hu King Eng, who adored him but did not wish to be like him. She selected a different role model for herself: a female American doctor who ran a nearby hospital. Hu aspired to become a physician, and she pursued this dream with monomaniacal ambition.

10

Hybrid Healers

American-trained Chinese Women in Medicine

It was not easy being married to Hu Yong Mi. Mrs. Hu had bound feet, which severely impaired her mobility. Yet frequent movement was precisely what her husband asked her to do. Early in his career, missionaries warned Hu that his vocation would demand regular and exhausting travel. Before committing, Hu asked his wife if she were willing to accept a life on the move. "It matters not to what place," she dutifully replied. "I will go with you." Mrs. Hu was a strong woman who possessed a high threshold for discomfort; however, her experience with Hu tested her Christian faith, physical health, and psychological well-being. His first assignment took them to a remote village where the people lived in squalor. "In front of their houses I saw piles of refuse," Hu described. Inside them "all was very dirty," with humanity coinhabiting spaces with "pigs, cattle, fowls, sheep." Mrs. Hu caught malaria. Her first daughter died from a disease, and her second daughter, King Eng, nearly perished from the same sickness. Illness was not the only threat. At the East Street Church, Mrs. Hu suffered "persecutions beyond the power of pen to narrate," wrote Sarah Sites, alluding to the horrifying incident where she had been violated (Chapter 4). Despite her trials, Mrs. Hu remained devoted to her husband and his work. Since Hu expected his whole family to pitch in, she and her children actively proselytized among the local women wherever he was stationed.[1] When he asked her to cast demons out of the possessed, she performed exorcisms.[2]

Being Hu's daughter also brought challenges. King Eng's youth coincided with the early years of her father's ministry, when he tried to win followers in hostile environments. She recalled lying awake in bed, listening to "the murmur of her father's voice" as he explained the "Jesus way" to a potential convert. To thwart his efforts, violent men would gather outside and hurl stones through the windows. Sleepless nights were not unusual in the household of Hu Yong Mi. The disadvantages of having such a father were obvious: the family never stayed put for long and they lived in perpetual fear. But there were also advantages. Judging foot-binding to be cruel and unchristian, Hu ordered his wife to abort the process with King Eng.[3] And arriving at the conviction that girls should be educated, he placed his daughter in the best school available. He even supported her dream of becoming a doctor.

Along with Hu King Eng, this chapter examines two other Chinese women who pursued careers as physicians after unconventional upbringings: Ida Kahn and Mary Stone. All three received Christian educations in China before availing themselves of missionary resources to study medicine in the United States. Like Yung Wing, Wong Kong-chai, and Yen Yung Kiung, they emerged from the process as hybrid individuals. As such, they attracted favorable attention in both Christian publications and the mainstream press. To observers, their marvelous transformations presented clear evidence of the power of American institutions to improve Chinese people. The three became "new women"—female counterparts to the "new men" Yung, Wong, and Yen. But Hu, Kahn, and Stone did not regard themselves as laboratory experiments. All along, their ambition had been to heal the sick, not support a theory. Nevertheless, they contributed to the wave of institution-building in China by opening not just hospitals but medical and nursing schools. Like the male hybrids, they became driven to extend the blessing of Western education to the next generation of Chinese.

Hu King Eng

The Doctor Dream

By the time King Eng reached school age, her father had already had his epiphany in regard to female education. He enrolled his daughter in the Woolston School, where she excelled. Upon passing all grade levels and graduating, she had reached the pinnacle of female education in China, but also a dead end. There was nowhere else to go academically—at least, nowhere obvious. At this point, King Eng drifted into the sphere of a relatively new missionary, Sigourney Trask.[4] After graduating from the Pittsburgh Female College, Trask claimed to have received a call from God. Her story of a divine summons directing her to overseas missions is something we have encountered before, it being standard fare in missionary autobiographies. But Trask deviated from the usual narrative. Instead of shipping out immediately, she elected to pursue a medical degree first. She studied at the Woman's Medical College of the New York Infirmary, the same school that would train Mary Niles. In 1874, Dr. Trask embarked for Foochow under the auspices of the WFMS.[5] Impressed by Trask's early success, the WFMS funded a state-of-the-art hospital on an island off of Foochow's coast.[6] "The building is . . . probably the best for the purpose in China," a pleased Trask commented after the facility opened in 1877. "It is a noble building, for a noble work, and I know it will be a great power for good."[7] Chinese authorities agreed. After one year, local officials and the provincial governor began supporting the hospital with donations. At the 1877 conference in Shanghai, Stephen Baldwin promoted both the hospital and its head physician.[8]

Esther Baldwin, Stephen's wife, visited the hospital daily to assist Trask. Her observations, shared in a report to the WFMS, shed light on the unique role that the hospital played in society in addition to its medical contribution. It offered Chinese women a safe zone where they could find temporary respite from their troubling lives. On any given day, Baldwin would listen as recovering women lamented their woeful circumstances. "We people are very wretched—haven't enough to eat or wear," an "unhappy-faced woman" complained. After noting the recent flood and cholera epidemic, the unhappy woman asked Baldwin "what great affliction will descend upon us this year?" Though Baldwin refrained from predicting the future, she tried as best she could to steer the conversation toward one who might alleviate suffering—God. Baldwin also described her efforts to comfort a frightened girl recovering from a traumatic surgery—Trask had surgically removed both her legs. While convalescing, the girl confronted both her new life as an amputee and her diminished position in the eyes of her mother-in-law. The latter, after purchasing her for her son, no longer wanted her.[9] Fortunately, the hospital was able to take in the "crippled" girl.[10] That same report announced that Trask had taken on her first medical student.

It was not long before King Eng asked Trask to train her as well. In the mind of King Eng, Trask cut an impressive figure: she had earned a degree typically obtained by men, managed a large institution, possessed strong Christian faith, and wielded the miraculous power to heal. A few years later, King Eng described the pivotal exchange with her father in which she had committed herself to a life in medicine. As Hu Yong Mi preached in church, he inadvertently provoked his daughter with three simple words: "every body sin." King Eng was taken aback. *Everybody?* Considering herself innocent, she confronted her father.

> I asked my father have I sinned? My father say—yes! I say—Why I never kill anybody—then my father told me . . . yes! You sin. Then I say I sorry—I cry. My father say—You better not sorry—you pray

God—and he take away my sin and make me so happy. Then my father say, God take away your sin . . . do you want to do something for God? I say, O, father, so long a time I want to study medicine and help sick people, then he say—You go pray God. He will help you—In three months I went to Foochow Hospital and learn.[11]

When King Eng shared this account, she was just starting to learn English (the Woolston School had opposed English when she was enrolled). Nevertheless, the story reveals Hu's shrewd intellect. At her father's urging, she accepted that she had sinned even if she had not committed murder. She also followed through obediently on his suggestion that she pray for forgiveness, and she felt tremendous gratitude to God as a result. Her father next urged her to do something for God to repay Him for cleansing her soul. At this point, her story took an interesting turn. Somewhat cleverly, she floated medicine—the career she had dreamed about for years—as the best way to thank God. Given that there were, in all of China, zero female doctors practicing Western medicine at this time (Kerr's experiment was just beginning), Hu's proposal was radical to say the least. But Hu Yong Mi could not disapprove even if he had wanted to. His daughter, after all, had followed the procedure that he had laid out to receive sanction from God.

The ambitious Hu threw herself into her training with Sigourney Trask. "I am now a medical student in the woman's hospital," she wrote to Ruth Sites, the daughter of Nathan and Sarah, who had returned to America for school.[12] Trask recognized that she had a special talent on her hands. By 1883, Hu's rapid progress led Trask to conclude that her pupil required more education than even Trask could provide. This realization prompted Trask to make a special request of the WFMS. "Probably the most remarkable thing in all Chinese history," the WFMS recorded in its annual report, "was the appeal . . . asking that . . . Hu King Eng," of whom "Dr. Trask speaks in the highest terms, be brought to this country" to study medicine. In calling the request the "most remarkable thing in all Chinese history," the WFMS was exaggerating. That said, its hyperbole spoke to the excitement sparked by Trask's letter. It inspired society members to fantasize about a glorious future in which Hu would "lift the womanhood of China to a higher plane."[13] After the Philadelphia branch promised funding, Hu, just eighteen years old, departed for America.[14]

Education in America

In the United States, Hu King Eng made the deliberate decision not to adopt American dress. One week after arriving, she appeared at a meeting held by her sponsor, the Philadelphia WFMS. A newspaper reported that an "almond-eyed girl, with rather pretty features, and wearing the richly embroidered ... skirt and silk slippers of ladies of rank in China" had "attracted universal attention" at the meeting.[15] Hu made a short speech in Chinese, which was translated by Sarah Sites, then on furlough with her husband.[16] Hu also got to know Sarah Keen, secretary of the Philadelphia WFMS, who would become a close friend.[17] When Hu asked Keen about appropriate attire in America, the latter advised her to "dress as she pleased." Overhearing this advice, Sarah Sites interjected, presenting the other side of the debate. If you eschew American styles in favor of Chinese dress, Sarah warned, "people will stare at you, and the boys will run after you and call you names." After considering this point, Hu countered with a rebuttal. "When you come to my China," she observed, "the boys holler at you" and "call you 'foreign devil,'" but "you do not wear Chinese dress." After Sarah conceded that she did not, Hu had won the point: "Then I not wear American dress."[18]

Hu spent the summer studying English with the Sites family before traveling to Ohio Wesleyan, Nathan's alma mater. Both she and Ruth Sites matriculated in the fall of 1884.[19] In college, Hu behaved differently than Yung Wing had at Yale three decades earlier. By refusing missionary aid, Yung prevented Christianity from dominating his life. This opened up a void in his identity, creating space for a high degree of Americanization. He dressed like his Caucasian friends, played sports, and embraced individualism. Having rejected the missionary path, his ultimate purpose in life remained unknown, though he harbored a vague aspiration to uplift China. In stark contrast, the self-assured Hu never deviated from a straightforward plan that she was fond of repeating to anyone who would listen: "I work hard, then I go back my China, make everybody well, and help their bodies: then I talk to them about Jesus."[20] Given the total clarity of her purpose, Hu had come to America not to explore the culture but to acquire a specific knowledge set. She may even have viewed Americanization as counterproductive. It had the potential, after all, to leave her stuck halfway between two cultures and to hinder her ability to relate to Chinese patients. Instead of Americanizing, Hu assiduously cultivated and proudly projected her Chinese identity. Ohio Wesleyan graduates, an alumna recalled, all remembered the "exotic blossom, whose silk-embroidered costumes, constructed in Chinese fashion, made her an object of interest."[21]

Hu also expressed her Christian faith by proselytizing on campus. Typically, when a Chinese Christian visited America, the individual instantly became (whether liking it or not) Exhibit A—living and breathing evidence of what missionaries could accomplish in China. As such, the Chinese Christian came across as a passive entity, someone who had been acted upon. Hu reversed the script. She stood before the college community *not as an example of a converted Chinese* but, more forcibly, as a *converter of Americans*.

Her evangelical talent manifested itself during her first year, when Ohio Wesleyan held a college-wide assembly to commemorate the Day of Prayer. After the president finished his remarks, Hu approached the rostrum in "full native costume" to address six hundred students. For twenty minutes, she described her experience in America, explaining how Jesus's loving presence sustained her with her parents being so far away. Many students were already "brushing away the tears" when Hu, "in her soft, clear voice," exhorted all to "Come to Jesus, just now." The following evening at a revival, Hu capitalized on her momentum. As a student knelt in prayer, trying to find God in her heart, Hu got down on her knees beside the young woman, inserting herself in the conversion process. That student joined the church, as did sixty others.[22] "She had a great influence over the girls," a peer observed, "and during our revival seasons she usually led more to Christ than any other girl." When visiting campus, the mother of a student converted by Hu expressed her astonishment at the role reversal. "Little did I think when I was giving money for the work in China," she confessed, "that a Chinese girl would come to this country and be the means of leading my daughter to Christ."[23] Hu convinced one student, Maude Simons, to commit not just to Christianity but to foreign missions. "It took one from a heathen land," Simons wrote, "to win my stubborn heart."[24] Hu had inherited her father's uncanny ability to win people over.

Missionary organizations were not blind to Hu's talent. During her vacations, organizers invited her to events that showcased her before the Christian community.[25] Hu always knew exactly what to do. At a gathering in New York, she "spoke feelingly" as she recounted what was, by this time, a well-rehearsed autobiography. The group learned of her lifelong passion to heal the sick, her debate with her father on sin, and her emotional decision to voyage to America. Hu's speech crescendoed with a dramatic appeal to the audience to pray for her as she pursued her dream. "And I hope you will all remember me," she entreated, "and pray for me that I get through my school very soon and reach my country . . . not only to help to heal their bodies, but also that their souls may be saved." When the speech ended, guests wiped away the tears as they always did when Hu spoke.[26]

Dr. Hu

In 1888, Hu graduated from college, traveled to Philadelphia, moved in with Sarah Keen, and matriculated at the Woman's Medical College of Pennsylvania. Two years into the program, she caught a terrible fever and had to withdraw. After recovering, she learned that her father had fallen gravely ill (tuberculosis), and she decided to join Ruth Sites, who was then returning to China. Back in China, missionaries wondered whether six years of "luxuries" in America had changed Hu. This was not idle speculation: Yung Wing, Yen Yung Kiung, Charlie Soong, and the students of the CEM had all experienced severe reentry crises. Defying the trend, Hu slid easily back into Chinese life. She took care of her ailing father and resumed working at the Foochow Hospital.[27] Reunited with her family and reintegrated into Chinese life, Hu perhaps wondered if returning to America to complete medical school was worth the effort.

But if she entertained doubts, her hospital work soon renewed her faith in her original plan. According to one account, Hu met with a "remarkable reception" as "sick women came to her in great numbers" after hearing she could cure them through "arts she had learned in America." The experience confirmed Hu's assumption that she could "wield great influence" among Chinese women as a healer if she could finish her degree. But that was not her only discovery. She also recognized that younger Chinese women were evolving in a way that rendered them receptive to her influence. "The Chinese women," Hu declared, "are waking up" and becoming "progressive in their ideas." Some of them now sought the same medical education that had transformed Hu herself. Thus, if Hu could finish medical school, she could teach the next generation of female doctors.[28] Sarah Sites's recollections corroborate this account of Hu's epiphany. Hu left her hospital work in Foochow, Sites wrote, with a "clearer knowledge of the special preparation she needed" for "her future work among her people" as both physician and teacher.[29] In 1892, a reenergized Hu returned to America. She completed her coursework and graduated in 1894. In 1895, she returned to China to launch her practice.[30]

The American press, which found Hu fascinating, devoted substantial coverage to this culminating moment of her personal quest. Newspapers dubbed her the "Miracle Lady,"[31] or sometimes the "Miracle Worker,"[32] and included sketches of her physical appearance that featured her Chinese dress. One paper ran the headline "New Woman Invades China."[33] Indeed, many observers saw Hu as the prototype for a new Chinese woman, just as Yung Wing had once epitomized the new Chinese man. Fascinated by her hybrid identity, multiple newspapers printed lengthy articles that told her origin story. Such stories recounted how Hu fused her Chinese core ("she is pure blooded Chinese") with Christianity and Western medicine.[34] Her ability to hold Chinese culture and American medicine in graceful equipoise proved irresistible to the American press.

Back in Foochow, Hu looked to consummate her dream by establishing her own medical practice. She began by returning to the Foochow Hospital, which Dr. Ellen Lyon now headed. When Lyon departed on furlough, Hu took charge just as Wong Fun had done in John Kerr's absence.[35] In 1899, she became the head and resident physician of a different medical facility, the

Woolston Memorial Hospital, located inside the city.[36] Early on, Hu encountered unexpected prejudice from Chinese patients. "When I first took up my work," she recalled, "people came and said they wanted a foreign doctor." It turned out her gender was not the problem—it was her race. From an adjacent room, Hu would overhear her Bible-women trying to explain to finicky patients that Dr. Hu had studied overseas. But many remained adamant. "No, I don't want a Chinese student," they insisted, "I want a foreign doctor." At this point, Hu would step out and, before her astonished assistants, direct the people to the nearest white physician.[37] Why did Hu choose not to argue? Having faith in herself, she knew that she would eventually win over the community with her performance. She did exactly that. Within months, she was receiving a steady flow of patients (2,620 during her first year). She also began training her first medical students, a group that included her younger sister.[38] In 1904, Hu had a home for herself built on Black Rock Hill, a scenic spot overlooking the city. Her choice of location was symbolic: it was the very site where, forty years earlier, a mob had attacked the residence of her father's mentor, Carlos Martin.[39] In 1910, she reported seeing an astounding 24,702 patients, adding that 810 of them "have received the Word with joy." She also raised the money to build a dispensary on Black Rock Hill, with much of the funding coming from Chinese donors.[40] Christian missions—medical missions especially—had earned a degree of acceptance among the Chinese.

Ida Kahn and Mary Stone

Gertrude Howe's Experiment

Hu King Eng was not the only Chinese woman to study overseas, achieve a degree of fame, and establish a practice in China. Ida Kahn and Mary Stone followed the trailblazing Hu. However, no one would have predicted this outcome for the two girls back in 1883. That year Gertrude Howe, following her spat with John Hykes, had removed the girls from Jiujiang and taken them to Chongqing. There she attempted to resurrect her missionary career by running a school. At first, the new setting pleased Howe and seemed ripe for evangelical harvest. In 1885, she penned a letter to the WFMS pleading for reinforcements generally and a woman doctor specifically. In Chongqing, Howe promised, a female physician would find one of the "grandest opportunities on the face of the whole earth."[41] But it did not take long for the situation to darken. A year later, Howe would send a series of letters to the WFMS describing how she and her teenage girls had narrowly escaped with their lives.

Howe's missionary experience in Chongqing reached its high-water mark in June of 1886 when her school held closing exercises. Before an audience of missionaries and Chinese residents, the schoolgirls read essays, performed recitations, and sang songs to show what they had learned. At this same time, hundreds of young men were streaming into the city to take the state examinations. Since some students were, in Howe's words, "riotous," their arrival elicited "the dread of the city people." She also suspected that local officials, charged with keeping the peace, were "afraid" of the students. If so, these fears proved to be well-founded. All around the city, students posted placards of an "inflammatory nature." Foreigners were erecting buildings, the placards proclaimed, "on a spot where they disturbed a dragon" and the "result would be calamity." Though the calamity did come, it was caused not by a dragon but by the students themselves. A mob looted the home of a missionary and set fire to a Catholic cathedral. Fortunately for Howe, she and her girls never encountered the mob up close. With the help of Chinese friends, they escaped the city and hid until they could board a boat bound for Shanghai.[42] From the attic of one hiding place, Howe peered through the "crevices" and saw "the sky lurid with the flames of the burning debris of the cathedral."[43]

After the conflict with Hykes and the harrowing experience in Chongqing, Howe recognized the need for less drama. Hoping for a fresh start, she returned to Jiujiang where she learned about the sad developments at the school she had founded: the missionary wife who had replaced her had failed, and the school had shut its doors. The good news was that the WFMS now wished Howe to breathe life back into the school. In retaking the reins, Howe surprisingly had the confidence of John Hykes, who had moved past the dispute and vowed to support her efforts. "I tell you frankly that I am glad she is back," he wrote, "and I shall do everything in my power to help her." Reconciled with Hykes and reinstalled at the school, Howe finally achieved the stability that would allow her to focus on her girls. She provided Ida Kahn and Mary Stone with a Western education rich in math and science. Howe's goal, after all, was to honor her commitment to Stone's father by preparing the girl for medical school overseas. Since Kahn studied the same material, she found herself ready for medical school too. In 1892, the WFMS agreed to fund the educations of both girls in America, as it had several years earlier with Hu King Eng.[44]

The plan was for Stone and Kahn to attend the University of Michigan's medical school. Before they could be admitted, however, the university required that they demonstrate proficiency in relevant academic subjects by passing an entrance examination. As evidence of the rigor of Howe's home-based instruction, the girls passed easily and matriculated in 1892.[45] What would the experience hold? When Michigan had first opened its doors to women in 1870, the state regents had voted to segregate men and women in the medical school. Gertrude Howe, one of the first female students, took the same courses as her male peers but did so in separate classrooms. This arrangement did not last for long. Forced to compensate instructors for teaching their classes twice (once to men and once to women), the university came to view gender segregation as costly and inefficient. After just one year, Michigan integrated all classes except for Anatomy.[46] Though Howe did not complete the program, a Canadian graduate earned fame as a missionary physician in China. In 1879, Leonora Howard cured the wife of Li Hongzhang, the most powerful official in China after Zeng Guofan's death.[47]

Ida Kahn and Mary Stone would also become famous in China. However, the two struggled early at Michigan. According to Connie Shemo, they "found their new environment intimidating," lived with Howe for the first two years, and dreaded the "terrible terrors" of laboratory work. But over time they adjusted and started to excel socially and academically. Concerning the latter, they earned high marks and graduated near the top of their class, finishing second and third.[48] Socially, they cooked Chinese meals for friends, lifted dumbbells in the gymnasium, and joined the choral music club.[49] Kahn was elected class secretary. They also made an interesting decision with regard to dress. Whereas Yung Wing had worn American clothes at Yale and Hu King Eng had maintained Chinese dress at Ohio Wesleyan, Kahn and Stone struck a middle position. They wore American clothes on routine days but donned Chinese outfits on holidays and special occasions. This decision perhaps reflected their hybrid identities; they had grown up in China in the home of an American parent. Not surprisingly, they wore Chinese gowns at their graduation ceremony in 1896.[50]

Drs. Stone and Kahn

Like Yung Wing forty years earlier, Stone and Kahn monopolized attention at graduation. When the two walked across the platform to receive their diplomas, they received an unexpected "outburst of enthusiasm" and "applause" as students, faculty, and the audience honored them with an "ovation."[51] "Their future career will be watched with every expectation of their eminent success," remarked James Angell, the University of Michigan's president and the former American Minister to China. The author of a lengthy and adoring newspaper article on Kahn and Stone predicted that the Chinese people would reject them when they returned home. They will be called "new women," she explained, "and their compatriots will gravely shake their queues and roll their almond eyes" when they try to practice medicine. China's society was not ready, she contended, for something as radical as a Chinese woman trained in Western medicine.[52]

This author missed the mark. In the summer of 1896, Kahn and Stone received clinical training in Chicago, spending time at several hospitals under the supervision of Dr. I. N. Danforth before embarking for home. They would be returning to China as medical missionaries under the auspices of the WFMS.[53] Upon reaching Jiujiang, Kahn and Stone met with an overwhelming reception described in detail in the *China Medical Missionary Journal*. Their Chinese friends, hearing of their imminent arrival, planned a rousing welcome complete with fireworks. When the vessel arrived, the pyrotechnics attracted curious city residents, who swarmed the waterfront to "get a glimpse" of the "women doctors." "Are they Chinese women?" asked some in the crowd, while others inquired, "Is it true they have been studying for four years in a foreign land?" But the most crucial question centered on their medical ability: "Can they heal the sick?" It did not take long for the community to learn the answer. Though missionaries had planned a period of rest for Stone and Kahn, patients started to materialize at their doorstep on the third day following their return. From there the numbers only increased.[54]

After one month, Kahn and Stone were summoned to a challenging case that would reveal their utility. According to the *China Medical Missionary Journal*, a woman carrying twins had delivered one infant when "all action ceased." The second baby remained unborn, and family members "were at a loss to know what to do." Panicking, someone got the idea to send for Kahn and Stone. When the two arrived, they discovered that they were second in line; the family had previously engaged a "native doctor of highest repute." This doctor had already arrived in his sedan chair dressed in "satin and silk." After inspecting the mother, he informed the family that "he could do nothing for the woman." Noting the presence of Stone and Kahn, he advised the family to place their trust in them. "They have crossed mountains and seas to study about these matters," he said before departing. Addressing the sister physicians, the family requested a "guarantee" that the mother would live. Refusing to make any promises, Stone and Kahn turned to the patient. They delivered the second child safely and saved the mother; the first child, born before they arrived, died. Three days later, the appreciative family invited them to a feast.[55]

The case demonstrated China's need for medical practitioners like Kahn and Stone. Though the account does not mention midwives, it is a near certainty, given what we know about standard birthing practice at the time, that at least one midwife had assisted before complications arose. Though satisfactory for routine deliveries, midwives sometimes lacked the training to adjust should something go wrong. When the family realized that lives were at risk, its first reaction was to call the best male physician practicing Chinese medicine. But he too proved inadequate. He recognized immediately that the case would require invasive action on a female patient, something that he was not trained to do (or dressed to do). Even if he had possessed the training, Chinese custom forbade him, as a male doctor, from close contact with the female patient's body. In this way, the case exposed a gaping need in childbirthing. Difficult deliveries required a new kind of healer, one never before seen in Jiujiang: a female doctor trained in Western obstetrics and its surgical procedures.

Though the article's author identified Stone and Kahn's value, other missionaries were slow to view them as equals. The missionary community did not invite them to reside in its compound, a clear indication of their ambiguous status: their colleagues perceived them less as missionary doctors and more as native women.[56] If they could not join the other missionaries, where did they live? "After we returned to China," Mary Stone remembered, "Miss Howe left the beautiful home of the missionaries and came to live in a little Chinese home that she built for us out of her own money." As they had done in Michigan, the two lived with their mother. The missionary community's bias also infected the sisters' assignment. Though the two wished to launch practices immediately, other missionaries—Howe included—believed that first they should apprentice under an established doctor in a hospital.[57] "After they have several months of hospital practice in other mission hospitals," one missionary wrote, "we hope to have a place ready for them to begin work."[58] But Kahn and Stone insisted they were ready right away. Opposing any kind of apprenticeship, they pointed out that other graduates of American medical schools were not discouraged from practicing on their own. Kahn also feared that she would lose face among the Chinese if placed in a position subordinate to white doctors. The "Chinese will think I have not learned my business," she said, adding that she preferred to "begin with a dispensary on a small scale and learn from my own practice."[59]

Kahn and Stone followed this course. They rented a modest "Chinese dwelling," measuring twenty-eight by twenty-one feet, and opened their own hospital. Unfortunately, it failed to meet even their most basic needs in terms of size and sanitation. "Our tiny hospital is crammed full" of patients, wrote Stone, who admitted to packing twenty-one people into the small space. An "observer might think that we carried home but a slight idea of hygiene." The facility was also unbearable in the summer. Unprotected from the sun by tree cover, the structure got progressively hotter throughout the day, becoming an "oven" by evening. Frustrated by the inadequate space, Stone called on the "women of America to build our new hospital," but acknowledged that, sadly, "not a letter comes" bearing good news. They would simply have to make do until fortune favored their courageous effort.[60]

It did. Back in the summer of 1896, Stone had greatly impressed I. N. Danforth, who supervised her clinical training. "She won the hearts of all with her charming ways," he wrote, "and got everything she wanted."[61] What she wanted now was a better facility, and Danforth agreed to supply support. He did so not only because he admired Stone but also because his recently deceased wife, a longtime WFMS member, had believed passionately in medical missions.[62] After Stone and Kahn sent their expectations for the structure to Chicago, Danforth commissioned an architect to generate an architectural plan. Soon construction began on the Elizabeth Skelton Danforth Memorial Hospital, a massive edifice composed of white granite and limestone. When the hospital opened in 1900, visitors passed through an impressive "pillared entrance" and then beheld a state-of-the-art facility complete with reception room, solarium, library, dark room, offices, veranda, and recovery area. The crown jewel, however, was the operating room, which featured a skylight, sterilizing room, operating table, and supply room stocked with drugs, instruments, and microscopes. "The operating room . . . is our pride," Kahn shared, "because it is so light."[63] Last, the hospital included a garden that, according to Stone, combined "Chinese taste" and "Christian sympathy." It provided the institution with a fitting symbol of the hybrid identities of the two physicians.[64]

Conclusion

In 1903, Kahn received a request from the gentry of Nanchang, the provincial capital, to bring Western medicine to their city. Within a decade, she was presiding over a large medical compound that included a hospital, a garden, and a home where she resided with Gertrude Howe. How did she handle the costs of running this large institution? Though continuing to receive WFMS support, Kahn mainly tapped the resources of local Chinese, who voluntarily provided monetary support.[65] Every year, her institution became less foreign and more indigenous. Back in Jiujiang, the school that Howe had started, renamed the Rulison-Fish School, underwent an expansion after 1900, adding facilities, increasing enrollments, and becoming an elite institution for girls. It also indigenized by hiring its strongest graduates as teachers.[66]

At the Danforth Hospital, Mary Stone assumed sole leadership. On her initiative, the hospital took on an additional function: nurse training. For years, Stone had informally prepared women to assist in the hospital; now she wished to institutionalize the process by starting a nursing school.[67] When Danforth learned of her ambitious plan, he offered to send an American nurse to help. Her answer, when it came, surprised him. Very politely, she replied that she did not seek the help of an American nurse. Missionaries, of course, were famous for complaining that they did not have enough resources; they seldom turned down offers from benefactors. Why did Stone decline Danforth's generosity?[68]

The rest of her letter explained why. Stone "feared" that the presence of an American nurse would lead to the misperception that Chinese women were incapable of managing on their own and required "help from America."

For Stone, a school that failed to become indigenous might do some good at the *local* level, but it would ultimately undermine China's *national* aspiration toward self-sufficiency. The letter went on to reveal the titanic dual ambition animating Stone's nurse-training plan. She intended to persuade Chinese women "that they are able to do things of which they have never dreamed." At the same time, her school would "show the people of other nations" that long-benighted Chinese women had only "lived such narrow lives" because no one had presented them with the "opportunity to develop their native powers."[69] Stone, in essence, was having the same epiphany as Hu King Eng. Chinese women, by acquiring Western medical training in indigenous institutions, could experience a collective awakening and achieve what Stone called a "new consciousness."[70] In the first two decades of the twentieth century, more than two hundred Chinese women would follow in the footsteps of Hu, Stone, and Kahn by studying medicine in the United States.[71]

11

Extroverted Evangelists

The Student Volunteer Movement and the YMCA

In the summer of 1886, William Ashmore sat reading the newspaper in his home in Wollaston, Massachusetts. On furlough, Ashmore was trying to heal from the trauma of the previous two years, which had been as hard as any in his thirty-five-year career in Asia. The sequence of tragic events began in Swatow one summer day in 1884. Gazing out over the ocean, Ashmore discerned a mysterious black dot in the sky. As the "little speck of a cloud" rapidly "increased in size," he realized that a major storm was approaching. When the typhoon made landfall, it was ferocious: it "smashed all our boats" and "made us tremble for our dwelling-houses." But the hurricane-force winds were just the beginning of trouble for Ashmore, who described that summer as "stormy, both literally and figuratively." Shortly after the typhoon, a cholera breakout devastated the region. And when that threat finally ebbed, missionaries faced a paroxysm of antiforeign violence. This time, the French war with China over Tonkin (northern Vietnam) triggered the outrage. Deeming the countryside "unsafe," missionaries stayed home and assumed a "defensive" stance. As summer bled into autumn, the anti-Christian violence intensified. Ashmore reported that "mandarin manipulation" incited "mobs" that "began the work of destroying chapels" and "looting the houses of Christians." Amid such hostility, Ashmore had no choice but to close the girls' school and cancel all junkets by Bible-women. "It was no use to send them out," he explained, as only "violence and rudeness awaited them."[1] Then in December, *annus horribilis* dealt Ashmore one final blow: his son, a minister in Minnesota, died at a young age.[2]

The year may have ended but the pain did not. His son was not the only family member to perish. Throughout the decade, Ashmore had witnessed the deteriorating health of Eliza, his wife and companion for over two decades. In 1885, her precarious condition compelled the couple to return to America as the "only chance of prolonging her life." By the time they boarded the vessel, Eliza had become so "feeble" as to prompt fears that she could not "endure a voyage." She survived the journey but just barely, then died shortly after the couple reached Massachusetts.[3] Ashmore was alone.

He had also reached a crossroads. Now in his sixties, Ashmore felt his physical strength and stamina diminished by over three decades of toil, stress, and sickness in Asia. His worn-out body, in other words, was sending the unambiguous signal that the time had come to retire. But the wails from his aching body were contested by his resilient mind, which refused to quit and yearned to leap back into the fray. Indeed, it was Ashmore's indomitable spirit that inspired colleagues to call him "the fighting saint."[4] The "hardest task for his self-control," wrote a friend who understood Ashmore's body-mind divide, "was to refrain from activity when years weighed him down."[5] Ashmore was conflicted.

Chance would tip the scales in favor of action. One morning in July of 1886, as Ashmore sat reading the *Springfield Republican,* his eyes alighted upon a stunning article. Almost every day that month, the paper would print a story about a Christian camp for college students being held in the north of Massachusetts in Northfield.[6] The paper reported that every day "scores of wide awake college boys," representing about 100 colleges, were "pouring in" to Northfield to spend three weeks in pastoral New England studying the Bible, singing hymns, attending lectures, and engaging in Christian activities. The paper predicted that over 250 students would attend.[7] As Ashmore read, he probably believed that Providence was communicating directly to him. In his mind, there was no such thing as a coincidence. As evangelical energy surged through his aging frame, Ashmore recognized that he could wallow on the sidelines no longer; he made immediate plans to travel to Northfield. But more than merely attending, Ashmore imagined himself playing a crucial role. He saw Northfield as an electric field of potential that, if left alone, might not generate anything lasting. According to the newspaper, the "aim" of scheduled events was "to familiarize the students with the use of the Bible" and convince them to "carry back" to campus the "good influences."[8] *Good influences? What did that mean?* The agenda was far too bland, vague, and diffuse for Ashmore. He resolved to redirect the youthful idealism toward a single well-defined purpose. He would tell them about foreign missions.

Thanks to the efforts of Ashmore and others, the Northfield retreat gave birth to a new missionary recruitment program—the Student Volunteer

Movement (SVM). The SVM plays a pivotal role in our story because it effected an infusion of recent college graduates into China missions. Along with expanding the missionary ranks, the SVM brought a new personality type to China. For decades, most missionaries had emerged from the same mold. Raised in small agricultural villages where the church dominated intellectual life, these volunteers favored a harsh brand of evangelism that cast the missionary as a crusader against the dark forces of heathenism.[9] They were content to labor for God alone, under tough conditions, in a forbidding land. But the SVM recruits embodied the traits of a younger generation. Recent college graduates, they tended to be social, gregarious, and worldly. Few found austerity and extreme self-denial appealing as a way of life. They also expressed new preferences with respect to the work itself. Less enamored with itinerant preaching than their predecessors, the new recruits eschewed junkets on mules in favor of the newer models unveiled at the 1877 conference. They also gravitated toward the YMCA, which made an aggressive bid to establish itself in China after 1890. Much like the WFMS, the SVM fueled the expansion of China missions near century's end.

Robert Mateer and Luther Wishard

Robert Mateer possessed the right set of traits for China's evolving Christian missions. In some ways, he was better suited for the work than his older brother, who possessed old-fashioned ideas about work and women. In the early 1880s, Robert traveled with Hunter Corbett to the inland city of Weixian, where he established a mission station largely by himself. While there, he dedicated his effort toward improving education for girls. Most of the schools, he wrote, did "little more than teach [girls] to read" and failed to "wake up the minds and ambitions."[10] Robert secured the funding to open a high school for girls in the city.[11] Why this focus on girls? Robert held progressive ideas on women's education that approximated those of Elizabeth Fisher. He also surpassed his brother in the area of interpersonal skills. As missions shifted their focus away from itinerant preaching and toward institution-building, they began to value social organization above pure individualism. It was while studying at Princeton that Robert found within himself the ability to mobilize people, plan events, forge networks, and lead organizations. The discovery of these latent gifts required a little luck. Robert happened to board with the dynamic Luther Wishard.

Luther Wishard was born into a devout Christian family that lived in a log cabin in rural Indiana. He acquired his belief in community-based religion after his father returned from a convention in Indianapolis where Dwight Moody had spoken passionately about the YMCA. Wishard recalled his father as being "so charged with spiritual electricity that he magnetized everybody with whom he came in contact." One such person was Wishard himself. While studying at Hanover College in Indiana, Wishard joined the local YMCA branch. In 1875, he transferred to Princeton, where he met with disappointment upon learning that the campus had no connection to the local YMCA. Such an affiliation, he believed, could help reduce the "gownishness" and "exclusiveness of college life." Wishard also believed that students could profit from "contact with active Christian businessmen" who would, in turn, benefit from "the steady inflow of men from colleges." The relationship, in sum, would be mutually advantageous.[12] As Wishard later discovered, Princeton was not an outlier; most colleges lacked connections to their local YMCA chapters. Though just an undergraduate, Wishard had the inspired idea to bring the YMCA movement—its community focus, wholesome activities, spirit of volunteerism, and Christian faith—to all college campuses.

To convert the idea into a reality, Wishard and his Princeton friends, a group that included Robert Mateer, planned a conference to attract like-minded students from multiple colleges. In 1877, delegates from twenty-one colleges arrived in Louisville, Kentucky, to attend a series of meetings over which Wishard presided. Working together, the students hammered out the blueprint for a national organization that would connect all college campuses under the auspices of the YMCA.[13] The "scheme," in Wishard's words, would "bind the Colleges together in Christian sympathy."[14] More specifically, the students agreed to publish a magazine, hold conferences, and link their campuses together through a system of "intercollegiate correspondence and inter-visitation." Who would oversee all of this infrastructure? The delegates turned in unison to Wishard to serve as the first collegiate secretary of the YMCA. Looking back at the genesis of the organization, Wishard credited not himself but rather his ability to work in harmony with an institution. "The one thing needful, the *sine qua non* for the proposed movement," he wrote, "was not only a man" but "a great college behind the man."[15] He could not have succeeded, in other words, without the support of Princeton and his fellow students. It was the coordinated efforts of people within institutions, not the lonely exertions of individuals, that changed the world. That was Luther Wishard's philosophy.

Robert Mateer studied his roommate's behavior as the latter reinvented college life in America. It was an astonishing achievement, and one that showed what one could accomplish with collegiality, networking, leadership, and personal magnetism. Three years later, he would try his own hand at event-planning. After graduating from Princeton in 1878, Robert matriculated into Princeton Seminary. He had by this time decided to follow in his older brother's footsteps by becoming a missionary in China. While immersed in his theological studies, Robert made an insight that would provide the seed for his own Wishard-style project. He knew that, at any given time, there were about three thousand students enrolled in seminaries across the country. Given their Christian faith and advanced scriptural knowledge, these students were natural candidates for foreign missions. Yet at present there did not exist an interseminary organization to promote missions. A seminary student, as a result, might pass through his entire degree program without once considering missions! It was a glaring lacuna that Robert was determined to address. After selling his idea to two other students, the threesome mailed letters to all American seminaries sharing the essential idea. The letter asserted that "a *genuine missionary revival* is needed . . . among theological students." It proposed creating a "permanent system of interseminary correspondence on the subject of missions." The hypothetical system would expose seminary students to the missionary profession before they graduated and embarked on ministerial careers.[16]

After receiving a favorable response, Robert started planning in earnest. From Wishard's example, he knew that a conference presented the best vehicle to launch a movement. In 1880, he arranged for representatives from a dozen seminaries to gather in New York for a conference-planning session. This group agreed to hold a major conference that fall at Rutgers Seminary. Wishard, who attended the meeting, spoke approvingly. "We recently attended a conference of theological students," he wrote, in which the purpose was "to give an impulse to the missionary spirit" in seminaries. In October, 250 students from thirty-two seminaries met at Rutgers. Robert Mateer, who served as conference chair, read a paper detailing how students could stimulate interest in missionary careers by coordinating with other students, their own institution, other seminaries, and overseas missionaries. The *Christian Intelligencer*, which covered the event, called it "a grand success" in ways the students may not have understood. "It may be gravely doubted," the newspaper observed, "whether the young men themselves were quite aware how the missionary work had sunk out of sight." The conference also made history: it marked the first national meeting of students focused exclusively on the promotion of foreign missions. Wishard, who was prone to hyperbole when excited, lauded the conference as "one of the most remarkable events in the history of the Christian Church." Though that was an overstatement, he did not exaggerate when he declared that the event "owes its origin, growth, and wonderful consummation to one young man . . . who goes in a few months . . . to China." That man was Robert Mateer.[17]

A Crossroads for Missions

After Mateer's conference ended, Wishard proceeded to oversell the conference's expected impact on missionary recruitment. The event, he predicted, would trigger "a turning to mission fields as had not been witnessed since the days of the apostles."[18] That did not happen, at least not immediately. In fact, in the early 1880s, missionary advocates bemoaned Americans' failure to provide foreign missions with robust support. In 1881, N. G. Clark, who succeeded Rufus Anderson at the American Board of Commissioners for Foreign Missions (the ABCFM), identified a disturbing trend: the number, size, and wealth of churches were all expanding in the Gilded Age, but the "missionary effort has not kept pace." Indeed, foreign missions were actually shrinking relative to other church functions. The once energetic Americans, Clark concluded, were sliding into lethargy as far as missions were concerned.[19]

This alarming trend raised a troubling question: was a once enthusiastic public now doubting the continued relevance of missions in the modern world? According to historian Valentin Rabe, the priorities of the churchgoing public shifted in the Gilded Age. In the late 1800s, America's rapid industrialization attracted vast immigrant streams from Russia, eastern Europe, and southern Europe. Many of these newcomers moved to large urban centers—such as New York, Chicago, and Pittsburgh—where they faced impoverished conditions in overcrowded tenements. The overwhelming nature of the urban crisis convinced many Americans to turn their attention away from foreign missions and toward the domestic front. As the urban-immigrant poor eclipsed "heathen" souls as the appropriate focus for church resources, the missionary verged on becoming a quaint "relic" from a bygone era.[20] Hoping to forestall that fate, Clark called for a revitalization movement. "There must be the awakening of a profounder missionary spirit throughout the land," he urged, to remind the nation that "this is emphatically the missionary age."[21]

Others agreed that foreign missions had reached a critical juncture. In 1886, A. T. Pierson, a Presbyterian minister and missions advocate, published *The Crisis of Missions*. The book amounted to a call to arms. Pierson warned that global evangelism had reached a point of "crisis," which he defined as a "combination of grand opportunity and great responsibility." Presuming the Second Coming to be imminent, Pierson argued that God had been conspicuously busy as of late leveling barriers to the Gospel. After imperial wars had opened once-closed countries like China, the marvels of industry and technology—railroads, canals, steamships, and telegraphs—allowed missionaries easier access to millions of previously out-of-reach souls. God, in short, had done His part. Would missionaries do theirs? Would they seize the chance afforded by so many "open doors"? For Pierson, the stakes could not be any higher: the response to the crisis would determine whether the movement culminated with "glorious success" or succumbed to "awful failure."[22]

Moody Meets Wishard

In the 1880s, something happened that nobody expected. In the United States, foreign missions abruptly caught fire on college campuses. Why did students suddenly gravitate toward a career thought to be, if not moribund, then at least old-fashioned? The story begins with Dwight Moody. Moody was a hulking man and charismatic evangelist who had achieved a national reputation spearheading revivals in cities after the Civil War. Newspapers hailed Moody for restoring Christian morality to civic spaces plagued by the typical problems associated with urban-industrial life. Possessing no education beyond the fourth grade, Moody had succeeded—despite very real struggles with grammar—by bringing to religion the same pep, optimism, and boosterism that worked in business.[23] Starting in 1879, Moody shifted his formidable energies to education in an effort to ignite Christian zeal in the young. He founded two schools—one for girls and one for boys—in Northfield, Massachusetts, the town of his birth.[24]

Moody also supported the YMCA. A local Christian association had been there for him in the 1850s when, at age seventeen, he had left the farm to try to make it in Boston. "I am going to join the Christian Association tomorrow night," he wrote his mother. "There I shall have a place to go . . . and I can have all the books I want to read and only have to pay one dollar a year." After moving west later that decade, Moody served as president of the YMCA's Chicago chapter. His heavy involvement with the YMCA eventually brought him into contact with Luther Wishard, the organization's collegiate secretary. In 1886, Moody sat down with Wishard for what would be a fateful meeting. For years, Wishard had dreamed of organizing "a great summer assembly" of college students. "I . . . told him," Wishard recalled, "how I had longed for such a conference of college men and how fully . . . I would cooperate in working up a gathering of them."[25] Wishard hoped to persuade Moody to preside over a summer program for college students on the campus of the new boys' school in Northfield—Mount Hermon.[26]

After Moody agreed to the proposition, Wishard shifted his energies to promotion. He sent out letters to all college YMCA chapters, inviting each to send at least one delegate to Northfield that July. "The object of the school," Wishard explained, "will be the study of the Bible" in daily exercises conducted by Moody himself.[27] Though Bible study was important, Moody recommended limiting it to two hours each day. Moody, who had a short attention span himself, believed that a minister who spoke too often and for too long on matters of theology risked chloroforming the people he hoped to inspire. "Any minister that preaches twice on Sundays, and then gives a long lecture in the prayer-meeting," he said, "will kill any church in this country."[28] After the reasonable-length Bible studies ended, students would fill the remaining hours of the day with "wholesome recreation"—sports and games, swimming and boating, and climbing in nearby mountains. The camp would be accessible by train, and the cost per student would not exceed $5 a week. After the initial mailing, Wishard made visits to college campuses to ensure robust participation. At Princeton, he met with Robert Wilder, an earnest young man interested in missions, who hesitated to commit. The persuasive Wishard secured Wilder's commitment by "pointing out the tremendous opportunity . . . for spreading the missionary cause." Wishard's words would be prophetic: Wilder would play a role in turning the Christian retreat into an engine of missionary recruitment.[29]

The Birth of the SVM

Though Moody had agreed to host the event, he did so with apprehension. His fears had nothing to do with the merits of Wishard's plan to recruit young people for Christian service. Undergraduates, he felt sure, could bring not only energy and idealism but also *numbers* to his movement. In the decades following the Civil War, college enrollment exploded in America, going from 16,600 students attending 209 colleges in 1860 to 44,133 students attending 415 colleges in 1890. By 1900, the undergraduate population had passed 100,000.[30] Though there was no arguing the demographics, Moody doubted his own ability to inspire this particular group. Self-conscious about his own meager schooling, Moody worried that his message would not appeal to a collegiate audience. In July of 1886, as the students started to arrive at Mount Hermon (251 students representing 89 colleges), their presence heightened Moody's feelings of inadequacy. He panicked. He sent a desperate telegram to A. T. Pierson, urging the latter to come immediately to buttress the event with his intellectualism.[31] If Moody failed, Pierson could rescue the camp with erudite discourses on theology.

When Pierson arrived, he found that Moody's fears were unfounded. The students had taken an instant liking to Moody, a lovable bear of a man who led them in prayer and joined in their sports and games. Though Moody turned out not to need Pierson, the latter discovered his role when Robert Wilder approached him with a request. "There are ten or twelve of us who have decided to devote our lives to God as foreign missionaries," Wilder said, "and we want you to give us a missionary address." On the evening of July 16, Pierson stood before a gathering and drew a crude map of the world on a chalkboard. He then proceeded to repeat the big insight from his book: since the hand of God was systematically removing obstacles to evangelism, Christians must seize the opportunity by venturing out as missionaries.[32] It was possibly during this address that Pierson first uttered the phrase that would become the "watchword" for the nascent missionary movement: "the evangelization of the world in this generation."³³ Regardless, Pierson's pitch, which infused foreign missions with carpe diem urgency, electrified the students.

Despite its impassioned rhetoric, Pierson's address possessed one shortcoming: it was abstract. Having never served overseas, Pierson could present the foreign missionary only in idea form—as a sterile intellectual concept rather than a flesh-and-blood human being. What was needed was a real missionary, one recently returned from a distant land. Enter William Ashmore. To some students, Ashmore's unexpected appearance verged on the miraculous—an act of Providence. To others, it perhaps seemed as if the collective will of the group had conjured him out of thin air. In reality, Ashmore, after seeing the conference written up in the newspaper, had rushed to Northfield to participate. "As soon as we found a live missionary among us," Wilder recalled, "we asked him to address some of the delegates."³⁴ Thrilled to have a purpose again, Ashmore obliged.

If Pierson kindled interest in foreign missions, Ashmore fanned the flames into a roaring fire. Speaking on a Friday night, Ashmore recounted how, in the 1860s, he founded the Baptist mission in Swatow with a mere two converts, both illiterate men. The local community dismissed the two men as fools and "warned their children that if they accepted the faith of the foreign devils they would become just such wrecks of humanity." Ashmore then listed the multiple forms of persecution he had endured: "mobs," "sacked dwellings," "fights with mandarins," "bushels of stones," and "curses by thousands." Though the hardships were formidable, Ashmore insisted that his perseverance had paid off. He claimed to have over 1,000 converts at work in 200 villages dispersed across 5,000 square miles—a swath of land comparable in size to Connecticut. Despite the impressive gains, Ashmore stressed that foreign missions remained in desperate need of manpower. College graduates must now channel their "strength, time," and "talents," not toward the acquisition of "money and pleasure and worldly success" but rather "into work for human souls."³⁵ Pierson, who witnessed Ashmore's address, reported that he "held the audience spell bound." As word of Ashmore's inspiring oratory spread, he earned himself a second appearance the following Tuesday.³⁶

This time, Ashmore did not hold back. Speaking for over an hour, he delivered a rousing call to arms that Pierson described as "overwhelming." Ashmore argued that the church had, to its great detriment, softened its views as of late, losing "the idea" of Christianity as a "war for Christ." Ashmore, who favored militant religion, called on the young men to resurrect the "Bible idea" of a "conquest of the world." "With what weapons," Ashmore asked, continuing his martial metaphor, "does God propose to carry on this war?" Just as a soldier brings his gun to battle, the missionary carries the New Testament "in his pistol pocket."³⁷ "Be willing to be brave, to bear the hardship," Ashmore exhorted, and to "obey" Christ's mandate: "Go ye forth and preach the gospel to every creature." Anyone who chooses not to heed Christ's command, Ashmore warned, must face his own conscience. "The Burden of proof is on you."[38]

The pressure was on. After listening to the speeches, the students responded not with applause but with something far more indicative of deep emotional impact—total silence. "We went out of that meeting not discussing the speeches," recalled John Mott of Cornell. "Everybody was quiet" because they were "moved to the depths of their souls." Overwhelmed by the novel feelings roiling inside of them, students fled to a nearby grove of trees where they prayed for guidance. "The grove ... was the scene that night of battles," Mott wrote, "in which the unselfish and heroic in men won the victory." Indeed, a conference never intended as a recruiting ground for foreign missions had become exactly that. At the start of the conference, fewer than a dozen students had expressed interest in missionary careers; after the speeches of Ashmore and Pierson, the young men toppled like dominoes. "One after another, men came to the decision to volunteer," remembered Mott, until the final day of the conference when the number crested at ninety-nine. As the ninety-nine knelt together in prayer, another student materialized, bringing the total to one hundred.[39]

When the conference ended, Wishard acted quickly to convert the explosive event into a sustained movement. The following year, he and his associates toured the United States, visiting 162 colleges and seminaries in an effort to recruit men and women. When their haul of 2,106 volunteers exceeded their most optimistic projections, the SVM was born. Wishard next tapped John Mott to take over his role as recruiter in the United States. With Mott at the helm, the SVM enjoyed a level of success that is best expressed through numbers. Up until 1870, the United States had produced only about 2,000 Protestant missionaries. In 1890, when the SVM remained in its infancy, only 934 Americans were laboring in a foreign mission field. We start to see the effect of the SVM in 1900, when America could boast of 5,000 active missionaries. By 1915, that number nearly doubled, reaching 9,000. In the 1920s, the SVM contributed about half of the 14,000 missionaries stationed overseas.[40] In China, statistics paralleled the national trend: the number of American missionaries rose from 210 in 1877 to 1,304 in 1907.[41]

The YMCA

Why did Luther Wishard step away from the SVM so shortly after its creation? He was preparing to embark on a world tour to promote the Intercollegiate YMCA.[42] Wishard was more responsible than anyone for establishing the YMCA in China. In the 1870s and 1880s, he had made a name for himself by bringing the YMCA to American colleges and by linking these chapters in a nationwide network. The YMCA could augment student life on campuses, he passionately believed, by encouraging student leadership and promoting a wholesome Christian lifestyle consisting of Bible study, social organization, sports, and community engagement. While focusing his energies on the domestic front, Wishard did contemplate the possibility that the YMCA might spread internationally using the existing infrastructure of Protestant missions. In 1883, he shared this idea with his friend Harlan Beach, who was headed to Tengchow. Beach pledged to do "everything in his power" to plant the seed, which he did.[43] Two years later, the Anglo-Chinese College of Foochow (Chapter 12) opened what it (mistakenly) called the first YMCA chapter "ever organized in China."[44] These isolated successes gave Wishard hope that the YMCA could take hold in China. However, he would not know for sure until he saw China for himself.

In April of 1890, Wishard visited China on his way to India. As he traveled along the coast, he met with old friends from the SVM now working in missions. At the same time, he performed reconnaissance, scouting cities and colleges as possible YMCA sites. In May he attended the missionary conference in Shanghai, having obtained in advance an invitation to pitch the YMCA before the gathering.[45] In crafting his comments, Wishard chose his words carefully. He knew that the grizzled veterans in the audience, feeling protective of their methods, might put forward opposition. Shrewdly, he presented himself not as a brash upstart forcing unwanted change on missionaries but rather as a deferential young man seeking their counsel. "I desire to learn from the missionaries," he announced, "whether the time [for the YMCA] has come." He acknowledged the church "as the only agency adapted to general missionary work" and expressed his satisfaction with "existing missionary methods." Having assured his audience that he posed no threat, Wishard explained his objective. He endeavored not to change missions but to enhance them with YMCA chapters that complemented their ongoing work. Finally, he promised to proceed only if missionaries themselves welcomed a partnership: "We stand ready to co-operate with the missionaries when, and only when, they ask for our cooperation." Wishard had struck exactly the right chord. At a conference known for cantankerous debates, not a single missionary registered disapproval.[46] The body even passed a resolution approving YMCA work.[47]

Wishard returned to America eager to press ahead. After persuading the YMCA to commit to China, he hunted for the right person to establish a beachhead. Given that his plan was to utilize existing missionary infrastructure, he settled on a young man who understood it well. Born on a houseboat in Zhejiang Province in 1870, Willard Lyon spent the first decade of his life in the mission of his father, D. N. Lyon. In 1891, he enrolled in the College of Wooster in Ohio, where he was elected president of the YMCA chapter. After college, he worked for the SVM in Chicago while studying in seminary. He was preparing, to his father's delight, to be a minister. When Wishard approached Lyon, the latter expressed grave doubts about his fitness for the work before declining the offer. Though Lyon's mind appeared made up, it wasn't. A year later, he wrote Wishard to reverse his decision. A divine influence "came over me suddenly as a thunderclap," Lyon vividly wrote, and caused his "prejudices" against going to China to "vanish like the mist before the sun." There remained, however, one hurdle: his father. A pure evangelist, D. N. Lyon had staunchly opposed the new missionary models unveiled at the 1877 conference. At Willard's request, Wishard wrote to D. N. Lyon to explain the YMCA's role in China, hoping that Lyon would become moved to support his son. Though Wishard excelled at persuasion, he could not budge the elder Lyon. Willard "has taken vows," Lyon adamantly insisted, and must not deviate from his plan to become a minister. Lyon also critiqued the YMCA's strategy of building on existing missions. It was foolish, he believed, to settle for this redundancy when YMCA men could better serve the cause by venturing "into the darkness" to "kindle a new fire" among the "millions in China who have never heard the name of Jesus." When Willard embarked for China in 1895 as the YMCA's first secretary, he did so without his father's "consent."[48]

Based in Tianjin, Lyon attempted to lay the groundwork for a national YMCA movement. Given that he was but one man (and one who did not, as of yet, speak Chinese well), progress was slow. In between language lessons, he tried to open new chapters while stimulating activity in the handful of existing chapters. By 1896, he was monitoring eleven YMCA chapters.[49] That year, he received a shot in the arm when John Mott visited China, bringing with him his personal charm, inexhaustible energy, and formidable networking ability. Mott's itinerary in China formed a small segment of a larger world tour. His ambitious goal was to stitch Christian student associations everywhere into a single fabric with global coverage. As Mott and Lyon traveled together, they stopped at numerous colleges (Chapter 12), performing an act of creation each time and leaving in their wake twenty-two new YMCA chapters. Reaching Shanghai, they attended an event they had organized—the first national convention of the Chinese YMCA. At the conference, they brought the disparate student associations together under a National Committee, which chose Lyon as its first head. Though Lyon was, of course, American, the YMCA did not wish to enter China as a foreign institution. To ensure indigenous leadership, the National Committee mandated that at least half of its members must be Chinese (at its second convention, in 1899, all officers would be Chinese except two).[50] When Mott departed China, he left behind a transformed organization. "He visited practically all the higher institutions of learning," a Chinese student recalled of the exhilarating moment, demonstrating to students "the advantages of union with the worldwide brotherhood of Christian students." In this way, Mott "influenced thousands of individual student lives" by infecting them with the "spirit of Christian unity."[51]

Back in Tianjin, a reinvigorated Lyon resumed work. He came to see his role in China in a vaguely karmic way as rectifying the moral deficit caused by the Chinese Exclusion Act. "America has excluded the Chinaman from her own borders," Lyon wrote, "and therefore Christian America owes . . . to China the true love that exists in the Christlike hearts."[52] In 1897, he launched a monthly magazine, *The Chinese Intercollegian*, designed to foster "esprit de corps" among Chinese student groups while also connecting them with "students of the rest of the world." But as exciting as the magazine was, it pushed an already overwhelmed Lyon to the brink of exhaustion. "I am in sore need of help," he bluntly stated in a report.[53] Help arrived when the YMCA sent three men to China: Robert Gailey, Robert Lewis, and Fletcher Brockman. In their effort to promote a healthy Christian lifestyle, Lewis and Gailey stressed physical education. Gailey, a former college football player at Princeton, brought to China a congenial nature and zest for living (along with prodigious eating ability). He taught Chinese students to play football and became a favorite among them.[54] Lewis, who would head the YMCA in Shanghai, built a gym and introduced basketball.[55] Each young man possessed a gregarious nature, a sunny disposition, and a gift for social organization. They existed in sharp contrast to the austere missionaries of previous decades.

Brockman also exemplified this new kind of missionary. Like Lyon, he provided the YMCA with a tangible link to the missionary past. Born in 1867, Brockman spent his youth in the cotton fields of rural Georgia. In the late 1870s, his parents moved the family to Atlanta so that he and his siblings could attend school. There he met Laura Haygood before she departed for China. In 1887, he started at Vanderbilt, missing Charlie Soong by a couple of years. Soong was gone but not forgotten: Brockman discovered that an entire folklore surrounded Soong in the collective memory of the college. When John Mott and Robert Wilder visited Vanderbilt to recruit for the SVM, Brockman signed up. He also heard Young J. Allen speak on campus. "His address at Vanderbilt was masterly," Brockman said of Allen. "He had an exalted opinion of the Chinese people." Though Brockman planned to go to China through the SVM, he first worked for seven years for the YMCA, becoming its national secretary. Unlike others in his circle, Brockman held onto the conservative vision of missions as a war against heathenism. When the time came to embark for China, that vision suffused his mind. "The religious leaders of China were hostile to Christianity," he thought at the time, "and I must meet them" in a "fight to the finish between light and darkness."[56] Brockman saw himself as heading into combat.

It would not take long for him to abandon this militaristic vision. When Brockman reached Shanghai in 1898, Lyon greeted him at the harbor and promptly took him to see Laura Haygood. Brockman located Charlie Soong, with whom he became "intimate friends." As close as the two were, Soong kept one colossal secret from Brockman. "It was years later before I learned that he was then the financial head of Sun Yat-sen's revolutionary efforts," wrote Brockman, who professed amazement that Soong had "silently carried" the "staggering burden" for so many years. Brockman also forged a lasting relationship with Young J. Allen, whom he regarded as a venerable sage with his long beard and flowing white hair. At some point, it occurred to Brockman that none of his new friends were militant, and he began to revise his preconceived notions of the Chinese. "In the first letter" home, "I announced my surrender of any sense of Anglo-Saxon superiority over the Chinese."[57]

Brockman's respect for Chinese people only strengthened when he started to work with them on YMCA business. He described his attempt to handle a financial crisis at the Hong Kong chapter. The organization's largest benefactor, a "Mr. Li," had suddenly gone bankrupt, leaving the YMCA without funds to run its programming. At an emergency meeting, Brockman showed up prepared to deliver a "set speech" that would urge members to look to their "faith" for the answer. Partway into his speech, Brockman was interrupted by Tong Kai-son, the chapter's chairman and one of Yung Wing's former students. "You tell us to have faith," Tong said, "but we are business men. We have to pay our debts in dollars. If you could turn your faith into dollars, it would be all right." Though Tong's tone was polite, Brockman understood that a Chinese had challenged his authority. Instead of becoming defensive, Brockman engaged in "some rapid and thorough searching of heart" before responding. "You are quite right, Mr. Tong," Brockman conceded. Faith is of "no use" in these circumstances.

Shifting gears, Brockman pledged to find the money somehow—but where? The group could think of no other Chinese Christian to appeal to for a donation. The only name that came up was Feng Hwa-chen, a man Brockman called the "famous Confucianist." Just a few years earlier, Brockman would have dismissed such a notion out of hand: Confucianists, after all, were the sworn enemies of missions. But China had changed him, and a more open-minded Brockman set up an interview with Feng, who turned out to be quite reasonable. "You gentlemen have come across the Pacific Ocean to help our young men," Feng said. "The least that we Chinese can do is to provide the funds."[58] Brockman got his money. But in the process, he had obtained something of greater value—self-knowledge. The incident revealed to him the degree to which he had evolved with respect to his treatment of the Chinese. His exchange with Tong suggests his willingness to respect a Chinese leader. And his acceptance of Feng's money shows that his prejudice against Confucianism was rapidly fading.

Establishing themselves just before 1900, Lyon, Brockman, Gailey, and Lewis represented the new missionary type who would shape Christian institutions in twentieth-century China. But what sort of influence would they seek and how would they achieve it? Shirley Garrett, who wrote a history of the YMCA in China, credits these pioneers with creating a fresh dynamic in their interactions with the Chinese that anticipated the Peace Corps volunteers of the 1960s. First, they dropped the cold solemnity that had characterized the tone of earlier missionaries and that so many Chinese found repellant. Instead, they exuded a warm optimism as they promoted their sunny brand of Christianity and the social uplift it could bring. Second, they chose not to exhort the Chinese, abandoning the entire concept of missions as a one-way communication. They envisioned the YMCA as a locus of "cultural exchange," a space designed to facilitate the "subtle blending of institutions and ideas." Last, they believed in "indigenizing" their organization by cultivating Chinese for leadership positions. Though nearly all missionaries planned to leave behind Chinese-controlled institutions, most saw this as a far-off goal. The YMCA, in contrast, accelerated the process. It wished to see an organization that was, in Garrett's words, "self-propagating, self-governing, and self-supporting as quickly as possible." In addition to Tong Kai-son, at least two other CEM students—T'ang Shao-yi and Liang Tunyen—played instrumental leadership and advisory roles in the YMCA. They were joined by large numbers of Chinese businesspeople, government officials, college educators, and student organizers who lent their time, money, and expertise toward developing the YMCA in the early twentieth century.[59]

Conclusion

Though the YMCA and the SVM were separate organizations, they shared substantial overlap. Missionaries who headed to China through the SVM often contributed to the YMCA when they got there. And Wishard, Mott, Wilder, and Lyon worked for both, sometimes simultaneously, because they saw their goals as compatible. Indeed, both organizations reflected in outlook the progressive turn made by their churches in the Gilded Age. It was at this time that the Social Gospel emerged in America in response to the myriad problems caused by the nation's rapid urbanization and industrialization. Instead of concentrating exclusively on saving souls, Christians increasingly targeted social problems like poverty, alcoholism, unclean tenements, malnutrition, and inadequate schooling. The Social Gospel, according to Harold Rabinowitz and Greg Tobin, "focused not only on the purification of the human soul, but the purification of human society."⁶⁰ When missionaries affiliated with the SVM or the YMCA carried the Social Gospel to China, their conception of the work changed: along with saving souls, missions should alleviate suffering and uplift Chinese society.⁶¹ Inspired by this broad view of missions, the new recruits regarded preaching about sin as somewhat crude, narrow, and outdated. In contrast, the newer models aligned well with their priorities. Of all the new institutions in China, there was one that attracted them the most—the college.

12

Ivory Pagodas

The Rise of Christian Colleges

Early in 1888, Nathan Sites and Sia Sek Ong boarded a steamship bound for America. Sia's colleagues in Foochow had chosen him to represent them in New York at the General Conference of the Methodist Episcopal Church. Sites would serve as his translator. When the ship reached San Francisco, the pair met with an immediate obstacle. Port authorities, enforcing the Chinese Exclusion Act (1882), barred Sia's entry. It was only after Sites explained the special circumstances to a judge that Sia was allowed into the country.[1] Safely in San Francisco, Sia composed a formal letter of introduction to the Methodist Episcopal Church. Likening the church to a Confucian family, Sia cast the Foochow branch in the role of a deferential child approaching a revered parent. "Your humble servant," he wrote, "comes as a little child, leaning on the parental knee, to convey hearty words of filial greeting . . . to the mother Church."[2]

Once the conference got underway, Sia stopped deferring. He spoke his mind and voted his conscience on issues confronting the church. When the all-male body voted on a proposal to open the conference to women, Sia cast his ballot in favor. His experience in Foochow had compelled him to revise his views on female potential. His side lost.[3] The docket also included a debate on the possible creation of a new position, the "Missionary Bishop," who would oversee churches in Asia. Rising to his feet, Sia delivered a six-paragraph oration arguing against the proposal. "If this General Conference decides to send . . . a Missionary Bishop to China, we must submit," Sia asserted, but "I feel it is not the desire of the people."[4] He lost again. In the ensuing election to determine who the first bishop would be, a total of 410 votes were cast, with the winner earning 286. Sia Sek Ong received one vote. Quite possibly, he voted for himself.[5]

After the conference, Sia toured the United States. A man who previously had not ventured outside his province beheld the American West and Niagara Falls as well as multiple cities, factories, churches, and colleges.[6] Visiting Sites's alma mater, Ohio Wesleyan, Sia received an honorary degree at the same commencement that saw Hu King Eng graduate.[7] He toured other colleges too, such as Depauw University in Indiana, where he was asked what impressed him most about the institution. "The fact that so many hundreds of young men and young women can study here together," he said of Depauw, which had started admitting women after the Civil War. During his travels, Sia gazed with awe upon the myriad manifestations of the Industrial Revolution. "There were great revelations to him," Stephen Baldwin wrote, "in the immense factories, the machine shops, the railways, and . . . all the great, busy, bustling life of the young republic." For Sia, the progress was thrilling to behold but also tinged with sorrow. After he returned to Foochow, Esther Baldwin innocently asked him to compare China and the United States. With profound sadness, Sia exclaimed, "Your country is alive; my country is dead!"[8]

It was a devastating conclusion to draw. But Sia used it as a source of invigoration, not discouragement. He prepared a lecture on America and delivered it in Foochow's churches. In each congregation, Sia "awakened intense interest as he told of the wonderful things he had seen." As audiences listened spellbound, "one wonder after another was brought to view." But Sia's purpose was not to astound. His lecture had a point. He claimed to have found "evidences of the superiority of Christianity" in America's "progress."[9] Progress followed the Gospel, Sia indicated, because a Christian society provided the foundation that made progress possible. For Chinese listeners, Sia offered a message of hope. His implication was that if they dedicated themselves to spreading Christianity, they could expect the future to bring not just more churches but *all of the modern marvels* Sia had vividly described—factories, railroads, hospitals, and colleges.

The college, more than any other institution, embodied Chinese dreams. For centuries, the Chinese had viewed education as the ladder to status in a Confucian society. For this reason, the Chinese did not require much convincing to accept the concept of a college; unlike the church, it slid easily into an existing slot in the people's aspirations. Colleges also appealed to those who decried China's vulnerability, revealed during painful wars with foreign powers. To those critics, the college seemed to offer, under one roof, all the academic disciplines that contributed to the West's military and industrial might: science, math, and engineering. Fittingly, when Sia returned to

China, he carried a symbol of Western learning that rivaled the crucifix in potency. During his American tour, several churches had raised money to send him home with a state-of-the-art telescope that, in Nathan Sites's words, revealed "the wonderful works of God in the sun, moon and planets." Where would the costly instrument go? Sia installed it in Foochow's Anglo-Chinese College.[10]

When that institution opened in 1881, it formed part of a small wave of new colleges founded by missionaries. That wave included St. John's College in Shanghai and Tengchow College in Shandong. Each college, in its early years, faced the challenge of defining its identity. This was no easy task because it required the college somehow to remain true to the mission's evangelical objective while also appealing to the Chinese community, which often cared little for Christianity. In each case, a college's identity hinged on its answer to two questions: should the college aggressively promote Christianity, and should it offer English instruction? Before 1895, Christian colleges grew but only slowly. That year, however, China's loss to Japan in a war sparked a national search for answers that conferred sudden relevance upon the Christian colleges and the modern education they offered. With surging enrollments, the colleges entered their takeoff periods. Becoming magnets for missionaries who wished to teach, coach, and administrate, the Christian colleges mirrored the YMCA in bringing to China a new type of missionary at century's end.

St. John's College

The story of missionary colleges begins with a man with a long name who had traveled a long distance. Samuel Isaac Joseph Schereschewsky was born in Russian Lithuania in 1831, emigrated to America in 1854, and sailed to China as a missionary in 1859. His peregrinations were not purely geographic. He had also undertaken a spiritual journey, starting out life as a Jew and converting to Christianity in New York, where he ascended the leadership ranks of the Episcopal Church. In 1859, Bishop William Boone, after dropping Yen Yung Kiung off at Kenyon, presided over the ceremony that promoted Schereschewsky to deacon before the two embarked together for China. One year later in Shanghai, Boone ordained him priest. But in China, Schereschewsky's career stalled. In the 1870s, he reported to his bishop that, after twelve years in the field, his effort to win converts was "without any apparent result so far." Able to claim only "one family and a lad," he doubted whether he was suited for the evangelical side of missions.[11] Had his life's long journey been in vain?

One aspect of missions work excited Schereschewsky. He had begun to compose what he hoped would be the definitive Mandarin translation of the

Old Testament. Possessing almost preternatural powers of concentration, he could prosecute the meticulous work for hours without taking breaks. The bishop, when he visited, marveled at the intellectual stamina of a man who could engage a Chinese copyist from morning until 5 P.M., release the exhausted man from his labor, gulp down a cup of tea, and then continue with a second copyist late into the night. His proclivity toward total immersion in his work tested his wife's patience. She recalled many nights in which she, after retiring alone, would awaken at 2 A.M. to an empty bed. She would find her husband huddled in his cold study, "repeating Chinese phrases to himself," oblivious to the fact that the fire had gone out.[12] Schereschewsky may have lacked the charisma of an evangelist, but he excelled at the intellectual side of his work.

In 1875, the Episcopal Church turned to Schereschewsky to fill the vacant bishop's position in Shanghai. When missionaries stationed there heard that he was under consideration, they did not doubt the man but did question the fit. "I have always supposed him a bookworm," responded William Boone Jr., the son of the former bishop, "and not a *worker among men.*" "He is very clever in books," wrote another, but he looks upon the Chinese "as a Brahmin does a pariah." Though colleagues feared his cerebral nature might distance him from the Chinese, the church favored him. It faced a problem, however, in that Schereschewsky himself wished to decline the position. Content with translations work, he did not covet the high-profile role. When the church approached him again in 1877, he expressed openness to the idea but stipulated that his acceptance was contingent upon the church's approval of one condition—it must commit $100,000 toward the founding of a college. "Since missions have been established in China," he pointed out, "not a *single* college has been established."[13] Now was the time to rectify the glaring omission. Why did Schereschewsky place a college at the center of his vision? Himself a scholar, he believed that "mission work must do more than convert blind beggars"; it should also appeal to the Chinese intellect. More practically, he recognized that missionaries could not spread Christianity in China by themselves; that mammoth task would require a constantly replenishing supply of native pastors. A college could fill this need by reliably churning out "hearty and efficient coworkers." His demand met, Bishop Schereschewsky launched an ambitious plan to found St. John's.[14]

In 1878, he purchased a merchant's estate, a fourteen-acre plot called "Jessfield" located five miles from Shanghai, accessible by road and river. Since Jessfield's existing structures were insufficient to sustain a college, Schereschewsky ordered the construction of new buildings to serve as dormitories, classrooms, and faculty residences. To ensure a steady flow of students, he envisioned the college as an extension of the two mission-run boys' schools in Shanghai—Baird Hall and Duane Hall. Going further, he had the students and faculty of these schools relocated to the new campus, where they became the preparatory department for the college. At the same time, the two mission-run girls' schools, Bridgman School and Emma Jones School, were also removed to the campus, where he consolidated them into St. Mary's Hall. Schereschewsky appointed Wong Kong-chai's daughter, Wong Woo-ngoo, to serve as headmistress of St. Mary's. Though male and female students would inhabit the same campus, they would not take classes together or even see one another. St. John's would practice strict segregation of the sexes.[15] As education migrated to Jessfield, Schereschewsky had to decide what to do with the vacated buildings in Shanghai. Though he might have sold them, he hesitated to do so on the hunch that Shanghai real estate would rise in value. He opted instead to hold the properties and lease them out.[16]

Schereschewsky's extensive construction plan included a house for Yen Yung Kiung. This decision reflected not only the bishop's respect for the Kenyon alumnus but also his understanding that the fortunes of St. John's would rest on Yen's shoulders. It was true that the bishop could count on several Chinese to help with the college. Along with Yen and Wong Kong-chai, he could avail himself of Hong Niok Woo, who in 1854 had voyaged to America onboard the *Susquehanna* as cabin boy for a surgeon from Pennsylvania. In America, Woo stayed with the doctor in Lancaster, learned the printing trade, became a U.S. citizen, and served in the Union Army. When the romantic adventurer returned to Shanghai in 1864, the mission found his versatility highly useful: he taught in schools, handled printing jobs, managed churches, preached sermons, assisted with medical work, and raised money in the Chinese community.[17] As handy as Woo was, only Yen understood how to organize a college capable of meeting the needs of Chinese students. It was Yen who, in September of 1879, stood on campus greeting Baird Hall and Duane Hall students as they arrived by river with their trunks. After moving them into their dorm, he commemorated the historic moment with a short speech. He "exhorted" the boys to study hard and keep active religious lives. He also reminded them that their "subscribers," the American donors sponsoring their scholarships, had taken a substantial "interest" in the new institution.[18]

On the first day of class, the fifty students learned that St. John's would follow a strict schedule imported from Yen's alma mater. "I keep Kenyon hours," Yen wrote, meaning that he had broken each day into timed units of productive activity:

6:45 A.M. Prayers, and, immediately after, breakfast.
8 A.M. to 12 P.M. Study and recitation.
12 P.M. Dinner.
12 P.M. to 2 P.M. Recess.

2 to 5 P.M. Study and recitation.
5 P.M. Prayers and supper.
7:30 to 8:30 P.M. Study.

Yen's "Kenyon hours" get to the heart of his personal interest in the college. He had always felt fortunate that, during his formative years, he had benefited from a Kenyon education. With St. John's, he was determined to extend to Chinese youths a similar experience. While St. John's remained inchoate, Yen endeavored to imprint Kenyon's values and structures upon the shapeless institution.[19]

To become a legitimate college, St. John's needed money—much more than it had in its coffers. To raise money, the school tried some creative fundraising ideas. It reached out to Kenyon alumni and invited them to join something called the "Kiung League," a club of donors who covered Yen's salary with their contributions. "I recalled the time when I came in your midst, a boy stranger," a grateful Yen wrote the Kiung League, and you "took me in," becoming "not only my generous patrons, but true friends."[20] As clever as the Kiung League was, it was indicative of the financial challenges faced by the college. In a free school, there was obviously no revenue to be had from tuition. And since Schereschewsky had poured the start-up money into the physical edifice, little remained for what must go inside—teachers, books, and equipment. Just four missionaries taught courses—Schereschewsky, Yen, William Boone, and Daniel Bates.[21] Yen, who was something of a polymath, handled History, Geography, Mathematics, Hydrostatics, and Astronomy.[22] Viewing the situation as unsustainable, Bates pleaded with Americans to donate money. "Is there not someone who will build for us a college chapel?" he asked, requesting also a telescope, a library, and books to put in it.[23] When Bates departed after a year, he left the college even more shorthanded, prompting Schereschewsky to describe Yen and Boone as "overtaxed."[24]

Given the college's urgent needs, it is somewhat curious that Schereschewsky would seek his own replacement mere months after the school's opening. But in 1880, that is exactly what he attempted. "I have done what I could," he wrote church members, "and now what I need is a *thoroughly-trained* professor to place at the head of the College."[25] Why did the founder wish to step down when the college most needed him? The job was draining him. Unlike translating texts, college management forced Schereschewsky to work with people, some of whom exasperated him. For example, when he made the executive decision to move the city schools to Jessfield, he inadvertently ignited a feud with Mary Nelson, head of the Emma Jones School. In a rage she stormed into his campus office and a heated exchange ensued, one filled with shouting and foot-stomping. Nelson did not hesitate to go over the bishop's head, mailing complaint letters to the home church. "It made my heart sick," Nelson lugubriously wrote, to see the city buildings, which previously had housed wholesome Christian schools, now shamefully leased for money. On this "holy ground," she claimed to have witnessed appalling things like opium dens, commerce on the Sabbath, and other foul sights that "make your blood run cold." Schereschewsky, she prophesied, would answer for his greed on Judgment Day. It was later revealed that, for years, Nelson had run a boardinghouse surreptitiously. Her real motive in opposing the bishop was to protect not a "holy ground" but her secret profit center. Though her machinations were exposed, this conflict exhausted Schereschewsky, as did others. When a male missionary at a girls' school was accused of impregnating a student, the bishop rushed over to appease the furious parents. It turned out the man was innocent, but Schereschewsky's handling of the potentially explosive incident siphoned off still more of his dwindling strength.[26]

Frustrations always attend an ambitious project such as what Schereschewsky was attempting. As long as the overall balance between progress and problems tipped favorably toward the former, he could persevere with his plan. But as good news slowed and vexations multiplied, the bishop started to wear down. His powers of concentration abandoned him, and he became temperamental and moody.[27] In the summer of 1881, Schereschewsky complained of extreme discomfort from the oppressive heat. When other symptoms materialized, doctors concluded he had suffered a stroke. Though he recovered somewhat, he was never the same again, and his active days in Shanghai were over. In 1884, William Boone officially replaced him as bishop and college head. On what did Schereschewsky blame his deteriorating condition? "I forfeited my health" managing the college and mission, he said, "and have [since] been at death's door." He had founded China's first Christian college, but at terrible cost. It nearly killed him.[28]

Fortunately for St. John's, the bishop's untimely exit provided the nadir. In ensuing years, the school recovered. Enrollments rose to a healthy plateau of about eighty students and stayed there throughout the 1880s. But these consistent numbers belied a high degree of academic flux as different programs within the college saw rising and falling fortunes. At its inception, Schereschewsky imagined St. John's primarily as a minister-training institution that would also teach Chinese classics and Western subjects. In keeping with these priorities, he devised a tripartite academic structure featuring three programs. Along with a Theology Program, he built a College Program, which comprised Chinese and Western Studies, and a Preparatory division, which was essentially a high school. But the school's actual trajectory deviated from the founder's vision. Over time, students gravitated away from Chinese Studies and Theology and toward two programs not included in the blueprints: Medicine and English.[29]

In its early years, St. John's maintained an ambivalent stance toward English. The original plan called for Chinese, not English, to be the medium of instruction.[30] However, an unexpected development in 1880 prompted a change in course: Chinese merchants made a request. A "number of applications have been received," the college reported, "from merchants who desire an English course for their sons with a view to business." While acknowledging that English classes were "not directly in the line of our purposed work," the college nevertheless concluded that "their desires should be met."[31] In 1881, Yen announced that St. John's had opened up a "paying department" in response to the merchants' "pressing demand." Unlike the scholarship students, the boys who matriculated into this new "Anglo-Chinese Department" would pay for English courses, room, and board.[32] Yen was of two minds on the issue. Part of him questioned the wisdom of catering to students for whom a "business knowledge" of English "is all they care for." At the same time, he believed that English, acting like a "wedge," could "open a general desire for liberal education."[33] Practical young men who enrolled to learn English would sample Western learning and develop a taste for it. In short, the liberal arts education that had transformed Yen at Kenyon would reach them too.

English did transform the college, but not in the manner Yen had hoped. "It is regretted," he wrote in 1884, that "the English language and not liberal learning is what is sought."[34] Though English did not bolster the liberal arts, it did attract high-profile Chinese families. The head of the China Merchants Steam Navigation Company, a top military official, and Li Hongzhang all enrolled sons or nephews in the Anglo-Chinese Department.[35] The scions of the rich and powerful brought money and prestige to St. John's, but their presence on campus came with a downside: they demanded special treatment above what the scholarship boys received. Wishing to avoid a two-tiered student body, college leaders faced a difficult decision. On the one hand, they did not wish to eliminate English, because it generated revenue. On the other hand, they recognized that the for-profit department perpetuated an invidious class distinction among students. To resolve the problem, the college made a change in 1884 that would alter its course forever: it closed the Anglo-Chinese Department while designating English as the medium of instruction college-wide.[36]

With this decisive action, St. John's reinvented itself. It ceased being a training school for ministers with a curious moneymaking appendage and emerged as a Christian college offering a liberal arts education taught in English.[37] The new English focus forced the college to add faculty. In the early 1880s, it hired Koeh Ah Szi, a Kenyon graduate, and Esther Spencer, a missionary.[38] Spencer innovated in English instruction, developing new pedagogical methods and writing textbooks.[39] It was also at this time that Yung Wing's boys returned to China after the closure of the CEM. With their unique educations and English fluency, they fit perfectly into the college's new curricular framework. Yen hired five of them to teach at St. John's, and also brought in a graduate of the Mateers' school.[40]

Like English, medicine had not figured into Schereschewsky's original plan. Medicine's rise within the college started when Henry Boone, William Boone's brother and Wong Kong-chai's childhood friend, returned to China in 1880 after finishing medical school. Boone saw missionaries like himself as bringers of progress. "These Chinese are waking up," he wrote with zeal. "They are crying out for education" and "want to study mathematics, civil engineering," and "medicine and surgery." To satisfy the "new generation," Boone started building a medical program.[41] He began by training a small number of St. John's graduates at the mission hospital in Shanghai.[42] To stimulate interest in medicine at St. John's, he partnered with Yen to give weekly lectures at the college. "Chemical lectures were given every Saturday morning," Yen reported, with "Dr. Boone making the experiments and I giving the explanations."[43] The medical program expanded after Boone successfully treated a seriously ill patient. While the patient convalesced, his relative, Lee Chu Bing, visited the hospital and came away impressed. "I was struck with its order and cleanliness," Lee said, "and also by the fact that the poorest received the same . . . care as the rich." The "hospital is a worthy institution, and I wish to help it." Lee did exactly that. He purchased a Shanghai city block, tore down the houses, and raised the money needed to erect St. Luke's Hospital. After its construction, Chinese merchants and officials fully supported the institution, obviating the need for mission funds. In the 1890s, Boone formally linked the two institutions by establishing a dual-site medical program: for two years students would take science courses at St. John's, before transferring to St. Luke's to train under Boone.[44]

Much of this development took place under a capable new administrator. Francis Hawks Pott arrived in 1886, was appointed headmaster in 1888, and would run the college for over fifty years. The irony, given the length of his tenure, was that Pott did not imagine a career in college administration—at least, not at first. He wished to evangelize in the conventional style. But once the reluctant educator started at St. John's, he discovered latent ability. St. John's also allowed him to work with Chinese people and indulge his interest in Chinese culture. That interest had originated in New York when, while studying Theology, he offered a Sunday school class to Chinese laundry workers. "I became anxious to learn about these strangers in our midst," he wrote, "and to read books about China." In China, he immersed himself in the culture: he mastered the language, ate Chinese food, wore Chinese clothes, and braided his hair into a queue. In 1888, he married Wong Kong-chai's daughter, Wong Woo-ngoo, the headmistress of St. Mary's.[45]

Though Pott adopted Chinese customs, he did not "go native," an expression implying the complete abandonment of one's own culture. Crucially, he never deviated from his primary objective, which was to instill Christian values, the ability to think, and a love for science. Using a hands-on approach, he endeavored to elevate the institution to the level of an American Christian college. Since such institutions have mottos, he coined one for St. John's: "Light and Truth."[46] He also promoted physical exercise, inaugurating semi-annual athletic contests. "They were held on the lawn in front of the Chapel," Pott wrote, "and naturally were of a somewhat primitive character." But they evolved to the point where Pott could claim St. John's as "the first institution in China to introduce organized athletic sports."[47] Pott also believed in faculty-student interaction outside of class. Once each week, the Potts hosted the students at their residence. "On Saturday nights I have my weekly reception," he explained, with "class by class coming to spend a few hours in play . . . with the usual light refreshments." When he detected waning religious interest among students, he took action by starting a choir, mandating attendance at daily chapel, and requiring participation in Bible classes. To see if his measures were having any effect, he periodically gathered together students to quiz them on the Bible. He found some student responses "disheartening," such as that angels were "little Buddhas" or that Mary was Jesus's disciple. But he remained, on the whole, encouraged that most students were acquiring the essential tenets of Christianity.[48]

Pott also insisted on discipline. Before his arrival, the college had been accused of negligence after some boys were caught gambling with dice and dominoes in the dormitory.[49] Every night, Pott paced the dormitory hallways to prevent mischief and catch night owls; every weekend he personally inspected student dorm rooms.[50] During his first year as head, he expelled eleven students, eight for breaking rules and three for poor academic performance. Last, he enforced the segregation of the sexes. "St. Mary's was . . . separated from the boys by a thick and high bamboo fence," an alumnus recalled. "We could hear the girls but could not see them."[51] After a decade of challenges, by 1890 Pott had China's first Christian college on solid footing.

The Anglo-Chinese College

When St. John's attached the name "Anglo-Chinese" to its for-profit English program, it did not pluck the name out of thin air. It borrowed the name from another Christian college launched in Foochow in 1881. The story of that college's founding begins with Tiong Ahok, a wealthy merchant who believed in charity. Whenever disaster struck his community—fire, flood, disease—he would act swiftly with aid.[52] He also believed in building institutions that served the public welfare. Though not a church member, he often attended Methodist Episcopal services and had befriended its missionaries. In December of 1880, he floated an idea before two missionaries. What if he were to donate money to start a college? By happenstance, Robert Maclay, a former Foochow missionary now stationed in Japan, arrived for a visit at this same time. Twenty years earlier, Maclay's recruiting speech in Ohio had won a commitment from Nathan Sites. Now he shared news of a successful Christian college in Japan and recommended a comparable institution for Foochow.[53] His idea achieved confluence with both Tiong Ahok's offer and the combined will of the Chinese ministers, who advocated for more higher learning. At a meeting held on January 19, 1881, missionaries, Chinese pastors, and Tiong Ahok agreed to form a college. Like the mission's churches, the college would adhere to the self-support model: the Chinese would support the institution through tuition. In the weeks that followed, Frank Ohlinger sparked the school's genesis: he formally accepted Tiong Ahok's gift, purchased land, appointed a board of trustees, and set tuition rates. He also assumed the presidency of the Anglo-Chinese College (ACC).[54]

Ohlinger's role as catalyst notwithstanding, it was the Chinese pastors who strongly wished to see this institution built. The missionaries themselves failed to reach consensus. Though Ohlinger and Sites favored opening a college, other missionaries resisted the idea. To understand their opposition, we must remember that education as a missionary model remained largely untested in 1881. Only four years had elapsed since Calvin Mateer's stirring defense of schools at the 1877 conference. Even though he had won some support, most of his backers valued schools only as a means to a loftier end—the conquest of China by Christianity. To them, a school was but a piece of bait intended to lure Chinese families into a zone of church influence. The education it provided was of secondary importance. Foochow's Chinese pastors differed in one crucial respect: they did not subordinate education to the Gospel. That was because, for them, conversion was supposed to bring not only religion but, in Dana Robert's words, "expectations for a new way of life." This new life included a cultivated mind.[55] Both sides, in sum, favored education, but they did so with strikingly different priorities. For some missionaries, a college that valued knowledge for its own sake went too far.

It also cost too much money. The debate surrounding higher education notwithstanding, a more practical concern threatened the ACC in its early years: the fledgling college faced a fiscal shortfall. The most pressing need was for a dormitory, the continued absence of which threatened the school's viability. Without a dorm, the school could accept only local students, of whom a finite number existed (forty-five enrolled in the first year). Fewer students meant less tuition revenue, the lifeblood of a self-supporting school. Ohlinger sought donations to help carry the school through its early years. "Until we receive $5,000 from some source [for a dorm]," Ohlinger wrote his home base, "we must continue to refuse admission to those who do not live in the immediate vicinity." A desperate Ohlinger even played to the vanity of potential donors by allowing them to affix their names to any edifice they funded: "You have the privilege of naming these halls." Ohlinger also appealed to their nobler selves, reminding donors what kind of human being the college intended to produce. A few graduates will always be "vagabonds," Ohlinger joked, but many more will find employment in the foreign community, likely as diplomats or merchants. A larger group still, he predicted, will imbibe the school's mission by dedicating their careers to education or the ministry. Vocations aside, nearly all graduates will become "true angels of mercy" who care for "this suffering people."[56]

Though he made no promises with regard to conversions, Ohlinger offered assurances that the school's Christian values would rub off on its students (the occasional "vagabond" excepted). That said, it appeared early on as if something more spiritually transformative might take place on campus. In 1882, Christianity unexpectedly caught fire, creating an electric atmosphere. "A gracious revival has spread among the students," the annual report stated, "till this institution . . . has all the ring of a Methodist camp-meeting, with its mourners' bench and its shouting testimonies."[57] What sparked the revival? Possibly, it had something to do with the regular visits of Chinese ministers. According to Ohlinger, students who had "never been in a Christian chapel" would "listen with rapt attention" to Sia Sek Ong or Hu Sing-Mi (Hu Yong Mi's brother).[58] But the awakening proved ephemeral. The revival came and went without making any lasting impact, and the school limped along with low enrollment. In 1883, Ohlinger stepped down from the presidency.

To replace Ohlinger, the board did not reach into the missionary pool in Foochow. Instead, it appointed an outsider with strong scholarly credentials: George Smyth, a graduate of Drew Theological Seminary, who excelled at Ancient Greek.[59] During his first year, Smyth detected a trend when he studied the profiles of the sixty-seven students: most were sons of church members. Based on the data, he deduced that the college existed to serve this demographic.[60] It was not long, however, before he revised the college's mission. Like any administrator, Smyth understood the indispensable nature of money. And in 1886, when the "term closed with not a dollar in the treasury," he acknowledged the urgency of the situation.[61] Since the college's financial fortunes depended on tuition, in order to survive it needed to attract more students. The college could no longer afford to appeal only to Christian families. Smyth had to widen the net.

Smyth adopted two measures. First, he delicately crafted the college's mission so as to attract non-Christian parents while still satisfying Christian stakeholders. Specifically, he continued to celebrate the school's Christian identity, because such words pleased American churchgoers; their donations were crucial in the short term when the new college required facilities and equipment. He dropped aggressive evangelical rhetoric, however, because it repelled prospective Chinese families whose tuitions would be counted upon to sustain the school in the long term. Finding a middle ground that could please such different constituencies was not easy. In an article for a missionary magazine, Smyth went to great lengths to explain his Christian—but not evangelical—vision. "Our college is a Christian school," he stated emphatically, noting that some students enjoyed Sunday-school lessons with Elizabeth Fisher. That said, "we . . . do nothing to force the students to become Christians" and do not engage in "propaganda." Anticipating criticism, Smyth defended the ACC against those who would fault the college for "doing nothing directly to Christianize the people." "We are educating," Smyth insisted, "and educating is part of the work of the church."[62]

Despite Smyth's best efforts, the ACC was failing to convince Chinese parents that the education it offered was worth the price. In 1885, Smyth could count just over forty students, fewer than the number the school had started with and a precariously low number for a tuition-driven institution.[63] The uninspiring enrollment figures reflected an overall lack of enthusiasm for the college in the Chinese community. In 1886, Smyth used a sequence of negatives to describe the spiritless closing ceremonies: "no long commencement orations," "no fine singing," and no "immense assemblage of gentlemen and ladies to applaud their favorites." Smyth held out hope that events might inspire more enthusiasm in the future "when the school becomes popular."[64] But the school had yet to demonstrate its value to the Chinese and so faced a cloudy future.

Tengchow College

Founded just after the ACC in 1882, Tengchow College enjoyed a more auspicious start. Not self-supporting, the college did not depend on tuitions and so did not have to try as hard to sell itself to the community. But if the college had required tuition-payers, it could have easily attracted them. That is because Calvin and Julia Mateer's system was earning a high reputation among Chinese for offering a rigorous but practical education. Indeed, graduates were launching successful careers in teaching, translating, business, and trade. And as alumni enjoyed increasing prosperity and status, they became more visible in their communities.[65] As such, they were walking advertisements for the system that had educated them.

Its education in demand, Tengchow College could afford to be selective in admissions. The college could subject applicants to a month of entrance examinations and interviews and still achieve maximum enrollment (seventy students). It even turned applicants away.[66] More students "want to come than we can possibly receive," Mateer wrote. "We try to take the best, rejecting all who are not bright and promising." But rapid growth brought immediate challenges in terms of facilities and personnel. To solve the problem of insufficient space, Mateer bought buildings on two adjacent properties. And after requesting help from his board, he anxiously awaited the arrival of Watson Hayes, who would teach math and science. "We . . . hope he will hurry and reach China," Mateer wrote in 1882, and "prove to be the right man."[67] He was. The "aim of the college," Hayes asserted, ought to be "the training up of scholarly, efficient, cultured, self-reliant and reliable men."[68] Calvin Mateer could not have said it better himself.

Unlike other new colleges, Tengchow did not have to invent an identity. That was because Mateer could simply extend the culture and curriculum of the boarding school to the higher grade levels. The college required students to take courses in three subject areas: Chinese Classics, Western Studies, and Religious Instruction. Chinese Classics consumed more student hours than the other two areas (Religion accounted for only six of the fifty-six total courses).[69] In Chinese Classics, Tengchow was able to keep pace with government schools. In mathematics and sciences, it surpassed all competitors. Its advantage lay chiefly in Calvin Mateer and Watson Hayes. In the opinion of both men, a kind of sclerotic scholasticism clogged the arteries of Chinese learning. To clear the blockage, they prescribed heavy doses of "brain energizing" math and science. All students were required to take Algebra, Geometry, Trigonometry, Calculus, Conic Sections, Surveying, Navigation, Physics, Chemistry, Astronomy, Geology, and Physiology.[70]

Though all Christian colleges taught science, Tengchow College possessed one remarkable feature that set it apart. Calvin Mateer had built the most advanced laboratory and mechanical workshop in China.[71] His purpose was to show students that science's abstract concepts led to real-world applications that could propel a nation forward, transform its economy, and improve human life. "The successful teaching of these sciences requires apparatus," he wrote, without which "science seems to the student like a dream."[72] Outside of class, Mateer used the workshop to provide hands-on education for his mechanically inclined students. "There he taught some of his most skillful students," Hunter Corbett recalled, "to make model engines, dynamos, electric trollies, [and] telegraph outfits."[73]

To keep abreast of new inventions, Mateer availed himself of any opportunity to study machinery. While on furlough in 1893, he visited the World's Columbian Exposition (the "World's Fair") in Chicago where he haunted the Electricity Building and Machinery Hall. He "spent days," recalled Corbett, who was also there, "making drawings, measurements, and so forth, of the most complex machinery." Mateer intended to use these sketches to build the machines himself back in Tengchow.[74] Though high-caliber students gravitated toward Mateer, so too did young men who, while less academically gifted, enjoyed tinkering with machines. Mateer used his workshop to train the college dropouts, many of whom went on to become machinists, electricians, photographers, and ironworkers. In this way, the workshop functioned as a de facto vocational school.[75]

In addition to its laboratory, Tengchow College possessed one other distinguishing feature. It set Chinese as the medium of instruction even for Western subjects; English was forbidden. For Mateer, this policy was a matter of conviction. He saw English as, in a word, *perilous*. When Chinese students learned English, it opened a portal into their minds, allowing dark and dangerous ideas to enter. "The young men of China are mad to learn English," Mateer wrote, but with English comes "books and newspapers, sowing the seeds of agnosticism, and skepticism and rationalism." Mateer was determined to prevent these Godless ideologies from infecting young minds.[76] As long as instructors taught in Chinese, Mateer could regulate the flow of knowledge. For any edifying academic subject, such as Algebra or Chemistry, he could produce a Chinese-language textbook. Conversely, he could block any Western ideas he deemed destructive to the nation's morality simply by refusing to produce a translation. This was about control. Of course, the pathway Mateer chose was a laborious one, because every unit of valuable Western knowledge had to be painstakingly translated before it could be taught. But the colossal undertaking was justified, Mateer insisted, because it allowed the missionary to regulate the information streaming into China. Hard work was the price one paid to be intellectual gatekeeper.

Mateer decried English for one other reason. At the 1890 missionary conference, he provoked a heated debate by submitting an incendiary paper that laid out, step by step, how English corrupts Chinese minds and souls. After a year or two of English, Mateer explained, a student figures out that his basic literacy affords him an opportunity for employment in the nearby treaty port. Seeking a shortcut to wealth, the restless young man quits college prematurely and absconds to the "market which pays so well." In the treaty port, he does secure a lucrative position but also finds himself besieged by the temptations of treaty-port life. His work exposes him to the foreign community's "good living and fine clothes," and "the wreck of his moral character is the common result." As his "habits and ideas of life take on a foreign coloring," he loses "sympathy with the plain and frugal habits" of his fellow Chinese. Becoming like a foreigner himself, he can no longer relate to his own people. In the final analysis, the Christian college—despite good intentions—has succeeded only in producing the worst sort of Sino-Western hybrid: a dissipated young man who loves wealth and luxury, not God and science.

Though Mateer did not refer to the ACC by name, that college's representatives perceived his essay as a thinly veiled attack. Incensed, they stood up one by one to dispute Mateer's theory of moral degeneration, impugn his denigration of their work, and defend English instruction. Frank Ohlinger, the former president of the ACC, stated that he disapproved of anyone who would engage in the "disparagement of one department," referring to English, so as "to give prominence to another department," in this case Chinese. Ohlinger also contested Mateer's assertion that English must not be taught because it opened the Chinese mind to dangerous ideas. Making a nautical analogy, Ohlinger asked whether anyone would seek to "abolish the Pacific Ocean because it floats pirates as well as merchantmen?" Mateer had stirred up a hornet's nest. Near the end of the session, he offered conciliatory remarks to mollify his offended colleagues and preserve comity. He did not, however, retreat from his main contention: English brought ruin.[77]

One could fault Mateer, as his peers did, for gratuitously instigating discord. After all, he might have simply accepted that two different models would shape Christian colleges. But Mateer saw his action as warranted by the pivotal nature of the present moment in Chinese higher education. In coming years, new colleges would be sprouting up across China—that was all but certain. What remained uncertain was the model these new institutions would follow. Would colleges pattern themselves after Tengchow College, with its Mandarin-only policy, or the ACC, and its commitment to English? Mateer was acutely aware that Young J. Allen had already opened the Anglo-Chinese College of Shanghai.[78] With his polemics, Mateer hoped to warn educators against making an egregious mistake they would regret.

In predicting the future, Mateer expected to see *gradual expansion* in higher education. It did not occur to him in 1890 that an external event might accelerate the growth. But that is what happened in 1895 when China lost a war with Japan. The humiliating defeat ignited among Chinese a search for answers that thrust Christian colleges into the spotlight before a suddenly attentive nation.

The Sino-Japanese War and Its Aftermath

In the 1890s, earthshaking change convulsed through Asia. For centuries, China occupied the central position of a tributary system that provided Asia with order. In this system, China and nearby Asian states—Korea, Thailand, Vietnam, and at one time Japan—behaved much like a Confucian family. In such a family, the father presides over his wife and children, providing virtuous guidance and setting an example of moral rectitude. They reciprocate by deferring to him and accepting their place within the hierarchy. As the patriarch of Asian states, China cast a civilizing influence over subordinate nations by teaching them Confucian values and statecraft. Those nations reciprocated by sending emissaries bearing tribute to the Forbidden City.[79] According to Immanuel C. Y. Hsü, Korea impressed China the most. While living under China's "cultural shadow," the Koreans "modeled their institutions and way of life after China's" and understood their relationship with China as "serving the great."[80]

Japan had once been a member of the family. But starting in the 1870s, Japan looked to a new authority for its ideas—the West. Japan did not, however, adopt everything its new mentor offered, shrewdly electing to pick and choose. As one British adviser to China explained, Japan placed Western knowledge into a "sieve" and "sifted out the parts useful to her," such as "the sciences and the art of war," before tossing the rest into the "dustbin." In this way, Japan underwent a rapid modernization program unlike any the world had ever seen. The "world now comprehends the startling fact," wrote the U.S. Secretary of the Navy, "that this small island kingdom ... has within a few decades stridden over ground traversed by other nations only within centuries."[81] In 1894, Japan challenged China's longstanding domination of the Korean Peninsula. Earning decisive victories on land and at sea, Japan defeated China in surprisingly easy fashion and, in 1895, dictated the terms of the Treaty of Shimonoseki.[82]

In the war's aftermath, shockwaves rippled through Asia, Europe, and America. In Asia, the war effected a new order in which Japan seized the apex position. "Seldom, perhaps never," observed a stunned American missionary, "has the civilized world so suddenly and completely reversed an estimate of a nation." In poignant contrast, China endured a demotion in global status every bit as dramatic as Japan's rise. "For the Chinese," wrote historian S. C. M. Paine, "the war kicked the bottom out of their world." Of course, China had by this time already absorbed crushing defeats from European nations. However, the loss to Japan inflicted far more psychic damage, Paine argued, because "defeat at the hands of an alien civilization could be discounted whereas defeat by a member of the Confucian order could not." To lose a war to a Western nation, in other words, hurt China but did not provoke an existential crisis; China could still claim cultural superiority over warlike Europeans and thus retain control of the Asian family of nations. Far worse was an internal challenge to its authority: a formerly subordinate member of the family rising up to strike down the father. That is what Japan had done. The Confucian hierarchy could not survive the trauma of a major rebellion from within the family—and so it toppled.[83]

China's newly exposed vulnerability left it ripe for exploitation. It was at this historic moment that Europeans started referring to China as the "Sick man of Asia"—a feeble nation tottering on the brink of collapse. "The perception of Chinese weakness," Paine wrote, "led to far more aggressive intrusions by the foreign powers."[84] No longer content merely to trade and enjoy extraterritoriality, the Western powers looked to carve up China. They "cut the China melon into . . . spheres of interest," wrote Hsü, "within which they constructed railways, opened mines, established factories," and "operated banks."[85] This new era of intensified imperialism depressed Chinese officials and intellectuals. "Our country can no longer survive in this world," wrote Hunan's governor.[86] Yen Yung Kiung, now approaching age sixty, also sank into gloom. "I am afraid" he wrote after the war, that China will be "divided like a watermelon among the foreign powers."[87] Though he believed deeply that Christianity and Western education could regenerate China, the war and the accelerated imperialism that ensued convinced him that he would not live to see China's rise. "Well, my sons," he said, trying to sound hopeful, "I am sorry that I shall not in my lifetime have the chance of seeing our country become rich and powerful, but you of the younger generation will . . . witness a New China."[88]

After the war, Yen was too old to act (he died in 1898). For other Chinese intellectuals, the war's shocking result sounded an alarm. Many viewed the military loss through the lens of Social Darwinism, a philosophy that had already gained traction in the West. The ideas of Herbert Spencer, a well-known Social Darwinist, first entered Chinese intellectual discourse in 1882. That year, Yen translated some of Spencer's works into Chinese while teaching at St. Johns.[89] In 1895, Yan Fu published a new translation of Spencer that Chinese intellectuals seized upon and applied to China's predicament. Extrapolating from Spencer's famous phrase "survival of the fittest," intellectuals wondered if China was indeed fit enough to fend off aggressive foreign powers. And if not, how could the country address its weakness? In this way, Spencer helped justify reform movements during the twilight of the Qing Dynasty.[90] "The doctrine of the survival of the fittest is on the lips of every thinking Chinese," wrote Yen's son, W. W. Yen, "and its grim significance is not lost on a nation that seems to be the center of the struggle in the Far East."[91]

For Huang Naishang, the war altered the course of his life. Ever since the 1870s, Huang had conversed with Young J. Allen, his friend and mentor, about the reforms that could revitalize China. The war infused these discussions with urgency. In 1894, Huang received the dreadful news that his younger brother, who had joined the Chinese navy on his suggestion, perished when a Japanese vessel torpedoed his ship. The combined impact of this personal loss and his nation's larger humiliation energized Huang, strengthening his conviction that only radical reform could save the nation. Indeed, Huang later identified the war as the "pivotal" juncture in his life. "I witnessed the aggressive encroachment of the foreigners, the weak defense . . . of our nation, the corruption of the administrative officers," and "the decadence . . . of the society," he said before adding with resolve: "I strongly desire to devote myself to my nation." Though committed to reforming China, Huang would no longer work through the church, his passion for Christianity having abated. "As far as religion is concerned," he wrote, "I . . . adopt a lukewarm attitude." In 1898, Huang attempted to insert his voice more forcibly in the government by taking the state examination in Beijing (he had failed in 1895). In the capital, he met two prominent Chinese reformers—Kang Youwei and Liang Qichao.[92] Kang advocated many of the same reforms as Huang. This was not surprising since both men had imbibed from the same intellectual well. On a trip to Shanghai in the 1880s, Kang had purchased all existing issues of Young J. Allen's *Globe Magazine*.[93] In 1895, he reprinted many of Allen's articles in a paper published by his Society for National Rejuvenation.[94]

In this reform climate, some intellectuals gave serious attention to missionaries and their institutions. Young J. Allen, for example, had long advocated for women's education and had recently opened the McTyeire School. In 1897, Liang Qichao published an essay in which he too seized upon women's education as the key. He argued, as Connie Shemo explains, that Chinese society had systematically degraded its women mentally, by denying them access to knowledge, and physically, by crippling them through footbinding. Weak Chinese women had inevitably produced weak sons, unfit to stand up to foreign aggression. It followed, given his logic, that any reform initiative must target women. Liang imagined a regenerated Chinese society in which educated Chinese women raised strong sons able to resist foreign incursion. To sell his idea, Liang needed an exemplar, a flesh-and-blood Chinese female who embodied the traits of his new woman. He chose Ida Kahn. With her overseas education and medical practice, she provided the role model that others could emulate. In the essay, Liang described at length her graduation ceremony at Michigan. To him, the event proved not only that a Chinese woman could handle a rigorous Western education but also that the Chinese, as a race, were not inferior to Caucasians.[95]

But Michigan was far away. Realistically, few Chinese students could hope to attend an American college or medical school. For this reason, if China were to undergo national revitalization through Western education, its young people would have to attend institutions closer to home. In an intellectual climate suddenly open to change, many Chinese looked seriously for the first time at Christian colleges. Such colleges, after all, had been quietly operating for years right under their noses.

Colleges Ascendant

In January of 1895, three Japanese vessels cruised into the Bohai Sea to subject the city of Tengchow to surprise bombardment. About twenty shells landed near Tengchow College, with one whistling over the head of Calvin Mateer. When the warships returned the next day, Watson Hayes—either bravely or foolishly—paddled out among the behemoths in a sampan. To signal his neutrality and peaceful intentions, he hoisted both the Stars and Stripes and the white flag of surrender. Though his objective was to board a vessel and persuade its officers to cease the attack, the Japanese ignored the little boat and its occupant. Unable to effect negotiation, Hayes returned to shore.[96] St. John's was also touched by the war. In 1894, the school heard the "gratifying news" that a former student had performed heroically on a Chinese battleship during the Battle of the Yalu River. Though Japanese vessels destroyed most of the Chinese fleet, the student's valor received mention in a popular American magazine.[97] On campus, several concerned students approached Pott, the St. John's headmaster, with a novel request. "Naturally, at a time when their country was engaged in war," Pott wrote, "the students took a keen interest in military affairs, and were anxious to be instructed in military drill." An enthusiast for physical fitness, Pott welcomed the idea, as did F. C. Cooper, a new science professor. Cooper assembled a volunteer corps that used bamboo poles instead of rifles. Before long, the school was requiring military drills for all students.[98]

When the war ended, the popular perception of Christian colleges changed overnight. Previously, the Chinese had viewed the colleges either as risky options for desperate or destitute parents or as niche schools that catered only to Chinese Christians. But in the war's aftermath, the Chinese saw these institutions in a new light—as incubators of modernization. The colleges offered rigorous training in the exact subjects the Chinese now coveted in their quest for national renewal: science, math, engineering, and (sometimes) English.

St. John's College

After the war, optimism suffused the reports coming out of St. John's. In 1896, the college announced a surge in applications as the "demand for education" of the type the college offered had become "larger than ever."[99] "One reason for the greater interest in higher education was the result of the war," Pott wrote. "It was logical to conclude that Japan's superior strength was largely due to . . . modern education."[100] The influx of students coincided with a major campus upgrade launched before the war. During a furlough in 1892, Pott raised $20,000 for new construction projects, proving conclusively that the once reluctant administrator possessed a gift for fundraising.[101] After Pott returned to China, Hong Niok Woo, the U.S. Civil War veteran, reached out to the Chinese community for additional contributions. "You know the education of our young men has my heart and soul," wrote one Chinese donor, because "it is they who can reform our country."[102] Though Pott staggered construction over several years, the new buildings eventually included Schereschewsky Hall, a large structure consisting of a dormitory, a dining hall, and classrooms. Science Hall, which came next, reflected the growing prestige of science among students.[103] Yen Hall, completed after 1900 (and after Yen Yung Kiung's death), included dorm space for 150 students, faculty residences, administrative offices, an assembly hall, and a library. Built in a "semi-Chinese" style, Yen Hall's architecture reflected the hybrid identity of the man it memorialized. And since clock towers always enhanced a campus, Cooper built one to remind students to go to class.[104] At an unveiling of new structures, the Shanghai bishop declared that St. John's, having proven itself to be "more than an experiment," was contributing to the emergence of "New China."[105]

Along with its physical complex, St. John's started to resemble a traditional American college in other ways. The emphasis on physical culture favored by Cooper and Pott expanded. In the 1890s, the school offered tennis, track, baseball, and football. Just after 1900, St. John's led a consortium of colleges in forming the China Intercollegiate Athletic Association. Pott referred to annual football contests with rival Nanyang College as the "Harvard and Yale games of the Far East." Along with sports, St. John's acquired other hallmarks of the American college. The decade gave birth to *The Echo*, a student-run magazine that claimed to be "the first paper published in the Orient by Chinese youths in a tongue foreign to them." Students enjoyed other opportunities for extracurricular activities. Along with the Shakespeare Club, Photography Club, and Glee Club, there was a Literary and Debating Society that one alumnus recalled fondly. The experience, he said, taught the student "to think on one's feet before an audience" and to avoid any grammar issue that "weakens the argument or renders the speech absurd in the eyes of critical fellow-students." A sensational new form of recreation appeared in 1895 when F. C. Yen (Yen's nephew) peddled around campus on an amazing machine—the bicycle. W. W. Yen (Yen's son) joined the faculty in 1900. Recently graduated from the University of Virginia, he brought a clear vision of an American college and, in Pott's words, "proved a tower of strength."[106] He was not an anomaly. As other qualified Chinese joined the faculty, staff, and administration in the early twentieth century, St. John's gradually ceded control to the Chinese.[107]

The Anglo-Chinese College

The rapid development of St. John's was not unique. When hostilities ended, the ACC also entered its takeoff period. In 1895, George Smyth observed sudden interest in the school, which he attributed to the "general awakening caused by the Chino-Japanese war."[108] Sia Sek Ong's son studied at the ACC before heading to America to earn medical and dental degrees.[109] However, it was in the following year that the ACC felt the full effects of China's awakening. "We are crowded to overflowing," the college noted in 1896, reporting enrollment over 200. "The dormitory could not accommodate all who wished to come in."[110] This was good news, especially given the meager enrollments of the 1880s. That being said, Smyth realized that, by turning away qualified applicants, the college was missing out on further growth. Needing additional dorm space and classrooms, he turned to the Chinese community, which answered by contributing funds for a new building.[111] "We have built a fine new dormitory for the college with money given by the Chinese," Smyth announced the following year. "Not a dollar of foreign money has gone into it."[112] The dorm, Smyth proudly claimed, offered "striking proof of the interest of Chinese in the college."[113] The new residence hall did not solve the space problem for long. Just months later, Smyth was again reporting dormitories "full to the brim" as enrollments climbed to 366, a staggering number given that the college achieved it while rejecting 180 applicants.[114] "There are too many people for the space," Smyth complained, adding that "we have simply no privacy at all."[115]

As problems go, this was a good one to have. Indeed, it suggested the Chinese community's full embrace of the ACC. If further evidence were needed, the college reached a remarkable fiscal milestone in 1898: the ACC derived all financial support from Chinese tuitions and donations.[116] Not a single missionary dollar contributed to school operations or construction projects. The college had achieved, in short, its objective of being self-supporting. The Chinese expressed their support in other ways. In 1897, Smyth gave a formal tour of the campus to Foochow's highest-ranking officials, a group that included the Literary Chancellor, the head of the province's educational department. "They remained three hours," he recounted, "visited the class rooms, carefully inspected the work, and spoke encouragingly to both students and teachers." When the Literary Chancellor made a follow-up visit to share his favorable assessment, Smyth understood the significance. "Lest I seem to any to be making too much of the favor of the officials," he explained, "let me add that it is difficult to do anything in China without [their] approval."[117] Graduation ceremonies also attracted Chinese dignitaries. Recall that, in 1886, Smyth presided over a lifeless closing ceremony that the Chinese happily skipped. In 1898, the city's elite citizens not only attended the event, they remained afterward to dine at Smyth's residence. "All this showed how different was the feeling toward the college from that which prevailed ten years ago," Smyth wrote, "when no man of high social or official position would think of countenancing . . . a Christian institution. Verily times have changed."[118]

Times had changed, and the ACC was not alone in benefiting from them. Its students enjoyed stronger career prospects after graduation because employers accorded greater respect to their degrees. Smyth admitted that, in previous years, a diploma from the ACC "was not considered worth much." It had now become so "valuable" as to entice former dropouts to return to school to finish up. In 1899, Smyth reported proudly that "all our graduates are at work." Though many entered government offices or trading firms, others became teachers. After the war, there was demand for anyone who could teach Western subjects and English; Smyth constantly fielded requests from other schools wishing to hire his graduates.[119] Though he placed many, he wisely held onto the best students, such as Ding Maing-Ing, who would head the Mathematics Department for forty years.[120] As Smyth tried to fulfill these requests, he discovered that demand exceeded his supply. It was another good problem to have.[121]

Tengchow College

Tengchow College could also boast of a strong record in placing graduates in teaching positions. Though the two schools resembled one another on the surface, different motivations actuated their teacher placement programs. The ACC benignly viewed teacher placement as serving the interests of both the graduating student and the hiring institution. Less innocently, Calvin Mateer's program advanced his larger objective to subvert the Confucian leadership. Mateer understood well the stunning nature of the historic moment: the loss to Japan had eroded the nation's confidence not only in its ruling class, rendering it vulnerable, but also in the very idea systems that underpinned Chinese civilization. Now was the time to strike, and Mateer moved to capitalize by deploying his chosen instrument of change—teacher placement. At a missionary education conference held in 1899, he made no attempt to disguise his designs. "If we, as educators," he baldly stated, "are able to supply the best teachers in the market and who are at the same time Christian men, *we will control China socially, politically, and religiously*" (emphasis added).[122]

How exactly did the plan to "control China" work? Tengchow educated cohorts of young men in what Irwin Hyatt has called Mateer's "intelligence system": science, math, engineering, and Chinese classics. After a student graduated, Mateer would hold onto him for two or three years, assigning him classes to teach while he remained under Mateer's supervision. Mateer retained indefinitely the best of his former students, such as Chou Li-wen. As their numbers grew, they gradually filled the faculty ranks, meaning that the school was slowly indigenizing. Most graduates, however, would teach elsewhere after Mateer located positions for them in Christian and government schools.[123] Carrying the "intelligence system" with them, Mateer's acolytes would, in his words, "plant and nurture the new intellectual life that is coming into China." It was, to be sure, an ambitious plan. But could Mateer really execute it? At the 1899 conference, he revealed that he already had. "I have . . . within the last year," he announced, "furnished eight professors to the Imperial university in Peking and four to that in Nanking, besides many others teaching in private schools, all of whom are staunch Christians." "I need not conceal the fact," he said with contentment, "that I take no small satisfaction in these things."[124]

As essential as Calvin Mateer was to the success of Tengchow, the period after the war witnessed a changing of the guard. In 1895, Watson Hayes assumed leadership of the college.[125] Two years later, Henry Luce joined the faculty. Who was Henry Luce? In the late 1880s, Luce saw Robert Wilder speak at his church in Scranton, Pennsylvania. Present at the genesis moment of the SVM, Wilder was now out mustering support for it.[126] Intrigued but not persuaded by Wilder, Luce attended Yale with every intention of pursuing a career in law. The plan changed after he befriended Horace Pitkin, a charismatic Christian student who led the SVM at Yale. Inspired by Pitkin, Luce decided to forsake a legal career and join the SVM. Specifically, Luce set his sights not just on China but on Shandong Province after hearing about the educational work of someone named Calvin Mateer. After graduating from Yale, Luce toured college campuses to recruit for the SVM while studying at divinity school. In 1897, he requested Tengchow College for his assignment—and got his wish. He worked under Calvin Mateer who, in 1898, baptized his newborn son—Henry Robinson Luce.[127]

Hardworking and willing to learn, Luce ostensibly appeared to present the perfect lieutenant for Calvin Mateer. But in reality, Luce epitomized the next evolution in the missionary movement, which was shifting away from the personality type exemplified by Mateer. Mateer, as a colleague described him, "possessed a *rugged strength* of character" that achieved results through a "Spartan . . . ability to endure hardships" and a "scorn for the amenities . . . of modern life."[128] Content to labor alone, Calvin Mateer could concentrate for hours on meticulous translations work, embark on long and lonely itinerating tours, or disappear into his workshop for a solitary day with machines. Like others in his generation, Mateer was driven by that intense individualism that one needed in order to found an institution in the face of stiff resistance. Luce was hardwired differently. He possessed a set of traits well-suited for the next phase in missions: to take an existing institution and place it on a new and grander trajectory. His gifts made him, in historian Irwin Hyatt's words, "the perfect second generation man."[129]

What exactly were his traits? Luce evinced an extroverted missionary style that contrasted sharply with Mateer's individualism. An affable man, he thrived in the company of others and believed in the collective power of people to achieve results through coordinated action. His successful attempt to introduce basketball epitomized his talent for social organization. Convinced of the sport's many benefits, he taught students the rules and arranged the first game. During that contest, students drifted listlessly on the court, too self-conscious to put forth effort in front of peers. As Luce hollered a steady stream of encouragement, unresponsive students allowed the ball to drop to the floor when it was passed to them. Refusing to quit, Luce continued his basketball boosterism and eventually the sport gained traction: Chinese students started to bring as much competitive spirit to games as American collegians.[130] Mateer could never have coaxed Chinese students to love basketball.

Luce could also identify the potential in others and unlock it. After 1900, he organized the campus event that launched the career of the college's most famous graduate—the evangelist Ding Li Mei. Ding spent his youth in schools run by the Mateers. When a boy, he studied under Julia Mateer, whom he called his "spiritual mother." Ascending within the Mateer system, he matriculated at Tengchow College, where he learned science under Watson Hayes.[131] Earning his degree in 1892, he taught at the college before joining the first cohort of a new theological school that Calvin Mateer opened in 1895. After graduating, Pastor Ding preached the Gospel for several years.[132] Recognizing the uncanny ability lodged in Ding, Luce called him "a young man of marked spiritual power." In 1909, Luce wondered if Ding might help him reverse a disturbing trend on campus: fewer students were choosing ministerial careers. "For some time," Luce wrote, "we have been concerned with our failure to lead an adequate number of college men into the ministry." Luce arranged for Ding to visit his alma mater.[133]

But Luce did not merely invite Ding and step back: he choreographed the event. To allow Ding's revival to proceed without distraction, Luce closed down other campus functions. He suspended classes, canceled club meetings, and reserved academic spaces for religious introspection. "Students were asked not to enter the Main College Building and Converse Science Hall," Luce wrote, "unless for the purpose of Bible study or prayer." Crucially, Luce also scheduled Ding for multiple prayer meetings and set aside rooms where Ding could hold "personal interviews" with students who felt something stirring inside them. Many of them did. Though Ding's effect was at first slow to manifest itself, the revival soon gathered steam. "The list of those deciding for the ministry increased to twenty, and then thirty," Luce wrote, adding that the event reminded him of the "early days" of the SVM. Before long, Ding's awakening became self-propelling, requiring no manipulation whatsoever from Luce. "The list increased to sixty and then to eighty," Luce continued, there being "no legitimate way to stop the tide" and "no reason for doing so." Though the "strain" left Ding "physically exhausted,"[134] his revival claimed 116 people.[135] Ding enjoyed similar success on other campuses, often securing between 100 and 200 students. "Mr. Ding's stay with us," a missionary noted, "has completely changed the atmosphere of the school." In 1915, Ding sparked a revival in Hunan Province that reaped 1,200 converts.[136] Recognizing that there were insufficient numbers of Chinese ministers to serve Christian communities, Ding founded the Chinese Student Volunteer Movement for the Ministry. As the name implies, Ding used the SVM as a model for his creation and employed the same strategy: he visited college campuses to recruit students for the ministry.[137] The man who became known as "the Moody of China" (in reference to Dwight Moody) got his start when Luce detected his potential and orchestrated a campus revival.[138]

Luce's organizational talent allowed him to undertake large-scale projects the likes of which Calvin Mateer could not imagine. By his second year, Luce had come to believe both that the college possessed untapped potential and that Tengchow, or rather the city's remote location, was holding the institution back. Why not move the college to a more accessible city like Jinan, the provincial capital?[139] Luce broached the idea to Mateer, who responded with discouragement. Undeterred, Luce forged ahead. Though he failed to secure Jinan as the college's new home (at least, not at first), he was, through compromise, able to move the institution to the centrally located city of Weixian in 1904. It was a stunning achievement, one that required the persuasive Luce to win over skeptics, raise funds, and oversee a difficult logistic operation. Calvin Mateer could never have pulled off such a feat. About a decade later, Luce topped himself: he spearheaded both the college's move to Jinan and the construction there of a vast complex. To succeed, Luce had to conduct an aggressive fundraising campaign in the United States, work with government officials in China, harmonize the American architectural firm with the Chinese builders, and oversee construction on-site.[140] His orchestration of people, companies, government, and capital surpassed not just the abilities but the dreams of old-guard missionaries. Luce, it turns out, was not just a missionary-educator. He was a missionary-impresario.

Conclusion

This chapter has described the origins and traced the rise of three Christian colleges. Before 1900, those colleges were joined by others: the Anglo-Chinese College of Shanghai, Nanking Christian College, Hangchow Presbyterian College, Canton Christian College, and Nanking University.[141] Though each college followed a unique trajectory, two trends emerge when we view the institutions collectively. First, their Christian influence tended to grow weaker, not stronger, over time. While several forces were at work here, we can attribute some of the decline to Chinese preferences: most students chose these colleges for educational reasons and only tolerated Christianity.

In addition, the missionary-educators who entered China after 1890—often through the SVM or the YMCA—de-emphasized proselytization. Recall that many missionaries of the previous generation had either opposed education entirely or valued schools only as traps to ensnare Chinese families. By 1900, opinion had shifted on this issue to the point where most missionaries objected to this limited (even deceptive) vision of education. "We have no right to make a school a mere proselyting agency," the *Chinese Recorder* asserted in 1901. "It should not be considered a trap to catch heathen children" by deploying education as "mere bait." Schools should instead "deal honestly with our pupils and with their parents" and strive to be "the best in China from a strictly educational stand-point."[142]

This editorial also aligned itself with a second trend in missionary education. "We should teach English," the author argued, "because it develops and awakens the minds of the pupils." As colleges proliferated in China, the new institutions would emulate the ACC, not Tengchow College. Indeed, Calvin Mateer's bid to block English instruction ultimately failed. As a sign of the times, resistance to English collapsed even at Mateer's own college—the once impregnable citadel of Mandarin. Quite appropriately, it was a new missionary, not a member of the old guard, who ushered in the curricular revolution. Calvin Mateer must have positively bristled when, in 1908, Henry Luce introduced English to the college and assigned himself the first class.[143] Now an old man, Mateer watched helplessly as English infected the institution he and Julia had founded. As it turned out, English would be the last Henry Luce initiative that Calvin Mateer would see. He died later that year and was buried alongside Julia Mateer and John Nevius at the Christian cemetery in Zhifu.[144]

Conclusion

Into the Twentieth Century

In 1860, Protestants embarked on an evangelical errand in China that involved, with a few exceptions, male preachers traveling along circuits. By 1900, the unidimensional missionary movement had undergone a stunning transformation: it had diversified in method, earned much Chinese acceptance, expanded American women's roles, and liberalized somewhat with respect to evangelical imperatives. Most importantly, missionaries had erected schools, colleges, hospitals, and YMCA chapters and initiated indigenization at these institutions. The American missionary movement in China, in short, had reinvented itself.

Writing for *The Atlantic* after 1900, Chester Holcombe, a missionary turned diplomat, described the transformation of missions and their relations with the Chinese. His purpose was to disabuse critics who insisted upon clinging to the "old and familiar" characterization of the missionary as a "menace"—someone who tries "to force an alien and undesired religion upon the Chinese" in a way that is "offensive to officials and people alike." That accusation no longer held true. Once confined to the "treaty ports," Holcombe explained, missionaries now enjoy "intimate association with the native residents" in the "mud-walled villages and rural hamlets." They also, he continued, have won over China's rich and powerful. "Once suspicious of or openly hostile to" missions, elite Chinese now make large "donations to mission hospitals and schools." Though some "friction" remained, Holcombe could state emphatically that the "day of Chinese opposition to missionary work . . . has passed."[1]

On this point, history would prove Holcombe wrong: the twentieth century would bring more friction. That being said, Holcombe was right to claim that missions had entered a new era. Where does the story go from here? Through their institutions, missionaries unleashed into China an energy that pulsated through the country as the century drew to a close. Did the institutionalizing movement, born near the end of one century, expand and accelerate in the next? Did the missionaries themselves continue to evolve? Did the Chinese assume more control over these institutions? Detailed answers to these questions lie beyond the scope of this book. However, we can, by tracking a single family, convey the extent to which the trends that emerged before 1900 continued to shape missions in the twentieth century.

In 1868, John Linton Stuart volunteered for missions after hearing John Nevius speak at Princeton. Like many of the missionaries covered in this book, he stormed into China filled with fiery zeal, launching his itinerant ministry in Hangzhou. There his effort stalled. "After five years of incessant toil, traveling and hardship," his son later wrote, "his health failed and he was sent home." On Christmas Day in 1874, Stuart returned to China a married man, determined to reboot his mission with innovation—he hoped to reinvent himself as a missionary-educator. Unfortunately, his own colleagues scuttled his plans. The school he founded was "closed by the mission," his son recounted, "because its members felt that preaching rather than secular instruction was his proper function." Stuart had run afoul of that institutionalized prejudice against education that dominated Protestant missions in the 1870s. That same prohibition, however, did not apply to missionary wives, and so John's new wife, Mary Stuart, could run a school for girls without attracting censure. Struggling to find a direction, John looked admiringly at Calvin Mateer from afar. Somehow, Mateer had overcome the same vocational resistance that had defeated his school. To see his hero, John forced Mary and their sons to endure a 1,200-mile roundtrip journey to Tengchow on mules.[2]

Experiences like this were not atypical for the Stuart boys. Mishkids, as the children of missionary parents were called, often found themselves dragged into bizarre activities required by their parents' unusual careers. In 1887, John and Mary took the family to Mobile, Alabama, where Mary was from. For the boys, disembarking the steamship was like stepping out of a time machine; for the first time, they beheld modern things like locomotives. To drum up interest in China missions, the parents forced John Leighton Stuart, age eleven, and his siblings to perform. Before audiences, the children would parade about in Chinese outfits, demonstrate proper chopstick use, and sing "Jesus loves me, this I know" in Chinese. It was degrading. Mishkids also had to tolerate prolonged family separations. When the Stuart parents returned to China in 1888, John and one brother stayed behind, moved in with relatives, and attended school for the first time (their mother had homeschooled them in China). Since they dressed and spoke differently from their peers and knew nothing of American culture, they were made, in John's account, the "objects of verbal torture by schoolmates." They were also denied the "worldly pleasures" that their cousins enjoyed because their custodians regarded anything fun, like dancing or the theater, as unbefitting of the children of such "saintly" parents. "The whole Mobile experience," John recalled, "created an aversion for missionary life."[3]

Back in China, John and Mary Stuart attended the 1890 missionary conference. There they survived the collapsing platform at the group photograph, witnessed Adele Fielde's ignominious exit, and watched Calvin Mateer spar with the ACC about English instruction. They also took in a retrospective essay by Young J. Allen entitled "The Changed Aspect of China." To comprehend the previous thirty years, Allen drew a parallel with the American frontier. "The conquest" of China that started in 1860, he wrote, "may be likened to the conquest of primeval America." In the latter case, settlers used the "axe" to clear away the "luxuriant wild growth of centuries." In China, missionaries confronted "similar conditions" of a "moral character," the "elimination of which was necessary to the introduction of that higher civilization." That Allen wrote "civilization," rather than "Gospel," carried significance. For him, the American project in China had evolved to include not just churches but schools, colleges, hospitals, museums, and presses. But no such broad vision had animated missions during its pioneering phase. Back then, a group of stalwart missionaries had collided with fierce Chinese resistance. For years, Allen recalled, "We... preached *at* them, taught *at* them, but... had little access to them" because "our relation was lacking in reciprocity." But after three tough decades, Protestant missions had finally assumed a form that both sides could accept. The pioneering phase was over, and the era of "civilization" had begun.[4]

For John Linton Stuart, Allen's message perhaps provoked mixed emotions. Thus far, Stuart's career had been not a failed one exactly, but an undistinguished one. If he sought an explanation for the disappointment, he found it in Allen's frontier metaphor. Stuart had come to China when missions wanted pioneers to apply force, not teachers to design curricula. Compounding the difficulty, the Chinese in those days showed apathy, if not opposition, to the idea of Christian education. Even the redoubtable Mateers had barely kept their school afloat in the face of resistance from both the Chinese and their own board. The takeaway from Allen's essay, in other words, was that there was nothing intrinsically wrong with Stuart personally. It was just that his timing was off. He had come to China too early. If—by some magic—he could start over in 1890, he would encounter conditions more aligned with his aspirations. Indeed, Allen even scripted a hopeful line that, years earlier, would have been unthinkable: "It is a great thing to be a missionary to China."⁵ But it was too late for John Linton Stuart. If there were any silver lining, it was that his sons would fare better than their father.

Or would they? Back in America, John Leighton Stuart had no interest in China. None. He preferred the academic life. In 1892, he moved to Virginia to attend first a preparatory school and then Hampden-Sydney College. Away from Mobile, he luxuriated in the fact that nobody knew him. He could shed the "awful brand of being from China" and start anew. In college, he developed a passion for the Classics and got involved with the YMCA, serving as chapter president. Unfortunately, when the SVM learned of his childhood in China, its secretaries targeted him as a promising candidate (his words: "obvious victim") for foreign missions. Though Willard Lyon, Fletcher Brockman, and Henry Luce meant well and would become his "closest friends," at this juncture the pressure they applied "crystallized my most acute religious problem." That problem, in a nutshell, was that he was torn between two careers: should he become a minister or a Classics professor? His chief problem with the ministry was that it likely led to a missionary career, which would inevitably return him to China. And Stuart dreaded China.⁶

But why? Stuart only vaguely understood his profound China anxiety until one sleepless night at college. As he lay awake in bed listening to the clock tower chime off the hours, his overactive mind conjured up vivid memories of his childhood in Hangzhou. He realized why he instinctively cringed at the prospect of following in his father's footsteps:

> It is difficult to exaggerate the aversion I had developed against going to China as a missionary. It was not the country so much as what I conceived to be the nature of the life and work haranguing crowds of idle, curious people in street chapels or temple fairs, selling tracts for almost nothing, being regarded with amused or angry contempt by the native population, physical discomforts or hardships, etc., no chance for intellectual or studious interests, a sort of living death. . . . This had all been accentuated by the boyhood trials due to the peculiar missionary background which in varying forms had followed me ever since. In contrast was the delight of College and life in Virginia.

Stuart had grown up in China during the brutal pioneering era described by Allen. He had witnessed the rejection and futility of the missionary's miserable existence. Not wishing that "living death" for himself, he preferred the stately buildings, verdant lawns, and posh intellectualism of the American college. Who could blame him? After graduation, Stuart taught at his old high school before entering theological school in 1899. It was there that he made a separate discovery about himself that also seemed to disqualify him for missions. On the spectrum of religious belief, which ran from conservative "orthodoxy" at one end to "free inquiry" on the other, Stuart claimed "sympathy with the latter." He was too liberal-minded for a vocation dominated by rigid church dogma.[7]

But Stuart was working with outdated images of both China and the missionary. China had become more receptive and missionaries (at least some of them) had evolved. By 1890, Allen's pioneer era had ended, giving way to a period of institution-building that favored someone like Stuart, a flexible thinker who wished to teach at a lectern and work behind a desk. Indeed, the positive trends that Allen identified gathered momentum after 1890. We have already seen how the Sino-Japanese War (1894–1895) increased demand for Christian colleges. The Boxer Uprising (1900) further accelerated China's turn to Western knowledge—though it did not look that way at first. The Boxer Uprising was fueled by ancient supernatural beliefs, hostility to modernity, and rage toward imperialism. Boxers harassed missionaries (murdering a few), killed hundreds of Chinese Christians, burned churches to the ground, wrecked railroads and telegraph systems, and attacked the foreign legations in Beijing.[8] So violent was this convulsion that it appeared poised to set the missionary movement back many years, if not extirpate it entirely.

But that is not what transpired. Ironically, a movement intended to eliminate missionaries only made them stronger. Many Chinese viewed the Boxer Uprising as so barbaric as to prove beyond a doubt China's urgent need for enlightened modernization; a wantonly destructive movement like this, they believed, must never happen again. They turned collectively to missionary institutions—the college especially—for their expertise. "More and more people recognized the need to strengthen their country through Western knowledge," writes Pui-lan Kwok. "Upper class and rich families began to send their sons and daughters to learn English and the sciences in prestigious schools run by the missions," powering the "unprecedented growth" of missions after 1900.[9] At St. John's, Pott noticed a change in consciousness. The "inertia of China has been overcome," he observed, and the Chinese "are ready to receive new ideas." Pott likened the Chinese mind to a "huge" question mark: it hungered for the knowledge that colleges could provide. The "door of opportunity," he announced, is "opened to us wider than ever before."[10]

The Boxer Uprising also led to specific programs designed to give Chinese students access to American higher education. After an international military force suppressed the Boxers, the resulting Boxer Protocol required China to reimburse the foreign powers for damages. The United States was set to receive $25 million, more than twice the amount of the damages it could document. Outraged by both this unfair settlement and the continued injustice of the Chinese Exclusion Act, Chinese in coastal cities launched a boycott of American goods in 1905. To defuse the explosive situation, Liang Cheng, a former CEM student and now Chinese Minister to the United States, met with President Theodore Roosevelt and eventually engineered the return of the excess money to China. Crucially, that remission would take the form not of a lump sum but of scholarships to American universities and the founding of a new school in China to prepare students for study in the United States. That institution, Qinghua University, would be structured according to the American model and teach an American curriculum.[11] In a sense, history was repeating itself. Indeed, Liang Cheng—like Yung Wing after the Tianjin Massacre—had capitalized on an ugly international incident, using it to launch a Sino-American educational program. It was the sort of creative problem-solving that could only spring from the fertile mind of someone bearing a hybrid identity. That his remission plan was not controversial in either China or America reveals the extent to which times had changed. Nobody viewed the placement of Chinese students in American schools as a risky experiment in cultural chemistry that might go awry. Sure enough, it didn't. Over twenty years, the Boxer Indemnity Scholarship Program educated thirteen hundred students and produced, according to Wei-li Ye, "some of modern China's best scholars and educators, as well as prominent leaders in other walks of life."[12] Once the rarest of unicorns, someone like Yung Wing was becoming commonplace.

In 1904, John Leighton Stuart could no longer resist what seemed like inexorable forces pulling him back to China. He volunteered for missions work and was placed with his parents in Hangzhou. As he beheld the meager fruits of his father's work, he felt again that sickening dread. "I realized the feeble results of my father's life-long labors" and the "old aversion" returned.[13] When the mission assigned Stuart to a specific district, he struggled as a preacher just like his father had. He judged the work "repressive" and the people "the hardest to reach."[14] Stuart was in a rut, the same rut from which his father had never escaped.

But this was a new era in China missions, one that would afford the son opportunities denied the father. Just as the gloom started to descend on Stuart, by a stroke of luck he was offered a teaching position at a theological seminary in Nanjing. Though the prospect looked enticing, one hurdle remained: he needed his mission's approval. He found himself, in other words, in the same situation as his father, thirty years earlier, when the latter's own mission had dashed his dream. But missionary priorities had changed. When the mission put the matter to a vote, only one man opposed. Stuart moved to Nanjing, where he taught the New Testament and actively supported the YMCA.[15]

College teaching would not define his career. Between 1900 and 1920, higher education in China underwent a frenzied period of activity as new

Christian colleges emerged and existing schools consolidated into larger institutions.[16] These forces seized Stuart and carried him up the academic ladder. In 1918, the merger of Peking University and North China Union College resulted in the formation of Yenching University, which Stuart would lead for two decades. By accepting the presidency, Stuart achieved the next and final evolutionary stage of the missionary progression: "First I left preaching for teaching, and now I was leaving teaching for university administration!" His upward move reflects the remarkable degree to which institutions had transformed missions in a single generation. John Linton Stuart, pushed out of the classroom by his own mission, was forced to settle for a conventional preaching career. John Leighton Stuart exited the classroom on his own terms to accept the presidency of a university, a variety of institution that did not exist in China when his father started. John Linton Stuart rode atop mules to rural villages to distribute religious tracts to peasants. John Leighton Stuart traveled by steamship to New York to present annual reports to Yenching's board of trustees. The routine nature of these trips prompted Stuart to refer to them not as furloughs, like in the old days, but as "commuting."[17]

While in the United States, Stuart stalked donors. Though missions had always relied on fundraising, it too had evolved. In his father's era, small donations from multitudes of churchgoers funded the operation, with the occasional large gift from a benefactor supporting a new building. In contrast, Stuart tried to hook big fish, meeting with representatives of the Fords, Rockefellers, and other tycoons. To aid him in his "professional begging," Stuart hired his dynamic friend, Henry Luce, who had recently secured the capital to build a vast campus complex in Jinan. The two chased after money with the same fervor that the previous generation had pursued souls. During Stuart's presidency, Yenching's endowment reached $2.5 million (approximately $45 million today).[18] Armed with funds, Stuart expanded the university. Over two decades, enrollment grew from 103 to 1,156 students and the number of faculty from 25 to 137. Those faculty taught in a diverse array of academic programs housed in three colleges—Arts and Letters, Natural Sciences, and Public Affairs—and a School of Religion. If Yenching resembled an American university with its academic offerings, it exceeded many with its spectacular physical plant.[19]

Indeed, Stuart oversaw construction of a world-class campus outside of Beijing. To give the campus thematic unity, he conceived and executed a plan to erect buildings exhibiting a hybrid architecture, one that fused Chinese aesthetics with Western practicality. In each finished edifice, "graceful curves and gorgeous coloring" encased an inner structure composed of "reinforced concrete and equipped with modern lighting, heating and plumbing." Similarly, an ornate pagoda enveloped the functional water tower. On the campus lake there was an island on which one could stroll through a

Chinese pavilion decorated with "carved monoliths from nearby ruins"—all paid for with a gift from Luce's son, Henry Robinson Luce. Visitors regarded Yenching as "the most beautiful campus in the world," and Stuart described it as "fairer than my dreams."[20]

While pleasing to look at, the Chinese motifs also symbolized Stuart's vision for Yenching. He did not deploy them as a façade, a false front intended to fool the Chinese into accepting what was really an evangelical foreign institution. Whereas the sole purpose for John Linton's generation had been to conquer China for Christ, Christianity receded as a priority for John Leighton. He believed that the days when missionaries imposed religion were over. Though the public did perceive Yenching "generally as Christian," Stuart insisted that participation in religious activities be strictly voluntary. "There should be no required chapel attendance nor compulsory religious services," he wrote, adding that students who professed the Christian faith derived no advantage from doing so. Of course, some foreignness was unavoidable. Yenching did forge partnerships with Harvard, Princeton, Wellesley, and the Rockefeller-funded Peking Union Medical College.[21] But the Chinese coveted these prestigious relationships and did not view them as examples of foreign intrusion. Indeed, Chinese preferences mattered to Stuart, whose desire was that the Chinese "think of Yenching as . . . their own" and not "as an enterprise maintained for them by foreigners." He even imagined a day when the Chinese would assume control. "My original aim," he declared, was "for Chinese to take an increasing share in . . . leadership," yielding in the end "a Chinese university" that retained its "western origin largely as a historical memory." Toward this end, he hired Chinese faculty and filled the Board of Managers mostly with Chinese. W. W. Yen, the son of Yen Yung Kiung, served a term as chairman.[22] In this way, Stuart advanced a vision that reversed the delete-and-replace of his father's generation. Instead of the missionary colonizing the Chinese mind, the Chinese would colonize the missionary institution. That is, with one exception: Stuart himself never abdicated his position.[23]

In the 1920s, Stuart's own family afforded him the opportunity to reflect on three generations of change. Though his father had died in 1913, his mother lived until January 1925. On Christmas Day 1924, three weeks before her death, Mary celebrated fifty years in China. To honor her golden anniversary, Stuart held an open house at Yenching. As Mary greeted the students, she was reminded of how conditions had improved for girls since the opening of her school. "As these sophisticated college girls tripped gaily in with their boyfriends," Stuart wrote, "this dramatized for my mother the progress in education for girls."[24] Gone were the days of foot-binding, of widespread resistance to female education, and of heavy curtains dividing the sexes. A few years later, Stuart's son Jack broached the idea of becoming a missionary. At first, Stuart recoiled: the idea resurrected unpleasant memories of psychological turmoil from thirty years earlier. Almost as a knee-jerk reaction, he advised Jack to "resist" the tug of missions. But then he had second thoughts. After observing that his son possessed "none of my antipathy," it dawned on him that his son's memories, in contrast with his own, "were rather alluring."[25]

And why wouldn't they be? Stuart's son had not experienced the hardship of the pioneering days of missions, when cross-bearing men and women had charged into China with righteous fervor, utterly unprepared for what awaited them. His son had not witnessed the violent mobs, perishing children, and showers of stones. Jack had passed much of his childhood on Yenching's impressive campus where he had watched his prestigious father command respect, engage in global steamship travel, and host distinguished Chinese intellectuals and officials. This is not to say that missions work had become perfectly safe. Indeed, social and political movements continued to convulse the nation. However, missions had undergone a remarkable transformation, offering now the sorts of instutions—schools, colleges, hospitals, and YMCA chapters—that the Chinese wanted. For this reason, Stuart knew that Jack, if he chose this path, would not be subjected to the pain, loneliness, and fruitless toil that had defined the missionary experience of the past. That was all a distant memory.

Notes

INTRODUCTION

1. Pearl Buck, *Fighting Angel: Portrait of a Soul* (New York: Reynal & Hitchcock, 1936), 82, 90.
2. Buck, *Fighting Angel*, 12–13, 82, 90, 98.
3. Buck, *Fighting Angel*, 90–96.
4. B. A. Garside, *One Increasing Purpose: The Life of Henry Winters Luce* (New York: Fleming H. Revell, 1948), 79, 99–109, 121–123, 148, 152.
5. Daniel Bays, *A New History of Christianity in China* (Chichester, West Sussex, UK: Wiley-Blackwell, 2012), 70.
6. John King Fairbank, *The Great Chinese Revolution: 1800–1985* (New York: Harper & Row, 1986), 125.
7. What follows is a summary of Yen's life. Chapters 7 and 12 provide more detail.
8. Obituary, *Chinese Recorder* 29, no. 7 (July 1898): 357–358.
9. W. W. Yen, *East-West Kaleidoscope, 1877–1946: An Autobiography* (New York: St. John's University Press, 1974), 286.
10. See Emerson's 1841 essay, "Self-Reliance."
11. F. L. Pott, *St. John's University 1879–1929* (Shanghai: Kelly and Walsh, 1929), 18.
12. Yen, *East-West*, 3, 26, 31, 55.
13. Qian Yimin and Yan Zhiyuan, *Fuching Yen: A Pioneer of Chinese Modern Medicine* (Fudan University Press, 2011), 9, 16, 22–28, 40, 121, 133–135; Nancy Chapman, *The Yale-China Association: A Centennial History* (Hong Kong: Chinese University Press, 2001), 20.
14. See the Introduction to *Twentieth Century Colonialism and China: Localities, the Everyday, and the World*, Bryna Goodman and David Goodman, eds. (London: Routledge, 2012), 1–2.
15. Daniel Vukovich, "Postcolonialism, Globalization, and the 'Asia Question,'" in *The Oxford Handbook of Postcolonial Studies*, ed. Graham G. Huggan (Oxford: Oxford University Press, 2013), 594.

16. Goodman and Goodman, *Twentieth Century*, 3–5.

17. Marius Meinhof, Junchen Yan, and Lili Zhu, "Postcolonialism and China: Some Introductory Remarks," *InterDisciplines* 8, no. 1 (2017): 5.

18. William R. Hutchison, *Errand to the World: American Protestant Thought and Foreign Missions* (Chicago: University of Chicago Press, 1993), 90.

19. Dana Robert, "From Missions to Mission to Beyond Missions: The Historiography of American Protestant Foreign Missions Since World War II," *International Bulletin of Missionary Research* 18, no. 4 (1994): 148.

20. The experience of Philip West shows the extent to which the Vietnam War could color scholarship on missionaries. At the height of the war, West was writing his book on the missionary-founded Yenching University. "My first impression of Yenching," West wrote, "was that it represented a Western effort in China I could respect." However, his view on Yenching darkened when he realized that "the language used to justify the American effort in Vietnam sounded too much like the defense of missionary behavior in China." Philip West, *Yenching University and Sino-Western Relations, 1916–1952* (Cambridge, MA: Harvard University Press, 1976), ix–x.

21. Paul A. Varg, *Missionaries, Chinese, and Diplomats. The American Protestant Missionary Movement in China, 1890–1952* (Princeton, NJ: Princeton University Press, 1958), ix.

22. Buck, *Fighting Angel*, 54.

23. Guoqi Xu, *Chinese and Americans: A Shared History* (Cambridge, MA: Harvard University Press, 2014), 1–3.

24. Buck, *Fighting Angel*, 128–129, 230.

25. Introduction to Jonathan Spence, *To Change China: Western Advisers in China* (New York: Penguin Books, 1980).

26. Ryan Dunch, "Beyond Cultural Imperialism: Cultural Theory, Christian Missions, and Global Modernity," *History and Theory* 41, no. 3 (2002): 302.

27. Ryan Dunch, *Fuzhou Protestants and the Making of a Modern China 1857–1927* (New Haven, CT: Yale University Press, 2001).

28. Bays, *New History*, 1.

29. Daniel H. Bays and Ellen Widmer, eds., *China's Christian Colleges: Cross-Cultural Connections, 1900–1950* (Stanford, CA: Stanford University Press, 2009), xvi.

30. David Hollinger, *Protestants Abroad: How Missionaries Tried to Change the World but Changed America* (Princeton, NJ: Princeton University Press, 2017), 6.

31. Lian Xi, *The Conversion of the Missionaries: Liberalism in American Protestant Missions in China, 1907–1932* (University Park: Pennsylvania State University Press, 1997), xii–xii.

32. *Report of the Great Conference Held at Shanghai, April 5th to May 8th, 1907* (New York: American Tract Society, 1907), 771, 777, 780.

33. Buck, *Fighting Angel*, 88–89.

CHAPTER 1

1. Hunter Corbett, "The American Presbyterian Mission in Shantung During Fifty Years: 1861–1911," in *A Record of American Presbyterian Mission Work in Shantung Province, China*, 2nd ed. (1914). The photograph faces page 1.

2. Corbett, "American Presbyterian," 1–3.

3. John Heeren, *On the Shantung Front: A History of the Shantung Mission of the Presbyterian Church in the U.S.A., 1861–1940* (New York: Board of Foreign Missions, 1940), 57.

4. Corbett, "American Presbyterian," 1–3.
5. Corbett, "American Presbyterian," 1–3.
6. Heeren, *Shantung Front*, 93.
7. John Haddad, *America's First Adventure in China: Trade, Treaties, Opium, and Salvation* (Philadelphia: Temple University Press, 2013), 133–134, 151.
8. Jessie Lutz, "Attrition Among Protestant Missionaries in China, 1807–1890," *International Bulletin of Missionary Research* 36, no. 1 (2012): 23.
9. Paul Cohen, *China and Christianity: The Missionary Movement and the Growth of Chinese Antiforeignism, 1860–1870* (Cambridge, MA: Harvard University Press, 1963), 84–85, 128. For text of treaties, see *Compilation of Treaties in Force* (Washington, DC: U.S. Government Printing Office, 1904), 138, 144.
10. Haddad, *First Adventure*, 152–153.
11. Cohen, *China and Christianity*, 78, 84.
12. Ellsworth Carlson, *The Foochow Missionaries, 1847–1880* (Cambridge, MA: Harvard University Press, 1974), 106–110.
13. "Zongli Yamen Document on the Unequal Treaties," in *The Search for Modern China: A Documentary Collection*, ed. Pei-Kai Cheng, Michael Lestz, and Jonathan Spence (New York: W. W. Norton, 1999), 159. Cited in Bays, *New History*, 76.
14. Milton Stauffer, *The Christian Occupation of China: A General Survey of the Numerical Strength and Geographical Distribution of Christian Forces in China* (Shanghai: China Continuation Committee, 1922), Appendix E, lxxx–lxxxi.
15. Michael Schuman, *Confucius and the World He Created* (New York: Basic Books, 2015), 5–10.
16. Thomas Wilson, ed., *On Sacred Grounds: Culture, Society, Politics, and the Formation of the Cult of Confucius* (Cambridge, MA: Harvard University Press, 2002), 12.
17. Herbert A. Giles, trans., *Three Character Classic* (Shanghai, 1910).
18. Carlson, *Foochow Missionaries*, 70–72.
19. Schuman, *Confucius*, 103–105.
20. Benjamin Elman, "Political, Social, and Cultural Reproduction via Civil Service Examinations in Late Imperial China," *The Journal of Asian Studies* 50, no. 1 (1991): 8–10.
21. Cohen, *China and Christianity*, 82–83.
22. Wilson, *Sacred Grounds*, 2–3.
23. Kung-Chuan Hsiao, *Rural China: Imperial Control in the Nineteenth Century* (Seattle: University of Washington Press, 1960), 184–191.
24. Fairbank, *Great Chinese Revolution*, 125.
25. Alexander Michie, *Missionaries in China* (London: Edward Stanford, 1891), 36.
26. Stephen Johnson, "Notices of Fuchau," *Chinese Repository* 16 (November 1847): 526. Quotation partially cited in Carlson, *Foochow Missionaries*, 7.
27. William Ashmore, "Signs of the Coming Dawn in China," *Missionary Magazine* 44 (November 1864): 413. Paul Cohen used the term *cultural clash* to describe Christianity's relationship to Confucianism; Cohen, *China and Christianity*, 82.
28. *Records of the General Conference of the Protestant Missionaries of China Held at Shanghai, May 10–23, 1877* (Shanghai: Presbyterian Mission Press, 1878), 173.
29. Arthur Smith, "How Mission Work Looked When I Came to China," *Chinese Recorder* 55 (January 1924): 11.
30. Chester Holcombe, *The Real Chinese Question* (New York: Dodd, Mead, 1900), 87–88.
31. Sidney A. Forsythe, *An American Missionary Community in China, 1895–1905* (Cambridge, MA: Harvard University Press, 1971), 4.

32. James Craighead, *Hunter Corbett: Fifty-six Years Missionary in China* (New York: Revell Press, 1921), 34.

33. Annetta Mills, "Julia Brown Mateer," *Chinese Recorder* 28 (May 1898): 218.

34. Robert McCheyne Mateer, *Character-building in China: The Life-story of Julia Brown Mateer* (New York: Fleming H. Revell, 1912), 26–31; Craighead, *Corbett*, 54–58; Daniel Fisher, *Calvin Wilson Mateer: A Biography* (Philadelphia: Westminster Press, 1911), 63–69.

35. Craighead, *Corbett*, 61–63.

36. Heeren, *Shantung Front*, 91–92.

37. Corbett, "American Presbyterian," 7.

38. Heeren, *Shantung Front*, 91–93.

39. Fisher, *Mateer*, 73–79.

40. Corbett, "American Presbyterian," 8.

41. James Muller, *Apostle of China: Samuel Isaac Schereschewsky, 1831–1906* (New York: Morehouse, 1937), 44.

42. Craighead, *Corbett*, 81–82.

43. Craighead, *Corbett*, 85, 95.

44. Craighead, *Corbett*, 105–106.

45. Craighead, *Corbett*, 54–55, 110–117.

46. Kenneth Scott Latourette, *A History of Christian Missions in China* (New York: Russell & Russell, 1929), 469.

47. Everett Hunt, "The Legacy of John Livingston Nevius," *International Bulletin of Missionary Research* 15, no. 3 (1991): 120–124.

48. Helen Nevius, *Life of John Livingston Nevius: For Forty Years a Missionary in China* (New York: Fleming H. Revell, 1895), 71–73.

49. Helen Nevius, *Nevius*, 164.

50. Charles Creegan, *Pioneer Missionaries of the Church* (New York: American Tract Society, 1903), 207–208; John Nevius, *China and the Chinese* (New York: Harper & Brothers, 1869), 318.

51. Irwin Hyatt, *Our Ordered Lives Confess: Three Nineteenth Century Missionaries in East Shantung* (Cambridge, MA: Harvard University Press, 1976), 79.

52. Nevius, *China*, 316.

53. Nevius, *China*, 330–334.

54. Nevius, *China*, 334.

55. Nevius, *China*, 335.

56. Helen Nevius, *Nevius*, 224–226; Nevius, *China*, 390–396.

57. John Nevius, "Methods of Mission Work," *Chinese Recorder* 17 (August 1886): 301–303.

58. Fisher, *Mateer*, 15–17, 25–26.

59. Fisher, *Mateer*, 43, 50–52.

60. Robert Mateer, *Character-building*, 18.

61. Mills, "Mateer," 218.

62. Robert Mateer, *Character-building*, 19–21.

63. Fisher, *Mateer*, 319.

64. Fisher, *Mateer*, 107.

65. Hyatt, *Ordered Lives*, 150–151.

66. Fisher, *Mateer*, 110; Hyatt, *Ordered Lives*, 151.

67. Hyatt, *Ordered Lives*, 151–153.

68. Robert Mateer, *Character-building*, 30–31.

69. Fisher, *Mateer*, 116–118.
70. Hyatt, *Ordered Lives*, 148–149.
71. Fisher, *Mateer*, 121–122, 126–127.
72. Hyatt, *Ordered Lives*, 149.
73. Fisher, *Mateer*, 91–92.
74. Chauncey Goodrich, "In Memoriam of Rev. Calvin Mateer," *Chinese Recorder* 40 (January 1906): 35–44.
75. Fisher, *Mateer*, 184–191.
76. "Missionary Intelligence," *Chinese Recorder* 2 (October 1869): 144.
77. Fisher, *Mateer*, 184–191; Hyatt, *Ordered Lives*, 154.
78. Hyatt, *Ordered Lives*, 156.
79. Jessie Lutz, *China and the Christian Colleges, 1850–1950* (Ithaca, NY: Cornell University Press, 1971), 14–15.
80. Robert Mateer, *Character-building*, 19, 76, 128–129; Fisher, *Mateer*, 133; Hyatt, *Ordered Lives*, 160–164.
81. Fisher, *Mateer*, 134–135.
82. Hyatt, *Ordered Lives*, 162–164.
83. Robert Mateer, *Character-building*, 43.
84. Mills, "Mateer," 219.
85. *Death Blow to Corrupt Doctrines: A Plain Statement of Facts Published by the Gentry and People. Translated from the Chinese* (Shanghai, 1870), iii.
86. Cohen, *China and Christianity*, 45–47.
87. *Death Blow*, v–vi.
88. Robert Nield, *China's Foreign Places: The Foreign Presence in China in the Treaty Port Era, 1840–1943* (Hong Kong: Hong Kong University Press, 2015), 236–237.
89. *Death Blow*, iii–iv, 15–16, 22, 32–33. Though Nevius and Mateer are not listed on the pamphlet, sources point to their role as translators. See Cohen, *China and Christianity*, 46; Samuel H. Chao, "John Livingston Nevius (1829–1893): A Historical Study of His Life and Mission Methods" (Ph.D. diss., Fuller Theological Seminary, 1991), 123.
90. Cohen, *China and Christianity*, 49.
91. *Papers Relating to the Massacre of Europeans at Tien-tsin on the 21st of June, 1870* (London Harrison and Sons, 1871), 164–168.
92. Hyatt, *Ordered Lives*, 153.
93. *Papers Relating to the Massacre*, 164–168.
94. Hyatt, *Ordered Lives*, 152.
95. Cohen, *China and Christianity*, 45.
96. Carlson, *Foochow Missionaries*, 129.
97. "Shan-Sin-Fan," *Chinese Recorder* 4 (September 1871): 106–107.
98. Michie, *Missionaries*, 14; *Death Blow*, ix.

CHAPTER 2

1. Ashmore, "Signs of the Coming Dawn," 413.
2. Walter Sinclair Stewart, *Early Baptist Missionaries* (Philadelphia: Judson Press, 1926), 2:110.
3. "In Memoriam: William Ashmore," *Baptist Missionary Magazine* 89 (June 1909): 196.
4. William Ashmore, "The Early Days of the Swatow Mission," *Chinese Recorder* 28 (September 1897): 421–423.

5. S. Moore Sites, *Nathan Sites: An Epic of the East* (New York: Fleming H. Revell, 1912), 22–24, 109.

6. Wade Barclay, *History of Methodist Missions* (New York: Board of Missions of the Methodist Church, 1949), 3:374–380.

7. Robert Maclay, *Life Among the Chinese, With Characteristic Sketches and Incidents of Missionary Operations and Prospects in China* (New York: Carlton and Porter, 1861), 153; Carlson, *Foochow Missionaries*, 48–64.

8. Sites, *Nathan Sites*, 52.

9. Barclay, *Methodist Missions*, 380.

10. Sites, *Nathan Sites*, 43.

11. Carlson, *Foochow Missionaries*, 69–70.

12. Carlson, *Foochow Missionaries*, 119–120.

13. Sites, *Nathan Sites*, 188–94.

14. Carlson, *Foochow Missionaries*, 124.

15. Sites, *Nathan Sites*, 179–181, 197–200; "The Death of Belle Sites," *Heathen Woman's Friend* 12, no. 1 (July 1880): 82.

16. Leonard Warren, *Adele Marion Fielde: Feminist, Social Activist, Scientist* (New York: Routledge, 2002), 20.

17. Warren, *Fielde*, 13–14.

18. Helen Norton Stevens, *Memorial Biography of Adele M. Fielde: Humanitarian* (Philadelphia: Fielde Memorial Committee, 1918), 50–53.

19. Warren, *Fielde*, 20–23.

20. Stewart, *Early Baptist*, 108–109.

21. Warren, *Fielde*, 20–23.

22. Stevens, *Fielde*, 79.

23. Stevens, *Fielde*, 85.

24. Connie A. Shemo, "'So Thoroughly American': Gertrude Howe, Kang Cheng, and Cultural Imperialism in the Woman's Foreign Missionary Society, 1872–1931," in *Competing Kingdoms: Women, Mission, Nation, and the American Protestant Empire, 1812–1960*, ed. Barbara Reeves-Ellington, Kathryn Kish Sklar, and Connie A. Shemo (Durham, NC: Duke University Press, 2010), 122.

25. Warren, *Fielde*, 29.

26. Frederick Hoyt, "'When a Field was Found too Difficult for a Man, a Woman should be Sent': Adele M. Fielde in Asia, 1865–1890," *The Historian* 44, no. 3 (1982): 317–319.

27. Adele Fielde, "An Experience in Hasheesh-Smoking," *Therapeutic Gazette* 4, no. 7 (July 1888): 449–451.

28. Fielde, "Hasheesh-Smoking," 449–451; Stevens, *Fielde*, 291–295; Warren, *Fielde*, 40–41.

29. Warren, *Fielde*, 42.

30. Hoyt, "When a Field," 320.

31. Warren, *Fielde*, 42.

32. Stevens, *Fielde*, 102.

33. Hoyt, "When a Field," 323.

34. Warren, *Fielde*, 42–46.

35. Stewart, *Early Baptist*, 121.

36. *Memorial Volume of Denison University, 1831–1906* (Granville, OH: Denison, 1907), 32; Peter Szto, "The Accommodation of Insanity in Canton, China: 1857–1935" (Ph.D. diss., University of Pennsylvania, 2002), 144.

37. *Memorial Volume*, 32; Szto, "Accommodation," 144.
38. Stewart, *Early Baptist*, 107.
39. William Cadbury, *At the Point of a Lancet: One Hundred Years of the Canton Hospital* (Shanghai: Kelly and Walsh, 1935), 101.
40. Szto, "Accommodation," 145–150.
41. Harriet Noyes, *History of the South China Mission of the American Presbyterian Church 1845–1920* (Shanghai: Presbyterian Mission Press, 1927), 20; Cadbury, *Lancet*, 102.
42. Carolyn McCandliss, *Of No Small Account: The Life of John Glasgow Kerr, M.D., L.L.D.* (St. Louis, MO: Wanshang Press, 1996), 32.
43. G. H. Choa, *"Heal the Sick" was their Motto: The Protestant Medical Missionaries in China* (Hong Kong: Chinese University Press, 1990), 31–32.
44. Choa, *"Heal the Sick,"* 32–33.
45. *Medical Mission Series: Hospitals in China* (Philadelphia: Woman's Foreign Missionary Society of the Presbyterian Church, 1912), 3–4.
46. Iris Borowy, ed., *Uneasy Encounters: The Politics of Medicine and Health in China 1900–1937* (Frankfurt, Germany: Peter Lang, 2009), 10.
47. Choa, *"Heal the Sick,"* 35.
48. *Records . . . 1877*, 120.
49. McCandliss, *No Small Account*, 39.
50. Choa, *"Heal the Sick,"* 77. For a description of Kwan Ato, see Edward Gulick, *Peter Parker and the Opening of China* (Cambridge, MA: Harvard University Press, 1973), 149–150, 164.
51. McCandliss, *No Small Account*, 39.
52. Cadbury, *Lancet*, 102.
53. J. Y. Wong, *Deadly Dreams: Opium, Imperialism, and the Arrow War (1856–1860) in China* (Cambridge: Cambridge University Press, 1998), 100.
54. Cadbury, *Lancet*, 116; Charles Selden, "The Life of John G. Kerr: Forty-three Years Superintendent of the Canton Hospital," *Chinese Medical Journal* 49 (April 1935): 368.
55. Selden, "John G. Kerr," 371.
56. McCandliss, *No Small Account*, 183.
57. Warren Candler, *Young J. Allen: The Man Who Seeded China* (Nashville, TN: Cokesbury, 1931), 18–19, 22, 32.
58. Adrian Bennett, *Missionary Journalist in China: Young J. Allen and His Magazines, 1860–1883* (Athens: University of Georgia Press, 1983), 3–4, 7–8.
59. Bennett, *Missionary Journalist*, 9.
60. Bennett, *Missionary Journalist*, 9, 13–14.
61. Candler, *Allen*, 54–55.
62. Earl Cranston, "Shanghai in the Taiping Period," *Pacific Historical Review* 5, no. 2 (1936): 157–159; Caleb Carr, *The Devil Soldier: The Story of Frederick Townsend Ward* (New York: Random House, 1992), 12–13; Candler, *Allen*, 91.
63. Bennett, *Missionary Journalist*, 16, 24; Adrian Bennett and Kwang-Ching Liu, "Christianity in the Chinese Idiom: Young J. Allen and the Early Chiao-hui hsin-pao, 1868–1870," in *The Missionary Experience in China and America*, ed. John K. Fairbank (Cambridge, MA: Harvard University Press, 1974), 164.
64. Bennett, *Missionary Journalist*, 17, 22, 26.
65. For the institution's origins, see W. A. P. Martin, *A Cycle of Cathay or China, South and North* (New York: Fleming H. Revell, 1900), 293–327.
66. Bennett and Liu, 163–164; Bennett, *Missionary Journalist*, 26–27.
67. Candler, *Allen*, 94, 102–103.

68. Bennett and Liu, 165.
69. Bennett, *Missionary Journalist*, 32.
70. Nevius, *China*, 334.
71. Craighead, *Corbett*, 129.
72. William Ashmore, "Fallacies about Missionaries," *Baptist Missionary Magazine* 65 (February 1885): 117–121.
73. Anna Seward Pruitt, *The Day of Small Things* (Richmond, VA: Foreign Mission Board of the Southern Baptist Convention, 1929), 24–31.
74. William Bainbridge, *Along the Lines at the Front: A General Survey of Baptist Home and Foreign Missions* (Philadelphia: Westcott and Thomson, 1882), 144.
75. *Proceedings of the Southern Baptist Convention* (Atlanta, GA: Jas. P. Harrison, 1888), xxxiv. Cited in Hyatt, *Ordered Lives*, 50.
76. H. A. Tupper, *Decade of Foreign Missions, 1880–1890* (Richmond, VA: Foreign Mission Board of the Southern Baptist Convention, 1891), 402–404.
77. Hyatt, *Ordered Lives*, 79.
78. Lutz, "Attrition," 23–24.
79. Valentin Rabe, "Evangelical Logistics: Mission Support and Resources to 1920," in *The Missionary Experience in China and America*, ed. John K. Fairbank (Cambridge, MA: Harvard University Press, 1974), 59–60.
80. T. D. Woolsey, "Christian Missions and Some of their Obstacles," *New Englander and Yale Review* 33, no. 4 (1874): 778.
81. Helen Nevius, *Nevius*, 85–105, 428.
82. Nevius, *China*, 374–377.
83. Adele Fielde, "Missionary Policy," *National Baptist Magazine* (September 23, 1875), 1.
84. F. S. Turner, *The Missionary Problem* (London: Hodder and Stoughton, 1870), 6–12.
85. "Mr. Turner's Views on the 'Missionary Problem' Examined," *Chinese Recorder* 3 (December 1870): 169–172. For other reactions, see in the same volume pages 26–27, 231, and 358.
86. Turner, *Missionary Problem*, 7–8.

CHAPTER 3

1. John Nevius, *Demon Possession and Allied Themes: Being an Inductive Study of Phenomena of Our Own Times* (Chicago: Fleming H. Revell, 1894), 9–10.
2. Nevius, *Demon*, 42–43.
3. Andrew Kaiser, *Encountering China: The Evolution of Timothy Richard's Missionary Thought, 1870–1891* (Eugene, OR: Pickwick Publications, 2019), 39.
4. Timothy Richard, *Forty-Five Years in China* (New York: Frederick A. Stokes, 1916), 67–68.
5. Robert Coltman, "Demoniacal Possession—So Called," *China Medical Missionary Journal* 4, no. 2 (1890): 59.
6. Richard Von Glahn, *The Sinister Way: The Divine and the Demonic in Chinese Religious Culture* (Berkeley: University of California Press, 2004), 6–8, 12.
7. Von Glahn, *Sinister Way*, 5–6.
8. F. Galpin, "Notes Concerning the Chinese Belief of Evil and Evil Spirits," *Chinese Recorder* 5 (January–February 1874): 44–45.
9. Von Glahn, *Sinister Way*, 5–6, 13, 98.

10. Nevius, *Demon*, 9. Nevius was not the only confused missionary when it came to converts performing exorcisms. In Shanxi Province, England's China Inland Mission baptized a young man who called himself Hsi Shengmo—"the Overcomer of Demons." According to Alvyn Austin, the missionaries "did not know how to respond to this extraordinary individual" who "had nothing to do with the foreigners, except to report his exploits." Alvyn Austin, *China's Millions: The China Inland Mission and Late Qing Society, 1832–1905* (Grand Rapids, MI: William B. Eerdmans, 2007), 176–177.

11. Nevius, *Demon*, 12–15.

12. Nevius, *Demon*, 12–15.

13. D. P. Walker, *Unclean Spirits: Possession and Exorcism in France and England in the Late Sixteenth and Early Seventeenth Centuries* (Philadelphia: University of Pennsylvania Press, 1981), 6.

14. Nevius, *Demon*, 12–15.

15. Nevius, *Demon*, 30–36.

16. Nevius, *Demon*, 35–38.

17. Paul Cohen, *China Unbound: Evolving Perspectives on the Chinese Past* (New York: Routledge Curzon, 2003), 94–95.

18. Nevius, *Demon*, 88–92. An account also appears in Adele Fielde, *Pagoda Shadows: Studies from Life in China* (Boston: W. G. Corthell, 1884), 241–243.

19. Nevius, *Demon*, 88–92.

20. Xiaofei Kang, *The Cult of the Fox: Power, Gender, and Popular Religion in Late Imperial and Modern China* (New York: Columbia University Press, 2006), 97, 114.

21. Stevens, *Fielde*, 151–153.

22. Nevius, *Demon*, 45–57.

23. Nevius, *Demon*, 45.

24. *Annual Report of the Missionary Society of the Methodist Episcopal Church for the Year 1881* (New York: Missionary Society of the Methodist Episcopal Church, 1882), 67–68.

25. *Annual Report . . . Methodist Episcopal . . . 1882*, 54.

26. *Annual Report . . . Methodist Episcopal . . . 1883*, 57.

27. John Morrison Reid, *Missions and Missionary Society of the Methodist Episcopal Church* (New York: Eaton and Mains, 1895), 2:37.

28. *Annual Report . . . Methodist Episcopal . . . 1884*, 57–58.

29. Hu Yong Mi, *Way of Faith* (Cincinnati, OH: Curts and Jennings, 1896), 7, 15, 21.

30. Hu, *Way*, 16, 21.

31. Dunch, *Fuzhou Protestants*, 7.

32. Hu, *Way*, 16, 21.

33. Hu, *Way*, 9–10, 12–13.

34. Hu, *Way*, 10–12.

35. Margaret Burton, *Notable Women of Modern China* (New York: Fleming H. Revell, 1912), 15.

36. Reid, *Missions*, 1:405.

37. Hu, *Way*, 10–13.

38. Hu, *Way*, 52.

39. Hu, *Way*, 41–42, 56.

40. Hu, *Way*, 114–116.

41. Rania Huntington, *Alien Kind: Foxes and Late Imperial Chinese Narrative* (Cambridge, MA: Harvard University Asia Center, 2003), 1–4.

42. Kang, *Cult*, 14, 18.

43. Kang, *Cult*, 35. For an account of a Daoist exorcism, see Huntington, *Alien Kind*, 64–65.
44. Hu, *Way*, 178–181.
45. Hu, *Way*, 87–90.
46. Justus Doolittle, *Social Life of the Chinese* (London: Sampson Low, Son, and Marston, 1868), 217–218.
47. Hu, *Way*, 87–90.
48. Calvin Kingsley, *Round the World* (Cincinnati, OH: Hitchcock and Walden, 1870), 2:151.
49. Hu, *Way*, 136–144.
50. Dunch, *Fuzhou Protestants*, 11.
51. Hu, *Way*, 79.
52. Dunch, *Fuzhou Protestants*, 16.
53. Nevius, *Demon*, 168–174.
54. Nevius, *Demon*, 135–136.

CHAPTER 4

1. Hu, *Way*, 68.
2. Helen Nevius, *Nevius*, 231–232.
3. John Nevius, *San-Poh, or North of the Hills: A Narrative of Missionary Work in an Out-Station in China* (Philadelphia: Presbyterian Board of Publication, 1869), 19–20, 32–37.
4. Nevius, *San-Poh*, 39–41.
5. Helen Nevius, *Nevius*, 152–3.
6. Nevius, *San-Poh*, 43–44.
7. Nevius, *San-Poh*, 45–48, 117–118.
8. Nevius, *San-Poh*, 44–45.
9. John Nevius, *The Planting and Development of Missionary Churches* (New York: Foreign Mission Library, 1899), 9.
10. Nevius, *China*, 352–354.
11. John Nevius, "How Shall We Deal with New Converts," *Chinese Recorder* 17 (January 1886): 29–30.
12. Nevius, *China*, 352–354.
13. Helen Nevius, *Nevius*, 231–232.
14. Sia Sek Ong, *Sia Sek Ong and the Self-support Movement in Our Foochow Mission: The Story of His Life and Work Related by Himself* (New York: Missionary Society of the Methodist Episcopal Church, n.d.), 3–4; Dunch, *Fuzhou Protestants*, 8.
15. W. X. Ninde, *The Picket Line of Missions: Sketches of the Advanced Guard* (New York: Eaton & Mains, 1897), 156–157.
16. Sia Sek Ong, *Sia*, 5–8.
17. Sia Sek Ong, *Sia*, 5–8.
18. S. L. Baldwin, "Rev. Sia Sek Ong," *The Gospel in All Lands* (July, 1898), 310.
19. Sia Sek Ong, *Sia*, 11–12.
20. Ninde, *Picket Line*, 161.
21. Sia Sek Ong, *Sia*, 13–14.
22. Sia Sek Ong, *Sia*, 15–16.
23. *Chinese Recorder* 4 (November 1871): 168–170.
24. *In Memoriam, S. L. Binkley* (Barnesville, OH, 1887).

25. Kingsley, *Round the World*, 2:147.
26. S. L. Baldwin, *Ling Ching Ting, The Converted Opium-Smoker* (New York: Self-Supporting Missionary Publication Department, n.d.), Pamphlet.
27. Sites, *Nathan Sites*, 125–129.
28. "Ling Ching Ting, the Faithful Christian Preacher," *Gospel in All Lands* 11 (1885): 321.
29. Sites, *Nathan Sites*, 126–127.
30. Baldwin, *Ling Ching Ting*.
31. Baldwin, *Ling Ching Ting*.
32. Baldwin, *Ling Ching Ting*.
33. Sites, *Nathan Sites*, 128–129.
34. *Annual Conference of the Methodist Episcopal Church* (New York: Phillips & Hunt, 1879), 13.
35. Sites, *Nathan Sites*, 128–129.
36. Hu, *Way*, 196–200.
37. See entries for October 5 and 10, 1863, and January 19, 1864. Journal of C. R. Martin, Martin Missionary Collection, Special Collections, Middlebury College. Martin refers to Hu Yong Mi as "Tong Mi" in his journal.
38. This retelling of the incident draws from three sources: Hu Yong Mi's autobiography and the accounts by Mary Martin and Stephen Baldwin. Hu, *Way*, 106–113. Mary Martin's diary entry for January 18, 1864, and Baldwin's account written on January 22, 1864, in the Journal of C. R. Martin. The Journals of C. R. Martin and Mary Elisabeth Allen Martin, Martin Missionary Collection.
39. Baldwin's account.
40. Hu, *Way*, 113–114.
41. Kingsley, *Round the World*, 2:130–131.
42. "Speeches by Chinese Christians on Self Support," *Chinese Recorder* 4 (April 1872): 284–285.
43. Hu, *Way*, 113–114.
44. Diary entries for September 6, 1864, and March 13, 1865. Journal of Mary Martin.
45. Hu, *Way*, 114.

CHAPTER 5

1. Craighead, *Corbett*, 142–143.
2. Tracey L-D Lu, *Museums in China: Power, Politics, and Identity* (New York: Routledge, 2014), 41–43; Craighead, *Corbett*, 144.
3. Arthur Judson Brown, *New Forces in Old China* (New York: Fleming H. Revell, 1904), 225–226; Craighead, *Corbett*, 145–146, 150.
4. W. R. Moody, "A Missionary Museum," *Record of Christian Work* 19, no. 10 (October 1900): 775.
5. James Dennis, *Christian Missions and Social Progress: A Sociological Study of Foreign Missions* (New York: Fleming H. Revell, 1906), 135.
6. Brown, *New Forces*, 225–226; Craighead, *Corbett*, 145–146, 150.
7. Dennis, *Christian Missions*, 135.
8. Stevens, *Fielde*, 148–150.
9. Stewart, *Early Baptist*, 2:114.
10. Warren, *Fielde*, 62.
11. *Baptist Missionary Magazine* 53 (1873): 324.

12. Valerie Griffiths, "Biblewomen from London to China: The Transnational Appropriation of a Female Mission Idea," *Women's History Review* 17, no. 4 (2008): 531.
13. *Baptist Missionary Magazine* 54 (1874): 254.
14. Fielde, *Pagoda Shadows*, 142–143.
15. Ellen Xiang-Yu Cai, "The First Group of Chaoshan Biblewomen," in *Christianizing South China: Mission, Development, and Identity in Modern Chaoshan*, ed. Joseph Tse-Hei Lee (Cham, Switzerland: Palgrave Macmillan, 2018), 18–24.
16. *Baptist Missionary Magazine* 56 (1876): 175–176.
17. Adele Fielde, "The Training and Work of Native Female Evangelists," *Records of The General Conference of The Protestant Missionaries . . . 1890* (Shanghai: American Presbyterian Mission Press, 1890), 245.
18. Fielde, *Pagoda Shadows*, 142–153.
19. *Baptist Missionary Magazine* 60 (1880): 359–360.
20. *Baptist Missionary Magazine* 56 (1876): 175–176.
21. Fielde, *Pagoda Shadows*, 142–153.
22. Fielde, *Pagoda Shadows*, 141–142.
23. Warren, *Fielde*, 61.
24. Hoyt, "When a Field," 326.
25. Stevens, *Fielde*, 117–118.
26. Stevens, *Fielde*, 119.
27. Warren, *Fielde*, 70–71.
28. Warren, *Fielde*, 76.
29. Fielde, *Pagoda Shadows*, 180–183.
30. Fielde, *Pagoda Shadows*, 169–171.
31. *Baptist Missionary Magazine* 56 (1876): 175–176.
32. *Eighth Annual Report of the Woman's Foreign Missionary Society . . . for 1877–78* (New York: Charles A. Coffin, Steam Book and Job Printer, 1878), 22.
33. *Eleventh Annual Report of the Woman's Foreign Missionary Society . . . for 1879–80* (Chicago: R. R. McCabe, 1880), 27.
34. One U.S. dollar equaled 1,140 cash.
35. Reid, *Missions*, 1:390.
36. Sia Sek Ong, "Who is Jesus?" trans. S. L. Baldwin (New York: Phillips & Hunt, 1871).
37. Bennett, *Missionary Journalist*, 32, 59.
38. Bennett, *Missionary Journalist*, 48–56, 77.
39. Bennett and Liu, 170.
40. Bennett, *Missionary Journalist*, 77, 149.
41. Bennett, *Missionary Journalist*, 155.
42. Bennett and Liu, 172–173.
43. Bennett, *Missionary Journalist*, 118, 140.
44. Bennett and Liu, 115.
45. Anne Pi-Yau Pang, *Huang Naishang: A Chinese Christian Reformer in Late Qing and Early Republican China* (Sarawak, Malaysia: Sibu Foochow Association, 2008), 23–24; Yeap Chong Leng, *Wong Nai Siong and the Nanyang Chinese: An Anthology* (Singapore: Singapore Society of Asian Studies, 2001), 1.
46. Pang, *Huang Naishang*, 24–30.
47. Pang, *Huang Naishang*, 29–30, 39–40, 147.
48. Bennett, *Missionary Journalist*, 106, 111.
49. Hyatt, *Ordered Lives*, 157.

50. Hyatt, *Ordered Lives*, 157–158.
51. Rufus Anderson, *Foreign Missions: Their Relations and Claims* (New York: Charles Scribner, 1869), 98, 118.
52. Fisher, *Mateer*, 126.
53. Hyatt, *Ordered Lives*, 186–187.
54. Hyatt, *Ordered Lives*, 185.
55. Hyatt, *Ordered Lives*, 161, 167.
56. Hyatt, *Ordered Lives*, 167.
57. Evelyn Rawski, *Education and Popular Literacy in Ch'ing China* (Ann Arbor: University of Michigan Press, 1979), 52; Angela Ki Che Leung, "Elementary Education in the Lower Yangtze Region in the Seventeenth and Eighteenth Centuries," in *Education and Society in Late Imperial China, 1600-1900*, ed. Benjamin Elman and Alexander Woodside (Berkeley: University of California Press, 1994), 394–396.
58. Fisher, *Mateer*, 138–140.
59. Hyatt, *Ordered Lives*, 167.
60. Hyatt, *Ordered Lives*, 224.
61. Rawski, *Education*, 25–28, 95, 186; Woodside and Elman, "Afterword: The Expansion of Education in Ch'ing China," in *Education and Society*, 525–529.
62. Lutz, *Christian Colleges*, 50.
63. Hyatt, *Ordered Lives*, 166–167.
64. Hyatt, *Ordered Lives*, 168.
65. Fisher, *Mateer*, 212–213.
66. Selden, "John G. Kerr," 371.
67. Vaccinations predate Kerr's arrival. Cantonese people had received vaccinations as early as 1805 when a British physician introduced the concept. K. Chimin Wong and Lien-Teh Wu, *History of Chinese Medicine: Being a Chronicle of Medical Happenings in China from Ancient Times to the Present Period* (Shanghai: National Quarantine Service, 1936), 278–284.
68. Noyes, *South China Mission*, 21.
69. John Kerr, "Report of the Medical Missionary Society's Hospital in Canton for the Year 1875," in *Report of the Medical Missionary Society in China for the Year 1875* (Canton, China, 1876), 18.
70. Selden, "John G. Kerr," 371.
71. McCandliss, *No Small Account*, 178–179.
72. Yung Wing, *My Life in China and America* (New York: Henry Holt, 1909), 18–19, 28–23.
73. "Success of a Chinese Student in Edinburgh," *The Monthly Journal of Medical Science* 15 (August 1852): 231.
74. James Young Simpson, *Physicians and Physic: Three Addresses* (Edinburgh: Adam and Charles Black, 1856), 67.
75. Choa, *"Heal the Sick,"* 80–81.
76. Wong Fun, "Report of the Missionary Hospital in the Western Suburbs of Canton, for 1859–60," *Edinburgh Medical Journal* 6, no. 6 (December 1860): 578–584.
77. Wong and Wu, *Chinese Medicine*, 372.
78. "Medical Missionary Work at Canton," *Record of the Presbyterian Church in the United States of America* 20 (1869): 187.
79. Yi-Li Wu, *Reproducing Women: Medicine, Metaphor, and Childbirth in Late Imperial China* (Berkeley: University of California Press, 2010), 179–180.

286 / Notes to Chapter 5

80. Judith Walzer Leavitt, "The Growth of Medical Authority: Technology and Morals in Turn-of-the-Century Obstetrics," *Medical Anthropology Quarterly* 42 (Summer 2002): 231.
81. Cadbury, *Lancet*, 117.
82. Kerr "Report . . . 1874," 17.
83. John Kerr, "Medical Missionary Hospital Clinic at Canton, China," *The Medical and Surgical Reporter* 6 (August 1861): 405–406.
84. Richard and Dorothy Wertz, *Lying-In: A History of Childbirth in America* (New Haven, CT: Yale University Press, 1977), 139; Guangqiu Xu, *American Doctors in Canton: Modernization in China, 1835-1935* (New Brunswick, NJ: Transaction Publishers, 2011), 134.
85. Kerr, "Medical Missionary," 405–406.
86. Cadbury, *Lancet*, 117.
87. Kerr, "Report . . . 1865," 9.
88. Cadbury, *Lancet*, 122–124; Xu, *American Doctors*, 192–193; Wong and Wu, *Chinese Medicine*, 488.
89. Choa, *"Heal the Sick,"* 88.
90. Cadbury, *Lancet*, 125, 191.
91. Xu, *American Doctors*, 88–90.
92. McCandliss, *No Small Account*, 174, 179.
93. Cadbury, *Lancet*, 175–176.
94. Kerr "Report . . . 1875," 22.
95. J. C. Thomson, "Medical Publications in Chinese," *The China Medical Missionary Journal* 1, no. 3 (1887): 116–118.
96. Cadbury, *Lancet*, 189.
97. Luqing Zhang et al., "An Ethical Solution to the Challenges in Teaching Anatomy with Dissection in the Chinese Culture," *Anatomical Sciences Education* 1, no. 2 (2008): 56–57.
98. *The T'Ang Code: Specific Articles*, trans. Wallace Johnson (Princeton, NJ: Princeton University Press, 2014), 271.
99. Wong, "Report . . . 1867," 15–16.
100. Wong, "Report . . . 1867," 15–16.
101. Kerr, "Report . . . 1865," 21.
102. Wong, "Report . . . 1867," 15–16.
103. Cadbury, *Lancet*, 178.
104. Wong, "Report . . . 1867," 7.
105. Eric Riches, "The History of Lithotomy and Lithotrity," *Annals of The Royal College of Surgeons of England* 43, no. 4 (1968): 185–199.
106. Cadbury, *Lancet*, 127, 189.
107. Wong, "Report . . . 1867," 9.
108. Wong, "Report . . . 1867," 15.
109. Hunter Corbett, "The Spirit and Methods of Evangelization," in *Counsel to New Missionaries from Older Missionaries of the Presbyterian Church* (New York: Board of Foreign Missions of the Presbyterian Church, 1905), 55–56.
110. Hyatt, *Ordered Lives*, 176–179.

CHAPTER 6

1. *Records . . . 1877*, i.
2. Hyatt, *Ordered Lives*, 176.

3. *Records . . . 1877*, i–iii, 8–9.
4. *Records . . . 1877*, v.
5. Helen Nevius, *Nevius*, 319.
6. Paul Bohr, *Famine in China and the Missionary: Timothy Richard as Relief Administrator and Advocate of National Reform, 1876–1884* (Cambridge, MA: Harvard University Press, 1972), xv, 13–21.
7. Bohr, *Famine*, xv–xvi, 28–31, 42–43, 75, 113.
8. Helen Nevius, *Nevius*, 319–320, 326.
9. Bohr, *Famine*, 89, 92, 98–99, 114.
10. Helen Nevius, *Nevius*, 319–323, 330.
11. Helen Nevius, *Nevius*, 328–330.
12. For Nevius's estimates, see two sources: John Nevius, "Methods of Mission Work" *Chinese Recorder* 17 (February 1886): 56; and Helen Nevius, *Nevius*, 328–330.
13. Nevius, "Methods," 56.
14. Craighead, *Corbett*, 135.
15. Nevius, "Methods," 56.
16. *Foreign Missionary* 37 (February 1879): 262.
17. Hyatt, *Ordered Lives*, 177.
18. *Records . . . 1877*, 85.
19. *Records . . . 1877*, 30–32.
20. Ralph Wardlaw Thompson, *Griffith John: The Story of Fifty Years in China* (London: Religious Tract Society, 1906), 492–493.
21. *Records . . . 1877*, 171–174.
22. Hyatt, *Ordered Lives*, 180–181.
23. Irwin Hyatt Jr., "Protestant Missions in China, 1877–1890: The Institutionalization of Good Works," in Kwang-Ching Liu, *American Missionaries in China: Papers from Harvard Seminars* (Cambridge, MA: Harvard University Press, 1966), 98–102.
24. *Records . . . 1877*, 236–240.
25. Since Allen's remarks were left off the record, only those sentences by him that other missionaries repeated in their own remarks have been preserved. *Records . . . 1877*, 236–240.
26. *Records . . . 1877*, 153, 156.
27. Smith, "How Mission Work Looked," 93.
28. *Records . . . 1877*, 156–158.
29. Hoyt, "When a Field," 329.
30. *Records . . . 1877*, 144.
31. Hyatt, *Ordered Lives*, 13–22.
32. *Records . . . 1877*, 323–328.
33. *Records . . . 1877*, 331.
34. *Records . . . 1877*, 333–337.
35. *Records . . . 1877*, 283, 287, 292.
36. Selden, "John G. Kerr," 372.
37. John Kerr, "The Chinese Question Analyzed." Delivered in the Hall of the Young-Men's Christian Association, November 13th, 1877 (Pamphlet printed for the author).
38. *Records . . . 1877*, 115–117.
39. *Records . . . 1877*, 122.
40. Isaac Wiley, *China and Japan* (New York: Phillips & Hunt, 1879), 6, 223–224.
41. Ryan Dunch, "Mission Schools and Modernity: The Anglo-Chinese College, Fuzhou," in Glen Peterson, Ruth Hayhoe, and Yongling Lu, eds., *Education, Culture, and Identity in Twentieth-century China* (Ann Arbor: University of Michigan Press, 2001), 114.

42. Dana Robert, "The Methodist Struggle Over Higher Education in Fuzhou, China, 1877–1883," *Methodist History* 34, no. 3 (1996): 175–176.

43. "Letter of Rev. J. L. Nevius," *Foreign Missionary* 37 (April 1879): 349.

44. Irwin Hyatt, "The Missionary as Entrepreneur: Calvin Mateer in Shantung," *Journal of Presbyterian History* 49, no. 4 (1971): 316–317.

45. The lens was ten inches in diameter. Fisher, *Mateer*, 214, 239.

46. Calvin Mateer, "Missionary Work in and from Tungchow," *Presbyterian Monthly Record* 33 (October 1882): 348–349.

47. Charles Corbett, *Shantung Christian University* (New York: United Board for Christian Colleges in China, 1955), 24; Fisher, *Mateer*, 213–214. Cyrus Field was a distant relative of Adele Fielde. Warren, *Fielde*, 7.

48. Fisher, *Mateer*, 236.

49. Harold Isaacs, *Scratches on Our Minds: American Images of China and India* (New York: John Day, 1958), 98.

CHAPTER 7

1. John Graham, *Lavater's Essays on Physiognomy: A Study in the History of Ideas* (Berne, Switzerland: Peter Lang, 1979), 35; John B. Davies, *Phrenology Fad and Science: A 19th-Century American Crusade* (New Haven, CT: Yale University Press, 1955), 7.

2. "Yung Wing and the Chinese Educational Mission," *Phrenological Journal* 67 (December 1878): 288–291.

3. G. R. Williamson, *Memoir of the Rev. David Abeel* (Wilmington, DE: Scholarly Resources, 1972), 211, 218; William J. Boone, *Address in Behalf of the China Mission* (New York: W. Osborne, 1837).

4. Muriel Boone, *The Seed of the Church in China* (Philadelphia: United Church Press, 1973), 92.

5. Boone, *Seed*, 92–103.

6. Boone, *Seed*, 106.

7. *Spirit of Missions* 12 (January 1847): 21.

8. *Spirit of Missions* 30 (January 1865): 30.

9. Boone, *Seed*, 110–111.

10. Boone, *Seed*, 121–124.

11. *Spirit of Missions* 10 (October 1845): 348.

12. Boone, *Seed*, 95, 121–124.

13. Boone, *Seed*, 121–124.

14. Boone, *Seed*, 124, 127, 131.

15. William Tenney, ed., *Memoir of Mrs. Caroline P. Keith* (New York: D. Appleton, 1864), 133–134.

16. *Spirit of Missions* 52 (January 1887): 22.

17. Boone, *Seed*, 261.

18. *Spirit of Missions* 30 (February 1865): 72.

19. *Spirit of Missions* 30 (January 1865): 30.

20. *Spirit of Missions* 30 (November and December 1865): 476.

21. *Spirit of Missions* 37 (September 1872): 549.

22. *Spirit of Missions* 17 (November 1852): 405–406.

23. Boone, *Seed*, 176.

24. Edward Yihua Xu, "Westernization and Contextualization: A Study on Three Pioneering Chinese Pastors of the Sheng Kung Hui in China," in *Contextualization of*

Christianity: An Evaluation in Modern Perspective, ed. Peter Chen-Main Wang (Sankt Augustin, Germany: Monumenta Serica Institut, 2007), 187.

25. Arthur R. Gray and Arthur M. Sherman, *The Story of the Church in China* (New York: Domestic and Foreign Missionary Society, 1913), 47–52.

26. *Spirit of Missions* 17 (November 1852): 405.

27. *Spirit of Missions* 21 (February 1856): 85–86.

28. *Spirit of Missions* 21 (February 1856): 85–86.

29. Boone, *Seed*, 286–287.

30. *Spirit of Missions* 22 (January 1857): 35–36.

31. *Spirit of Missions* 22 (July 1857): 351.

32. Yung Wing, *My Life in China and America* (New York: Henry Holt, 1909), 2–13.

33. Liel Leibovitz and Matthew Miller, *Fortunate Sons: The 120 Chinese Boys Who Came to America, Went to School, and Revolutionized an Ancient Civilization* (New York: W. W. Norton, 2011), 54.

34. Yung, *My Life*, 2–13.

35. Yung, *My Life*, 18–19.

36. Edward J. M. Rhoads, "In the Shadow of Yung Wing: Zeng Laishun and the Chinese Educational Mission to the United States," *Pacific Historical Review* 74, no. 1 (2005): 24.

37. Yung, *My Life*, 2–13, 18–19.

38. Yung Wing to Samuel Wells Williams, April 13, 1849, box 1, series 1, Yung Wing Papers, Manuscript Collections, Yale University Library.

39. Edward Rhoads, *Stepping Forth into the World: The Chinese Educational Mission to the United States, 1872–1881* (Hong Kong: Hong Kong University Press, 2011), 149.

40. Edmund Worthy, "Yung Wing in America," *Pacific Historical Review* 34, no. 3 (1965): 267.

41. Yung, *My Life*, 28–33.

42. Yung to Williams, April 13, 1849, Yung Wing Papers.

43. Yung, *My Life*, 35–39.

44. Leibovitz, *Fortunate Sons*, 24–25.

45. Yung to Williams, December 25, 1850, Yung Wing Papers.

46. Leibovitz, *Fortunate Sons*, 24–25.

47. Yung, *My Life*, 37–40.

48. Worthy, "Yung Wing," 271–272; Leibovitz, *Fortunate Sons*, 25–26. Since American-style football had not been invented, the game probably resembled rugby.

49. Yung, *My Life*, 40.

50. "History and Outcome of the Chinese Educational Mission to the United States," *Chinese Times*, February 11, 1888, 87.

51. "Yung-Wing," *Portsmouth Journal of Literature and Politics*, November 25, 1854.

52. "Yung Wing's Grand Coup," *New York Herald*, May 5, 1872.

53. Yung, *My Life*, 41.

54. Yung, *My Life*, 49–51.

55. Yung, *My Life*, iii, 257.

56. *Biographical Memoranda Respecting All Who Ever Were Members of the Class of 1832 in Yale College* (New Haven, CT: Tuttle, Morehouse and Taylor, 1880), 33.

57. Yung, *My Life*, 59–67.

58. Yung, *My Life*, 70–73.

59. Linda Cooke Johnson, *Shanghai: From Market Town to Treaty Port, 1074–1858* (Stanford, CA: Stanford University Press, 1995), 320.

60. Stella Dong, *Shanghai: The Rise and Fall of a Decadent City* (New York: William Morrow, 2000), 34.
61. Yung, *My Life*, 70–73, 136.
62. Yung, *My Life*, 75.
63. Wright, *Last Stand*, 7–8, 11.
64. Wright, *Last Stand*, 14, 210–212, 242–248; Spence, *To Change China*, 146.
65. Yung, *My Life*, 140, 148–153.
66. Yung, *My Life*, 156–171.
67. Yung, *My Life*, iii, 170–175.
68. Yung, *My Life*, 177–181.
69. Rhoads, *Stepping*, 14–17.
70. B. G. Northrop, "Chinese Youth Coming to America," *New York Observer and Chronicle*, September 19, 1872.
71. Rhoads, *Stepping*, 61.
72. Rhoads, *Stepping*, 70, 78, 83–86.
73. Rhoads, *Stepping*, 145–151.
74. William Lloyd Phelps, *Autobiography with Letters* (New York: Oxford University Press, 1939), 83–86.
75. William Hung, "Huang Tsun-Hsien's Poem 'The Closure of the Educational Mission in America,'" *Harvard Journal of Asiatic Studies* 18 (June 1955): 54.
76. Rhoads, *Stepping*, 153–157. See also Li Enfu, "Why I am not a Heathen," *North American Review* 145 (September 1887): 306–307.
77. "The Chinese Students," *New Haven Register*, July 30, 1881.
78. "History and Outcome."
79. *Connecticut Courant*, June 6, 1874.
80. *Hartford Daily Courant*, May 7, 1872.
81. "Report of The Joint Special Committee to Investigate Chinese Immigration," *Report of Committees of the Senate of The United States for the Second Session of The Forty-Fourth Congress* (Washington, DC: U.S. Government Printing Office, 1877), 462–465.
82. Rhoads, *Stepping*, 80, 115, 133, 168.
83. Lian Xi, "Returning to the Middle Kingdom: Yung Wing and the Recalled Students of the Chinese Educational Mission to the United States," *Modern Asian Studies* 49, no. 1 (2015): 159–160.
84. Yung Shang Him, *The Chinese Educational Mission and Its Influence* (Shanghai: Kelly & Walsh, 1939), 10–11.
85. Rhoads, *Stepping*, 143, 160–163.
86. Xi, "Returning," 162.
87. Rhoads, *Stepping*, 143, 160–163.
88. Rhoads, *Stepping*, 173, 178.
89. Yung, *My Life*, 223.
90. Hung, "Huang Tsun-Hsien's Poem," 73.
91. Rhoads, *Stepping*, 184.
92. Rhoads, *Stepping*, 188, 201.
93. Xi, "Returning," 163.
94. Brief Typed Biography of Yen Yung Kiung, Special Collections and Archives, Kenyon College; Yen, *East-West Kaleidoscope*, 7.
95. Yimin, *Fuching Yen*, 3.
96. "A Brief Account of the Late Rev. Young King Yen's Fifty Years," Special Collections and Archives, Kenyon College. This eulogy was written in 1898 by a former classmate who knew Yen for fifty years.

97. Seiji Kodama, "Life and Work of Y. K. Yen, the First Person to Introduce Western Psychology to China," *Psychologia* 34, no. 4 (1991): 214–215.
98. Brief Typed Biography of Yen.
99. "A Short Sketch of the Late Rev. Yung Kiung Yen, M.A," Special Collections and Archives, Kenyon College.
100. "Extract from a Letter of Mr. J. T. Points," *Spirit of Missions* 20 (February 1855): 58–59.
101. Lydia Fay, "Hong Niok, Chinese Convert," *Spirit of Missions* 31 (November 1871): 532–535.
102. "Extract from a Letter of Mr. J. T. Points," *Spirit of Missions* 20 (February 1855): 58–59.
103. *The Gospel Missionary* 6 (February 1, 1856): 28–31.
104. "A Brief Account."
105. *Spirit of Missions* 23 (November–December 1858): 621.
106. Yen took forty-three courses, each of which were graded on a ten-point scale. He received twenty-five perfect scores of ten and two marks in the eight range, with remaining scores falling between nine and ten. Grades of Yen Yung Kiung, Special Collections and Archives, Kenyon College.
107. "A Glance at Chinese Primary Education," *Kenyon Collegian* (April 1860), 301–308; Special Collections and Archives, Kenyon College.
108. Carol Lee Hamrin, ed., *Salt and Light 2: More Lives of Faith that Shaped Modern China* (Eugene, OR: Pickwick Publications, 2010), 218.
109. Yen, *East-West Kaleidoscope*, 1.
110. "An Alumni Letter," *Kenyon Collegian* 33 (December 7, 1906): 67.
111. Kodama, "Life and Work," 217.
112. "A Short Sketch."
113. Kodama, "Life and Work," 217.
114. "A Short Sketch."
115. "A Short Sketch."
116. Kodama, "Life and Work," 217–218.
117. *Spirit of Missions* 32 (February 1867): 144–146.
118. *Spirit of Missions* 32 (November 1867): 803–804.
119. *Spirit of Missions* 33 (August 1868): 641–642.
120. *Spirit of Missions* 33 (September 1868): 697–698.
121. Boone, *Seed*, 268.
122. *Spirit of Missions* 34 (June 1869): 353–357.
123. Xu, "Westernization," 189.
124. *Spirit of Missions* 36 (September 1871): 437–438.
125. *Spirit of Missions* 37 (April 1872): 236–237.
126. Judith Liu, *Foreign Exchange: Counterculture behind the Walls of St. Hilda's School for Girls, 1929-1937* (Bethlehem, PA: Lehigh University Press, 2011), 219.
127. Hamrin, *Salt and Light 2*, 18.
128. Yen, *East-West Kaleidoscope*, 3, 8.
129. "A Short Sketch."
130. "A Short Sketch."
131. Yung Kiung Yen, "A Chinaman on Our Treatment of China," *The Forum* 14 (September 1892): 89.
132. Rhoads, *Stepping*, 169.
133. E. A. Haag, *Charlie Soong: North Carolina's Link to the Fall of the Last Emperor of China* (Greensboro, NC: Jaan Publishing, 2015), 45–48, 52–54.

134. Sterling Seagrave, *The Soong Dynasty* (New York: Harper & Row, 1985), 48.
135. Haag, *Soong*, 127–128.
136. Seagrave, *Soong*, 59–71.
137. W. W. Yen, "The Chinese Student's View," *Overland Monthly*, May 1911, 499.

CHAPTER 8

1. Frances Baker, *The Story of the Woman's Foreign Missionary Society of The Methodist Episcopal Church, 1869–1895* (Cincinnati, OH: Curts & Jennings, 1898), 13–18, 22.
2. R. Pierce Beaver, *All Loves Excelling: American Protestant Women in World Mission* (Grand Rapids, MI: William B. Eerdmans, 1968), 101–103.
3. Dana Robert, *American Women in Mission: A Social History of Their Thought and Practice* (Macon, GA: Mercer University Press, 1996), 129–134.
4. Pui-lan Kwok, *Chinese Women and Christianity 1860–1927* (Atlanta, GA: Scholars Press, 1992), 20.
5. Arthur Smith, *Village Life in China: A Study in Sociology* (New York: Fleming H. Revell, 1899), 262.
6. Robert, *American Women*, 129–134.
7. Baker, *Story*, 18.
8. Amanda Porterfield, *Mary Lyon and the Mount Holyoke Missionaries* (New York: Oxford University Press, 1997), 6.
9. Robert, *American Women*, 131.
10. Robert, *American Women*, 130.
11. "Mission Schools: Shall Heathen Children Be Taught?" *Heathen Woman's Friend* 9 (August 1876): 35–36; Robert, *American Women*, 130–132.
12. Sarah Woolston, "Feet Binding," *Records . . . 1877*, 132–137.
13. Robert, "Methodist Struggle," 176–177, 180–181.
14. J. T. Gracey, *Eminent Missionary Women* (New York: Eaton and Mains, 1898), 203–205. Esther Baldwin was the wife of missionary Stephen Baldwin.
15. Molly Spitzer Frost, "Unbinding Ties: Female Missionaries and Chinese Women in the Late Qing," *Methodist History* 41, no. 1 (2002): 335.
16. Margaret Burton, *The Education of Women in China* (New York: Fleming H. Revell, 1911), 42–43.
17. Robert, "Methodist Struggle," 176, 180–181.
18. Mary Isham, *Valorous Ventures: A Record of Sixty Six Years of the Woman's Foreign Missionary Society* (Boston: Woman's Foreign Missionary Society Methodist Episcopal Church, 1936), 168.
19. Sites, *Nathan Sites*, 109–113.
20. Robert, "Methodist Struggle," 179–180.
21. Isham, *Valorous Ventures*, 167–168.
22. Burton, *Notable*, 20–23.
23. Sites, *Nathan Sites*, 109–113.
24. Isham, *Valorous Ventures*, 167–168.
25. Robert, "Methodist Struggle," 181–186.
26. Robert, "Methodist Struggle," 181, 183, 187.
27. *Fourteenth Annual Report of the Woman's Foreign Missionary Society of the Methodist Episcopal Church for the Year 1883* (Columbus: Ohio State Journal Printing, 1884), 25.
28. Robert, "Methodist Struggle," 181, 183, 187.

29. Baker, *Story*, 266.
30. *Fourteenth Annual Report*, 24–25.
31. Robert, "Methodist Struggle," 176.
32. Connie A. Shemo, *The Chinese Medical Ministries of Kang Cheng and Shi Meiyu, 1872–1937: On a Cross-Cultural Frontier of Gender, Race, and Nation* (Bethlehem, PA: Lehigh University Press, 2011), 21–24.
33. Ruth Borodin, *Women at Michigan: The "Dangerous Experiment," 1870 to the Present* (Ann Arbor: University of Michigan Press, 1999), xxvii, 38.
34. Shemo, *Chinese Medical*, 22–24.
35. Shemo, *Chinese Medical*, 22–24.
36. *The Story of Ida Kahn and Mary Stone* (Boston: Woman's Foreign Missionary Society, 1912), Unpaginated pamphlet.
37. Shemo, *Chinese Medical*, 22–24.
38. Shemo, "Thoroughly American," 121–123.
39. "Beginning at the Beginning," *Heathen Woman's Friend* 14 (September 1882): 62–63.
40. Shemo, "Thoroughly American," 124.
41. Weili Ye, "'Nü Liuxuesheng': The Story of American-Educated Chinese Women, 1880s–1920s," *Modern China* 20, no. 3 (1994): 319.
42. Gertrude Howe, "Teaching English in Girls' Schools," *Records of the Third Triennial Meeting of the Educational Association of China* (Shanghai: Presbyterian Mission Press, 1900), 152.
43. Robert, *American Women*, 185–186.
44. "Beginning at the Beginning," *Heathen Woman's Friend* 14 (September 1882): 62–63.
45. Shemo, "Thoroughly American," 125.
46. Shemo, *Chinese Medical*, 24.
47. Robert, *American Women*, 186–187.
48. Shemo, *Chinese Medical*, 35.
49. Shemo, *Chinese Medical*, 27.
50. Eva Brewster, *Her Name Was Elizabeth: The Life of Elizabeth Fisher Brewster Christian Missionary to China: 1884–1950* (Mount Shasta, CA: Red Hart Press, 2019), 10–11, 27.
51. Brewster, *Elizabeth*, 12–13, 21, 27.
52. Brewster, *Elizabeth*, 16–18, 28–30.
53. Brewster, *Elizabeth*, 41–42.
54. Brewster, *Elizabeth*, 44–46.
55. Isham, *Valorous Ventures*, 172.
56. Brewster, *Elizabeth*, 44–46.
57. *Sixteenth Annual Report . . . 1885* (Columbus: Ohio State Journal Printing, 1886), 30.
58. Elizabeth Fisher, "The Enlightenment of Our Native Christian Women," *Chinese Recorder* 21 (September 1890): 392–393.
59. Jane Hunter, *The Gospel of Gentility: American Missionaries in Turn-of-the-Century China* (New Haven, CT: Yale University Press, 1984), 15.
60. Brewster, *Elizabeth*, 50–51.
61. Brewster, *Elizabeth*, 51.
62. Oswald Eugene Brown and Anna Muse Brown, *Life and Letters of Laura Askew Haygood* (Nashville, TN: Publishing House of the Methodist Episcopal Church, South, 1904), 11–15, 24–25, 29.

63. Heidi Ross, "'Cradle of Female Talent': The McTyeire Home and School for Girls, 1892-1937," in *Christianity in China: From the Eighteenth Century to the Present*, ed. Daniel Bays (Stanford, CT: Stanford University Press, 1996), 211–212.

64. M. Cristina Zaccarini, *The Sino-American Friendship as Tradition and Challenge: Dr. Ailie Gale in China, 1908-1950* (Bethlehem, PA: Lehigh University Press, 2001), 48.

65. Brown, *Haygood*, 94–95, 99–102, 107, 122.

66. Brown, *Haygood*, 133, 165, 176.

67. Brown, *Haygood*, 166–168, 174–176, 193–194, 217, 275.

68. Brown, *Haygood*, 176.

69. The daotai oversaw the courts, customs, law enforcement, and defense of the area. See Ross, "Cradle," 213–214.

70. Brown, *Haygood*, 277–282.

71. Brown, *Haygood*, 281.

72. Brown, *Haygood*, 283–286.

73. Seagrave, *Soong*, 97–98, 110–115.

74. Brown, *Haygood*, 283–286, 293.

75. Ross, "Cradle," 214.

76. "Adaline Kelsey's autobiography," Adaline Higbee Kelsey Papers (AHKP), Archives and Special Collections, Mount Holyoke College Collections.

77. Letter . . . describing her first six months as a missionary physician in China, from October 30, 1878, until April 1879, AHKP.

78. *Journal of Education* 17 (May 10, 1883): 300.

79. Letter . . . dated March 15, 1880, describing some of her experiences living as a missionary physician in China, AHKP.

80. Letter . . . describing her first six months.

81. Letter from Adaline Kelsey to her friends from the Mount Holyoke Female Seminary, Class of 1868, dated April 4, 1879, describing her life as a missionary physician in Chefoo, China, AHKP.

82. William Rankin, *Memorials of Foreign Missionaries of the Presbyterian Church* (Philadelphia: Presbyterian Board, 1895), 52–53.

83. Letter . . . March 15, 1880.

84. Letter . . . March 15, 1880.

85. Letter . . . March 15, 1880.

86. Letter . . . March 15, 1880.

87. Hyatt, *Ordered Lives*, 222–224.

88. Hyatt, *Ordered Lives*, 222–224.

89. Mateer Family Letters, Personal Collection of Donna Albino, accessed July 5, 2022, https://mtholyoke.com/dalbino/letters/mateer.html.

90. Hyatt, *Ordered Lives*, 221.

91. Membership would exceed three million by 1915. Zaccarini, *Sino-American Friendship*, 48.

92. Hunter, *Gospel*, xiii.

CHAPTER 9

1. "Women Students at the Medical College," *Medical News* (January 12, 1884).

2. Warren, *Fielde*, 82–84.

3. Warren, *Fielde*, 82–84.

4. Stevens, *Fielde*, 160–163, 274.

5. Regina Morantz-Sanchez, *Sympathy and Science: Women Physicians in American Medicine* (Chapel Hill: University of North Carolina Press, 1999), 76.
6. Stevens, *Fielde*, 160–163.
7. Stevens, *Fielde*, 147–154.
8. Carol Li Nie, "The Divergent Careers of Adele Marion Fielde and Catherine Maria Ricketts," in *Christianizing South China: Mission, Development, and Identity in Modern Chaoshan*, ed. Joseph Tse-Hei Lee (Cham, Switzerland: Palgrave Macmillan, 2018), 42.
9. Warren, *Fielde*, 97.
10. Nie, "Divergent Careers," 45–46.
11. Warren, *Fielde*, 101.
12. Nie, "Divergent Careers," 45–46.
13. Fielde, "Hasheesh-Smoking," 449–451. Warren, *Fielde*, 97–102.
14. *Records . . . 1890*, x.
15. Adele Fielde, "The Training and Work of Native Female Evangelists," *Records . . . 1890*, 247.
16. *Records . . . 1890*, 263–268.
17. "Letter of Rev. B. C. Henry," *The Foreign Missionary* 37 (July 1878): 56–58.
18. Kerr, "Report . . . 1880," 17.
19. Noyes, *South China Mission*, 27.
20. Xu, *American Doctors*, 136.
21. Harriet Noyes, *A Light in the Land of Sinim* (New York: Fleming H. Revell, 1919), 85.
22. Mary Fulton, *In as Much: Extracts from Letters, Journals, Papers, etc.* (West Medford, MA: Central Committee on the United Study of Foreign Missions, 1915), 54–55.
23. Noyes, *Sinim*, 85.
24. Kerr, "Report . . . 1879," 16.
25. Xu, *American Doctors*, 131.
26. Kerr, "Report . . . 1880," 20.
27. Noyes, *Sinim*, 86–90.
28. Xu, *American Doctors*, 115.
29. Worthy, "Yung Wing," 286.
30. Marie-Claire Bergère, *Sun Yat-Sen*, trans. Janet Lloyd (Stanford, CA: Stanford University Press, 1998), 25–27.
31. Nina Brown Baker, *Sun Yat-Sen* (New York: Vanguard, 1946), 37–40.
32. Sun Yat Sen, *Kidnapped in London* (Bristol, UK: J. W. Arrowsmith, 1897), 10.
33. Xu, *American Doctors*, 115.
34. Kerr, "Report . . . 1883," 10.
35. Xu, *American Doctors*, 138.
36. Cadbury, *Lancet*, 144–145.
37. Morantz-Sanchez, *Sympathy*, 64–75.
38. Morantz-Sanchez, *Sympathy*, 64–75.
39. Morantz-Sanchez, *Sympathy*, 145–147, 151, 179.
40. Jessie Lutz, *Pioneer Chinese Christian Women: Gender, Christianity, and Social Mobility* (Bethlehem, PA: Lehigh University Press, 2010), 268.
41. Michelle Renshaw, *Accommodating the Chinese: The American Hospital in China, 1880–1920* (New York: Routledge, 2005), 157.
42. Kerr, "Report . . . 1883," 10, 17–19.
43. Kerr, "Report . . . 1883," 9.
44. Noyes, *South China Mission*, 47.

45. Mary Niles, "Dispensary for Women and Children," *Report of the Medical Missionary Society in China for the Year 1885* (Canton, China: 1886), 20, 33.
46. Noyes, *Sinim*, 208.
47. "Report . . . 1889," 13–14.
48. See Reports for 1887 and 1888.
49. Mary Niles, "Five Days with the Doctor, October 20–24, 1891," *Woman's Work for Woman* 7 (March 1892): 64.
50. Fulton, *In as Much*, 13–14.
51. Fulton, *In as Much*, 13–18, 22.
52. Harriet Noyes to Emily Noyes (October 10, 1885), Noyes Collection, Wooster College, accessed July 5, 2022, http://noyesletters.org/items/show/440.
53. Fulton, *In as Much*, 21–25, 39.
54. Fulton, *In as Much*, 26–29.
55. Fulton, *In as Much*, 27–28, 32–33.
56. Fulton, *In as Much*, 31–33.
57. Fulton, *In as Much*, 34–36.
58. Cadbury, *Lancet*, 189.
59. Fulton, *In as Much*, 34–36.
60. Fulton, *In as Much*, 34, 37–38.
61. Fulton, *In as Much*, 38–39.
62. Noyes, *Sinim*, 89–90.
63. Mary H. Fulton, "Hackett Medical College for Women," *China Medical Journal* 23, no. 5 (1909): 324.
64. Xu, *American Doctors*, 142–143.
65. *The Seventy-Seventh Annual Report of the Board of Foreign Missions of the Presbyterian Church in the United States* (New York: Presbyterian Building, 1914), 178–179.
66. Connie Shemo, "'Her Chinese Attended to Almost Everything': Relationships of Power in the Hackett Medical College for Women, Guangzhou, China, 1901–1915," *Journal of American-East Asian Relations* 24, no. 4 (2017): 321–323.
67. Xu, *American Doctors*, 205–208.
68. Peter Szto, "Psychiatric Space and Design Antecedents: The John G. Kerr Refuge for the Insane," in *Psychiatry and Chinese History*, ed. Howard Chiang (London: Pickering & Chatto, 2014), 73, 82.
69. Szto, "Accommodation," 116–117.
70. Szto, "Psychiatric Space," 73, 82–84.
71. Szto, "Accommodation," 230–232.
72. Szto, "Psychiatric Space," 79–82.
73. Szto, "Psychiatric Space," 86–88.
74. Xu, *American Doctors*, 213.
75. Xu, *American Doctors*, 36–37.
76. McCandliss, *No Small Account*, 187.
77. Henry Boone, "The Medical Missionary Association of China: Its Future Work," *China Medical Missionary Journal* 1, no. 1 (March 1887): 1–3.
78. Hyatt, "Protestant Missions," 103–104.

CHAPTER 10

1. Burton, *Notable*, 17–20.
2. Hu, *Way*, 114–116.

3. Burton, *Notable*, 20–21.
4. Burton, *Notable*, 20–23.
5. Mary Wheeler, *First Decade of the Woman's Foreign Missionary Society* (New York: Phillips & Hunt, 1881), 168–172.
6. Baker, *Story*, 156–157.
7. Annie Gracey, *Medical Work of the Woman's Foreign Missionary Society: Methodist Episcopal Church* (Dansville, NY: A. O. Bunnell, 1881), 152.
8. Wheeler, *First Decade*, 173–174, 178.
9. *Eighth Annual Report of the Woman's Foreign Missionary Society. . . for 1877–78* (New York: Charles A. Coffin, Steam Book and Job Printer, 1878): 40–42.
10. *Ninth Annual Report . . . 1878–79* (Boston, 1879): 11–12.
11. Mary Wheeler, "Hu King Eng," *Christian Advocate* (May 20, 1886): 313.
12. "Letter No. II," *Missionary Review of the World* 6 (November 1883): 457.
13. *Fourteenth Annual Report . . . 1883* (Columbus: Ohio State Journal Printing, 1884), 26.
14. *Fifteenth Annual Report . . . 1884* (Columbus: Ohio State Journal Printing, 1885), 26.
15. The *Tribune* cites an article from the *Philadelphia Telegraph*: "A Chinese Woman Doctor," *New York Tribune*, May 9, 1884, 8.
16. "Public Meeting in Philadelphia," *Heathen Woman's Friend* 16 (July, 1884): 10.
17. Sarah Pripas-Kapit, "Piety, Professionalism and Power: Chinese Protestant Missionary Physicians and Imperial Affiliations between Women in the Early Twentieth Century," *Gender & History* 27, no. 2 (2015): 353.
18. "Hu King Eng Gone," *Philadelphia Inquirer*, December 1, 1890, 5.
19. Burton, *Notable*, 24–27.
20. Wheeler, "Hu," 313.
21. Burton, *Notable*, 28–29.
22. *Heathen Woman's Friend* 16 (April 1885): 233–234.
23. Burton, *Notable*, 31.
24. *Proceedings of the General Conference of Protestant Missionaries in Japan, Held in Tokyo, October 24–31, 1900* (Tokyo: Methodist Publishing House, 1901), 723–724.
25. Burton, *Notable*, 31–32.
26. See two accounts of the event: *Christian Advocate*, July 4, 1889, 428; and "Miss Hu King Eng," *The Gospel in All Lands* (New York: Hunt and Eaton, 1889), 429–430.
27. Burton, *Notable*, 34–36.
28. "First Chinese Woman Doctor," *Boston Daily Globe*, July 20, 1895.
29. S. Moore Sites, *Hu King Eng, M.D.* (Boston: Woman's Foreign Missionary Society, 1912), 3.
30. "First Chinese Woman Doctor."
31. "Miracle Lady," *Monmouth Evening Gazette* (Illinois), September 17, 1898. The name "Miracle Lady" remained attached to Hu twenty years later. Belle Brain, "Who's Who in Medical Missions," *Missionary Review of the World* 42 (October 1919): 748.
32. "Chang's Physician Was Graduated Here," *Philadelphia Inquirer*, October 10, 1897.
33. "New Woman Invades China," *Philadelphia Times*, June 13, 1897.
34. "First Chinese Woman Doctor."
35. Burton, *Notable*, 39–42.
36. Frances Baker, "Some Methodist Hospitals Abroad," *Christian Advocate*, May 21, 1908, 842.
37. Burton, *Notable*, 42.
38. Burton, *Notable*, 42–44.

39. Burton, *Notable*, 49, 65–66.
40. *Forty-First Annual Report of the Woman's Foreign Missionary Society of the Methodist Episcopal Church* (Boston: WFMS Publication Office, 1910), 164.
41. *Heathen Woman's Friend* 17 (July 1885): 12–13.
42. Gertrude Howe, "Riot Experiences," *Heathen Woman's Friend* 18 (January 1887): 171–173.
43. Howe, "Riot Experiences," *Heathen Woman's Friend* 18 (February 1887): 202–204.
44. Shemo, *Chinese Medical*, 35.
45. Shemo, *Chinese Medical*, 45.
46. Borodin, *Women at Michigan*, 14–15.
47. Margaret Negodaeff-Tomsik, *Honour Due: The Story of Dr. Leonora Howard King* (Ottawa: Canadian Medical Association, 1999), xiv, 22, 25, 56, 91–95, 125.
48. Shemo, *Chinese Medical*, 46–47.
49. Diana Crossways, "Two Learned and Lovely Chinese Girls," *Salt Lake Herald*, September 20, 1896.
50. Shemo, *Chinese Medical*, 46–47.
51. *Phillipsburg Herald* (Kansas), August 20, 1896.
52. Crossways, "Two Learned."
53. Shemo, *Chinese Medical*, 48.
54. "Drs. Ida Kahn and Mary Stone," *China Medical Missionary Journal* 10 (December 1896): 181–184.
55. "Drs. Ida Kahn and Mary Stone," 181–184.
56. Shemo, "Thoroughly American," 127–128.
57. Shemo, *Chinese Medical*, 48–49.
58. Burton, *Notable*, 127.
59. Shemo, *Chinese Medical*, 48–49.
60. Burton, *Notable*, 132–133, 171–172.
61. Burton, *Notable*, 168.
62. I. N. Danforth, "The Elizabeth Skelton Danforth Memorial Hospital at Kiu Kiang, China," *American Journal of Clinical Medicine* 18, no. 3 (March 1911): 273–277.
63. Burton, *Notable*, 138–139, 171–174.
64. Charles M. Dow, "A Business Man's View of Missionary Work in China," *Outlook* 93 (December 25, 1909), 958.
65. Shemo, *Chinese Medical*, 93.
66. *Thirty-Eighth Annual Report of the Northwestern Branch of the Woman's Foreign Missionary Society* (Chicago: Libby and Sherwood, 1908), 53; *Fortieth Annual Report of the Northwestern Branch of the Woman's Foreign Missionary Society* (Chicago: Libby and Sherwood, 1910), 43.
67. Shemo, *Chinese Medical*, 67.
68. Burton, *Notable*, 145, 212–213.
69. Burton, *Notable*, 145, 212–213.
70. Mary Stone, "What Chinese Women Have Done and Are Doing for China," *The China Mission Year Book* 5 (1914): 239–240.
71. Mark Noll, *Clouds of Witnesses: Christian Voices from Africa and Asia* (Downers Grove, IL: Intervarsity Press, 2011), 204.

CHAPTER 11

1. William Ashmore, "Swatow," *Baptist Missionary Magazine* 65 (July 1885): 272–274.
2. "Personal," *Baptist Missionary Magazine* 65 (February 1885): 29.

3. "Death of Mrs. Ashmore," *Baptist Missionary Magazine* 65 (September 1885): 353.
4. Stewart, *Early Baptist*, 105.
5. "In Memoriam: William Ashmore," *Baptist Missionary Magazine* (June 1909): 194–196.
6. Michael Parker, *The Kingdom of Character: The Student Volunteer Movement for Foreign Missions (1886–1926)* (New York: University Press of America, 1998), 2.
7. "Moody's School of College Students," *Springfield Republican*, July 7, 1886.
8. "Moody's School."
9. Clifton Jackson Phillips, *Protestant America and the Pagan World: The First Half Century of the American Board of Commissioners for Foreign Missions, 1810–1860* (Cambridge, MA: Harvard University Asia Center, 1969), 29–31.
10. John Stanley, "Christianity and Female Empowerment: The American Presbyterian Mission Schools in Weixian, Shandong Province (1883–1920)," *Global Asia Journal* 8 (2009): 14.
11. Obituary of Robert Mateer, *Chinese Recorder* 52 (October 1921): 707–710.
12. Charles Hopkins, *History of the YMCA in North America* (New York: Association Press, 1951), 276–277.
13. Clarence Shedd, *Two Centuries of Christian Movements: Their Origins and Intercollegiate Life* (New York: Association Press, 1934), 149–152.
14. Hopkins, *History*, 278.
15. Shedd, *Two Centuries*, 149–152.
16. Shedd, *Two Centuries*, 214–215.
17. Shedd, *Two Centuries*, 217–222.
18. Shedd, *Two Centuries*, 221–222.
19. N. G. Clark, "Our Great Trust," *Missionary Herald* 77 (November 1881): 430.
20. Rabe, "Evangelical Logistics," 59–60.
21. Clark, "Great Trust," 430.
22. Arthur T. Pierson, *The Crisis of Missions; or the Voice out of the Cloud* (New York: R. Carter, 1886), 273–274.
23. Bruce J. Evensen, "'It Is a Marvel to Many People': Dwight L. Moody, Mass Media, and the New England Revival of 1877," *The New England Quarterly* 72, no. 2 (1999): 252, 267–268.
24. James Findlay, "Dwight L. Moody, Evangelist of the Gilded Age: 1837–1899," *Church History* 30, no. 2 (1961): 232.
25. Shedd, *Two Centuries*, 229–231, 241–242.
26. Parker, *Kingdom*, 5–7.
27. Shedd, *Two Centuries*, 243–244, 247.
28. J. W. Hanson, *The Life and Works of the World's Greatest Evangelist, Dwight L. Moody* (Chicago: W. B. Conkey, 1900), 149.
29. Shedd, *Two Centuries*, 243–244, 247.
30. Roger Geiger, *The American College in the Nineteenth Century* (Nashville, TN: Vanderbilt University Press, 2000), 133, 269.
31. Dana Robert, *Occupy Until I Come: A. T. Pierson and the Evangelization of the World* (Grand Rapids, MI: William B. Erdmans, 2003), 140–141, 145–146.
32. Robert, *Occupy*, 146–148.
33. Dana Robert, "The Origin of the Student Volunteer Watchword: 'The Evangelization of the World in This Generation,'" *International Bulletin of Missionary Research* 10, no. 4 (1986): 146.
34. Parker, *Kingdom*, 2, 9.
35. Pierson, "Missionary Field," 262–264.
36. *Springfield Republican*, July 27, 1886.

37. Pierson, "Missionary Field," 262–264.

38. Parker, *Kingdom*, 2, 9.

39. Basil Matthews, *John R. Mott: World Citizen* (New York, Harper and Brothers, 1934), 59–60.

40. Parker, *Kingdom*, 11–13. See also unpaginated introduction.

41. *Records . . . 1877*, 487; *China Centenary Missionary Conference Records . . . 1907* (Shanghai: Conference Committee, 1907), 771.

42. Parker, *Kingdom*, 11–13.

43. Hopkins, *History*, 288.

44. G. B. Smyth, "The Anglo-Chinese College at Foochow," *Gospel in All Lands* (May 1886): 214–215.

45. Shirley Garrett, *Social Reformers in Urban China: The Chinese YMCA, 1895–1926* (Cambridge, MA: Harvard University Press, 1970), 42.

46. Luther Wishard, "The Young Men's Christian Association and Foreign Missions," *Records . . . 1890*, 141–144, 203, 432.

47. Garrett, *Social Reformers*, 43.

48. See Willard Lyon to Wishard, August 3, 1893, Willard Lyon to Wishard, May 12, 1894, and D. N. Lyon to Wishard, June 27, 1894, YMCA of the USA, International Division. Correspondence and Reports, undated and 1890–1891, 1893–May 1900, box 22, folder 3, University of Minnesota Libraries, Kautz Family YMCA Archives, accessed June 19, 2020, https://umedia.lib.umn.edu/item/p16022coll360:80995.

49. Willard Lyon, "Report of D. Willard Lyon, Second Quarter 1896," University of Minnesota Libraries, Kautz Family YMCA Archives, accessed June 09, 2020, https://umedia.lib.umn.edu/item/p16022coll358:6111.

50. Garrett, *Social Reformers*, 65–66.

51. The student, C. T. Wang, studied law at Yale and became a high-ranking government official. Matthews, *Mott*, 123–124.

52. Garrett, *Social Reformers*, 68.

53. Willard Lyon, "Report of D. Willard Lyon, First Quarter 1897," University of Minnesota Libraries, Kautz Family YMCA Archives, accessed June 09, 2020, https://umedia.lib.umn.edu/item/p16022coll358:4233.

54. Garrett, *Social Reformers*, 68–69.

55. Judy Polumbaum, "From Evangelism to Entertainment: The YMCA, the NBA, and the Evolution of Chinese Basketball," *Modern Chinese Literature and Culture* 14, no. 1 (2002): 188–189.

56. Fletcher Brockman, *I Discover the Orient* (New York: Harper and Brothers, 1935), 1, 7–10, 17.

57. Brockman, *I Discover*, 30–33.

58. Brockman, *I Discover*, 80–85.

59. Garrett, *Social Reformers*, 35, 57, 64–65, 79, 82–85.

60. Harold Rabinowitz and Greg Tobin, *Religion in America: A Comprehensive Guide to Faith, History, and Tradition* (New York: Sterling, 2011), 119.

61. Parker, *Kingdom*, 125–127. See also Terrill Lautz, "The SVM and Transformation of the Protestant Mission to China," in Bays and Widmer, *China's Christian Colleges*, 4.

CHAPTER 12

1. *Christian Advocate* (April 19, 1888): 264.

2. "Letter from Rev. Sia Sek Ong," *Gospel in All Lands* (May 1888): 229.

3. "Women are Not Laymen," *Trenton Times*, May 8, 1888.

4. *Christian Advocate* (May 31, 1888): 364.
5. *Journal of The General Conference of The Methodist Episcopal Church* (New York: Phillips & Hunt, 1888), 485.
6. "Visit of Sia Sek Ong," *Northern Christian Advocate*, July 12, 1888.
7. See *Zion's Herald* 66, no. 37 (September 12, 1888): 290; and 66, no. 28 (July 11, 1888): 218.
8. W. F. McDowell et al., *The Picket Line of Missions: Sketches of the Advanced Guard* (New York: Eaton & Mains, 1897), 177–180.
9. *Picket Line*, 180–181.
10. Nathan Sites, "What's in a Name? Sia Sek Ong," *Zion's Herald* 66, no. 31 (August 1, 1888): 243.
11. Muller, *Apostle*, 41–42, 47, 83–84.
12. Muller, *Apostle*, 85–86.
13. Muller, *Apostle*, 100–115.
14. Walter Satneck, *St. John's University, Shanghai, 1879–1950: Portrait of a Missionary University* (Dover, DE: Typescript at Virginia Theological Seminary, 1986), 27–28.
15. Mary Lamberton, *St. John's University Shanghai 1879–1951* (New York: United Board for Christian Colleges, 1955), 5, 7, 9, 13, 25–26, 61.
16. Irene Eber, *The Jewish Bishop and the Chinese Bible: S. I. J. Schereschewsky (1831–1906)* (Leiden, The Netherlands: Brill Academic Publishing, 1999), 133.
17. *Spirit of Missions* (June 1899), 259–261; William Wormer, "A Chinese Soldier in the Civil War," *Papers Read before the Lancaster County Historical Society* 25, no. 3 (1921): 52–54.
18. *Spirit of Missions* (February 1880): 61–62.
19. *Spirit of Missions* (February 1880): 61–62.
20. *Spirit of Missions* (January 1881): 34–36.
21. *Spirit of Missions* (March 1880): 95. Four Chinese professors taught Chinese classics. Pott, *St. John's*, 3.
22. *Spirit of Missions* (August 1883): 376.
23. *Spirit of Missions* (June 1880): 210.
24. *Spirit of Missions* (November–December 1881): 534.
25. *Spirit of Missions* (June 1880): 243.
26. Eber, *Jewish Bishop*, 138–141.
27. Eber, *Jewish Bishop*, 138–141.
28. Muller, *Apostle*, 168–176, 199–200.
29. Satneck, *St. John's*, 43–44, 82.
30. Pott, *St. John's*, 5.
31. *Spirit of Missions* (November–December 1880): 469.
32. *Spirit of Missions* (May 1881): 233–234.
33. *Spirit of Missions* (January 1883): 48–49.
34. *Spirit of Missions* (June 1884): 296.
35. *Spirit of Missions* (May 1883): 287.
36. Pott, *St. John's*, 5; Satneck, *St. John's*, 33; Lamberton, *St. John's*, 20.
37. Edward Yihua Xu, "Liberal Arts Education in English and Campus Culture at St. John's University," in Bays and Widmer, *China's Christian Colleges*, 109.
38. Pott, *St. John's*, 5.
39. *Chinese Recorder* 29, no. 11 (November 1898): 556.
40. Lamberton, *St. John's*, 28; *Spirit of Missions* (October 1883): 448–449; and *Spirit of Missions* (January 1883): 48–49.
41. *Spirit of Missions* (October 1883): 453.

42. *Spirit of Missions* (April 1881): 199.
43. *Spirit of Missions* (May 1881): 233–234.
44. *Spirit of Missions* (September 1901): 603–608.
45. Satneck, *St. John's*, 34–35, 143.
46. Satneck, *St. John's*, 35.
47. Pott, *St. John's*, 9.
48. Lamberton, *St. John's*, 25–31.
49. See *Correspondence in Connection with the Protest against the Consecration of Reverend W. J. Boone* (Shanghai, 1895); and Chloë Starr, "Rethinking Church through the Book of Common Prayer in Late Qing and Early Republican China," in *Christian Encounters with Chinese Culture: Essays on Anglican and Episcopal History in China*, ed. Philip Wickeri (Hong Kong: Hong Kong University Press, 2015), 92–94.
50. Pott, *St. John's*, 44–45, 48.
51. Lamberton, *St. John's*, 27, 61.
52. "Mrs. Tiong Ahok," *Heathen Woman's Friend* 23, no 5 (November 1891), 98–99.
53. Reid, *Missions*, 2:29–35.
54. Dunch, "Mission Schools," 115.
55. Robert, "Methodist Struggle," 183.
56. *Annual Report . . . Methodist Episcopal . . . 1881*, 63–65.
57. *Annual Report . . . Methodist Episcopal . . . 1882*, 31.
58. *Annual Report . . . Methodist Episcopal . . . 1881*, 63–65.
59. See *Northern Christian Advocate* (August 10, 1882, and November 23, 1882).
60. *Annual Report . . . Methodist Episcopal . . . 1883*, 59–60.
61. Smyth, "Anglo-Chinese College," 214–215.
62. Smyth, "Anglo-Chinese College," 214–215.
63. *Annual Report . . . Methodist Episcopal . . . 1885*, 49–50.
64. Smyth, "Anglo-Chinese College," 214–215.
65. Bays, *New History*, 76. Bays cites a 1995 study by Chinese scholars.
66. Hyatt, *Ordered Lives*, 183; Hyatt, "Missionary as Entrepreneur," 317.
67. Mateer, "Mission Work in and from Tungchow," 349.
68. Watson Hayes, "The Aim of a Christian School in China," *Records of the Third Triennial Meeting of the Educational Association of China* (Shanghai: Presbyterian Mission Press, 1900), 65.
69. Hyatt, *Ordered Lives*, 186–188.
70. Corbett, *Shantung Christian University*, 24–32.
71. Hyatt, *Ordered Lives*, 186.
72. Calvin Mateer, "What is the best Course of Study for a Mission School in China," *Records of the Second Triennial Meeting of the Educational Association of China* (Shanghai: Presbyterian Mission Press, 1896), 53.
73. Hunter Corbett, "In Memorium: Calvin Wilson Mateer," *Presbyterian Banner* 95 (November 26, 1908): 32–33.
74. Corbett, "In Memorium," 32–33.
75. Hyatt, "Missionary as Entrepreneur," 320.
76. Corbett, *Shantung Christian University*, 83–84.
77. For Calvin Mateer's essay and rebuttals, see *Records of The General Conference . . . 1890*, 456–467, 497–509.
78. *Gospel in All Lands* (January 18, 1883): 35.
79. Immanuel C. Y. Hsü, *China's Entrance into the Family of Nations: The Diplomatic Phase, 1858–1880* (Cambridge, MA: Harvard University Press, 1960), 5–7.

80. Immanuel C. Y. Hsü, *The Rise of Modern China* (New York: Oxford University Press, 2000), 332–333.
81. S. C. M. Paine, *The Sino-Japanese War of 1894–1895: Perceptions, Power, and Primacy* (Cambridge: Cambridge University Press, 2003), 1.
82. Hsü, *Rise*, 341–342.
83. Paine, *Sino-Japanese War*, 5, 16.
84. Paine, *Sino-Japanese War*, 4, 18.
85. Hsü, *Rise*, 344.
86. Pang, *Huang Naishang*, 53.
87. Kodama, "Life and Work," 224.
88. Yen, *East-West Kaleidoscope*, 286.
89. Ke Zunke and Li Bin, "Spencer and Science Education in China," in *Global Spencerism: The Communication and Appropriation of a British Evolutionist*, ed. Bernard Lightman (Leiden, The Netherlands: Brill, 2015), 81–82.
90. Jilin Xu, "Social Darwinism in Modern China," *Journal of Modern Chinese History* 6, no. 2 (2012): 182–184.
91. W. W. Yen, "The United States and China," *Overland Monthly*, May 1911, 474.
92. Pang, *Huang Naishang*, 42, 44, 54–55, 73.
93. Bennett, *Missionary Journalist*, 236–237.
94. Corbett, *Shantung Christian University*, 53.
95. Shemo, *Chinese Medical*, 6, 52–53. Liang did not support all varieties of hybrid Chinese. In a different essay, he decried the Chinese who worked with foreigners in the treaty ports: "They spoke the barbarian language and put on barbarian dress.... But when you asked them whether they had any knowledge of Western natural science, they had none." Garrett, *Social Reformers*, 47–48.
96. This account draws from two sources: Heeren, *Shantung Front*, 84; and Corbett, *Shantung Christian University*, 51–52.
97. Philo McGiffin, "The Battle of the Yalu," *Century Magazine* 50, no. 5 (August 1895): 602; *Spirit of Missions* (January 1896): 27–28.
98. Pott, *St. John's*, 12.
99. *Spirit of Missions* (March 1896): 119.
100. Pott, *St. John's*, 12.
101. Lamberton, *St. John's*, 36.
102. Pott, *St. John's*, 14.
103. Lamberton, *St. John's*, 36–38, 55–56.
104. Pott, *St. John's*, 12, 18.
105. *Spirit of Missions* (April 1895): 144–146.
106. Pott, *St. John's*, 9, 15, 17, 48–49, 59–60.
107. Satneck, *St. John's*, 120, 125.
108. *Annual Report ... Methodist Episcopal ... 1895*, 50–52.
109. Dunch, *Fuzhou Protestants*, 42–43.
110. *Gospel in All Lands* (August 1896): 387.
111. *Gospel in All Lands* (March 1897): 107.
112. *Gospel in All Lands* (July 1897): 341.
113. *Annual Report ... Methodist Episcopal ... 1897*, 109–11.
114. George Smyth, "Prosperity of the Anglo-Chinese College at Foochow," *Gospel in All Lands* (January 1899): 42–43.
115. S. L. Baldwin, "The Anglo-Chinese College at Foochow," *Gospel in All Lands* (September 1898): 405–406.

116. Eddy Lucius Ford, "The History of the Educational Work of the Methodist Episcopal Church in China" (Ph.D. diss., Northwestern University, 1936), 172–174. See also *Annual Report . . . Methodist Episcopal . . . 1897*, 109–111.

117. *Annual Report . . . Methodist Episcopal . . . 1897*, 109–111.

118. *Annual Report . . . Methodist Episcopal . . . 1898*, 104–105.

119. Smyth, "Prosperity."

120. Ford, "Educational Work," 172.

121. Smyth, "Prosperity."

122. Calvin Mateer, "Plans for the Future," *Third Triennial Meeting*, 123.

123. Hyatt, *Ordered Lives*, 203–205.

124. Mateer, "Plans for the Future," 122–123.

125. Charles Scott, "A Great Missionary's Fifty Years in China," *Sunday-School Times* (June 10, 1933), 388–389.

126. Garside, *Increasing Purpose*, 26.

127. Alan Brinkley, *The Publisher: Henry Luce and His American Century* (New York: Knopf, 2010), 7–12.

128. Goodrich, "In Memoriam," 35–44.

129. Hyatt, *Ordered Lives*, 228.

130. Garside, *Increasing Purpose*, 86, 105–106.

131. Timothy Tow, *Ting Li Mei: The First Chinese Evangelist* (Singapore: Far Eastern Bible College Press, 1988), 9–10.

132. Daniel Bays, "The Growth of Independent Christianity in China, 1900–1937," in *Christianity in China: From the Eighteenth Century to the Present* (Stanford, CA: Stanford University Press, 1996), 313.

133. Henry Luce, "China: The Moving of the Spirit," *All the World* (January 1910): 19–22.

134. Luce, "China."

135. C. E. Scott, "Ding, the Apostle of Shantung," *Missionary Review of the World* 34, no. 2 (February 1911): 125–27.

136. A. R. Kepler, *Ding Li Mei* (New York: Women's Board of Foreign Missions for the Presbyterial Church, 1915), 8–9.

137. Yihua Xu, "Birth, Growth, and Decline of the Chinese Student Volunteer Movement for the Ministry in 20th Century China," in *Christian Mission and Education in Modern China, Japan, and Korea: Historical Studies*, ed. Jan A. B. Jongeneel (Frankfurt, Germany: Peter Lang, 2009), 65–69.

138. O. Braskamp, "The Evangelist Ding Li Mei: The Moody of China," *Chinese Recorder* 47, no. 7 (July 1916): 497.

139. Brinkley, *Publisher*, 12.

140. Corbett, *Shantung Christian University*, 61, 68–69, 110–113.

141. Lutz, *Christian Colleges*, 531–533.

142. "No Mere Proselytizing Agencies," *Chinese Recorder* 31, no. 5 (May 1901): 249.

143. Corbett, *Shantung Christian University*, 81.

144. Goodrich, "In Memoriam," 44.

CONCLUSION

1. If the Chinese had mostly overcome their prejudice for outsiders, the same could not be said about Americans. Holcombe cited the "anti-Chinese mobs" that injured and harassed immigrants from China. Chester Holcombe, "The Missionary Enterprise in China," *The Atlantic*, September 1906, 348, 350–354.

2. John Leighton Stuart, *Fifty Years in China: The Memoirs of John Leighton Stuart, Missionary and Ambassador* (New York: Random House, 1954), 11–15.

3. Stuart, *Fifty Years*, 16–19.

4. *Records . . . 1890*, 11–20.

5. *Records . . . 1890*, 11.

6. Stuart, *Fifty Years*, 19–28.

7. Stuart, *Fifty Years*, 24, 28–29.

8. Diana Preston, *Besieged in Peking: The Story of the 1900 Boxer Rising* (London: Constable and Company, 1999), 29, 34–37.

9. Kwok, *Chinese Women*, 14. See also Hunter, *Gospel*, 3–4.

10. F. L. Hawks Pott, "Education," in *China Centenary Missionary Conference Records* (New York: American Tract Society, 1907), 62–63.

11. Madeline Hsu, "Chinese and American Collaborations through Educational Exchange during the Era of Exclusion, 1872–1955," *Pacific Historical Review* 83, no. 2 (2014): 320–322.

12. Weili Ye, *Seeking Modernity in China's Name: Chinese Students in the United States, 1900–1927* (Stanford, CA: Stanford University Press, 2001), 9–10.

13. Stuart, *Fifty Years*, 35.

14. Yu-Ming Shaw, *An American Missionary in China: John Leighton Stuart and Chinese-American Relations* (Cambridge, MA: Harvard University Asia Center, 1992), 23, 27.

15. Stuart, *Fifty Years*, 39–43.

16. William Fenn, *Christian Education in Changing China 1880–1950* (Grand Rapids, MI: William B. Eerdmans, 1976), 43.

17. Stuart, *Fifty Years*, 49–54, 57–58.

18. Stuart, *Fifty Years*, 56–58, 65.

19. Shaw, *American Missionary*, 50.

20. Stuart, *Fifty Years*, 56–57.

21. Shaw, *American Missionary*, 51; Stuart, *Fifty Years*, 63–69.

22. Stuart, *Fifty Years*, 51, 72, 106.

23. Stuart contended that donors insisted upon American leadership to ensure a continuation of the institution's Christian character and ties to missions. Shaw, *American Missionary*, 63–64.

24. Stuart, *Fifty Years*, 88.

25. Jack ultimately decided to be a Presbyterian minister in the United States. Stuart, *Fifty Years*, 91.

Bibliography

ARCHIVES, LIBRARIES, AND COLLECTIONS

Adaline Higbee Kelsey Papers. Archives and Special Collections. Mount Holyoke College Collections.
Kautz Family YMCA Archives. University of Minnesota Libraries.
Martin Missionary Collection. Special Collections. Middlebury College.
Mateer Family Letters. Personal Collection of Donna Albino.
Materials Relating to Yen Yung-Kiung. Special Collections and Archives. Kenyon College.
Noyes Collection. Special Collections. Wooster College.
Yung Wing Papers. Manuscript Collections. Yale University Library.

NEWSPAPERS AND PERIODICALS

All the World
American Journal of Clinical Medicine
Baptist Missionary Magazine
Boston Daily Globe
Century Magazine
China Medical Journal
China Medical Missionary Journal
China Mission Year Book
Chinese Medical Journal
Chinese Recorder and Missionary Journal
Chinese Repository
Chinese Times
Christian Advocate
Connecticut Courant

Foreign Missionary
Forum
Gospel in All Lands
Gospel Missionary
Hartford Daily Courant
Heathen Woman's Friend
Journal of Education
Medical and Surgical Reporter
Medical News
Missionary Herald
Missionary Magazine
Missionary Review of the World
Monmouth Evening Gazette
Monthly Journal of Medical Science
National Baptist Magazine
New Englander and Yale Review
New Haven Register
New York Herald
New York Observer and Chronicle
New York Tribune
North American Review
Northern Christian Advocate
Outlook
Overland Monthly
Philadelphia Inquirer
Philadelphia Telegraph
Philadelphia Times
Phillipsburg Herald
Phrenological Journal
Portsmouth Journal of Literature and Politics
Presbyterian Banner
Presbyterian Monthly Record
Record of Christian Work
Record of the Presbyterian Church in the United States of America
Salt Lake Herald
Spirit of Missions
Springfield Republican
Sunday-School Times
Therapeutic Gazette
Trenton Times
Woman's Work for Woman
Zion's Herald

CONFERENCE RECORDS AND ANNUAL REPORTS

Educational Association of China. Records of the First, Second, and Third Triennial Meetings.

Journal of The General Conference of The Methodist Episcopal Church for 1888.

Medical Missionary Society's Hospital in Canton. Annual Reports for 1865–1888.

Missionary Society of the Methodist Episcopal Church. Annual Reports for 1881–1900.
Northwestern Branch of the Woman's Foreign Missionary Society. Annual Reports for 1907–1910.
Proceedings of the Southern Baptist Convention for 1888.
Records of General Missionary Conference (Shanghai) for 1877, 1890, and 1907.
Woman's Foreign Missionary Society of the Methodist Episcopal Church. Annual Reports for 1877–1885.

BOOKS AND JOURNAL ARTICLES

Anderson, Rufus. *Foreign Missions: Their Relations and Claims*. New York: Charles Scribner, 1869.

Austin, Alvyn. *China's Millions: The China Inland Mission and Late Qing Society, 1832–1905*. Grand Rapids, MI: William B. Eerdmans, 2007.

Bainbridge, William. *Along the Lines at the Front: A General Survey of Baptist Home and Foreign Missions*. Philadelphia: Westcott and Thomson, 1882.

Baker, Frances. *The Story of the Woman's Foreign Missionary Society of The Methodist Episcopal Church, 1869–1895*. Cincinnati, OH: Curts & Jennings, 1898.

Baker, Nina Brown. *Sun Yat-Sen*. New York: Vanguard, 1946.

Baldwin, S. L. *Ling Ching Ting, The Converted Opium-Smoker*. New York: Self-Supporting Missionary Publication Department, n.d.

Barclay, Wade. *History of Methodist Missions*. 4 vols. New York: Board of Missions of the Methodist Church, 1949.

Bays, Daniel. "The Growth of Independent Christianity in China, 1900–1937." In *Christianity in China: From the Eighteenth Century to the Present*, 307–316. Stanford, CA: Stanford University Press, 1996.

———. *A New History of Christianity in China*. Chichester, West Sussex, UK: Wiley-Blackwell, 2012.

Bays, Daniel, and Ellen Widmer, eds. *China's Christian Colleges: Cross-Cultural Connections, 1900–1950*. Stanford, CA: Stanford University Press, 2009.

Beaver, R. Pierce. *All Loves Excelling: American Protestant Women in World Mission*. Grand Rapids, MI: William B. Eerdmans, 1968.

Bennett, Adrian. *Missionary Journalist in China: Young J. Allen and his Magazines, 1860–1883*. Athens: University of Georgia Press, 1983.

Bennett, Adrian, and Kwang-Ching Liu. "Christianity in the Chinese Idiom: Young J. Allen and the Early Chiao-hui hsin-pao, 1868–1870." In *The Missionary Experience in China and America*, edited by John King Fairbank, 159–196. Cambridge, MA: Harvard University Press, 1974.

Bergère, Marie-Claire. *Sun Yat-Sen*. Translated by Janet Lloyd. Stanford. CA: Stanford University Press, 1998.

Biographical Memoranda Respecting All Who Ever Were Members of the Class of 1832 in Yale College. New Haven, CT: Tuttle, Morehouse and Taylor, 1880.

Bohr, Paul. *Famine in China and the Missionary: Timothy Richard as Relief Administrator and Advocate of National Reform, 1876–1884*. Cambridge, MA: Harvard University Press, 1972.

Boone, Muriel. *The Seed of the Church in China*. Philadelphia: United Church Press, 1973.

Boone, William. *Address in Behalf of the China Mission*. New York: W. Osborne, 1837.

Borodin, Ruth. *Women at Michigan: The "Dangerous Experiment," 1870 to the Present*. Ann Arbor: University of Michigan Press, 1999.

Borowy, Iris, ed. *Uneasy Encounters: The Politics of Medicine and Health in China 1900–1937*. Frankfurt, Germany: Peter Lang, 2009.
Brewster, Eva. *Her Name Was Elizabeth: The Life of Elizabeth Fisher Brewster Christian Missionary to China: 1884–1950*. Mount Shasta, CA: Red Hart Press, 2019.
Brinkley, Alan. *The Publisher: Henry Luce and His American Century*. New York: Knopf, 2010.
Brockman, Fletcher. *I Discover the Orient*. New York: Harper and Brothers, 1935.
Brown, Arthur Judson. *New Forces in Old China*. New York: Fleming H. Revell, 1904.
Brown, Oswald, and Anna Muse Brown. *Life and Letters of Laura Askew Haygood*. Nashville, TN: Publishing House of the Methodist Episcopal Church, South, 1904.
Buck, Pearl. *Fighting Angel: Portrait of a Soul*. New York: Reynal & Hitchcock, 1936.
Burton, Margaret. *The Education of Women in China*. New York: Fleming H. Revell, 1911.
——. *Notable Women of Modern China*. New York: Fleming H. Revell, 1912.
Cadbury, William. *At the Point of a Lancet: One Hundred Years of the Canton Hospital*. Shanghai: Kelly and Walsh, 1935.
Cai, Ellen Xiang-Yu. "The First Group of Chaoshan Biblewomen." In *Christianizing South China: Mission, Development, and Identity in Modern Chaoshan*, edited by Joseph Tse-Hei Lee, 15–36. Cham, Switzerland: Palgrave Macmillan, 2018.
Candler, Warren. *Young J. Allen: The Man Who Seeded China*. Nashville, TN: Cokesbury, 1931.
Carlson, Ellsworth. *The Foochow Missionaries, 1847–1880*. Cambridge, MA: Harvard University Press, 1974.
Carr, Caleb. *The Devil Soldier: The Story of Frederick Townsend Ward*. New York: Random House, 1992.
Chao, Samuel. "John Livingston Nevius (1829–1893): A Historical Study of His Life and Mission Methods." Ph.D. diss., Fuller Theological Seminary, 1991.
Cheng, Pei-Kai, Michael Lestz, and Jonathan Spence, eds. *The Search for Modern China: A Documentary Collection*. New York: W. W. Norton, 1999.
Choa, G. H. *"Heal the Sick" Was Their Motto: The Protestant Medical Missionaries in China*. Hong Kong: Chinese University Press, 1990.
Cohen, Paul. *China and Christianity: The Missionary Movement and the Growth of Chinese Antiforeignism, 1860–1870*. Cambridge, MA: Harvard University Press, 1963.
——. *China Unbound: Evolving Perspectives on the Chinese Past*. New York: RoutledgeCurzon, 2003.
Compilation of Treaties in Force. Washington, DC: U.S. Government Printing Office, 1904.
Corbett, Charles. *Shantung Christian University*. New York: United Board for Christian Colleges in China, 1955.
Corbett, Hunter. "The American Presbyterian Mission in Shantung During Fifty Years: 1861–1911." In *A Record of American Presbyterian Mission Work in Shantung Province, China*. 2nd ed. 1914. Publisher not identified.
——. "The Spirit and Methods of Evangelization." In *Counsel to New Missionaries from Older Missionaries of the Presbyterian Church*. New York: Board of Foreign Missions of the Presbyterian Church, 1905.
Correspondence in Connection with the Protest against the Consecration of Reverend W. J. Boone as Missionary Bishop of the Protestant Episcopal Church of America in China: Also Letters Referring to the Wretched Management of the Mission. Shanghai, 1895.
Craighead, James. *Hunter Corbett: Fifty-six Years Missionary in China*. New York: Revell Press, 1921.

Cranston, Earl. "Shanghai in the Taiping Period." *Pacific Historical Review* 5, no. 2 (1936): 147–160.
Creegan, Charles. *Pioneer Missionaries of the Church.* New York: American Tract Society, 1903.
Davies, John B. *Phrenology Fad and Science: A 19th-Century American Crusade.* New Haven, CT: Yale University Press, 1955.
Death Blow to Corrupt Doctrines: A Plain Statement of Facts Published by the Gentry and People. Translated from the Chinese. Shanghai, 1870.
Denison University. *Memorial Volume of Denison University, 1831–1906.* Granville, OH: Denison, 1907.
Dennis, James. *Christian Missions and Social Progress: A Sociological Study of Foreign Missions.* New York: Fleming H. Revell, 1906.
Dong, Stella. *Shanghai: The Rise and Fall of a Decadent City.* New York: William Morrow, 2000.
Doolittle, Justus. *Social Life of the Chinese.* London: Sampson Low, Son, and Marston, 1868.
Dunch, Ryan. "Beyond Cultural Imperialism: Cultural Theory, Christian Missions, and Global Modernity." *History and Theory* 41, no. 3 (2002): 301–325.
———. *Fuzhou Protestants and the Making of a Modern China 1857–1927.* New Haven, CT: Yale University Press, 2001.
———. "Mission Schools and Modernity: The Anglo-Chinese College, Fuzhou." In *Education, Culture, and Identity in Twentieth-century China,* edited by Glen Peterson, Ruth Hayhoe, and Yongling Lu, 109–136. Ann Arbor: University of Michigan Press, 2001.
Eber, Irene. *The Jewish Bishop and the Chinese Bible: S. I. J. Schereschewsky (1831–1906).* Leiden, the Netherlands: Brill Academic Publishing, 1999.
Elman, Benjamin. "Political, Social, and Cultural Reproduction via Civil Service Examinations in Late Imperial China." *The Journal of Asian Studies* 50, no. 1 (1991): 7–28.
Evensen, Bruce. "'It Is a Marvel to Many People': Dwight L. Moody, Mass Media, and the New England Revival of 1877." *The New England Quarterly* 72, no. 2 (1999): 251–274.
Fairbank, John King. *The Great Chinese Revolution: 1800–1985.* New York: Harper & Row, 1986.
Fenn, William. *Christian Education in Changing China 1880–1950.* Grand Rapids, MI: William B. Eerdmans, 1976.
Fielde, Adele. *Pagoda Shadows: Studies from Life in China.* Boston: W. G. Corthell, 1884.
Findlay, James. "Dwight L. Moody, Evangelist of the Gilded Age: 1837–1899." *Church History* 30, no. 2 (1961): 232.
Fisher, Daniel. *Calvin Wilson Mateer: A Biography.* Philadelphia: Westminster Press, 1911.
Ford, Eddy Lucius. "The History of the Educational Work of the Methodist Episcopal Church in China: A Study of its Development and Present Trends." Ph.D. diss., Northwestern University, 1936.
Forsythe, Sidney. *An American Missionary Community in China, 1895–1905.* Cambridge, MA: Harvard University Press, 1971.
Frost, Molly Spitzer. "Unbinding Ties: Female Missionaries and Chinese Women in the Late Qing." *Methodist History* 41, no. 1 (2002): 329–341.
Fulton, Mary. *In as Much: Extracts from Letters, Journals, Papers, etc.* West Medford, MA: Central Committee on the United Study of Foreign Missions, 1915.
Garrett, Shirley. *Social Reformers in Urban China: The Chinese YMCA, 1895–1926.* Cambridge, MA: Harvard University Press, 1970.

Garside, B. A. *One Increasing Purpose: The Life of Henry Winters Luce*. New York: Fleming H. Revell, 1948.
Geiger, Roger. *The American College in the Nineteenth Century*. Nashville, TN: Vanderbilt University Press, 2000.
Goodman, Bryna, and David Goodman, eds. *Twentieth Century Colonialism and China: Localities, the Everyday, and the World*. London: Taylor and Francis, 2012.
Gracey, Annie. *Medical Work of the Woman's Foreign Missionary Society: Methodist Episcopal Church*. Dansville, NY: A. O. Bunnell, 1881.
Gracey, J. T. *Eminent Missionary Women*. New York: Eaton and Mains, 1898.
Graham, John. *Lavater's Essays on Physiognomy: A Study in the History of Ideas*. Berne, Switzerland: Peter Lang, 1979.
Gray, Arthur, and Arthur M. Sherman. *The Story of the Church in China*. New York: Domestic and Foreign Missionary Society, 1913.
Griffiths, Valerie. "Biblewomen from London to China: The Transnational Appropriation of a Female Mission Idea." *Women's History Review* 17, no. 4 (2008): 521–541.
Gulick, Edward. *Peter Parker and the Opening of China*. Cambridge, MA: Harvard University Press, 1973.
Haag, E. A. *Charlie Soong: North Carolina's Link to the Fall of the Last Emperor of China*. Greensboro, NC: Jaan Publishing, 2015.
Haddad, John. *America's First Adventure in China: Trade, Treaties, Opium, and Salvation*. Philadelphia: Temple University Press, 2013.
Hamrin, Carol Lee, ed. *Salt and Light 2: More Lives of Faith that Shaped Modern China*. Eugene, OR: Pickwick Publications, 2010.
Hanson, J. W. *The Life and Works of the World's Greatest Evangelist, Dwight L. Moody*. Chicago: W. B. Conkey, 1900.
Heeren, John. *On the Shantung Front: A History of the Shantung Mission of the Presbyterian Church in the U.S.A., 1861–1940*. New York: Board of Foreign Missions, 1940.
Holcombe, Chester. "The Missionary Enterprise in China." *The Atlantic*, September 1906.
———. *The Real Chinese Question*. New York: Dodd, Mead, 1900.
Hollinger, David. *Protestants Abroad: How Missionaries Tried to Change the World but Changed America*. Princeton, NJ: Princeton University Press, 2017.
Hopkins, Charles. *History of the YMCA in North America*. New York: Association Press, 1951.
Hoyt, Frederick. "'When a Field was Found too Difficult for a Man, a Woman should be Sent': Adele M. Fielde in Asia, 1865–1890." *The Historian* 44, no. 3 (1982): 314–334.
Hsiao, Kung-Chuan. *Rural China: Imperial Control in the Nineteenth Century*. Seattle: University of Washington Press, 1960.
Hsü, Immanuel C. Y. *China's Entrance into the Family of Nations: The Diplomatic Phase, 1858–1880*. Cambridge, MA: Harvard University Press, 1960.
———. *The Rise of Modern China*. New York: Oxford University Press, 2000.
Hsu, Madeline. "Chinese and American Collaborations through Educational Exchange during the Era of Exclusion, 1872–1955." *Pacific Historical Review* 83, no. 2 (2014): 314–332.
Hu, Yong Mi. *Way of Faith*. Cincinnati, OH: Curts and Jennings, 1896.
Hung, William. "Huang Tsun-Hsien's Poem 'The Closure of the Educational Mission in America.'" *Harvard Journal of Asiatic Studies* 18, no. 1/2 (1955): 50–73.
Hunt, Everett. "The Legacy of John Livingston Nevius." *International Bulletin of Missionary Research* 15, no. 3 (1991): 120–124.

Hunter, Jane. *The Gospel of Gentility: American Missionaries in Turn-of-the-Century China*. New Haven, CT: Yale University Press, 1984.
Huntington, Rania. *Alien Kind: Foxes and Late Imperial Chinese Narrative*. Cambridge, MA: Harvard University Asia Center, 2003.
Hutchison, William. *Errand to the World: American Protestant Thought and Foreign Missions*. Chicago: University of Chicago Press, 1993.
Hyatt, Irwin T., Jr. "The Missionary as Entrepreneur: Calvin Mateer in Shantung." *Journal of Presbyterian History* 49, no. 4 (1971): 303–327.
———. *Our Ordered Lives Confess: Three Nineteenth Century Missionaries in East Shantung*. Cambridge, MA: Harvard University Press, 1976.
———. "Protestant Missions in China, 1877–1890: The Institutionalization of Good Works." In *American Missionaries in China: Papers from Harvard Seminars*, edited by Kwang-Ching Liu, 93–126. Cambridge, MA: Harvard University Press, 1966.
In Memoriam, S.L. Binkley, A.M. Born February 17th, 1836. Died September 24th, 1887. Barnesville, OH, 1887.
Isaacs, Harold. *Scratches on Our Minds: American Images of China and India*. New York: John Day, 1958.
Isham, Mary. *Valorous Ventures: A Record of Sixty and Six Years of the Woman's Foreign Missionary Society*. Boston: Woman's Foreign Missionary Society, Methodist Episcopal Church, 1936.
Johnson, Linda Cooke. *Shanghai: From Market Town to Treaty Port, 1074–1858*. Stanford, CA: Stanford University Press, 1995.
Kaiser, Andrew. *Encountering China: The Evolution of Timothy Richard's Missionary Thought, 1870–1891*. Eugene, OR: Pickwick Publications, 2019.
Kang, Xiaofei. *The Cult of the Fox: Power, Gender, and Popular Religion in Late Imperial and Modern China*. New York: Columbia University Press, 2006.
Kepler, A. R. *Ding Li Mei*. New York: Women's Board of Foreign Missions for the Presbyterian Church, 1915.
Kerr, John. "The Chinese Question Analyzed." Speech delivered in the Hall of the Young Men's Christian Association, November 13th, 1877. Pamphlet printed for the author.
Kingsley, Calvin. *Round the World*. 2 vols. Cincinnati, OH: Hitchcock and Walden, 1870.
Kodama, Seiji. "Life and Work of Y. K. Yen, the First Person to Introduce Western Psychology to China." *Psychologia* 34, no. 4 (1991): 213–226.
Kwok, Pui-lan. *Chinese Women and Christianity 1860–1927*. Atlanta, GA: Scholars Press, 1992.
Lamberton, Mary. *St. Johns's University Shanghai 1879–1951*. New York: United Board for Christian Colleges, 1955.
Latourette, Kenneth Scott. *A History of Christian Missions in China*. New York: Russell & Russell, 1929.
Leavitt, Judith Walzer. "The Growth of Medical Authority: Technology and Morals in Turn-of-the-Century Obstetrics." *Medical Anthropology Quarterly* 42 (Summer 2002): 230–255.
Leibovitz, Liel, and Matthew Miller. *Fortunate Sons: The 120 Chinese Boys Who Came to America, Went to School, and Revolutionized an Ancient Civilization*. New York: W. W. Norton, 2011.
Leng, Yeap Chong. *Wong Nai Siong and the Nanyang Chinese: An Anthology*. Singapore: Singapore Society of Asian Studies, 2001.

Leung, Angela Ki Che. "Elementary Education in the Lower Yangtze Region in the Seventeenth and Eighteenth Centuries." In *Education and Society in Late Imperial China, 1600–1900*, edited by Benjamin Elman and Alexander Woodside, 381–416. Berkeley: University of California Press, 1994.

Li Nie, Carol. "The Divergent Careers of Adele Marion Fielde and Catherine Maria Ricketts." In *Christianizing South China: Mission, Development, and Identity in Modern Chaoshan*, edited by Joseph Tse-Hei Lee, 37–53. Cham, Switzerland: Palgrave Macmillan, 2018.

Liu, Judith. *Foreign Exchange: Counterculture behind the Walls of St. Hilda's School for Girls, 1929–1937*. Bethlehem, PA: Lehigh University Press, 2011.

Lu, Tracey L-D. *Museums in China: Power, Politics, and Identity*. New York: Routledge, 2014.

Lutz, Jessie. "Attrition Among Protestant Missionaries in China, 1807–1890." *International Bulletin of Missionary Research* 36, no. 1 (2012): 22–27.

———. *China and the Christian Colleges, 1850–1950*. Ithaca, NY: Cornell University Press, 1971.

———. *Pioneer Chinese Christian Women: Gender, Christianity, and Social Mobility*. Bethlehem, PA: Lehigh University Press, 2010.

Maclay, Robert. *Life Among the Chinese, With Characteristic Sketches and Incidents of Missionary Operations and Prospects in China*. New York: Carlton and Porter, 1861.

Martin, W. A. P. *A Cycle of Cathay or China, South and North*. New York: Fleming H. Revell, 1900.

Mateer, Robert. *Character-building in China: The Life-story of Julia Brown Mateer*. New York: Fleming H. Revell, 1912.

Matthews, Basil. *John R. Mott: World Citizen*. New York: Harper and Brothers, 1934.

McCandliss, Carolyn. *Of No Small Account: The Life of John Glasgow Kerr, M.D., L.L.D.* St. Louis, MO: Wanshang Press, 1996.

McDowell, W. F., et al. *The Picket Line of Missions: Sketches of the Advanced Guard*. New York: Eaton & Mains, 1897.

Medical Mission Series: Hospitals in China. Philadelphia: Woman's Foreign Missionary Society of the Presbyterian Church, 1912.

Meinhof, Marius, Junchen Yan, and Lili Zhu. "Postcolonialism and China: Some Introductory Remarks." *InterDisciplines* 8, no. 1 (2017): 1–25.

Michie, Alexander. *Missionaries in China*. London: Edward Stanford, 1891.

Morantz-Sanchez, Regina. *Sympathy and Science: Women Physicians in American Medicine*. Chapel Hill: University of North Carolina Press, 1999.

Muller, James. *Apostle of China: Samuel Isaac Schereschewsky, 1831–1906*. New York: Morehouse, 1937.

Negodaeff-Tomsik, Margaret. *Honour Due: The Story of Dr. Leonora Howard King*. Ottawa: Canadian Medical Association, 1999.

Nevius, Helen. *The Life of John Livingston Nevius: For Forty Years a Missionary in China*. New York: Fleming H. Revell, 1895.

Nevius, John. *China and the Chinese*. New York: Harper & Brothers, 1869.

———. *Demon Possession and Allied Themes: Being an Inductive Study of Phenomena of Our Own Times*. Chicago: Fleming H. Revell, 1894.

———. *The Planting and Development of Missionary Churches*. New York: Foreign Mission Library, 1899.

———. *San-Poh, or North of the Hills: A Narrative of Missionary Work in an Out-Station in China*. Philadelphia: Presbyterian Board of Publication, 1869.

Nield, Robert. *China's Foreign Places: The Foreign Presence in China in the Treaty Port Era, 1840–1943*. Hong Kong: Hong Kong University Press, 2015.
Ninde, W. X. *The Picket Line of Missions: Sketches of the Advanced Guard*. New York: Eaton & Mains, 1897.
Noll, Mark. *Clouds of Witnesses: Christian Voices from Africa and Asia*. Downers Grove, IL: Intervarsity Press, 2011.
Noyes, Harriet. *History of the South China Mission of the American Presbyterian Church 1845–1920*. Shanghai: Presbyterian Mission Press, 1927.
———. *A Light in the Land of Sinim*. New York: Fleming H. Revell, 1919.
Paine, S. C. M. *The Sino-Japanese War of 1894–1895: Perceptions, Power, and Primacy*. Cambridge: Cambridge University Press, 2003.
Pang, Anne Pi-Yau. *Huang Naishang: A Chinese Christian Reformer in Late Qing and Early Republican China*. Sarawak, Malaysia: Sibu Foochow Association, 2008.
Papers Relating to the Massacre of Europeans at Tien-tsin on the 21st of June, 1870. London Harrison and Sons, 1871.
Parker, Michael. *The Kingdom of Character: The Student Volunteer Movement for Foreign Missions (1886–1926)*. New York: University Press of America, 1998.
Phelps, William Lloyd. *Autobiography with Letters*. New York: Oxford University Press, 1939.
Phillips, Clifton Jackson. *Protestant America and the Pagan World: The First Half Century of the American Board of Commissioners for Foreign Missions, 1810–1860*. Cambridge, MA: Harvard University Asia Center, 1969.
Pierson, Arthur T. *The Crisis of Missions; or the Voice out of the Cloud*. New York: R. Carter, 1886.
Polumbaum, Judy. "From Evangelism to Entertainment: The YMCA, the NBA, and the Evolution of Chinese Basketball." *Modern Chinese Literature and Culture* 14, no. 1 (2002): 178–230.
Porterfield, Amanda. *Mary Lyon and the Mount Holyoke Missionaries*. New York: Oxford University Press, 1997.
Pott, F. L. *St. John's University 1879–1929*. Shanghai: Kelly and Walsh, 1929.
Preston, Diana. *Besieged in Peking: The Story of the 1900 Boxer Rising*. London: Constable and Company, 1999.
Pripas-Kapit, Sarah. "Piety, Professionalism and Power: Chinese Protestant Missionary Physicians and Imperial Affiliations between Women in the Early Twentieth Century." *Gender & History* 27, no. 2 (2015): 349–373.
Pruitt, Anna Seward. *The Day of Small Things*. Richmond, VA: Foreign Mission Board of the Southern Baptist Convention, 1929.
Rabe, Valentin. "Evangelical Logistics: Mission Support and Resources to 1920." In *The Missionary Experience in China and America*, edited by John King Fairbank, 56–90. Cambridge, MA: Harvard University Press, 1974.
Rabinowitz, Harold, and Greg Tobin. *Religion in America: A Comprehensive Guide to Faith, History, and Tradition*. New York: Sterling, 2011.
Rankin, William. *Memorials of Foreign Missionaries of the Presbyterian Church*. Philadelphia: Presbyterian Board, 1895.
Rawski, Evelyn. *Education and Popular Literacy in Ch'ing China*. Ann Arbor: University of Michigan Press, 1979.
Reid, John Morrison. *Missions and Missionary Society of the Methodist Episcopal Church*. New York: Eaton and Mains, 1895.

Renshaw, Michelle. *Accommodating the Chinese: The American Hospital in China, 1880–1920*. New York: Routledge, 2005.

"Report of The Joint Special Committee to Investigate Chinese Immigration." *Report of Committees of the Senate of The United States for the Second Session of The Forty-Fourth Congress*. Washington, DC: U.S. Government Printing Office, 1877.

Rhoads, Edward. "In the Shadow of Yung Wing: Zeng Laishun and the Chinese Educational Mission to the United States." *Pacific Historical Review* 74, no. 1 (2005): 19–58.

———. *Stepping Forth into the World: The Chinese Educational Mission to the United States, 1872–1881*. Hong Kong: Hong Kong University Press, 2011.

Richard, Timothy. *Forty-Five Years in China*. New York: Frederick A. Stokes, 1916.

Riches, Eric. "The History of Lithotomy and Lithotrity." *Annals of the Royal College of Surgeons of England* 43, no. 4 (1968): 185–199.

Robert, Dana. *American Women in Mission: A Social History of Their Thought and Practice*. Macon, GA: Mercer University Press, 1996.

———. "From Missions to Mission to Beyond Missions: The Historiography of American Protestant Foreign Missions Since World War II." *International Bulletin of Missionary Research* 18, no. 4 (1994): 146–162.

———. *Occupy Until I Come: A. T. Pierson and the Evangelization of the World*. Grand Rapids, MI: William B. Erdmans, 2003.

———. "The Origin of the Student Volunteer Watchword: 'The Evangelization of the World in This Generation.'" *International Bulletin of Missionary Research* 10, no. 4 (1986): 146–149.

Ross, Heidi. "'Cradle of Female Talent': The McTyeire Home and School for Girls, 1892–1937." In *Christianity in China: From the Eighteenth Century to the Present*, edited by Daniel Bays, 209–227. Stanford, CA: Stanford University Press, 1996.

Satneck, Walter. *St. John's University, Shanghai, 1879–1950: Portrait of a Missionary University*. Dover, DE: Typescript at Virginia Theological Seminary, 1986.

Schuman, Michael. *Confucius and the World He Created*. New York: Basic Books, 2015.

Seagrave, Sterling. *The Soong Dynasty*. New York: Harper & Row, 1985.

Shaw, Yu-Ming. *An American Missionary in China: John Leighton Stuart and Chinese-American Relations*. Cambridge, MA: Harvard University Asia Center, 1992.

Shedd, Clarence. *Two Centuries of Christian Movements: Their Origins and Intercollegiate Life*. New York: Association Press, 1934.

Shemo, Connie. *The Chinese Medical Ministries of Kang Cheng and Shi Meiyu, 1872–1937: On a Cross-Cultural Frontier of Gender, Race, and Nation*. Bethlehem, PA: Lehigh University Press, 2011.

———. "'Her Chinese Attended to Almost Everything': Relationships of Power in the Hackett Medical College for Women, Guangzhou, China, 1901–1915." *Journal of American-East Asian Relations* 24, no. 4 (2017): 321–346.

———. "'So Thoroughly American': Gertrude Howe, Kang Cheng, and Cultural Imperialism in the Woman's Foreign Missionary Society, 1872–1931." In *Competing Kingdoms: Women, Mission; Nation, and the American Protestant Empire, 1812–1960*, edited by Barbara Reeves-Ellington, Kathryn Kish Sklar, and Connie Shemo, 117–140. Durham, NC: Duke University Press, 2010.

Sia Sek Ong. *Sia Sek Ong and the Self-support Movement in Our Foochow Mission: The Story of His Life and Work Related by Himself*. New York: Missionary Society of the Methodist Episcopal Church, n.d.

———. "Who is Jesus?" Translated by S. L. Baldwin. New York: Phillips & Hunt, 1871.

Simpson, James Young. *Physicians and Physic: Three Addresses*. Edinburgh: Adam and Charles Black, 1856.
Sites, Sarah Moore. *Hu King Eng, M.D.* Boston: Woman's Foreign Missionary Society, 1912.
———. *Nathan Sites: An Epic of the East*. New York: Fleming H. Revell, 1912.
Smith, Arthur. *Village Life in China: A Study in Sociology*. New York: Fleming H. Revell, 1899.
Spence, Jonathan. *To Change China: Western Advisers in China*. New York: Penguin Books, 1980.
Stanley, John. "Christianity and Female Empowerment: The American Presbyterian Mission Schools in Weixian, Shandong Province (1883–1920)." *Global Asia Journal* 8 (2009): 1–42.
Starr, Chloë. "Rethinking Church through the Book of Common Prayer in Late Qing and Early Republican China." In *Christian Encounters with Chinese Culture: Essays on Anglican and Episcopal History in China*, edited by Philip Wickeri, 81–102. Hong Kong: Hong Kong University Press, 2015.
Stauffer, Milton. *The Christian Occupation of China; a General Survey of the Numerical Strength and Geographical Distribution of Christian Forces in China*. Shanghai: China Continuation Committee, 1922.
Stevens, Helen. *Memorial Biography of Adele M. Fielde: Humanitarian*. Philadelphia: Fielde Memorial Committee, 1918.
Stewart, Walter. *Early Baptist Missionaries*. 2 vols. Philadelphia: Judson Press, 1926.
Story of Ida Kahn and Mary Stone. Boston: Woman's Foreign Missionary Society, 1912.
Stuart, John Leighton. *Fifty Years in China: The Memoirs of John Leighton Stuart, Missionary and Ambassador*. New York: Random House, 1954.
Sun Yat Sen. *Kidnapped in London*. Bristol, U.K.: J. W. Arrowsmith, 1897.
Szto, Peter. "The Accommodation of Insanity in Canton, China: 1857–1935." Ph.D. diss., University of Pennsylvania, 2002.
———. "Psychiatric Space and Design Antecedents: The John G. Kerr Refuge for the Insane." In *Psychiatry and Chinese History*, edited by Howard Chiang, 71–90. London: Pickering & Chatto, 2014.
The T'Ang Code: Specific Articles. Translated by Wallace Johnson. Princeton, NJ: Princeton University Press, 2014.
Tenney, William, ed. *Memoir of Mrs. Caroline P. Keith*. New York: D. Appleton, 1864.
Thompson, Ralph Wardlaw. *Griffith John: The Story of Fifty Years in China*. London: Religious Tract Society, 1906.
Three Character Classic. Translated by Herbert Giles. Shanghai, 1910.
Tow, Timothy. *Ting Li Mei: The First Chinese Evangelist*. Singapore: Far Eastern Bible College Press, 1988.
Tupper, H. A. *Decade of Foreign Missions, 1880–1890*. Richmond, VA: Foreign Mission Board of the Southern Baptist Convention, 1891.
Turner, F. S. *The Missionary Problem: A Reply to "Missionary Theology," an article by the Rev. Edward White, published in the "Rainbow" of July 1, 1869*. London: Hodder and Stoughton, 1870.
Varg, Paul. *Missionaries, Chinese, and Diplomats. The American Protestant Missionary Movement in China, 1890–1952*. Princeton, NJ: Princeton University Press, 1958.
Von Glahn, Richard. *The Sinister Way: The Divine and the Demonic in Chinese Religious Culture*. Berkeley: University of California Press, 2004.
Vukovich, Daniel. "Postcolonialism, Globalization, and the 'Asia Question.'" In *The Oxford Handbook of Postcolonial Studies*, edited by Graham G. Huggan, 587–604. Oxford: Oxford University Press, 2013.

Walker, D. P. *Unclean Spirits: Possession and Exorcism in France and England in the Late Sixteenth and Early Seventeenth Centuries.* Philadelphia: University of Pennsylvania Press, 1981.
Warren, Leonard. *Adele Marion Fielde: Feminist, Social Activist, Scientist.* New York: Routledge, 2002.
Wertz, Richard and Dorothy. *Lying-In: A History of Childbirth in America.* New Haven, CT: Yale University Press, 1977.
West, Philip. *Yenching University and Sino-Western Relations, 1916–1952.* Cambridge, MA: Harvard University Press, 1976.
Wheeler, Mary. *First Decade of the Woman's Foreign Missionary Society.* New York: Phillips & Hunt, 1881.
Wiley, Isaac. *China and Japan.* New York: Phillips & Hunt, 1879.
Williamson, G. R. *Memoir of the Rev. David Abeel.* Wilmington, DE: Scholarly Resources, 1972.
Wilson, Thomas, ed. *On Sacred Grounds: Culture, Society, Politics, and the Formation of the Cult of Confucius.* Cambridge, MA: Harvard University Press, 2002.
Wong, Fun. "Report of the Missionary Hospital in the Western Suburbs of Canton, for 1859–60." *Edinburgh Medical Journal* 6, no. 6 (December 1860): 578–584.
Wong, J. Y. *Deadly Dreams: Opium, Imperialism, and the Arrow War (1856–1860) in China.* Cambridge: Cambridge University Press, 1998.
Wong, K. Chimin, and Lien-Teh Wu. *History of Chinese Medicine: Being a Chronicle of Medical Happenings in China from Ancient Times to the Present Period.* Shanghai: National Quarantine Service, 1936.
Woodside, Alexander, and Benjamin Elman. "Afterword: The Expansion of Education in Ch'ing China." In *Education and Society in Late Imperial China, 1600–1900*, 525–560. Berkeley: University of California Press, 1994.
Wormer, William. "A Chinese Soldier in the Civil War." *Papers Read before the Lancaster County Historical Society* 25, no. 3 (1921): 52–55.
Worthy, Edmund. "Yung Wing in America." *Pacific Historical Review* 34, no. 3 (1965): 265–287.
Wright, Mary. *The Last Stand of Chinese Conservatism: The T'ung-Chih Restoration, 1862–1874.* New York: Atheneum, 1966.
Wu, Yi-Li. *Reproducing Women: Medicine, Metaphor, and Childbirth in Late Imperial China.* Berkeley: University of California Press, 2010.
Xi, Lian. *The Conversion of the Missionaries: Liberalism in American Protestant Missions in China, 1907–1932.* University Park: Pennsylvania State University Press, 1997.
———. "Returning to the Middle Kingdom: Yung Wing and the Recalled Students of the Chinese Educational Mission to the United States." *Modern Asian Studies* 49, no. 1 (2015): 150–176.
Xu, Guangqiu. *American Doctors in Canton: Modernization in China, 1835–1935.* New Brunswick, NJ: Transaction Publishers, 2011.
Xu, Guoqi. *Chinese and Americans: A Shared History.* Cambridge, MA: Harvard University Press, 2014.
Xu, Jilin. "Social Darwinism in Modern China." *Journal of Modern Chinese History* 6, no. 2 (2012): 182–197.
Xu, Yihua. "Birth, Growth, and Decline of the Chinese Student Volunteer Movement for the Ministry in 20th Century China." In *Christian Mission and Education in Modern China, Japan, and Korea: Historical Studies*, edited by Jan A. B. Jongeneel, 65–80. Frankfurt, Germany: Peter Lang, 2009.

———. "Westernization and Contextualization. A Study on Three Pioneering Chinese Pastors of the Sheng Kung Hui in China." In *Contextualization of Christianity: An Evaluation in Modern Perspective*, edited by Peter Chen-Main Wang, 183–208. Sankt Augustin, Germany: Monumenta Serica Institut, 2007.

Ye, Weili. "'Nü Liuxuesheng': The Story of American-Educated Chinese Women, 1880s–1920s." *Modern China* 20, no. 3 (1994): 315–346.

———. *Seeking Modernity in China's Name: Chinese Students in the United States, 1900–1927*. Stanford, CA: Stanford University Press, 2001.

Yen, W.W. *East-West Kaleidoscope, 1877–1946: An Autobiography*. New York: St. John's University Press, 1974.

Yimin, Qian, and Yan Zhiyuan. *Fuching Yen: A Pioneer of Chinese Modern Medicine*. Shanghai: Fudan University Press, 2011.

Yung, Shang Him. *The Chinese Educational Mission and Its Influence*. Shanghai: Kelly & Walsh, 1939.

Yung, Wing. *My Life in China and America*. New York: Henry Holt, 1909.

Zaccarini, M. Cristina. *The Sino-American Friendship as Tradition and Challenge: Dr. Ailie Gale in China, 1908–1950*. Bethlehem, PA: Lehigh University Press, 2001.

Zhang, Luqing, et al. "An Ethical Solution to the Challenges in Teaching Anatomy with Dissection in the Chinese Culture." *Anatomical Sciences Education* 1, no. 2 (2008): 56–59.

Zunke, Ke, and Li Bin. "Spencer and Science Education in China." In *Global Spencerism: The Communication and Appropriation of a British Evolutionist*, edited by Bernard Lightman, 78–102. Leiden, the Netherlands: Brill Academic Publishing, 2015.

Index

Abeel, David, 139
Academy of Natural Sciences (Philadelphia), 189–190
Achung (medical student), 119
Acts of the Apostles as guide for missionaries, 125–126
Adam and Eve, 19–20
Adoption of children by Howe, 173–175
Agency of Chinese people, 6, 8, 11, 12; of Chinese ministers out on their own, 81; in Foochow, 132–134; Nevius on, 83, 84
Alcohol: Hu temptation by, 72; and temperance movement, 40
Allen, Mary (Houston), 53, 54
Allen, Young J., 52–54, 103–107; and Anglo-Chinese College of Shanghai, 251; and Brockman, 232, 233; early life of, 52; *Globe Magazine* of, 105–106, 127, 254; and Haygood, 179–180, 183; and Huang, 106–107, 253; and missionary conference (1877), 126–127; and missionary conference (1890), 265; publishing projects of, 104–107, 126–127; on role of Chinese women, 104, 179–180, 254; and Soong, 164, 165; and Stuart, 265–266; on textbook committee, 126; as Tongwen Guan teacher, 53–54, 104, 151
American Baptist Missionary Union, 45–47
American Board of Commissioners for Foreign Missions (ABCFM), 108, 168, 169, 225

Americanization: of CEM students, 154, 155, 156; Hu resistance to, 210; hybrid identity in, 142–143; of Wong, 142–143; of Yen, 7, 160, 161–162, 163; of Yung, 147, 148, 153, 210, 215
American Medical Association, 196–197
Analects, 19
Ancestor spirits, interventions of, 63
Ancestor worship in Confucianism, 20
Anderson, Rufus, 108, 225
Angell, James, 215
Anglo-Chinese College of Foochow, 245–248; English language in, 251, 262; funding of, 246–248, 257; and Ohlinger, 246–247, 251; and Sino-Japanese War, 256–258; Smyth as president of, 247–248, 256–258; telescope installed at, 238; YMCA chapter in, 230
Anglo-Chinese College of Shanghai, 251, 261
Anglo-Chinese Department in St. John's College, 243, 245
Anti-Christian sentiment, 4–6, 12, 59; agency of Chinese people in, 6, 11; Ashmore experience with, 39–40, 220, 228; in Boxer Uprising, 267; cemetery vandalism in, 16, 23; of Chinese officials, 5, 27, 30, 33, 42, 82; Corbett experience with, 23–25, 97; *Death Blow* stories in, 35–37; in family, 27–28, 34, 73, 76, 83; Fulton experience with, 200–202; in Guangdong Province, 37, 39–40, 116; in Hok-chiang district, 90–91;

Anti-Christian sentiment *(continued)*
  Holcombe on, 263–264; Howe experience with, 214; Hu experience with, 93–95, 206; Ling experience with, 90–91; Mateer experience with, 28–35; Nevius experience with, 26–28; in Ngu Kang, 76; pamphlets encouraging, 35–37; in San-poh, 84; in Shandong Province, 15–38; Sia experience with, 87–88; Sites experience with, 42–43; in southern regions of China, 39–59; and supernatural beliefs, 37, 76–77; Tianjin Massacre in, 35–36, 153; transition to institution-building in, 10–11; Zia experience with, 84
Apostles: miracles of, 126; as model for missionaries, 125–126
Ashmore, Eliza, 190, 221
Ashmore, William, 22, 39–40, 45, 54–55, 220–222; and Fielde, 47, 48, 100, 101, 102, 128, 192; and Kerr, 49; at Northfield conference of college students, 221, 228–229; and Student Volunteer Movement, 221–222; in Swatow, 22, 39–40, 45, 47, 48, 220, 228; training Chinese on Bible, 100
Astronomy: Allen publications on, 105; Mateer school instruction on, 111, 134, 135
Athletic activities. *See* Sports activities
Attrition rate of missionaries, 56
Austin, Alvyn, 281n10

Baird Hall, 239, 240
Baldwin, Caleb, 167
Baldwin, Esther, 169, 208, 237
Baldwin, Harriet, 167
Baldwin, Stephen, 41, 90, 91, 130, 208, 237
Baldwin Locomotive Works, Mateer visit to, 134
Bangkok, Fielde in, 45–47
Baptisms: Allen performing, 54; Corbett performing, 25; of Kwo, 65; of Ling, 90; of Liu, 64; of Luce, 259; Mateer performing, 31; of Sun Yat-sen, 195; Sydenstricker performing, 3; of Wong, 141, 142; Woo requesting, 159
Baptist missionaries, 12; and American Baptist Missionary Union, 45–47; single women as, 47
Baptist Missionary Magazine, 102
Baseball, 154, 157, 160, 256
Basketball, 3, 232, 260
Bates, Daniel, 241
Bays, Daniel, 3–4, 12
Beach, Harlan, 230
Beijing University, 1
Bennett, Adrian, 105

Bible: Acts of the Apostles in, 125–126; Ashmore training Chinese on, 100; exorcism references in, 64; Fielde questioning beliefs on, 189, 190; Fielde training Chinese women on, 100–103; Garden of Eden story in, 19–20, 144, 189; Hu study of, 78
Bible-women of Fielde, 100–103; conference presentations on, 127–128, 191–192; obstetrics training of, 189, 190; success of, 132
Bicycles, 256
Binkley, Samuel, 89–90
Bishop Boone Memorial School, 163
Black Rock Hill: Hu home on, 213; Martin home on, 92, 93, 213
Blackwell, Elizabeth, 196
Blindness: cataract surgery in, 200; of girls in Canton, school established for, 203
Blockley Hospital (Philadelphia), 188
Boone, Henry, 139, 141, 205, 244
Boone, Mary, 139
Boone, Phoebe, 140, 141
Boone, Sally, 139
Boone, William, 139–141, 238; at St. John's College, 241, 242; and Yen, 141, 158, 160, 161, 163, 238
Boone, William, Jr., 142, 162, 239
Boone Memorial School, 163
Borowy, Iris, 51
Boxer Indemnity Scholarship Program, 268
Boxer Protocol, 267
Boxer Uprising (1900), 267
Bridgman School, 240
Brockman, Fletcher, 232–234, 266
Brown, Arthur Judson, 98
Brown, Julia, 29–30. *See also* Mateer, Julia
Brown, Margaret (later Capp), 184, 185
Brown, Samuel, 113; and Yung, 145–146, 147, 149
Buck, Pearl, 2, 10, 11
Buddhism, 62, 71, 75

Cannibalism in Northern Chinese Famine, 122–123
Canton: female medical students in, 192–204; Niles school for blind girls in, 203; Refuge for the Insane in, 203–204; tornado damage in (1878), 192–193; True Light Seminary in, 193–194, 196, 202, 203
Canton Christian College, 261
Canton Hospital, 50; childbirth practices in, 114; Corbett visit to, 119–120; funding of, 115; gender disparity in patients of, 194; Kerr at, 51–52, 112–116, 119, 131, 189,

193–198; Kerr leave from, 118–119, 197–198; Niles at, 196–198; as progressive, 131
Capp, Edward, 184
Capp, Margaret, 184, 185
Cataract surgeries, 51, 112, 198, 200
Cattle demons, 77
CEM (Chinese Educational Mission), 153–157, 164; dissolution of, 156–157, 244
Cemeteries: Mateer fear of, 29; in Tengchow, vandalism of, 16, 23, 30; in Zhifu, 262
Central Medical College (Shanghai), 8
Cesarean section procedures, 114
Chang (bookseller), 42
Chen Lanbin, 153
Chen Sin Ling, 69
Chiang Kai-shek, 165
Chilcott, Cyrus, 45
Childbirth, 113–115; Bible-women trained on, 189, 190; Cesarean section in, 114; embryotomy in, 114–115, 197–198; Fielde interest in, 188–189, 190; Fulton practice in, 200; gender separation in, 113–114, 188–189, 216–217; Kahn and Stone practice in, 216; midwives in, 113, 114, 131, 216; Niles practice in, 197–198
China Famine Relief Fund, 123
China Intercollegiate Athletic Association, 256
China Medical Missionary Association, 205
China Medical Missionary Journal, 205, 216
China Merchants Steam Navigation Company, 243
Chinese Christian Home Mission, 155, 156
Chinese Christians: Bible-women of Fielde, 100–103; CEM students as, 155, 156; and demon-possession narratives, 65–66; on English language instruction, 171; exorcisms by, 63–65, 66, 68–71, 74–75, 281n10; in Foochow, empowerment of, 132–134; Hu King Eng, 207–213; Hu Yong Mi, 71–80, 81, 91–95; hybrid identity of (*see* Hybrid identity); Ling, 89–91; as Mateer school teachers, 109; Miao, 32–33; number of, compared to hardships of missionaries, 41, 44, 58; self-supporting programs of, 81–96; and Shanghai missionary conference, 132; Sia, 85–89, 103–104; Swun, 27–28; treaty protections for, 17–18, 33; Wang, 68–69; Wong, 139–144; and Woolston school controversy, 171; Yen, 161–163; Zia, 82–85
Chinese Educational Mission (CEM), 153–157, 164; dissolution of, 156–157, 244
Chinese Exclusion Act (1882), 164, 232, 236, 267

Chinese immigrants in U.S.: and Chinese Exclusion Act (1882), 164, 232, 236, 237; Loomis in support of, 155–156; opposition to, 130, 155, 164, 232, 236, 237
The Chinese Intercollegian, 232
Chinese language: Allen study of, 53; Corbett study of, 23–24; Mateer school using, 108–109, 111; Mateer study of, 30; medical terminology in, 205; Nevius study of, 60; South China Medical School using, 116; Tengchow College using, 250; textbook translation into, 250; time required for proficiency in, 56
Chinese medicine, 49, 50–51; childbirth in, 113–114; Wong using Western medicine and, 143
Chinese Question, 155
Chinese Recorder, 58, 125, 262
Chinese Revolution (1911), 165, 195
Chinese Student Volunteer Movement for the Ministry, 261
Chinese supernaturalism, 60–80. *See also* Supernatural and demon beliefs
Chinese women: childbirth practices (*see* Childbirth); foot-binding of (*see* Foot-binding); in medicine, 193–194, 199, 205, 206–219; reform proposals after Sino-Japanese War, 254; traditional gender roles of (*see* Gender roles in Chinese culture)
Choa, G. H., 50
Cholera epidemic, 15–16, 95, 220
Chongqing, Howe in, 175, 213–214
Chou Li-wen, 111, 258
Chou Wen-yuan, 109, 111
Christian Association, 226
Christian colleges, 236–262; Anglo-Chinese College, 238, 245–248, 256–258; St. John's College, 238–245, 255–256; Sino-Japanese War affecting demand for, 254–261, 267; Tengchow College, 238, 248–251, 258–261. *See also specific colleges*
Christian Intelligencer, 224
Christianity: as alternative source of authority, 82, 83; and Chinese culture, 82; and Confucianism, 5, 21, 58, 86–87, 143–144; *Death Blow* stories on, 35–37; as exclusive religion, 5, 21–22, 27; and exorcisms, 63–65, 66, 68–71, 74–75, 281n10; God in (*see* God); and opium, 42; resistance to (*see* Anti-Christian sentiment); sin beliefs in, 19–20; and supernatural beliefs, 61, 62, 63–66, 70, 71
The Church News, 104–105

Civil service examination: Confucian canon in, 20, 157; as goal of education, 111; Huang taking, 107, 254
Civil War (U.S.), 141, 179; affecting funding of missionary activities, 53, 54, 56, 161; college enrollment after, 227; and single women as missionaries, 167; Yung machinery purchase during, 152
Clark, N. G., 225
Clothing and dress: of CEM students, 154; of Gutzlaff, 145; of Hu King Eng, 209–210, 211, 212, 215; of Kahn, 215; of Kelsey, 184; of native doctor, 216; of Stone, 215; of Stuarts, 265; of Yung, 148, 215
Cohen, Paul, 36
Colleges and universities: Anglo-Chinese College, 238, 245–248, 256–258; Christian, 236–262; in institution-building approach, 1, 3, 13; St. John's College, 7–8, 238–245, 255–256; Sino-Japanese War affecting demand for, 255–261, 267; Student Volunteer Movement and YMCA missionaries from, 220–235; Tengchow College, 238, 248–251, 255, 258–261. *See also specific colleges*
Colonialism, 9
Colonial modernity, 9
Coltman, Robert, 62
Conference of 1877 (Shanghai). *See* Missionary conference of 1877
Conference of 1890 (Shanghai). *See* Missionary conference of 1890
Confucianism, 5, 82; Allen on, 53, 104–105; Brockman on, 233, 234; and CEM students, 156, 157; and Chinese culture, 21; of Chinese officials, 5, 20, 27; and Christianity, 5, 21, 58, 86–87, 143–144; delete-and-replace approach to, 21–22; education in, 237; family in, 20, 28, 147, 163; and fox demon, 75; Great Way in, 143–144; Huang on, 106; innate goodness of humanity in, 19, 20; and international relations of China, 252; Mateer on, 109, 258; missionaries providing alternatives to, 6; resentment toward, 83; and self-strengthening initiative, 151, 153; social order in, 6, 19–21, 82, 83, 86, 99, 252; state-sponsored lectures on, 21; Wong on, 143–144
Confucius (551–479 B.C.), 19, 117
Connecticut Courant, 157
Conversions: by Allen, 104, 127; by Ashmore, 228; of CEM students, 155, 156; by Ding, 261; in education as missionary model, 246, 247; family opposition to, 27–28, 34,
73, 83; in famine relief efforts, 124–125; in Foochow, by Methodist Episcopal Mission, 41; by Hu King Eng, 211; by Hu Yong Mi, 79–80; of Hu Yong Mi, 72–74; joy in, 73; in medical missionary of Kerr, 52; of Miao by Mateer, 32–33; of missionaries to Oriental life, 12; number of, compared to hardships of missionaries, 41, 44, 58; of Sia, 87; and supernatural beliefs, 61, 65–66, 70; of Swun by Nevius, 27–28; by Yen, 163
Cooper, F. C., 255, 256
Corbett, Hunter, 22–25; Canton Hospital visit, 119; early life of, 22; on exorcism at haunted house, 62; hostile reactions to, 24–25; itinerant missionary of, 24–25, 97, 124; and Kerr, 119; language study of, 23–24; and Mateer (Calvin), 110, 249, 250; and Mateer (Robert), 222; museum of, 97–98, 122
Corbett, Lizzie Culbertson, 23, 24
Corbett, Ross, 24
Crawford, Martha, 55–56
Crawford, T. P., 128–130
The Crisis of Missions (Pierson), 225
Culbertson, Lizzie (later Corbett), 23, 24
Cultural imperialism, 10, 11, 12

Danforth, I. N., 216, 217–218
Danforth, Joshua, 15
Danforth, Mrs. Joshua, 15
Danforth Memorial Hospital, 218
Daoism, 62, 75, 93
Darwin, Charles, 189
Darwinism, 189, 190; social, 253
David Gregg Hospital for Women and Children, 202
Dean, William, 45, 46, 47
Death angel, 56
Death Blow to Corrupt Doctrines, 35–37
Delete-and-replace model, 21–22, 61, 66, 270
Demon beliefs, 60–80. *See also* Supernatural and demon beliefs
"Demoniacal Possession in China" (Richard), 61–62
Demon-possession narrative, 66
Denison University, 48
Depauw University, 237
Depression of 1873, 56
Ding Li Mei, 260–261
Ding Maing-Ing, 258
Diphtheria, 52
Dodd, Samuel, 130
Dog demons, 77
Domestic abuse of women, 99, 100, 102
Dong, Stella, 150

Drought conditions, Northern Chinese Famine in, 122, 123
Duane Hall, 239, 240
Dunch, Ryan, 12, 79

East Street Church: Huang preaching at, 106; Hu Yong Mi and riot at, 92–95, 206
The Echo, 256
Edkins, Joseph, 127
Education, 1; ABCFM opposition to, 168; and agency of Chinese, 11; of Allen, 52, 105; Allen in, 53–54, 104, 105; of Bible-women of Fielde, 101, 128; in bicultural settings, 12; Boxer Uprising affecting, 267–268; in Chinese Educational Mission, 153–157; in Christian colleges, 236–262; for civil service examination, 111; on Confucian canon, 21; English language instruction in (*see* English language instruction); of Fielde, 189; Fielde in, 101; Fisher in, 175–179; gender segregation in, 214–215, 240, 245, 270; of Haygood, 179; Haygood in, 179–183; of Howe, 173; Howe in, 173–175, 179, 213–214; of Hu King Eng, 207–211, 237; and hybrid identity, 137–165; of Kahn, 207; of Kelsey, 183; of Kerr, 48; in Kerr medical school, 115–117, 130–131, 132; of Luce, 3; Luce in, 3, 259–261; of Mateer, 29; in Mateer school, 33–35, 107–112, 125–126, 134–135, 167, 222, 260; in McTyeire school, 180–183, 254; memorization in, 109–110; in Mingdao Women's School, 101; as missionary model, 11, 12, 107–112, 125–126, 167, 246, 262; and modernization of China, 135, 148, 255; in Moody schools, 226; of Niles, 196; number enrolled in, 126; number of schools in, 12; Sino-Japanese War affecting demand for, 255–261, 267; of Sites, 40; and status in Confucian society, 237; of Stone, 207; Stone in, 218–219; Stuart in, 264, 268–269; textbooks for, 126 (*see also* Textbooks); in Tongwen Guan school, 53–54, 104, 151; traditional Chinese pedagogy in, 109–110; of Trask, 207–208; WFMS in, 167, 168–173; of Wong Fun, 113; Wong Kong-chai in, 142; Woolstons in, 168–173, 175; of Yen, 160–161, 238; Yen in, 7–8, 163; of Yung, 137–138, 144–148, 159; Yung in, 152–157
Elizabeth Skelton Danforth Memorial Hospital, 218
Embryotomy, 114–115, 197–198
Emma Jones School, 240, 241
Emory College, Allen at, 52, 105
England, China Inland Mission from, 281n10

English language instruction, 262; in Anglo-Chinese College, 251, 262; in Fisher school, 178; Mateer opposition to, 250–251, 262, 265; Ohlinger on, 251; in St. John's College, 243–244; in Woolston school, 171, 172, 209
Episcopal missionaries, 12
Evangelical models of missionary work, 13
Exorcisms, 61, 206; by Chinese Christians, 63–65, 66, 68–71, 74–75, 281n10; Corbett on, 62; in Kucheng District, 70; by spirit-mediums, 64, 69
Expansionism, Western, 9
Extraterritoriality right, 9, 18, 149, 150

Facial features, physiognomy of, 137–138
Fairbank, John King, 5, 21
Family: in Confucianism, 20, 28, 147, 163; opposition to Christianity in, 27–28, 34, 73, 76, 83
Famine, Northern Chinese (1876–1879), 122–125
Fay, Lydia, 159
Feng Hwa-chen, 233–234
Field, Cyrus, 135
Fielde, Adele Marion, 44–48, 99–103, 167, 188–192; and Ashmore, 47, 48, 100, 101, 102, 128, 192; in Bangkok, 45–47; Bible-women of (*see* Bible-women of Fielde); criticism of China, 57–58; hashish experience, 46, 191; at missionary conferences, 127–128, 132, 191–192, 265; resignation of, 191, 192; social activism of, 44; in Swatow, 47, 57, 99–103, 132; on women and demons, 66–68
Fighting Angel: Portrait of a Soul (Buck), 2
Filial piety in Confucianism, 20
First Opium War (1839–1842), 17, 136, 145; Boone arrival in China at time of, 139; rights of foreigners after, 17, 149; treaty ports after, 17, 41
Fisher, Elizabeth, 175–179, 222, 248; conference presentation of, 178–179; death of father, 176; early life of, 176; travel for student recruiting, 177–178
Five colors (yellow, green, red, black, white), 76
Five directions (North, East, South, West, Middle), 76
Five elements (wood, water, metal, earth, fire), 50, 76
Five Rulers (Ngu-ta), 76–77
Foochow: Anglo-Chinese College in (*see* Anglo-Chinese College of Foochow); Binkley in, 89; cholera and dysentery in, 95; East Street Church in, 92–95, 106,

Foochow *(continued)*
  206; empowerment of Chinese pastors in, 132–134; Fisher in, 175–179; hospital in, 208, 212; Hu King Eng medical practice in, 212; Hu Yong Mi in, 61, 71–80, 92–95; Johnson in, 22; Maclay in, 40; Methodist Episcopal Mission in, 41, 132; opium use in, 133; self-supporting programs in, 81, 85–86, 89, 92–95, 132–134; Sia in, 85–86, 89, 236, 237; supernatural beliefs in, 61, 71–80; Trask in, 208; as treaty port, 17, 41; Wiley in, 132–133; Woolstons in, 168–173, 175; YMCA chapter in, 230
Foochow Shipyard, 151
Football, 148, 154, 232, 256, 289n48
Foot-binding, 206; end of, 270; Fielde on, 99, 103; Howe on, 175; of Hu King Eng, 170, 207; Jones on, 143; Liang on, 254; Woolston on, 169
Foreigners: extraterritoriality right of, 9, 18, 149, 150; hostility toward, 94, 200–202; ignorance of native ideas and customs, 82; opium trade of, 42; vampire rumors on, 34, 35
Forsythe, Sidney, 22
Fox demon, 74–75
Franklin, Benjamin, 26
Friends Hospital (Philadelphia), 203–204
Fudan University, 8
Fujian Province, 12; Foochow in *(see* Foochow); opium addiction in, 42; rumors about missionaries in, 37
Fulton, Albert, 198–203
Fulton, Edith, 199
Fulton, Florence, 199
Fulton, Mary, 189, 198–203
Funding: American Civil War affecting, 53, 54, 56, 161; of Anglo-Chinese College, 246–248, 257; of Canton Hospital, 115; and Chinese Christians on mission payroll, 87, 88; Crawford on, 129, 130; of famine relief, 123–124; of Foochow hospital, 208; of Hu King Eng dispensary, 213; of Hu Yong Mi church, 94–95; of institution-building, 136; of Kahn medical education, 214; of Kelsey mission, 183; magazines encouraging donations for, 102; of Mateer mission, 120, 125, 134–135; of McTyeire school, 181, 183; of Nanchang hospital, 218; of Niles school for blind girls, 203; of Refuge for the Insane, 203; of St. John's College, 239, 240, 241, 255; self-supporting programs in *(see* Self-supporting programs); Sia approach to, 88–89, 103–104, 106; of Stone medical education, 214; of Tengchow College, 261; of Woo education, 159; of Woolston school, 170; of Yenching University, 269, 270; of Yen education, 159, 161; of YMCA in China, 233–234; of Yung education, 147, 161, 210

Gailey, Robert, 232, 234
Games of chance, Hu temptation by, 72
Garden of Eden, 19–20, 144, 189
Garrett, Shirley, 234
Gauld, William, 131
Gayley, Charles, 15
Gayley, Samuel, 15, 16
Gayley, Sarah Mills, 15, 16
Gender roles in Chinese culture, 167–168, 170; Allen on, 104, 179–180, 254; in Confucian social order, 20, 67, 99; Fielde on, 99–100, 128; Fisher on, 178; and health care, 113–114, 188–189, 194, 195–196, 197, 198, 216–217; Kelsey on, 186; at McTyeire school opening reception, 181–182; and power of spirit-mediums, 67–68; reform proposals after Sino-Japanese War, 254; Woolstons on, 171
Gender segregation: in education, 214–215, 240, 245, 270; at McTyeire school opening reception, 181–182; in obstetrics, 113–114, 188–189, 216–217; in worship, 178
Ghosts, beliefs in, 5, 60, 62. *See also* Supernatural and demon beliefs
Gilded Age, 3, 225, 234
The Globe Magazine, 105–106, 127, 254
God (Christian), 5; Ashmore belief in, 39; in contests with other gods, 8, 75–77, 79; Corbett belief in, 23; Crawford belief in, 56; Fisher belief in, 177; Hu belief in, 73, 78, 79, 209; Kerr belief in, 48, 49, 51; missionaries responding to call of, 5, 10, 17, 23, 37, 38, 41; and opium trade, 17; Sites belief in, 41, 43
Gods and deities, belief in, 5, 8, 60, 62, 75–77, 79. *See also* Supernatural and demon beliefs
The Good Earth (Buck), 2
Goodman, Bryna, 9
Goodman, David, 9
Grant, Ulysses S., 157
Granville Literary and Theological Institution, Kerr at, 48–49
Great Way, 143–144
Gregg Hospital for Women and Children, 202
Guangdong Province: Ashmore mission in, 22, 39–40, 45; Shan Sin Fan scare in, 37, 116; Swatow in *(see* Swatow)
Guangxi Province, Fultons in, 198–202
Guiping, Fultons in, 198–202

Gulangyu, 139, 140
Gunboats, and military protection of missionaries, 9, 30, 107
Gutzlaff, Mary, 144, 145

Hackett Medical College for Women, 202, 203
Hager, Charles, 195
Hair style of men, 2, 146, 154
Halcomb, Mattie, 55, 56
Hammond, Charles, 146–147
Hands-off approach in Nevius Plan, 84–85
Han Dynasty, 75
Hangchow Presbyterian College, 261
Hangzhou, Stuart family in, 264, 266, 268
Hankow, Yen mission in, 163
Hanover College, Wishard at, 223
Happer, Andrew, 128
Hartford CT, Chinese Educational Mission in, 153–157
Hashish, Fielde experience with, 46, 191
Hayes, Watson, 249, 255, 259, 260
Haygood, Laura, 179–183; and Allen, 179–180, 183; Atlanta school of, 179; and Brockman, 232, 233; conference contribution (1890), 191; leadership style of, 182; and McTyeire school in Shanghai, 180–183
Healing system in Chinese medicine, 50
The Heathen Woman's Friend (magazine), 168, 174
Hell, 68
Herbal remedies in Chinese medicine, 49, 50, 51
Hoag, Lucy, 173
Ho Ching, 18
Hok-chiang district, 90–91, 92
Holcombe, Chester, 22, 263–264
Hollinger, David, 12
Holmes, Samuel, 36
Hong Kong, Fielde arriving in, 44
Hong Xiuquan, 53
Houston, Mary (later Allen), 53, 54
Howard, Leonora, 215
Howe, Gertrude, 173–175, 179; children adopted by, 173–175; in Chongqing, 175, 213–214; Haygood compared to, 182; and Hykes, 175, 213, 214; in Jiujiang, 173–175, 213, 214; and Kahn, 173, 174, 213–215, 217, 218; Kelsey compared to, 186; and Stone, 174, 213–215, 217; and Woman's Foreign Missionary Society, 173–175, 213, 214
Hsi Shengmo ("the Overcomer of Demons"), 281n10
Hsü, Immanuel C. Y., 252, 253
Huang Kaijia, 157

Huang Naishang, 106–107, 253–254; and Allen, 106–107, 253; on Sino-Japanese War, 253–254
Hu King Eng, 205, 206–213; education of, 170, 207–211, 237; hybrid identity of, 207, 212; and Trask, 207–209; at Woolston school, 170, 207, 209
Humanity, innate goodness and sin of, 19–20
Hunan Province: Ding in, 261; hostility to foreigners in, 19
Hunter, Jane, 178, 187
Hu Po Mi, 73
Hu Sing Mi, 73, 247
Hutchison, William, 9
Hu Yong Mi, 81, 205, 206–207; conversion to Christianity, 72–74; early life of, 71; and East Street Church and riot, 92–95, 206; fox demon encounters, 74–75; and Huang, 106; Ling in dream of, 91–92; marketing Christianity in rural areas, 78–80; and Martin, 92–95; and rain in Lek Tu village, 75–76; Satan beliefs, 73, 77–79; self-confidence of, 132; and self-support model, 81, 91–95, 132; on sin, 72, 77, 208–209; supernatural beliefs of, 61, 71–80, 92; training female evangelists, 170; violent attack on family and, 93–94, 206; wife of, 94, 206, 207
Hu Yong Mi, Mrs., 94, 206, 207
Hyatt, Irwin, 33, 186, 258, 259
Hybrid identity, 11, 13, 137–165, 207; in adoptions, 174; of CEM students, 157, 212; of Hu King Eng, 207, 212; of Kahn, 207, 215, 218; of Stone, 207, 215, 218; of Wong, 142–144, 207; of Yen, 7, 160–164, 207, 212, 256; of Yung, 149–152, 153, 207, 212
Hykes, John, 175, 213, 214

Imperialism, 9–10; after Sino-Japanese War, 253; cultural, 10, 11, 12; missionaries as beneficiaries of, 9; spiritual, 9, 10
Incense burning, 62, 68
Industrial Revolution, 237
Infant girls killed by parents, 99, 102, 173, 200
Institution-building model of missions, 1, 3–5, 12, 97–120; Allen publications in, 103–107, 126–127; of Corbett, 97–98; education in, 11, 12, 107–112, 125–126, 246, 262; Fielde and Bible-women in, 99–103, 127–128; funding of, 136; Kerr medical missionary in, 112–119, 120, 130–131; of Luce, 3, 4; stereotypes on Chinese affecting, 136; transition to, 4, 5–6, 10–11
"Intelligence system" of Mateer, 258–259

Itinerant missionary work, 4, 5–6, 17; ABCFM supporting, 168; of Corbett, 24–25, 97, 124; of Mateer, 31–32, 33, 108, 125; of Nevius, 26–27; of Stuart, 264, 269; of Sydenstricker, 2–3

Jacobi, Mary Putnam, 196
Japan: Maclay stationed in, 246; modernization of, 252; Perry expedition to, 159; and Sino-Japanese War, 238, 251–261
Jefferson College, Mateer at, 29
Jefferson Medical College, Kerr at, 49, 51, 204
Jesus: Binkley beliefs on, 89–90; Fielde training Bible-women on, 101; Hu King Eng beliefs on, 211; Hu Yong Mi beliefs on, 73, 78, 79; Ling beliefs on, 90–91; Sia beliefs on, 88, 104
Jewell, Carrie, 177
Jiangxi Province, Howe in, 173–175
Jinan, Tengchow College moved to, 261
Jiujiang, Howe in, 173–175, 213, 214
John, Griffith, 125, 126
Johnson, Linda, 150
Johnson, Stephen, 22
Jones, Caroline, 143, 144
Jones School, 240, 241
Julia M. Turner Training School for Nurses, 202

Kahn, Ida, 173, 174, 207, 213–218; hospital of, 217–218; hybrid identity of, 207, 215, 218; and Liang, 254
Kamli-Fau Hospital, 113
Kang, Xiaofei, 67, 75
Kang Aide, 173. See also Kahn, Ida
Kang Youwei, 254
Kao-yai, Nevius famine relief headquarters in, 123, 124
Keen, Sarah, 210, 211
Kellogg, Mary, 153
Kelsey, Adaline, 183–186, 187
Kenyon College, and Yen, 7, 160, 238, 240–241, 243
Kerr, Abby (Kingsbury), 49, 50, 51
Kerr, Isabella (Mosley), 51, 52, 197
Kerr, John, 48–52, 112–119, 120, 193–198; and Ashmore, 49; at Canton Hospital, 51–52, 112–116, 119, 131, 189, 193–198; and China Medical Missionary Association, 205; and Corbett, 119; early life of, 48; medical school of, 115–117, 130–131, 132, 189, 193–194; medical textbooks of, 116–117; and Mui, 193–194; number of surgeries performed by, 51, 112; personal losses of, 51, 52, 112; Refuge for the Insane established by, 203–204; and Shanghai missionary conference (1877), 130–131, 132; temporary leave from hospital, 117–119, 197–198; and Wong Fun, 113–115, 116, 118–119
Kerr, Martha (Noyes), 193, 198, 203
Kiangnan Arsenal, 126, 151, 152
Kingsbury, Abby (later Kerr), 49, 50, 51
Kiung League, 241
Koeh Ah Szi, 243
Korea, 251, 252
Kucheng District, demon possession incident in, 69–71
Kung, H. H., 165
Kwan Ato, 51, 112, 116
Kwo, as case of demon possession, 64–65
Kwok, Pui-lan, 267

Lavater, Johann, 137
Leavitt, Walzer, 114
Lee Chu Bing, 244
Legal protection of missionaries, 17–19, 42; of Corbett, 25; extraterritoriality right in, 9, 18, 149, 150; of Martin and Hu, 94; of Mateer, 30–31, 107; of Sites, 43
Lek Tu village, calls for rain in, 75–76
Leng (assistant of Nevius), 64–65
Lenin, Vladimir, 9
Leung Kin Cho, 118, 199, 201
Lewis, Robert, 232, 234
Liang Cheng, 268
Liang Qichao, 254
Liang Tunyen, 234
Li Enfu, 155
Li Hongzhang, 157, 215, 243
Ling Ching Ting, 89–91; Hu dream of, 91–92
Lithotomy and lithotrity for urinary calculi, 118–119
Liu Chong-ho, 64
Li Yu Mi, 86
London Mission Society, 113
Loomis, Augustus, 155–156
Luce, Henry Robinson, 2, 259, 270
Luce, Henry Winters, 2, 3, 13; and Ding, 260–261; and English language instruction, 262; institution-building approach of, 3, 4; and Mateer, 259, 261; organizational talent of, 261; and Stuart, 266, 269; in Student Volunteer Movement, 5, 259, 260; and Tengchow College, 259–261, 262
Lu Haodong, 195
Lu Sin-sang, 83
Lutz, Jessie, 56, 197
Lyon, D. N., 125, 127, 230, 231

Lyon, Ellen, 212
Lyon, Mary, 168, 183
Lyon, Willard, 230–232, 234; and Brockman, 233; and Mott, 231; and Stuart, 266; in Tianjin, 231, 232; and YMCA in China, 231

Machinery: Mateer interest in, 134–135, 249–250, 259; at Tengchow College, 249–250; Yung purchasing for Zeng, 151–152
Maclay, Robert, 40–41, 246
Magazines: Allen publishing, 104–107, 126–127; encouraging donations for missionary work, 102
Malaria, 206
Martin, Carlos, 92–95, 213
Martin, Lucius, 95
Martin, Mary, 93, 94, 95
Mateer, Calvin, 22, 23, 28–33, 82; on Allen publications, 127; boarding school of, 33–35, 107–112, 120, 260; on Confucianism, 109, 258; and Corbett, 110, 249, 250; on Crawford, 130; and *Death Blow* stories, 35–36, 37; death of, 262; and Ding, 260; early life of, 28–29; educational model of, 167; on English language instruction, 250–251, 262, 265; on famine relief, 125; on Fielde, 192; funding of mission, 120, 125, 134–135; furlough in U.S., 134–135; individualism of, 259; itinerant ministry of, 31–32, 33, 108, 125; and Kelsey, 183–186; language study of, 30; legal and military protection of, 30–31, 107; and Lillian Mateer, 186–187; and Luce, 259, 261; machinery interest of, 134–135, 249–250, 259; and Miao, 32–33, 108; and missionary conference (1877), 121, 125–126, 134, 167, 246; and missionary conference (1890), 250–251, 265; opposition to preaching of, 30–32; on self-supported approach, 130; *shentza* travel of, 31; and Stuart, 264; teacher placement program of, 258–259; and Tengchow College, 134–135, 248–251, 255, 258–259; on textbook committee, 126; textbooks of, 250; theological school of, 260
Mateer, Julia, 23, 29–30, 33–35, 262; boarding school of, 33–35, 107–112, 120, 260; and Ding, 260; early life of, 29; and Kelsey, 184, 185; and Tengchow College, 248
Mateer, Lillian, 186–187
Mateer, Robert, 186, 222, 223–224
Mayers, W. F., 36
McGavock, Mrs. Willie Harding, 180
McTyeire school, 180–183, 254

Medical missionary work, 204–205; Chinese participation in, 131; of Kahn, 216; of Kerr, 48–52, 112–119, 120, 130–131; of Stone, 216
Medical schools: Fielde attending, 189; Fulton establishing, 202–203; gender segregation in, 194, 195, 196; Howe attending, 173; Kelsey attending, 183; of Kerr, 115–117, 130–131, 132, 189, 193–194; Niles attending, 196; St. John's College as, 244
Medical services, 12, 13, 188–219; in childbirth, 113–115, 188–189; in Chinese and Western medicine compared, 50–51, 113–114; Fielde concerns about, 188–192; Fulton providing, 198–203; Gauld on Chinese involvement in, 131; gender discrimination in, 197; gender roles affecting, 113–114, 188–189, 194, 195–196, 197, 198, 216–217; Hu King Eng providing, 205, 211–213; Kahn providing, 215–218; Kelsey providing, 184, 185; Kerr providing, 48–52, 112–119, 130–131, 193–194, 203–204; Mui providing, 193, 199; Niles providing, 195–198, 203; number of patients receiving, 205; Stone providing, 215–218; Trask providing, 208; for urinary calculi, 118–119
Meinhof, Marius, 9
Memorization in traditional Chinese education, 109–110
Mental health care in Refuge for the Insane, 203–204
Merchant foreigners in China, 37
Methodist Episcopal Church: Foochow mission of, 41, 132; Hu family joining, 73; Maclay as preacher for, 40, 41; New York conference of (1888), 236–237
Methodist missionaries, 12
Miao Hua-yu, 32–33, 108
Midwives, 113, 114, 131, 216
Military protection of missionaries, 17–18; of Fultons, 201; gunboats in, 9, 30, 107; of Mateer, 30–31, 107
Mills, Charles, 15–16
Mills, Lucy, 15
Mills, Rose, 15–16
Mills, Sarah, 15, 16
Mingdao Women's School, 101
Mingxin school, 203
Miracles performed by Apostles, 126
Mishkids, life of, 264–265
Missionary conference of 1877 (Shanghai), 5, 13, 121–136; Allen at, 126–127; Baldwin at, 208; Crawford at, 128–130; Fielde at, 127–128, 132; impact of, 131–135; Kerr paper

Missionary conference of 1877 *(continued)* presented at, 130–131; Mateer at, 125–126, 246; Sites at, 128, 129–130; textbook committee established in, 126; Woolston at, 169

Missionary conference of 1890 (Shanghai), 191–192; Allen at, 265; Fielde at, 191–192, 265; group photograph at, 191, 265; Mateer at, 250–251, 265; Stuarts at, 265; Wishard at, 230

Missionary models: Acts of the Apostles as basis of, 125–126; Allen publications in, 103–107, 126–127; Bible-women of Fielde in, 100–103, 127–128; conference presentations on (1877), 121–136; delete-and-replace, 21–22, 61, 66, 270; education in, 11, 12, 107–112, 125–126, 167, 246, 262; evangelical, 13; institution-building, 97–120 (*see also* Institution-building model of missions); itinerant (*see* Itinerant missionary work); medical (*see* Medical missionary work); Nevius Plan in, 81, 82–85, 86; self-supporting programs in (*see* Self-supporting programs); single women in, 166–187; transformation of, 4–6, 10–11, 263–264, 271

The Missionary Problem (Turner), 58

Missionary stations, number of, 12, 18–19

Modernization, 9; and colonial modernity, 9; education in, 135, 148, 255; institutions contributing to, 1; of Japan, 252

Monson Academy, 113, 145–146

Moody, Dwight, 154–155, 156, 261; schools established by, 226; and Wishard, 222–223, 226–227; and YMCA, 222, 226

Moore, Sarah, 41. *See also* Sites, Sarah

Morantz-Sanchez, Regina, 196

Morrison School, 113, 145

Mosley, Isabella (later Kerr), 51, 52, 197

Mott, John, 229, 231–232, 234

Mount Hermon school, 226, 227

Mount Holyoke Female Seminary: and Kelsey, 183–184, 185; and Lyon, 168, 183; and Mateer (Lillian), 186

Mui Ah-Kwai, 193–194, 199

Museum and Gospel Hall of Corbett, 97–98, 122

Nanchang, Kahn managing hospital in, 218

Nanjing theological seminary, Stuart teaching at, 268

Nanking Christian College, 261

Nanking Treaty, 17

Nanking University, 261

Nanyang College, 256

The National Baptist, 57–58

Nationalism, 7, 10

Nelson, Mary, 241–242

Nelson, Robert, 162

Nevius, Helen, 26, 28, 124

Nevius, John, 26–28, 35–37, 54, 262; cynicism in U.S. about work of, 56–57; and *Death Blow* stories, 35–36, 37; on Fielde, 192; itinerant ministry of, 26–27; on Mateer school, 134; and Nevius Plan, 81, 82–85; in Ningbo, 26, 60; and Northern Chinese Famine (1876–1879), 122–125; planning missionary conference, 121, 122; resistance to work of, 26–28; respect for Chinese agency, 83; self-discipline and rules of, 26; and Stuart, 264; on supernatural and demon beliefs, 60, 61–66, 68, 80; at Zhifu event, 61–62

Nevius Plan, 81, 82–85; compared to self-support program, 81–82, 86

New China, 7, 253, 256

New York conference of Methodist Episcopal Church (1888), 236–237

Ngu Kang, opposition to Christianity in, 76

Ngu-ta (Five Rulers), 76–77

Nie Qigui, 182

Niles, Mary, 189, 195–198, 203

Ningbo: Methodist Episcopals in, 41; Nevius in, 26, 60, 83, 84; as treaty port, 17

Niu Shangzhou, 164, 165

North China Herald, 151

North China Union College, 269

Northern Chinese Famine (1876–1879), 122–125

Northfield MA: Ashmore in, 221, 228–229; conference of Christian college students in, 221, 226–229; Moody founding schools in, 226

Northrup, B. G., 153

Noyes, Harriet, 193–194, 199

Noyes, Martha (later Kerr), 193, 198, 203

Observatory and telescope at Mateer school, 135

Obstetrics, 113–115, 188–189. *See also* Childbirth

Ohio Wesleyan: Hu King Eng at, 210, 211, 215, 237; Sia visit to, 237; Sites at, 40, 210, 237

Ohlinger, Frank, 69–70, 106, 107; and Anglo-Chinese College, 246–247, 251; on English language instruction, 251; on self-supporting programs, 133

Opium use, 69; and Christianity, 42; in Foochow, 133; in Fujian Province, 42; Hu temptation by, 72; of Ling, 89, 90; priest

desperate for money for, 23; Swun addiction to, 27, 28
Opium Wars, 8; First (see First Opium War); Second (1857–1860), 5, 17, 35–36, 51–52; treaty arrangements after (see Treaty arrangements after Opium Wars)
The Origin of Species (Darwin), 189
Ovarian surgeries, women performing, 193, 197

Pagoda Shadows (Fielde), 102
Paine, S. C. M., 252, 253
Pamphlets, anti-Christian, 35–37
Pang, Anne Pi-Yau, 106
Parker, Edwin, 166
Parker, Lois, 166
Parker, Peter, 49–50, 51
Partridge, S. B., 127
Peace Corps, 234
Peking Union Medical College, 1, 8, 270
Peking University, 269
Perry, Matthew, 159
Phelps, William, 154
Phrenological Journal, 137
Phrenology, 137
Physiognomy, 137–138
Pierson, A. T., 225, 227–228, 229
Pirates, Ling as, 89, 90
Pitkin, Horace, 259
Pittsburgh Female College, Trask at, 207
Points, John T., 158, 159
Ports, treaty, 9, 17, 41, 150
Pott, Francis Hawks, 244–245, 255, 267
Presbyterian Board of Foreign Missions, 26
Presbyterian missionaries, 12; Zhifu meeting (1874), 121
Pride of Chinese, 136
Princeton Theological Seminary: Corbett at, 23; Luce at, 3; Mateer at, 223–224; Nevius at, 26
Princeton University: Mateer at, 222, 223; Nevius speaking at, 264; Wishard at, 223; Yenching University partnership with, 270
Prostitutes, Hu temptation by, 72
Publications: of Allen, 104–107, 126–127, 254; encouraging donations for missionary work, 102; textbooks (see Textbooks)

Qing Dynasty, 8; Confucian social order in, 20; education in, 110; famine during, 123; fox demon in, 75; gender roles in, 20, 67; hair style of men in, 2, 146, 154; overthrow of, 165; reform movements in, 253; self-strengthening initiative in, 151–152, 153; and Taiping Rebellion, 53
Qinghua University, 1, 8, 268
Quakers, 204

Rabe, Valentin, 225
Rabinowitz, Harold, 234
Rain, calls for, 75–76, 79
Reformed Chinese, Yen as, 160
Refuge for the Insane, 203–204
Reincarnation, 68
Renshaw, Michelle, 197
Resistance to Christianity. *See* Anti-Christian sentiment
Rhoads, Edward, 153, 154, 156
Richard, Timothy, 61–62, 122, 123
Robert, Dana, 10, 167, 171, 246
Rong Kui, 156
Rong Shangqian, 157
Roosevelt, Theodore, 268
Rulison-Fish School, 218
Rural and interior areas: Allen waiting to travel in, 53; anti-Christian sentiment in, 5, 22; first access of foreigners to, 1, 5, 14, 17; Fisher in, 177–178; Fulton in, 198–199; Hu strategy in, 78–80; itinerant ministry in (see Itinerant missionary work); Kelsey in, 184; Nevius Plan on, 85; number of missionary stations in, 19; as rejective society, 22; supernatural and demon beliefs in, 5, 8, 13, 60–80; treaty arrangements providing access to, 4–5, 9, 16, 17, 18–19, 53; Yen mission in, 163
Rutgers Seminary, 224

Salary: from mission payrolls, 87–88; of women, compared to men, 46
Sandford, E. T., 30
San-poh district, 83–84
Satan, 62; Hu beliefs on, 73, 77–79
Schereschewsky, Samuel Isaac Joseph, 238–242, 244
Schereschewsky Hall of St. John's College, 256
Science, 11; Allen publications on, 105, 126, 127; Allen teaching, 53; Fielde study of, 189–190; Howe curriculum on, 174, 175; at Mateer school, 111, 126, 134, 135; role in missionary work, 6, 126, 127; at St. John's College, 256; at Tengchow College, 249, 260
Séances, 67–68
Second Opium War (1857–1860), 5, 17, 51–52; and Tianjin Massacre, 35–36
Self-strengthening initiative, 151–152, 153, 156

Self-supporting programs, 81; of Anglo-Chinese College, 246–247, 257; compared to Nevius Plan, 81–82, 86; conference organization of, 133; Crawford on, 129, 130; of Hu Yong Mi, 81, 91–95, 132; of Ling, 89–91; Ohlinger on, 133; of Sia, 85–89, 103–104, 130, 132; Sites on, 81, 129–130, 132, 133; of YMCA, 234

Semicolonialism, 9, 149

Shandong Province: charitable schools in, 110; cholera epidemic in, 15–16, 23; Corbett in, 22–25; frequent deaths in, 56; Kelsey in, 183–186; Mateers in, 22, 23, 28–37, 183–186; Nevius in, 26–28, 35–37, 60, 81; resistance to missionaries in, 15–38; supernatural and demon beliefs in, 60, 65; Tengchow College in, 238 (see also Tengchow College)

Shanghai: Allen in, 53, 104, 251; Anglo-Chinese College of, 251, 261; McTyeire school in, 180–183; missionary conference of 1877 in (see Missionary conference of 1877); missionary conference of 1890 in (see Missionary conference of 1890); St. John's College in, 238–245 (see also St. John's College); St. Luke's Hospital in, 244; Schereschewsky in, 238–242; Tongwen Guan school in, 53–54, 104, 151; as treaty port, 17, 150; Wong in, 144, 205; YMCA in, 231, 232, 233

Shanghai Daily News, Allen as editor at, 104

Shanghai Medical College of Fudan University, 8

Shan Sin Fan scare, 37, 116

Shanxi Province, 281n10

Shemo, Connie, 174, 203, 215, 254

Shentza travel of Mateer, 31

Shih Mei-yu, 174. *See also* Stone, Mary

Sia Sek Ong, 236–238; and Anglo-Chinese College, 247; education of son, 256–257; and Foochow school for girls, 171; at Methodist Episcopal Church conference (1888), 236–237; self-supporting church of, 85–89, 103–104, 106, 130, 132; and Sites, 86, 87, 88, 106, 236; tour of U.S., 236–237

Silver Flower (Bible-woman), 102

Simons, Maude, 211

Simpson, James Young, 113, 114

Sin: Binkley on, 89–90; Hu on, 72, 77, 208–209; as innate in humanity, 19–20; Ling on, 90–91

Single women as missionaries, 5, 13, 47, 48, 132, 166–187

Sino-Japanese War, 238, 251–252, 267; aftermath of, 252–261; and Anglo-Chinese College, 256–258; and St. John's College, 255–256; Tengchow bombardment in, 254–255; and Tengchow College, 255, 258–261

Sites, Belle, 43–44

Sites, Nathan, 40–44, 209; and founding of Anglo-Chinese College, 246; and Huang, 106; and Hu King Eng, 210; impulsively joining temperance actions, 40; and Ling, 90, 91; and Maclay, 40–41, 246; on opium addiction, 69; on self-supporting programs, 81, 129–130, 132, 133; and Shanghai missionary conference (1877), 128, 129–130; and Sia, 86, 87, 88, 106, 236; on telescope at Anglo-Chinese College, 238; training female evangelists, 170; violent attack on, 42–43; in Yen-p'ing, 42–44

Sites, Ruth, 209, 210, 211

Sites, Sarah, 41, 42, 44, 206, 209, 212; and Fielde, 103; and Hu King Eng, 210; and Ling, 90, 91; as Woolston school leader, 170

Smith, Arthur, 22, 110, 127–128, 167

Smyth, George, 247–248, 256–258

Social Darwinism, 253

Social Gospel, 234–235

Social order: Confucian, 6, 19–21, 82, 83, 86, 99, 252; gender roles in, 20, 67, 99 (see also Gender roles in Chinese culture)

Society for National Rejuvenation, 254

Soong, Charlie, 164–165, 182–183, 212; and Brockman, 233; and Sun Yat-sen, 165, 233; at Vanderbilt, 232

Soong, T. V., 165

Soong Ai-ling, 165

Soong Ching-ling, 165

Soong Mei-ling, 165

South China Medical School, 115–118; female students at, 193–194

Southern Methodist Episcopal Mission, Allen joining, 53

Southern Woman's Foreign Missionary Society (SWFMS), 180, 181

Speed (Bible-woman), 102–103

Spence, Jonathan, 11

Spencer, Esther, 243–244

Spencer, Herbert, 253

Spirit-mediums, 63, 64; demon possession of, 65, 66–68; exorcisms performed by, 64, 69; power and influence of, 67; women as, 64, 65, 66–68

Spiritual imperialism, 9, 10

Sports activities: of CEM students, 154, 157; Gailey organizing, 232; Luce organizing, 3; at St. John's College, 245, 256; at Tengchow

College, 260; of Yen, 160; at YMCA in Shanghai, 232; of Yung Wing, 148
Stereotypes on Chinese, 136
St. John's College, 238–245; Anglo-Chinese Department in, 243, 245; curriculum in, 242–244; daily schedule in, 240–241; English language instruction in, 243–244; extracurricular activities in, 256; funding of, 239, 240, 241, 255; medical training in, 244; and Pott, 244–245, 255–256, 267; and Schereschewsky, 238–242, 244; Schereschewsky Hall of, 256; and Sino-Japanese War, 255–256; and Yen, 7–8, 163, 240–241, 243, 244, 253, 256; Yen Hall of, 8, 256
St. Luke's Hospital (Shanghai), 244
St. Mary's Hall, 240, 245
Stone, Mary (Shih Mei-yu), 174, 207, 213–219; hospital of, 217–218; hybrid identity of, 207, 215, 218; nursing training program of, 218–219
Stuart, Jack, 270–271
Stuart, John Leighton, 264–265, 266–271
Stuart, John Linton, 264–266, 269, 270
Stuart, Mary, 264, 265, 270
Student Volunteer Movement, 5, 13, 220, 221–222, 234–235; beginning of, 227–229, 259; and Brockman, 232; Chinese model of, 261; and Luce, 5, 259, 260; and Lyon, 231; number of missionaries from, 229; and Social Gospel, 234–235; and Wishard, 229, 230
Sun Wen (later Sun Yat-sen), 195
Sun Yat-sen, 165, 195, 233
Supernatural and demon beliefs, 60–80; adaptability of, 62; on ancestor spirits, 63; of anti-Christians, 37, 76–77; and Christianity, 61, 62, 65–66, 70, 71; contests with Christian God in, 8, 75–77, 79; in death of child, 87; demon-possession narrative in, 66; in everyday events, 63; exorcisms in, 62, 63–66, 206; fear of bamboo dragon in, 103; of Hu Yong Mi, 61, 71–80, 92; interventions of supernatural beings in, 63; in Kucheng District, 69–71; Nevius on, 60, 61–66, 68, 80; power and proximity of supernatural beings in, 63; Richard presentation on, 61–62; in rural areas, 5, 8, 13, 60, 62–63, 74, 75–76; women possessed by demons in, 64–65, 66–68, 69, 74–75
Surgical procedures, 51; for cataracts, 51, 112, 198, 200; Cesarean section in, 114; Chinese woman performing, 193; embryotomy in, 114–115, 197–198; Kerr performing, 51, 112,
119; Niles performing, 197–198; Trask performing, 208; for urinary calculi, 118–119
Survival of the fittest, 253
Susquehanna, 159, 240
Swatow: Ashmore in, 22, 39–40, 45, 47, 48, 220, 228; Fielde in, 47, 57, 99–103, 132; medical missionary in, 51; typhoon in, 220
Swun (language teacher of Nevius), 27–28
Sydenstricker, Absalom, 1–3, 4; appearance of, 2; itinerant ministry of, 2–3; respect for Chinese, 11; robbery and attack on, 13–14; spiritual imperialism of, 10
Syle, Edward, 144
Szto, Peter, 203, 204

Taiping Rebellion (1850–1864), 53, 123, 151
T'ang Shao-yi, 234
Tan Yaoxun, 156
Telescope: at Anglo-Chinese College, 238; at Mateer school, 135
Temperance movement, 40
Tengchow: bombardment in Sino-Japanese War, 254–255; cemetery vandalism in, 16, 23, 30; Corbett family in, 23; fear of massacre in, 36; Gayley and Danforth families in, 15, 16; Kelsey in, 185; Mateers in, 23, 30, 34–35, 36, 109, 134–135, 185
Tengchow College, 238, 248–251; curriculum in, 249; funding of, 261; and Luce, 259–261, 262; and Mateer, 134–135, 248–251, 255, 258–259; and Sino-Japanese War, 255, 258–261
Tenney, Caroline, 141
Textbooks: Chinese language, Mateer producing, 250; committee established on, 126; medical, Kerr producing, 116–117; in Woolston school, 170
Thailand, missionaries in, 45
Thomson, Elliott, 142
Three Character Classic, 19, 53
Tianjin: Lyon in, 231, 232; massacre in, 35–36, 153
Tianjin Treaty, 17–18; expansion of missionary activities after, 18–19, 26, 53; protections afforded by, 17–18, 33
Tiong Ahok, 245–246
Tobin, Greg, 234
Tong Kai-son, 233, 234
Tongwen Guan, Allen teaching at, 53–54, 104, 151
Tornado damage in Canton (1878), 192–193
Townsend, Robert, 30
Trask, Sigourney, 207–209

Treaty arrangements after Opium Wars, 9, 17–19; extraterritoriality right in, 9, 18, 149, 150; interior travel of missionaries in, 4–5, 9, 16, 17, 18–19, 53; legal protection in (*see* Legal protection of missionaries); military protection in, 17–18 (*see also* Military protection of missionaries); port system in, 9, 17, 41, 150
Treaty of Nanking, 17
Treaty of Shimonoseki, 252
Treaty of Tianjin, 17–18; expansion of missionary activities after, 18–19, 26, 53; protections afforded by, 17–18, 33
Treaty of Wangxia, 18
Treaty ports, 9, 17; Foochow as, 17, 41; racial hierarchy in, 150; Shanghai as, 17, 150
True Light Seminary, 194, 202, 203; Mui at, 193–194; Niles at, 196
Tu, Mr. (teaching Nevius Chinese language), 60, 61
Tuberculosis, 211
Turner, F. S., 58, 59
Turner Training School for Nurses, 202
Twichell, Joseph, 154
Typhoid fever, 44, 45
Typhoon in Swatow, 220

Universities. *See* Colleges and universities
University of Edinburgh, Wong Fun studying medicine at, 113, 146
University of Michigan medical school, 173, 214–215
University of Pennsylvania, 190
Urinary calculi treatment, 118–119

Vampires, rumors on foreigners as, 34, 35
Vanderbilt University, 232
Varg, Paul, 10
Vietnam War, 274n20
Von Glahn, Richard, 62, 63
Vukovich, Daniel, 9

Wachusett (U.S.S.), 30, 31
Wang Wu-Fang, exorcisms performed by, 68–69
Webster, Daniel, 156
Weixian: Mateer mission in, 222; Tengchow College moved to, 261
Wellesley College, 43
Wen Bingzhong, 154, 157, 164, 165
Wesleyan Female College, 179, 183
West, Philip, 274n20
Western imperialism and expansion, 9

Western medicine: childbirth in, 113–115, 216–217; Chinese women trained in, 209–219; compared to Chinese medicine, 50–51, 113; surgery in, 51; Wong using Chinese medicine and, 143
Western Theological Seminary, Mateer at, 29
Wheeler, Francis, 175
Widmer, Ellen, 12
Wilder, Robert, 227, 228, 232, 234, 259
Wiley, Isaac, 132–133
Williams, Samuel Wells, 146, 147
Wishard, Luther, 222–223, 224, 226–227, 234; and Lyon, 230–231; and Moody, 222–223, 226–227; at Shanghai missionary conference (1890), 230; and Student Volunteer Movement, 229, 230; and YMCA, 223, 229–231
Woman's Foreign Missionary Society (WFMS), 5, 13, 166, 167–173, 187; and ABCFM, 168, 169; adoptions banned by, 174; education focus of, 167, 168–173; and Fisher, 175–179; founding of, 166, 168; and Haygood, 179–183; and Howe, 173–175, 213, 214; and Hu King Eng, 209, 210; and Kahn, 216, 218; Southern chapter of, 180, 181; and Stone, 216; and Trask, 208; and Wheeler, 175; and Woolston school controversy, 168–173, 175
Woman's Medical College of Pennsylvania, 189, 198, 211
Woman's Medical College of the New York Infirmary, 183, 196, 208
Women, 5, 13; Allen on role of, 104, 179–180, 254; Bible-women of Fielde (*see* Bible-women of Fielde); in Confucian social order, 20, 67, 99; demon possession cases involving, 64–65, 66–68, 69, 74–75; domestic abuse of, 99, 100, 102; Fielde, 45–48, 167, 188–192; Fisher, 175–179; foot-binding of (*see* Foot-binding); Fulton, 198–203; Haygood, 179–183; Howe, 173–175; Hu King Eng, 205, 206–213; Kahn, 213–218; Kelsey, 183–186; in medicine, 188–219; Mui, 193–194; Niles, 195–198, 203; salary of, compared to men, 46; single women as missionaries, 5, 13, 47, 48, 132; as spirit-mediums, 64, 65, 66–68; Stone, 213–219; in temperance movement, 40; in Tianjin Massacre, 35; and traditional gender roles (*see* Gender roles in Chinese culture); and WFMS, 166, 167–173 (*see also* Woman's Foreign Missionary Society); Woolston sisters, 168–173. *See also specific women*

Wong Fun, 112–115, 145, 146; in charge of hospital and medical school, 118–119; embryotomy performed by, 114–115, 198; medical education in Scotland, 113, 146; at South China Medical School, 116
Wong Kong-chai, 138, 139–144, 159, 205; American experience with Boone family, 140; baptism of, 141, 142; death of family members, 140–141, 142; hybrid identity of, 142–144, 207; and St. John's College, 240; and Yen, 162, 240
Wong Shing, 113, 145, 146
Wong Woo-ngoo, 240, 245
Woo, Hong Niok, 159, 240, 255
Woolsey, T. D., 56
Woolston, Beulah, 169, 175; controversy concerning school of, 168–173
Woolston, Sarah, 169, 171, 175; controversy concerning school of, 168–173
Woolston Memorial Hospital, 213
Woolston school, 168–173; curriculum changes in, 170–171, 172; English language instruction in, 171, 172, 209; Hu King Eng at, 170, 207, 209
World's Fair in Chicago (1893), 249–250
Wu, Yi-li, 113
Wuchang, Yen mission in, 163
Wu Zideng, 156

Xenophobia, 42, 92, 200
Xi, Lian, 12
Xiamen, 17, 41
Xu, Guangqiu, 194, 204
Xu Guoqi, 11

Yale College: Luce at, 3, 259; Yung at, 147–148, 149, 159, 160
Yale Medical School, 8
Yalu River Battle, 255
Yan, Junchen, 9
Yan Fu, 253
Yang He-ding, 158, 159–160
Yangtze Navy, 151
Ye, Wei-li, 268
Yek Ing Kwang, 69
Yen, F. C., 8, 256
Yen, W. W., 8, 163, 165, 253, 256, 270
Yenching University, 269–270, 274n20

Yen Hall of St. John's College, 8, 256
Yen-p'ingm Sites in, 42–44
Yen Yung Kiung, 6–8, 13, 138, 157–164; as archetype, 7, 160; and Boone, 141, 158, 160, 161, 163, 238; on Chinese education system, 162–163; education of, 6–7, 158, 160–161, 238; hybrid identity of, 7, 160–164, 207, 212, 256; influence of, 7–8; justice concerns of, 164; and Kenyon College, 7, 160, 238, 240–241, 243; Kiung League funding salary of, 241; on New China, 7, 253; as Reformed Chinese, 160; and St. John's College, 7–8, 163, 240–241, 243, 244, 253, 256; on Sino-Japanese War, 253
Yin and yang in Chinese medicine, 50
YMCA (Young Men's Christian Association), 1, 13, 222–223, 226, 229–235; and Brockman, 232–234; funding of, 233–234; leadership positions of Chinese in, 234; and Lyon, 231; and Moody, 222, 226; self-supporting goal of, 234; and Social Gospel, 234–235; and Stuart, 266, 268; and Wishard, 223, 229–231
Yung Shang Him, 156
Yung Wing, 113, 137–138, 144–157; bullied by Scotchman, 149–150; declining funding for education, 147, 161; early life of, 144–145; educational mission of, 152–157, 165; education of, 144–148, 151, 159; experience in U.S., 145–148, 153; hybrid identity of, 149–152, 153, 207, 212; marriage of, 153; mustache of, 148, 149; personal losses of, 147; purchasing manufacturing equipment, 151–152; and self-strengthening initiative, 151–152, 153; and Sun Yat-sen, 195; and Tong, 233; and Zeng, 151–152

Zeng Guofan, 151–152, 157, 215
Zhejiang Province, 83
Zhifu, 23; cholera epidemic in, 15–16; Christian cemetery in, 262; Corbett in, 23–24, 97–98; Presbyterian missionary meeting in (1874), 121; Richard presentation on demons in, 61–62
Zhu, Lili, 9
Zia Ying-tong, 82–85
Zion's Herald, 106
Zongli Yamen, 18, 30

John R. Haddad is Professor of American Studies and Popular Culture at Penn State Harrisburg. He is the author of *The Romance of China: Excursions to China in U.S. Culture, 1776–1876* and *America's First Adventure in China: Trade, Treaties, Opium, and Salvation* (Temple).

www.ingramcontent.com/pod-product-compliance
Lightning Source LLC
Chambersburg PA
CBHW022009300426
44117CB00005B/91